MW01493514

EARLY GREEK PHILOSOPHY

VII

LCL 530

EARLY GREEK PHILOSOPHY

VOLUME VII

LATER IONIAN AND ATHENIAN THINKERS

PART 2

EDITED AND TRANSLATED BY

ANDRÉ LAKS AND GLENN W. MOST

IN COLLABORATION WITH
GÉRARD JOURNÉE

AND ASSISTED BY
LEOPOLDO IRIBARREN

HARVARD UNIVERSITY PRESS
CAMBRIDGE, MASSACHUSETTS
LONDON, ENGLAND
2016

First published 2016

LOEB CLASSICAL LIBRARY® is a registered trademark
of the President and Fellows of Harvard College

Library of Congress Control Number 2015957358
CIP data available from the Library of Congress

ISBN 978-0-674-99708-0

*Composed in ZephGreek and ZephText by
Technologies 'N Typography, Merrimac, Massachusetts.
Printed on acid-free paper and bound by
The Maple-Vail Book Manufacturing Group*

CONTENTS

LATER IONIAN AND
ATHENIAN THINKERS
PART 2

27. ATOMISTS (LEUCIPPUS, DEMOCRITUS)

The ancient 'successions' (cf. **DOX. T20**) present Leucippus as a disciple of Zeno (**P2, P3**) on account of the interest they share in the question of indivisibility; but otherwise his is a personality that we cannot grasp. Most often, when he is mentioned he is associated with Democritus, in the wake of Aristotle, but what belongs to each of the two thinkers is not indicated explicitly. However, the ancient reports (cf. especially **D30**) do suggest that Leucippus supplied the general principles—the indivisible atoms and the void—of a system that Democritus went on to elaborate further and above all to amplify considerably by the range of his own research in all the fields of knowledge. In any case, it is hardly possible to treat the two thinkers separately from each other.

About Democritus we are much better informed. We know that he came from Abdera, a village in Thrace to which his name remains indissolubly linked (whereas in the case of Leucippus the ancient tradition hesitates between Miletus and Abdera). The chronological indications are complicated: one dating sets his birth earlier, in 472/68 BC, another later, in 460/56; his longevity is well attested, and he certainly outlived Socrates, who was in any case his near contemporary.

Democritus' original works were as diverse as they were numerous, as is indicated by the transmitted catalog of his writings (even if this includes a certain number of apocryphal titles); but from these there survive only isolated terms and expressions and a few sentences (the ethical maxims that are attributed to him pose a special problem; see below). His writings must have disappeared quite early; one sign of this is that Simplicius, our major source for citations of the principal early Greek philosophers, does not seem to have had access to any of his works. But the doxographical reports concerning his doctrine of principles and his natural philosophy are abundant, and some of them are very detailed. This can be seen as an effect of the very special attention paid him by Aristotle, and following him by Theophrastus, an attention owing principally to three factors: the force and coherence of his doctrine; the abundance and sophistication of his causal explanations (Democritus himself placed his research under the banner of 'aetiology'); and the encyclopedic character of his work, in which Aristotle was able to recognize an undertaking of the same range as his own.

Democritus' ethical fragments pose an insoluble problem because of the many uncertainties that weigh upon the ca. 228 quotations transmitted in Stobaeus' *Anthology* under the name of Democritus and, in some cases, under that (otherwise unknown) of Democrates. These quotations, which most often take the form of maxims or advice, are presented without context; besides those that are assigned to Democrates, others appear in other anthologies, where they are attributed to other people, for example Epictetus or Maximus the Confessor. Some are of a con-

siderable banality. It is hard to avoid the impression that most of these fragments have been attributed to Democritus for what might be called honorific reasons. From this perspective, they belong rather to the history of his reception, or indeed of his pseudepigraphic reception, which in any case is known to have been abundant. But it would be just as risky to attach them exclusively to this tradition as to attribute them in their entirety to Democritus himself. Rather than trying systematically to distinguish the authentic from the inauthentic—an undertaking for which no satisfactory criteria are available—we have chosen to print the great majority of these maxims in italics, in order to indicate their problematic character. The few exceptions are due to their closeness, semantic or doctrinal, to texts that there is no particular reason to distrust.

BIBLIOGRAPHY

Editions and Translations

W. Leszl. *I Primi Atomisti* (Florence, 2009).

S. Luria. *Democritea* (Leningrad, 1970). Italian translation by A. Krivushina (Milan, 2007).

C. C. W. Taylor. *The Atomists: Leucippus and Democritus* (Toronto, 1999).

Collection of Articles

P.-M. Morel and A. Brancacci, eds. *Democritus: Science, the Arts, and the Care of the Soul* (Leiden-Boston, 2007).

On the Catalog of His Writings

W. Leszl. "Democritus' Works: From Their Titles to Their Contents," in Morel and Brancacci, eds., pp. 11–76.

On the Alchemical Tradition

M. Martelli. *Scritti alchemici. Pseudo-Democrito, con il commentario di Sinesi. Edizione critica del testo greco, traduzione e commento* (Paris-Milan, 2011).

OUTLINE OF THE CHAPTER

P

ATOMISTS (LEUCIPPUS, DEMOCRITUS)

ATOMISTS (LEUCIPPUS, DEMOCRITUS)

ATOMISTS
(LEUCIPPUS [67 DK],
DEMOCRITUS [68 DK])

For Leucippus, references to DK take the form 67 Ax or Bx; for Democritus, references are generally by only Ax, Bx, or Cx.

P

Leucippus (P1–P5)
Family and city (P1)

P1

a (< 67 A1) Diog. Laert. 9.30

Λεύκιππος Ἐλεάτης, ὡς δέ τινες, Ἀβδηρίτης, κατ᾽ ἐνίους δὲ Μιλήσιος[1] [. . . = **P2**].

[1] Μιλήσιος recc.: μήλιος mss.

b (< 67 A8) Simpl. *In Phys.*, p. 28.4–5

Λεύκιππος δὲ ὁ Ἐλεάτης ἢ Μιλήσιος (ἀμφοτέρως γὰρ λέγεται περὶ αὐτοῦ) [. . . = **D32**].

ATOMISTS
(LEUCIPPUS, DEMOCRITUS)

P

Leucippus (P1–P5)
Family and City (P1)

P1

a (< 67 A1) Diogenes Laertius

Leucippus of Elea, but of Abdera according to other people, and according to some, of Miletus [. . .].

b (< 67 A8) Simplicius, *Commentary on Aristotle's* Physics

Leucippus, of Elea or of Miletus (for both are said about him) [. . .].

Teachers (P2–P5)

P2 (< 67 A1) Diog. Laert. 9.30

[. . . = **P1**] οὗτος ἤκουσε Ζήνωνος.

P3 (< 67 A10) (Ps.-?) Hippol. *Ref.* 1.12.1

Λεύκιππος δὲ Ζήνωνος ἑταῖρος [. . .].

P4 (67 A5) Tzetz. *Chil.* 2.980

[. . .] Λευκίππου [. . .] τοῦ μαθητοῦ Μελίσσου [. . .].

P5 (< 67 A5) Iambl. *VP* 104

[. . .] μαθητεύσαντες τῷ Πυθαγόρᾳ πρεσβύτῃ νέοι, Φιλόλαός τε καὶ Εὔρυτος, [. . .] Λεύκιππός τε καὶ Ἀλκμαίων [. . .].

Democritus (P6–P56)
Family and City of Origin (P6–P8)

P6 (< A1) Diog. Laert. 9.34

Δημόκριτος Ἡγησιστράτου, οἱ δὲ Ἀθηνοκρίτου, τινὲς Δαμασίππου, Ἀβδηρίτης ἤ, ὡς ἔνιοι, Μιλήσιος.

P7 (< A40) (Ps.-?) Hippol. *Ref.* 1.13.1

[. . . = **P18**] Δημόκριτος Δαμασίππου, Ἀβδηρίτης [. . . = **P18**].

ATOMISTS (LEUCIPPUS, DEMOCRITUS)

Teachers (P2–P5)

P2 (< 67 A1) Diogenes Laertius

[. . .] he studied with Zeno.

P3 (< 67 A10) (Ps.-?) Hippolytus, *Refutation of All Heresies*

Leucippus, companion of Zeno [. . .].

P4 (67 A5) Tzetzes, *Chiliades*

Leucippus [. . .] the disciple of Melissus [. . .].

P5 (< 67 A5) Iamblichus, *Life of Pythagoras*

[. . .] young disciples of the aged Pythagoras: Philolaus and Eurytus, [. . .] Leucippus and Alcmaeon [. . .].

Democritus (P6–P56)
Family and City of Origin (P6–P8)

P6 (< A1) Diogenes Laertius

Democritus, son of Hegesistratus; but other people say, of Athenocritus; certain ones, of Damasippus; he was from Abdera, or according to some people, from Miletus.

P7 (< A40) (Ps.-?) Hippolytus, *Refutation of All Heresies*

[. . .] Democritus, son of Damasippus, of Abdera [. . .].

P8 (< A2) *Suda* Δ.447

Δημόκριτος [. . .] Ἀβδηρίτης ἐκ Θρᾴκης [. . .].

Chronology (P9–P15)

P9 (B5) Diog. Laert. 9.41

γέγονε δὲ τοῖς χρόνοις, ὡς αὐτός φησιν ἐν τῷ Μικρῷ
διακόσμῳ, νέος κατὰ πρεσβύτην Ἀναξαγόραν, ἔτεσιν
αὐτοῦ νεώτερος τετταράκοντα. συντετάχθαι δέ φησι
τὸν Μικρὸν διάκοσμον ἔτεσιν ὕστερον τῆς Ἰλίου
ἁλώσεως τριάκοντα[1] καὶ ἑπτακοσίοις.

[1] τρία <καὶ ἑξή>κοντα Mansfeld

P10 (< A1) Diog. Laert. 9.41

γεγόνοι δ᾽ ἄν, ὡς μὲν Ἀπολλόδωρος ἐν Χρονικοῖς
[*FGrHist* 244 F36a], κατὰ τὴν ὀγδοηκοστὴν Ὀλυμπιάδα, ὡς δὲ Θράσυλλος ἐν τῷ ἐπιγραφομένῳ Τὰ πρὸ
τῆς ἀναγνώσεως τῶν Δημοκρίτου βιβλίων [Test. 18a
Tarrant], κατὰ τὸ τρίτον ἔτος τῆς ἑβδόμης καὶ ἑβδο-
μηκοστῆς Ὀλυμπιάδος, ἐνιαυτῷ, φησί, πρεσβύτερος
ὢν Σωκράτους. εἴη ἂν οὖν κατ᾽ Ἀρχέλαον τὸν Ἀναξαγόρου μαθητὴν καὶ τοὺς περὶ Οἰνοπίδην· καὶ γὰρ
τούτου[1] μέμνηται [. . . = **P26**].

[1] τούτων Reiske

P8 (< A2) *Suda*

Democritus [. . .] an Abderite who came from Thrace
[. . .].

Chronology (P9–P15)

P9 (B5) Diogenes Laertius

With regard to chronology, he was, as he himself says in
his *Small World System,* **"young when Anaxagoras was
old,"** being younger than him by forty years. And he says
that the *Small World System* was composed 730 years after
the fall of Troy.[1]

---

[1] If we accept the date of 1184/83 for the fall of Troy, as established by Eratosthenes (and by Apollodorus following him),
then this work will have been written in 454/53, but that date is
too early. Mansfeld lowers it to 421/20 by correcting 730 to 763.
It remains uncertain whether this computation goes back to Democritus himself or, as Mansfeld thinks, to Apollodorus (in which
case Apollodorus would be the subject of "he says").

P10 (< A1) Diogenes Laertius

He would have been born, at least according to Apollodorus in his *Chronology,* during the 80th Olympiad [=
460/56 BC]; but according to Thrasyllus, in his book entitled *Preliminaries to Reading Democritus' Books,* it was
during the third year of the 77th Olympiad [= 470/69], and
he was, he says, one year older than Socrates. So he would
be a contemporary of Archelaus, the disciple of Anaxagoras, as well as of Oenopides; and in fact he mentions this
latter [. . .].

P11 (< A2) *Suda* Δ.447

Δημόκριτος [. . .] γεγονὼς ὅτε καὶ Σωκράτης ὁ φιλόσοφος, κατὰ τὴν οζ′ Ὀλυμπιάδα, οἱ δὲ κατὰ τὴν π′
φασίν.

P12 (A4) Eus. *Chron.* (Cyr., Hier.; cf. *Chron. Pasch.*)

a Cyrill. Alex. *Jul.* 1.15

ἑβδομηκοστῇ Ὀλυμπιάδι φασὶ γενέσθαι[1] Δημόκριτον
καὶ Ἀναξαγόραν, φιλοσόφους φυσικούς [. . .].

[1] γενέσθαι] ἐγνωρίζοντο *Chron. Pasch.* 317.5, clari habentur
Hier. p. 107, 15

b Hier. *Chron.*, p. 114.7

[ad Ol. 86.1] Democritus Abderites et Empedocles et
Hippocrates medicus Gorgias Hippiasque et Prodicus et
Zeno et Parmenides philosophi insignes habentur.[1]

[1] insignes habentur] γενέσθαι Cyrill. Alex. *Jul.* 1.15

c Hier. *Chron.*, p. 117.17

[ad Ol. 94.4] Democritus moritur.

P13 (A5) Diod. Sic. 14.11.5

περὶ δὲ τὸν αὐτὸν χρόνον καὶ Δημόκριτος ὁ φιλόσοφος ἐτελεύτησε βιώσας ἔτη ἐνενήκοντα.

P11 (< A2) *Suda*

Democritus [. . .] born at the same time as Socrates the philosopher, during the 77th Olympiad [= 472/68]; but other people say, during the 80th [= 460/56].

P12 (A4) Eusebius, *Chronicle*

a (Cyril of Alexandria)

They say that it was during the 70th Olympiad [= 500/496] that Democritus and Anaxagoras, natural philosophers, were born [. . .].

b (Jerome)

[86th Olympiad, 1st year = 436] Democritus of Abdera, Empedocles, Hippocrates the doctor, Gorgias, Hippias, Prodicus, Zeno, and Parmenides, philosophers, are considered famous.

c (Jerome)

[94th Olympiad = 404/400] Democritus dies.

P13 (A5) Diodorus Siculus

About the same time [Ol. 94.1 = 404] the philosopher Democritus died, after having lived for ninety years.

P14 (< A6) Ps.-Luc. *Long.* 18

Δημόκριτος μὲν ὁ Ἀβδηρίτης ἐτῶν γεγονὼς τεττάρων
καὶ ἑκατὸν [. . . = **P54**] ἐτελεύτα.

P15 (< A1) Diog. Laert. 9.43

[. . . = **P51**] ἀλυπότατα τὸν βίον προήκατο, ὥς φησιν
ὁ Ἵππαρχος [*FGrHist* 1109 F1], ἐννέα πρὸς τοῖς ἑκατὸν
ἔτη βιούς.

Reported Teachers and Travels (P16–P22)
Greek Teachers and Oriental Ones? (P16–P20)

P16 (< A1) Diog. Laert.

a 9.34

οὗτος μάγων τινῶν διήκουσε καὶ Χαλδαίων, Ξέρξου
τοῦ βασιλέως τῷ πατρὶ αὐτοῦ ἐπιστάτας καταλιπόν-
τος, ἡνίκα ἐξενίσθη παρ᾽ αὐτῷ, καθά φησι καὶ Ἡρό-
δοτος· παρ᾽ ὧν τά τε περὶ θεολογίας καὶ ἀστρολογίας
ἔμαθεν ἔτι παῖς ὤν. ὕστερον δὲ Λευκίππῳ παρέβαλε
καὶ Ἀναξαγόρᾳ κατά τινας [. . .].

b 9.35–36

φησὶ δὲ Δημήτριος ἐν Ὁμωνύμοις [Frag. 29 Mejer] καὶ
Ἀντισθένης ἐν Διαδοχαῖς [*FGrHist* 508 F12 = Frag. 12
Giannattasio Andria] ἀποδημῆσαι αὐτὸν καὶ εἰς Αἴγυ-
πτον πρὸς τοὺς ἱερέας γεωμετρίαν μαθησόμενον καὶ

P14 (< A6) Ps.-Lucian, *Long-lived Men*

Democritus of Abdera died after having lived for 104 years [. . .].

P15 (< A1) Diogenes Laertius

[. . .] he abandoned life without any suffering, as Hipparchus says, after having lived for 109 years.

Reported Teachers and Travels (P16–P22)
Greek Teachers and Oriental Ones? (P16–P20)

P16 (< A1) Diogenes Laertius

a

He studied with certain Magi and Chaldeans, as King Xerxes had left supervisors with his father when he had been his guest, as Herodotus reports [cf. 7.109, 8.120]; he learned theology and astronomy from them while he was still a boy. Later he met Leucippus, and, according to some people, Anaxagoras [. . .].

b

Demetrius in his *Homonyms* and Antisthenes in his *Successions* say that he traveled to the priests in Egypt in order to learn geometry, and went to the Chaldeans in

πρὸς Χαλδαίους εἰς τὴν Περσίδα καὶ εἰς τὴν Ἐρυ-
θρὰν θάλασσαν γενέσθαι. τοῖς τε γυμνοσοφισταῖς
φασί τινες συμμῖξαι αὐτὸν ἐν Ἰνδίᾳ καὶ εἰς Αἰθιοπίαν
ἐλθεῖν. [. . . = **P37b**]

P17 (< A2) *Suda* Δ.447

Δημόκριτος [. . .] φιλόσοφος, μαθητὴς κατά τινας
Ἀναξαγόρου καὶ Λευκίππου, ὡς δέ τινες καὶ Μάγων
καὶ Χαλδαίων Περσῶν·[1] ἦλθε γὰρ καὶ εἰς Πέρσας καὶ
Ἰνδοὺς καὶ Αἰγυπτίους καὶ τὰ παρ᾽ ἑκάστοις ἐπαι-
δεύθη σοφά.

  [1] <καὶ> Περσῶν Bernhardy

P18 (< A40) (Ps.-?) Hippol. *Ref.* 1.13.1

Δημόκριτος δὲ Λευκίππου γίνεται γνώριμος. Δημόκριτος [. . . = **P7**] πολλοῖς συμβαλὼν γυμνοσοφισταῖς ἐν
Ἰνδοῖς καὶ ἱερεῦσιν ἐν Αἰγύπτῳ καὶ ἀστρολόγοις καὶ
ἐν Βαβυλῶνι μάγοις.

P19 (A13) Cic. *Fin.* 5.19.50

quid de Pythagora? quid de Platone aut de Democrito
loquar? a quibus propter discendi cupiditatem videmus
ultimas terras esse peragratas.

Persia and the Red Sea. Some people say that he associated with the gymnosophists in India and that he went to Ethiopia. [. . .]

P17 (< A2) *Suda*

Democritus [. . .] philosopher, according to some people a disciple of Anaxagoras and Leucippus, according to others also of the Magi and of the Persian Chaldeans. For he went to Persia, India, and Egypt, and was educated in the wisdom of each of them.

P18 (< A40) (Ps.-?) Hippolytus, *Refutation of All Heresies*

Democritus becomes a companion of Leucippus. Democritus [. . .] having met many gymnosophists in India, priests in Egypt, and astronomers and Magi in Babylonia.

P19 (A13) Cicero, *On Ends*

Why should I speak of Pythagoras? Why of Plato or Democritus? We see that, because of their desire to learn, these men traveled through the very farthest countries.

P20 (0.3.21 Leszl) Diod. Sic. 1.98.3

ὑπολαμβάνουσι δὲ καὶ Δημόκριτον παρ᾽ αὐτοῖς ἔτη
διατρῖψαι πέντε καὶ πολλὰ διδαχθῆναι τῶν κατὰ τὴν
ἀστρολογίαν.

Pythagoreans? (P21)

P21 (< A1) Diog. Laert. 9.38

δοκεῖ δέ, φησὶν ὁ Θράσυλλος [Test. 18b Tarrant], ζη-
λωτὴς γεγονέναι τῶν Πυθαγορικῶν [. . . = **P24**]. πάντα
δὲ δοκεῖν παρὰ τούτου λαβεῖν καὶ αὐτοῦ δ᾽ ἂν ἀκηκοέναι, εἰ μὴ τὰ τῶν χρόνων ἐμάχετο. πάντως μέντοι
τῶν Πυθαγορικῶν τινος ἀκοῦσαί φησιν αὐτὸν Γλαῦ-
κος ὁ Ῥηγῖνος [Frag. 5 Lanata], κατὰ τοὺς αὐτοὺς χρό-
νους αὐτῷ γεγονώς. φησὶ δὲ καὶ Ἀπολλόδωρος ὁ Κυ-
ζικηνὸς [74.2 DK] Φιλολάῳ αὐτὸν συγγεγονέναι.

Visit to Athens? (P22)

P22 (< A1, B116) Diog. Laert.

a 9.36

δοκεῖ δέ, φησί [*scil.* Dem. Magn. Frag. 29 Mejer], καὶ
Ἀθήναζε ἐλθεῖν καὶ μὴ σπουδάσαι γνωσθῆναι, δόξης
καταφρονῶν. καὶ εἰδέναι μὲν Σωκράτη, ἀγνοεῖσθαι δὲ
ὑπ᾽ αὐτοῦ· "ἦλθον" γάρ, φησίν, "εἰς Ἀθήνας καὶ οὔ-
τις με ἔγνωκεν."

P20 (≠ DK) Diodorus Siculus

They [i.e. the Egyptians] suppose that Democritus too [scil. like Lycurgus, Plato, Solon, and Pythagoras] spent five years with them learning many things about astronomy.

See also **R115, R125**

Pythagoreans? (P21)

P21 (< A1) Diogenes Laertius

"He seems," says Thrasyllus, "to have been an emulator of the Pythagoreans" [. . .]. And it seems that he took over everything from him [i.e. Pythagoras] and that he would have studied with him if the chronology had not prevented it. Glaucus of Rhegium, who lived at the same time as him [i.e. Democritus], says that in any case he studied with one of the Pythagoreans. And Apollodorus of Cyzicus too says that he spent time with Philolaus.

Visit to Athens? (P22)

P22 (< A1, B116) Diogenes Laertius

a

He [i.e. Demetrius of Magnesia in his *Homonyms*] says that he seems to have gone to Athens too and not to have tried to be recognized, since he despised glory; and that he knew Socrates, but was not known by him, for he said, **"I came to Athens and no one recognized me."**

See also **P39**

b 9.37

Δημήτριος δὲ ὁ Φαληρεὺς ἐν τῇ Σωκράτους ἀπολογίᾳ
μηδὲ ἐλθεῖν φησιν [Frag. 93 Wehrli] αὐτὸν εἰς Ἀθήνας.
τοῦτο δὲ καὶ μεῖζον, εἴγε τοσαύτης πόλεως ὑπερεφρό-
νησεν, οὐκ ἐκ τόπου δόξαν λαβεῖν βουλόμενος, ἀλλὰ
τόπῳ δόξαν περιθεῖναι προελόμενος.

References to Other Thinkers (P23–P26)
Thales

See **THAL. P2, R1**

Anaxagoras (P23)

P23 (< A1, cf. B5) Diog. Laert. 9.34–35

Φαβωρῖνος δέ φησιν ἐν Παντοδαπῇ ἱστορίᾳ [Frag. 81
Amato] λέγειν Δημόκριτον περὶ Ἀναξαγόρου ὡς οὐκ
εἴησαν αὐτοῦ αἱ δόξαι αἵ τε περὶ ἡλίου καὶ σελήνης,
ἀλλὰ ἀρχαῖαι, τὸν δ' ὑφῃρῆσθαι· διασύρειν τε αὐτοῦ
τὰ περὶ τῆς διακοσμήσεως καὶ τοῦ νοῦ, ἐχθρῶς
ἔχοντα πρὸς αὐτόν, ὅτι δὴ μὴ προσήκατο αὐτόν. πῶς
οὖν κατά τινας ἀκήκοεν αὐτοῦ;

Pythagoreans (P24)

P24 (< A1) Diog. Laert. 9.38

[. . .] ἀλλὰ καὶ αὐτοῦ Πυθαγόρου μέμνηται, θαυμάζων
αὐτὸν ἐν τῷ ὁμωνύμῳ συγγράμματι [. . . cf. **P21**].

b

But Demetrius of Phalerum in his *Defense of Socrates* says that he did not even come to Athens. This is something that is even greater, if it is true that he despised so great a city, not wishing to derive glory from a place, but preferring to bestow glory on it.

References to Other Thinkers (P23–P26)
Thales

See **THAL. P2, R1**

Anaxagoras (P23)

P23 (< A1, cf. B5) Diogenes Laertius

Favorinus reports in his *Miscellaneous History* that Democritus said about Anaxagoras that the opinions he expressed about the sun and moon were not his own but were ancient, and that he had stolen them; and that he tore to pieces what he said about the cosmic ordering and mind, displaying hostility toward him because he had not accepted him to his company. So how could he have been his student, as some people maintain? [= **ANAXAG. R1**]

See also **ANAXAG. R2**

Pythagoreans (P24)

P24 (< A1) Diogenes Laertius

[Scil. Thrasyllus says,] "[. . .] in fact he mentions Pythagoras himself, expressing admiration for him in the treatise that bears his name [. . .]."

31

Xeniades of Corinth (P25)

P25 (B163) Sext. Emp. *Adv. Math.* 7.53

Ξενιάδης δὲ ὁ Κορίνθιος, οὗ καὶ Δημόκριτος μέμνηται [. . . = **XENI. D1**].

Other 5th Century Thinkers (P26)

P26 (< A1) Diog. Laert. 9.42

[. . . = **P10**] καὶ γὰρ τούτου μέμνηται. μέμνηται δὲ καὶ τῆς περὶ τοῦ ἑνὸς δόξης τῶν περὶ Παρμενίδην καὶ Ζήνωνα, ὡς κατ᾽ αὐτὸν μάλιστα διαβεβοημένων, καὶ Πρωταγόρου τοῦ Ἀβδηρίτου [. . .].

Alleged Direct Disciples (P27–P28)
Protagoras (P27)

P27 (A9) Athen. *Deipn.* 8.354C

ἐν δὲ τῇ αὐτῇ ἐπιστολῇ ὁ Ἐπίκουρος [Frag. 172 Usener] καὶ Πρωταγόραν φησὶ τὸν σοφιστὴν ἐκ φορμοφόρου καὶ ξυλοφόρου πρῶτον μὲν γενέσθαι γραφέα Δημοκρίτου· θαυμασθέντα δ᾽ ὑπ᾽ ἐκείνου ἐπὶ ξύλων τινὶ ἰδίᾳ συνθέσει ἀπὸ ταύτης τῆς ἀρχῆς ἀναληφθῆναι ὑπ᾽ αὐτοῦ καὶ διδάσκειν ἐν κώμῃ τινὶ γράμματα, ἀφ᾽ ὧν ἐπὶ τὸ σοφιστεύειν ὁρμῆσαι.

ATOMISTS (LEUCIPPUS, DEMOCRITUS)

Xeniades of Corinth (P25)

P25 (B163) Sextus Empiricus, *Against the Logicians*

Xeniades of Corinth, whom Democritus mentions [. . .].

Other 5th Century Thinkers (P26)

P26 (< A1) Diogenes Laertius

[. . .] and in fact he mentions this latter [i.e. Oenopides]. He also mentions the doctrine of the One held by Parmenides and Zeno, as they were very much talked about during his time, as well as Protagoras of Abdera [. . .].

Alleged Direct Disciples (P27–P28)
Protagoras (P27)

P27 (A9) Athenaeus, *Deipnosophists*

In the same letter [scil. *On Occupations*] Epicurus also says that Protagoras the sophist started out as a porter and wood-carrier, and then first became Democritus' personal secretary. The latter admired him for a particular way he had of assembling pieces of wood, and from this starting point he took him on and he taught him how to read in some village; from this he received the impulse toward becoming a sophist [cf. **PROT. P5–P7**].

Hippocrates (P28)

P28 (< A10) *Suda* I.564

Ἱπποκράτης [. . .] μαθητὴς γέγονε [. . .] ὡς δέ τινες
Δημοκρίτου τοῦ Ἀβδηρίτου, ἐπιβαλεῖν γὰρ αὐτὸν νέῳ
πρεσβύτην.[1]

[1] νέον πρεσβύτῃ ed. Porti

Character (P29–P48)
Intelligence (P29)

P29 (< A92) Sen. *Quaest. nat.* 7.3.2

Democritus [. . .], subtilissimus antiquorum omnium
[. . .= **D100**].

Experience (P30)

P30 (< B15) Agathem. *Geogr.* 1.1.2 (*GGM* 2.471.12)

[. . .] Δημόκριτος, πολύπειρος ἀνὴρ [. . . = **D112**].

Withdrawal and Self-Discipline (P31–P32)

P31 (< A1) Diog. Laert. 9.36

[. . . = **P16b**] λέγει δὲ [Dem. Magn. Frag. 29 Mejer] ὅτι
τοσοῦτον ἦν φιλόπονος, ὥστε τοῦ περικήπου δω-
μάτιόν τι ἀποτεμόμενος κατάκλειστος ἦν· καί ποτε

ATOMISTS (LEUCIPPUS, DEMOCRITUS)

Hippocrates (P28)

P28 (< A10) *Suda*

Hippocrates [. . .] became the student [. . .] according to
some people, of Democritus of Abdera; for he [i.e. Hip-
pocrates] became attached to (?) him [i.e. Democritus]
when the latter was young while he himself was an old
man.

Character (P29–P48)
Intelligence (P29)

P29 (< A92) Seneca, *Natural Questions*

Democritus [. . .], the most subtle of all the ancients [. . .].

Experience (P30)

P30 (< B15) Agathemerus, *A Sketch of Geography in
Epitome*

[. . .] Democritus, a man of great experience [. . .].

Withdrawal and Self-Discipline (P31–P32)

P31 (< A1) Diogenes Laertius

[. . .] He [i.e. Demetrius in his *Homonyms*] says that he
was so industrious that he divided off a little room from
the garden around the house and locked himself inside;

τοῦ πατρὸς αὐτοῦ πρὸς θυσίαν βοῦν ἀγαγόντος καὶ
αὐτόθι προσδήσαντος, ἱκανὸν χρόνον μὴ γνῶναι, ἕως
αὐτὸν ἐκεῖνος διαναστήσας προφάσει τῆς θυσίας καὶ
τὰ περὶ τὸν βοῦν διηγήσατο.

P32 (< A1) Diog. Laert. 9.38

ἤσκει δέ, φησὶν ὁ Ἀντισθένης [FGrHist 508 F13 =
Frag. 13 Giannattasio Andria], καὶ ποικίλως δοκιμάζειν
τὰς φαντασίας, ἐρημάζων ἐνίοτε καὶ τοῖς τάφοις ἐν-
διατρίβων.

The Eyes as a Hindrance (P33–P35)

P33 (A22) Cic. Tusc. 5.39.114

Democritus luminibus amissis alba scilicet discernere et
atra non poterat, at vero bona mala, aequa iniqua, honesta
turpia, utilia inutilia, magna parva poterat, et sine varietate
colorum licebat vivere beate, sine notione rerum non
licebat. atque hic vir impediri etiam animi aciem aspectu
oculorum arbitrabatur, et cum alii saepe, quod ante pedes
esset, non viderent, ille in infinitatem omnem peregrina-
batur, ut nulla in extremitate consisteret.

P34 (< A23) Aul. Gell. Noct. 10.17.1

Democritum philosophum in monumentis historiae Grae-
cae scriptum est, virum praeter alios venerandum auc-

and once when his father tied up an ox there that he had brought for sacrifice, he did not notice it for a long time until his father woke him up on account of the sacrifice and told him about the ox.

P32 (< A1) Diogenes Laertius

Antisthenes [scil. of Rhodes] reports that he trained himself and tested his sense impressions in many ways, sometimes withdrawing into solitude and spending time among the tombs.

The Eyes as a Hindrance (P33–P35)

P33 (A22) Cicero, *Tusculan Disputations*

When Democritus lost his eyesight he was not able to distinguish white and black—but certainly he was able [scil. to distinguish] good and evil, just and unjust, noble and shameful, useful and useless, big and small, and he was able to live happily, deprived of the variety of colors, but he was not able to do so without an idea of things. And this man even thought the acuity of his mind was hindered by the vision of his eyes, and whereas other people often do not see what is right in front of their feet, he traveled throughout all of infinity without stopping at any limit.

P34 (< A23) Aulus Gellius, *Attic Nights*

In the records of Greek history it is written that Democritus the philosopher, a man worthy of veneration beyond all others and enjoying an ancient authority, deprived him-

toritateque antiqua praeditum, luminibus oculorum sua
sponte se privasse, quia existimaret cogitationes commen-
tationesque animi sui in contemplandis naturae rationibus
vegetiores et exactiores fore, si eas videndi inlecebris et
oculorum impedimentis liberasset.

P35 (A27) Plut. *Curios.* 12 521C–D

ὅθεν ἐκεῖνο μὲν ψεῦδός ἐστι, τὸ Δημόκριτον ἑκουσίως
σβέσαι τὰς ὄψεις ἀπερεισάμενον εἰς ἔσοπτρα πυρω-
θέντα καὶ τὴν ἀπ' αὐτῶν ἀνάκλασιν δεξάμενον, ὅπως
μὴ παρέχωσι θόρυβον τὴν διάνοιαν ἔξω καλοῦσαι
πολλάκις, ἀλλ' ἐῶσιν ἔνδον οἰκουρεῖν καὶ διατρίβειν
πρὸς τοῖς νοητοῖς, ὥσπερ παρόδιοι θυρίδες ἐμφραγεῖ-
σαι.

Attitude Toward Money and Public
Recognition (P36–P39)

P36 (0.3.17 Leszl) Sen. *Prov.* 6.2

Democritus divitias proiecit onus illas bonae mentis
existimans.

P37

a (A16) Ael. *Var. hist.* 4.20

Δημόκριτον τὸν Ἀβδηρίτην λόγος ἔχει τά τε ἄλλα
γενέσθαι σοφὸν καὶ δὴ καὶ ἐπιθυμῆσαι λαθεῖν, καὶ ἐν

self voluntarily of the sight of his eyes because he thought that the ideas and reflections of his mind would be more lively and precise for contemplating natural causes if he freed them from the temptations of seeing and from the obstacles of the eyes.

P35 (A27) Plutarch, *On Curiosity*

[. . .] it is a fabrication that Democritus voluntarily extinguished the vision of his eyes by staring at a blazing mirror and receiving its reflection so that they would not disturb his thought by often summoning it to go outward but instead would leave it inside to keep the house and to occupy itself with intelligibles, as though they were windows to the street that had been shut.

See also **R111**

Attitude Toward Money and Public Recognition (P36–P39)

P36 (≠ DK) Seneca, *On Providence*

Democritus rejected riches, thinking that they are a burden for the health of the mind.

P37

a (A16) Aelian, *Historical Miscellany*

It is reported that Democritus of Abdera was wise in many regards and above all in his desire to escape notice, and

ἔργῳ θέσθαι πάνυ σφόδρα τοῦτο. διὰ ταῦτά τοι καὶ
πολλὴν ἐπῄει γῆν. ἧκεν οὖν καὶ πρὸς τοὺς Χαλδαίους
ἐς Βαβυλῶνα καὶ πρὸς τοὺς μάγους καὶ τοὺς σοφι-
στὰς τῶν Ἰνδῶν. τὴν παρὰ τοῦ Δαμασίππου τοῦ πατρὸς οὐσίαν ἐς τρία μέρη νεμηθεῖσαν τοῖς ἀδελφοῖς
τοῖς τρισί, τἀργύριον μόνον λαβὼν ἐφόδιον τῆς ὁδοῦ,
τὰ λοιπὰ τοῖς ἀδελφοῖς εἴασε. διὰ ταῦτά τοι καὶ Θεόφραστος αὐτὸν ἐπῄνει [Frag. 513 FHS&G], ὅτι περιῄει
κρείττονα ἀγερμὸν ἀγείρων Μενέλεω καὶ Ὀδυσσέως.
ἐκεῖνοι μὲν γὰρ ἠλῶντο, αὐτόχρημα Φοινίκων ἐμπό-
ρων μηδὲν διαφέροντες· χρήματα γὰρ ἤθροιζον, καὶ
τῆς περιόδου καὶ τοῦ περίπλου ταύτην εἶχον τὴν πρόφασιν.

b (< A1) Diog. Laert. 9.35–36

[. . . = **P16b**] τρίτον τε ὄντα ἀδελφὸν νείμασθαι τὴν
οὐσίαν· καὶ οἱ μὲν πλείους φασὶ τὴν ἐλάττω μοῖραν
ἑλέσθαι τὴν ἐν ἀργυρίῳ, χρείαν ἔχοντα ἀποδημῆσαι,
τοῦτο κἀκείνων δολίως ὑποπτευσάντων. [36] ὁ δὲ Δημήτριος [Frag. 29 Mejer] ὑπὲρ ἑκατὸν τάλαντά φησιν
εἶναι αὐτῷ τὸ μέρος, ἃ πάντα καταναλῶσαι.

P38 (A15) Phil. *Vita contemp.* 14

Ἀναξαγόραν καὶ Δημόκριτον Ἕλληνες ᾄδουσιν, ὅτι
φιλοσοφίας ἱμέρῳ πληχθέντες μηλοβότους εἴασαν
γενέσθαι τὰς οὐσίας.

that he put this into practice very much. And that is why he traveled around much of the earth; and so he went to the Chaldeans, Babylonia, the Magi, and the sages of India [cf. **P16–P20**]. And when the estate of his father Damasippus was divided into three portions for the three brothers, he took only the money, to pay for his travels, and left the rest for his brothers. That is why Theophrastus praised him, for he traveled around amassing a better collection than Menelaus and Odysseus had [cf. *Od.* 3.301, 4.80, 90]: for these latter had wandered without differing at all from Phoenician merchants, since they had gathered riches, and this has been the reason for their travels by land and by sea.

b (< A1) Diogenes Laertius

[. . . = **P16**] [scil. and some people say] that he was the third brother and divided the family estate; and most people say that he chose the smaller share, the one that consisted in money, since he needed this for the sake of his travels—and they [i.e. his brothers] had cunningly guessed he would do so. Demetrius says that his share was greater than one hundred talents and that he spent it all.

P38 (A15) Philo, *On the Contemplative Life*

The Greeks sing the praises of Anaxagoras and Democritus because these men, struck by a desire for philosophy, left their estates to be grazed by sheep.

P39 (< B116) Cic. *Tusc.* 5.36.104

"veni Athenas," inquit Democritus, **"neque me quis-
quam ibi adgnovit."** constantem hominem et gravem,
qui glorietur a gloria se afuisse.

His Passion for Causes (P40–P41)

P40 (< B118) Dionys. Alex. *Nat.* in Eus. *PE* 14.27.4

Δημόκριτος γοῦν αὐτός, ὥς φασιν, ἔλεγε βούλεσθαι
μᾶλλον μίαν εὑρεῖν αἰτιολογίαν ἢ τὴν Περσῶν οἱ βα-
σιλείαν γενέσθαι [. . .].

P41 (< A17a) Plut. *Quaest. conv.* 1.10 628C–D

[. . .] καὶ γὰρ ἐκεῖνος ὡς ἔοικε τρώγων σίκυον, ὡς
ἐφάνη μελιτώδης ὁ χυμός, ἠρώτησε τὴν διακονοῦσαν,
ὁπόθεν πρίαιτο· τῆς δὲ κῆπόν τινα φραζούσης, ἐκέλευ-
σεν ἐξαναστὰς ἡγεῖσθαι καὶ δεικνύναι τὸν τόπον·
θαυμάζοντος δὲ τοῦ γυναίου καὶ πυνθανομένου τί
βούλεται, "τὴν αἰτίαν," ἔφη, "δεῖ με τῆς γλυκύτητος
εὑρεῖν, εὑρήσω δὲ τοῦ χωρίου γενόμενος θεάτης"·
"κατάκεισο δή," τὸ γύναιον εἶπε μειδιῶν, "ἐγὼ γὰρ
ἀγνοήσασα τὸ σίκυον εἰς ἀγγεῖον ἐθέμην μεμελιτω-
μένον"· ὁ δ' ὥσπερ ἀχθεσθεὶς "ἀπέκναισας," εἶπεν,
"καὶ οὐδὲν ἧττον ἐπιθήσομαι τῷ λόγῳ καὶ ζητήσω
τὴν αἰτίαν," ὡς ἂν οἰκείου καὶ συγγενοῦς οὔσης τῷ
σικύῳ τῆς γλυκύτητος.

P39 (< B116) Cicero, *Tusculan Disputations*

"I came to Athens," said Democritus, **"and no one there recognized me"** [cf. **P22**]—a steadfast and serious man, who made it his glory that he avoided glory.

His Passion for Causes (P40–P41)

P40 (< B118) Dionysius, Bishop of Alexandria, in Eusebius, *Evangelical Preparation*

Democritus himself, as they say, stated that he would rather discover a single causal explanation (*aitiologia*) than become king of the Persians [. . .].

P41 (< A17a) Plutarch, *Table Talk*

[. . .] Apparently, when he was eating a cucumber its flavor seemed to him to taste like honey, so he asked his serving woman where she had bought it. When she indicated a certain garden, he got up and told her to lead him and to show him the place. The woman was surprised and asked him what he wanted, and he said, "I have to discover the cause of the sweetness, and I shall discover it by observing the place." "Then you can sit down," the woman said with a smile," for without noticing it I put the cucumber into a container that had been filled with honey." But he replied in irritation, "You have tried to fool me, and I shall stick nonetheless to what I said and I shall look for the cause," on the idea that the sweetness was inherent and innate to the cucumber.

The Encyclopedist (P42–P45)

P42 (< A1) Diog. Laert. 9.37

"εἴπερ οἱ Ἀντερασταὶ Πλάτωνός εἰσι," φησὶ Θράσυλλος [Test. 18c Tarrant], "οὗτος ἂν εἴη ὁ παραγενόμενος
ἀνώνυμος, τῶν περὶ Οἰνοπίδην καὶ Ἀναξαγόραν ἕτερος,[1] ἐν τῇ πρὸς Σωκράτην ὁμιλίᾳ διαλεγόμενος περὶ
φιλοσοφίας, ᾧ,[2] φησίν, ὡς πεντάθλῳ ἔοικεν ὁ φιλόσοφος. καὶ ἦν ὡς ἀληθῶς ἐν φιλοσοφίᾳ πένταθλος· τὰ
γὰρ φυσικὰ καὶ τὰ ἠθικὰ <ἤσκητο>,[3] ἀλλὰ καὶ τὰ
μαθηματικὰ καὶ τοὺς ἐγκυκλίους λόγους· καὶ περὶ
τεχνῶν πᾶσαν εἶχεν ἐμπειρίαν."

[1] <ἐριζόντων νεανιῶν> ἕτερος Marcovich e Plat. *Amat.* 132b1
et c1   [2] ᾧ BPF: <ἐν> ᾧ Reiske: οὗ Diels   [3] <ἤσκητο>
Casaubon e *Suda* II.971

P43 (B144) Philod. *Music.* 4.23 Col. 150.29–34

Δημ[ό]κριτος μὲν | τοίνυν, ἀνὴρ οὐ φυσιολογώ|τατος
μόν[ον] τῶν ἀρχαίων, ἀλλὰ καὶ τῶν ἱστορου|μένων
οὐδενὸς ἧττον πολυπράγμων [. . . = **D204**].

P44 (< B165)

a Cic. *Acad.* 2.23.73

quid loquar de Democrito? quem cum eo conferre pos-
sumus non modo ingenii magnitudine sed etiam animi, qui
ita sit ausus ordiri: "haec loquor de universis."

ATOMISTS (LEUCIPPUS, DEMOCRITUS)

The Encyclopedist (P42–P45)

P42 (< A1) Diogenes Laertius

"If indeed *The Rivals* is by Plato," says Thrasyllus, "he [i.e. Democritus] must be the unnamed man, different from Oenopides and Anaxagoras, who speaks about philosophy during the conversation with Socrates, the one for whom, he [scil. Socrates] says, the philosopher resembles a pentathlete [cf. Ps.-Plato, *Rivals* 136a]. And indeed he was in truth a real pentathlete in philosophy: for he ⟨practiced⟩ physics and ethics, and also mathematics and the subjects of general culture (*enkuklioi logoi*), and he had full practical experience in the arts and crafts."

P43 (B144) Philodemus, *On Music*

Democritus, a man who not only inquired into natural phenomena the most of any of the ancient philosophers but was also, in his curiosity, second to none of those we have heard of [. . .].

P44 (< B165)

a Cicero, *Prior Academics*

What shall I say of Democritus? To whom can we compare him for the extent not only of his intelligence but also of his courage—he who dared to begin with, "I say this about the totality of things."

45

EARLY GREEK PHILOSOPHY VII

b Sext. Emp. *Adv. Math.* 7.265

Δημόκριτος δὲ ὁ τῇ Διὸς φωνῇ παρεικαζόμενος, καὶ λέγων τάδε περὶ τῶν ξυμπάντων [. . . = **D26b**].

P45 (< B26f) Colum. *Agric.* 1 Praef. 32

[. . .] perfectum [. . .] agricolam, si quidem artis consummatae sit et in universa rerum natura sagacitatem Democriti vel Pythagorae fuerit consecutus [. . .].

*The Laughing Philosopher—or the
Crazy One?* (P46–P48)

P46 (A21) Sotion *Ira* 2 in Stob. 3.20.53

τοῖς δὲ σοφοῖς ἀντὶ ὀργῆς Ἡρακλείτῳ μὲν δάκρυα, Δημοκρίτῳ δὲ γέλως ἐπῄει.

P47 (0.3.11 Leszl) Ael. *Var. hist.* 4.20

ὅτι οἱ Ἀβδηρῖται ἐκάλουν τὸν Δημόκριτον Φιλοσοφίαν [. . .]. κατεγέλα δὲ πάντων ὁ Δημόκριτος καὶ ἔλεγεν αὐτοὺς μαίνεσθαι· ὅθεν καὶ Γελασῖνον αὐτὸν ἐκάλουν οἱ πολῖται. λέγουσι δὲ οἱ αὐτοὶ τὸν Ἱπποκράτην περὶ τὴν πρώτην ἔντευξιν ὑπὲρ τοῦ Δημοκρίτου δόξαν λαβεῖν ὡς μαινομένου· προϊούσης δὲ αὐτοῖς τῆς συνουσίας ἐς ὑπερβολὴν θαυμάσαι τὸν ἄνδρα.

b Sextus Empiricus, *Against the Logicians*

Democritus, who is compared with the voice of Zeus and who "says this about the totality of all things" [. . .].[1]

---

[1] These might be the opening words of *The Small World System*.

P45 (< B26f) Columella, *On Agriculture*

[. . .] the perfect [. . .] farmer, if he possesses consummate art and has acquired the sagacity of Democritus or Pythagoras in the domain of the universal nature of things [. . .].

> *The Laughing Philosopher—or the*
> *Crazy One?*[1] *(P46–P48)*

---

[1] Laughing Democritus is attested in many ancient texts; Democritus is opposed to Heraclitus, the weeping philosopher (cf. **HER. P12, R59**).

P46 (A21) Sotion, *On Anger* in Stobaeus, *Anthology*

Among the sages, Heraclitus was overcome by tears instead of by anger, and Democritus by laughter [= **HER. P12**].

P47 (≠DK) Aelian, *Historical Miscellany*

The Abderites called Democritus 'Philosophy' [. . .]. Democritus laughed at everyone and said they were crazy; and that is why his fellow citizens called him 'Laugher.' The same people say that when Hippocrates met him for the first time he thought that Democritus was crazy, but that as they spent more time together he came to admire the man enormously.

P48 (cf. C3) Ps.-Hipp. *Epist.* 17

a 9.348 Littré

τοῦτ᾽ ἐκεῖνο, Δαμάγητε, ὅπερ εἰκάζομεν, οὐ παρέκοπτε
Δημόκριτος, ἀλλὰ πάντα¹ ὑπερεφρόνεε, καὶ ἡμᾶς ἐσω-
φρόνιζε καὶ δι᾽ ἡμέων πάντας ἀνθρώπους. [. . .] καὶ
οὗτοι μέντοι ὧδε εἶχον ὡς ἐπὶ μαινομένῳ τῷ Δημοκρίτῳ, ὁ δὲ μετ᾽ ἀκριβείης τότε ὑπερεφιλοσόφεεν.

¹ πάντας aliqui mss.

b 9.352, 354, 356 Littré

ἐπεὶ δὲ ἐπλησίαζον, ἔτυχεν ὅτε ἐπῆλθον αὐτέῳ, τι¹ δή
ποτε γράφων ἐνθουσιωδῶς καὶ μεθ᾽ ὁρμῆς. [. . .]
[ΙΠ.] "καὶ πρῶτόν γε τί τοῦτο τυγχάνεις γράφων
φράζε." [. . .]
    ὁ δ᾽ ἐπισχὼν ὀλίγον, "περὶ μανίης," ἔφη. [. . .]
[ΙΠ.] "ἀλλὰ τί περὶ μανίης γράφεις;"
    "τί γάρ," εἶπεν, "ἄλλο, πλὴν ἥτις τε εἴη, καὶ ὅκως
ἀνθρώποισιν ἐγγίνεται, καὶ τίνα τρόπον ἀπολωφέοιτο·
τά τε γὰρ ζῷα ταῦτα ὁκόσα, ἔφη, ὁρῆς, τουτέου μέντοι γε ἀνατέμνω εἵνεκα, οὐ μισέων θεοῦ ἔργα, χολῆς
δὲ διζήμενος φύσιν καὶ θέσιν· οἶσθα γὰρ ἀνθρώπων
παρακοπῆς ὡς αἰτίη ἐπιτοπολὺ αὕτη πλεονάσασα,
ἐπεὶ πᾶσι μὲν φύσει ἐνυπάρχει, ἀλλὰ παρ᾽ οἷς μὲν
ἔλαττον, παρ᾽ οἷς δέ τι πλέον· ἡ δ᾽ ἀμετρίη αὐτέης

¹ ὅ ante τι del. Littré

P48 (cf. C3) Ps.-Hippocrates, *Letters*

a

It is, Damagetus, just as you and I [i.e. Hippocrates] guessed: Democritus has not gone mad, but he has been despising everything and has been bringing us, and through us all men, to our senses. [. . .] But these [i.e. all the Abderitans] were like this [scil. sad] because they thought that Democritus was crazy, but instead at that time he was devoting himself with great precision to the highest philosophy.

b

When [. . .] I [i.e. Hippocrates] approached, he [i.e. Democritus] happened, when I went up to him, to be writing something with inspiration and ardor. [. . .]
[Hippocrates:] "Tell me first what it is that you are writing."

He paused for a moment, then said, "About madness."
[. . .]
[Hippocrates:] "But what is it that you are writing about madness?"

"What else," he said, "than what it is, and how it befalls humans, and how it can be allayed. For all these animals," he said, "that you see—this is why I dissect them, not because I hate the works of god, but because I am investigating the nature and location of the bile. For, as you know, it is an excess of this that most often is the cause of frenzy in human beings, since it is present in all men by nature, but there is less of it in some, rather more in oth-

νοῦσοι τυγχάνουσιν, ὡς ὕλης ὅτε μὲν ἀγαθῆς, ὀτὲ δὲ
φαύλης ὑποκειμένης."

κἀγὼ, "νὴ Δία," ἔφην, "ὦ Δημόκριτε, ἀληθέως γε
καὶ φρονίμως λέγεις, ὅθεν εὐδαίμονά σε κρίνω τοσαύτης ἀπολαύοντα ἡσυχίης· ἡμῖν δὲ μετέχειν ταύτης
οὐκ ἐπιτέτραπται."

ἐρεομένου δὲ "διὰ τί, ὦ Ἱππόκρατες, οὐκ ἐπιτέτραπται;" "ὅτι," ἔφην, "ἢ ἀγροὶ ἢ οἰκίη ἢ τέκνα ἢ δάνεια
ἢ νοῦσοι ἢ θάνατοι ἢ δμῶες ἢ γάμοι ἢ τοιαῦτά τινα
τὴν εὐκαιρίην ὑποτάμνεται." ἐνταῦθα δὴ ὁ ἀνὴρ εἰς τὸ
εἰωθὸς πάθος κατηνέχθη, καὶ μάλα ἀθρόον τι ἀνεκάγ-
χασε, καὶ ἐπετώθασε, καὶ τὸ λοιπὸν ἡσυχίην ἦγεν.

c 9.360 Littré

[III.] "ἴσθι δὲ νῦν περὶ σέο γέλωτος τῷ βίῳ λόγον
δώσων."

ὁ δὲ μάλα τρανὸν ἐπιδών μοι, "δύο," φησὶ, "τοῦ
ἐμοῦ γέλωτος αἰτίας δοκέεις, ἀγαθὰ καὶ φαύλα· ἐγὼ
δὲ ἕνα γελῶ τὸν ἄνθρωπον, ἀνοίης μὲν γέμοντα, κε-
νεὸν δὲ πρηγμάτων ὀρθῶν, πάσῃσιν ἐπιβουλῇσι νη-
πιάζοντα, καὶ μηδεμιῆς ἕνεκεν ὠφελείης ἀλγέοντα
τοὺς ἀνηνύτους μόχθους, πείρατα γῆς καὶ ἀορίστους
μυχοὺς ἀμέτροισιν ἐπιθυμίῃσιν ὁδεύοντα, ἄργυρον
τήκοντα καὶ χρυσὸν, καὶ μὴ παυόμενον τῆς κτήσιος
ταύτης, αἰεὶ δὲ θορυβεύμενον περὶ τὸ πλέον, ὅκως
αὐτοῦ ἐλάσσων μὴ γένηται· καὶ οὐδὲν αἰσχύνεται λε-
γόμενος εὐδαίμων [. . .]."

ers. And its disproportion produces illnesses, as though its matter were sometimes beneficial, other times harmful."

I said, "By Zeus, Democritus, you are speaking truthfully and sensibly, and for this reason I consider you to be happy, since you enjoy such great tranquility. But as for me, it has not been granted to me to have a share in this."

Then he asked, "For what reason, Hippocrates, has it not been granted to you?" and I replied, "Because either fields or household or children or loans or illnesses or deaths or servants or marriages or other things of this sort deprive me of any opportunity for it." And then that man fell into his accustomed state, burst into gales of laughter and made fun of me, and afterward remained silent.

c

[Hippocrates:] "Know that you must now provide the world with an explanation of your laughter."

But he gave me a piercing glance and said, "You think that there are two reasons for my laughter, good things and bad ones. But in fact I laugh at only one thing, man, who is full of foolishness, empty of correctness, behaves like a baby in all his plans, suffers never-ending toils without gaining any advantage, travels the limits of the earth and boundless nooks and crannies because of his measureless desires, melts down silver and gold and never puts a stop to this greediness, always frantic to have more so that he never comes second (?)—and he is not ashamed to call himself happy [. . .]."[1]

[1] There are many echoes in the maxims of Democritus and those attributed to him; cf. e.g. **D228, D253,** etc.

Predictions (P49–P50)

P49 (A18) Clem. Alex. *Strom.* 6.32.2

Δημόκριτος δὲ ἐκ τῆς τῶν μεταρσίων παρατηρήσεως πολλὰ προλέγων Σοφία ἐπωνομάσθη. ὑποδεξαμένου γοῦν αὐτὸν φιλοφρόνως Δαμάσου τοῦ ἀδελφοῦ τεκμηράμενος ἔκ τινων ἀστέρων πολὺν ἐσόμενον προεῖπεν ὄμβρον. οἱ μὲν οὖν πεισθέντες αὐτῷ συνεῖλον τοὺς καρπούς (καὶ γὰρ ὥρᾳ θέρους ἐν ταῖς ἅλωσιν ἔτι[1] ἦσαν), οἱ δὲ ἄλλοι πάντα ἀπώλεσαν ἀδοκήτου καὶ πολλοῦ καταρρήξαντος ὄμβρου.

[1] ἔτι Victorius: ἔτη L

P50 (< A1) Diog. Laert. 9.42

φησὶ δ' Ἀθηνόδωρος ἐν ὀγδόῃ Περιπάτων[1] ἐλθόντος Ἱπποκράτους πρὸς αὐτὸν κελεῦσαι κομισθῆναι γάλα· καὶ θεασάμενον τὸ γάλα εἰπεῖν εἶναι[2] αἰγὸς πρωτοτόκου καὶ μελαίνης· ὅθεν τὴν ἀκρίβειαν αὐτοῦ θαυμάσαι τὸν Ἱπποκράτην. ἀλλὰ καὶ κόρης ἀκολουθούσης τῷ Ἱπποκράτει, τῇ μὲν πρώτῃ ἡμέρᾳ ἀσπάσασθαι οὕτω· "χαῖρε κόρη," τῇ δ' ἐχομένῃ· "χαῖρε γύναι"· καὶ ἦν ἡ κόρη τῆς νυκτὸς διεφθαρμένη.

[1] περιπάτων F: περὶ πάντων BP
[2] καὶ mss., corr. Casaubon

Predictions (P49–P50)

P49 (A18) Clement of Alexandria, *Stromata*

Democritus received the nickname 'Wisdom' because he made many predictions on the basis of his observation of the heavens. When his brother Damasus received him hospitably, he predicted from examining certain heavenly bodies that there would be a lot of rain. Some people believed him and gathered in the fruits (for it was summer and they were still in the plantations), but the others lost everything when it rained intensely and unexpectedly.

P50 (< A1) Diogenes Laertius

Athenodorus says in the 8th book of his *Walks* that when Hippocrates came to visit him [i.e. Democritus], he ordered that milk be brought; and when he had observed the milk he said that it came from a black, primiparous she-goat. Hippocrates was very surprised at his precision. Another time, a girl was accompanying Hippocrates; and on the first day he greeted her by saying, "Hello, maiden," but on the next day, "Hello, woman." And in fact the girl had been deflowered during the night.

The Circumstances of His Death (P51–P54)

P51 (< A1) Diog. Laert. 9.43

τελευτῆσαι δὲ τὸν Δημόκριτόν φησιν Ἕρμιππος
[Frag. 31 Wehrli] τοῦτον τὸν τρόπον. ἤδη ὑπέργηρων
ὄντα πρὸς τῷ καταστρέφειν εἶναι. τὴν οὖν ἀδελφὴν¹
λυπεῖσθαι ὅτι ἐν τῇ τῶν Θεσμοφόρων ἑορτῇ μέλλοι
τεθνήξεσθαι καὶ τῇ θεῷ τὸ καθῆκον αὐτῇ² οὐ ποιή-
σειν· τὸν δὲ θαρρεῖν εἰπεῖν καὶ κελεῦσαι αὑτῷ προσ-
φέρειν ἄρτους θερμοὺς ὁσημέραι. τούτους δὴ ταῖς
ῥισὶ προσφέρων διεκράτησεν αὑτὸν τὴν ἑορτήν·
ἐπειδὴ δὲ παρῆλθον αἱ ἡμέραι (τρεῖς δὲ ἦσαν), ἀλυπότατα τὸν βίον προήκατο [. . . = **P15**].

¹ ἀδελφιδῆν Reiske   ² αὐτῇ Reiske et Kühn (-ῇ F):
αὐτὴν BP

P52 (< A29) Athen. *Deipn.* 2.26 46E–F

Δημόκριτον δὲ τὸν Ἀβδηρίτην λόγος ἔχει διὰ γῆρας
ἐξάξαι αὑτὸν διεγνωκότα τοῦ ζῆν καὶ ὑφαιροῦντα τῆς
τροφῆς καθ᾿ ἑκάστην ἡμέραν, ἐπεὶ αἱ τῶν Θεσμοφο-
ρίων ἡμέραι ἐνέστησαν, δεηθεισῶν τῶν οἰκείων γυναι-
κῶν μὴ ἀποθανεῖν κατὰ τὴν πανήγυριν, ὅπως ἑορτά-
σωσι, πεισθῆναι κελεύσαντα μέλιτος ἀγγεῖον αὑτῷ
πλησίον παρατεθῆναι, καὶ διαζῆσαι ἡμέρας ἱκανὰς
τὸν ἄνδρα, τῇ ἀπὸ τοῦ μέλιτος ἀναφορᾷ μόνῃ χρώμενον, καὶ μετὰ τὰς ἡμέρας βασταχθέντος τοῦ μέλιτος ἀποθανεῖν.

The Circumstances of His Death (P51–P54)

P51 (< A1) Diogenes Laertius

Hermippus says that Democritus died in the following way. When he was already very old, he was near the end. Then his sister became upset because he was going to die during the festival of the Thesmophoria and she would not be able to perform the proper honors for the goddess. He told her to cheer up and ordered her to bring him hot loaves of bread every day. By applying these to his nostrils he managed to stay alive until the end of the festival; and when the days had passed (there were three of them) he abandoned life without any suffering [. . .].

P52 (< A29) Athenaeus, *Deipnosophists*

It is reported that Democritus of Abdera had decided to kill himself because of his old age, and that he was reducing his food every day. But when the days of the Thesmophoria were imminent and his female relatives asked him to stay alive during the festival, so that they could celebrate it, he was persuaded and ordered that a container of honey be set down near him. And by consuming only what evaporated from the honey, that man stayed alive long enough, and when the honey was removed after those days he died.

P53 (A24) Lucr. 3.1039–41

denique Democritum post quam matura vetustas
admonuit memores motus languescere mentis,
sponte sua leto caput obvius optulit ipse.

P54 (< A6) Ps.-Luc. *Long.* 18

Δημόκριτος μὲν ὁ Ἀβδηρίτης [. . . = **P14**] ἀποσχόμενος
τροφῆς ἐτελεύτα.

Honors (P55)

P55 (< A1) Diog. Laert. 9.39–40

ἐλθόντα δή φησιν [*FGrHist* 508 F14 = Antisth. Rhod.
Frag. 14 Giannattasio Andria] αὐτὸν ἐκ τῆς ἀποδημίας
ταπεινότατα διάγειν, ἅτε πᾶσαν τὴν οὐσίαν κατανα-
λωκότα· τρέφεσθαί τε διὰ τὴν ἀπορίαν ἀπὸ τἀδελφοῦ
Δαμάσου. ὡς δὲ προειπών τινα τῶν μελλόντων εὐδο-
κίμησε, λοιπὸν ἐνθέου δόξης παρὰ τοῖς πλείστοις
ἠξιώθη. νόμου δὲ ὄντος τὸν ἀναλώσαντα τὴν πα-
τρῴαν οὐσίαν μὴ ἀξιοῦσθαι ταφῆς ἐν τῇ πατρίδι,
φησὶν ὁ Ἀντισθένης, συνέντα, μὴ ὑπεύθυνος γενηθείη
πρός τινων φθονούντων καὶ συκοφαντούντων, ἀναγνῶναι αὐτοῖς τὸν Μέγαν διάκοσμον, ὃς ἁπάντων αὐτοῦ
τῶν συγγραμμάτων προέχει· καὶ πεντακοσίοις ταλάν-
τοις τιμηθῆναι· μὴ μόνον δέ, ἀλλὰ καὶ χαλκαῖς εἰ-
κόσι· καὶ τελευτήσαντα αὐτὸν δημοσίᾳ ταφῆναι, βιώ-

P53 (A24) Lucretius, *On the Nature of Things*

> And finally, after his ripe old age had warned Democ-
> ritus
> That the mental impulses of his memory were
> deteriorating,
> Of his own free will he delivered himself up to death.

P54 (< A6) Ps.-Lucian, *Long-lived Men*

Democritus of Abdera [. . .] died by starving himself.

Honors (P55)

P55 (< A1) Diogenes Laertius

He [i.e. Antisthenes of Rhodes] says that when he re-
turned from his travels he lived in extreme poverty, since
he had spent all his wealth; and that because of his lack of
means he was supported by his brother Damasus. But he
enjoyed a high reputation because he predicted some future events; and in consequence he was considered worthy
of divine honor by most men. Antisthenes says that there
was a law forbidding anyone who had squandered his patrimony to be buried in his fatherland; and Democritus,
knowing this, so as to avoid being made liable to render
an account by anyone who might envy and prosecute him,
gave them a reading of his *Great World System,* which is
the greatest of all of his treatises. And he was rewarded
with five hundred talents, and not only with that, but also
with bronze statues; and when he died he was buried at
public expense, after he had lived for over one hundred

σαντα ὑπὲρ τὰ ἑκατὸν ἔτη. ὁ δὲ Δημήτριος τοὺς συγγενέας αὐτοῦ φησιν [Frag. 30 Mejer] ἀναγνῶναι τὸν Μέγαν διάκοσμον, ὃν μόνον ἑκατὸν ταλάντων τιμηθῆναι. ταῦτα δὲ καὶ Ἱππόβοτός φησιν [Frag. 21 Gigante].

years. But Demetrius says that it was his relatives who gave the reading of his *Great World System,* and that it was awarded only one hundred talents; and Hippobotus says the same thing.

Iconography (P56)

P56 (≠ DK) Koch, "Ikonographie," in Flashar, Bremer, Rechenauer (2013), I.1, pp. 225, 226.

ATOMISTS
(LEUCIPPUS [67 DK],
DEMOCRITUS [68 DK])

For Leucippus, references to DK take the form 67 Ax or Bx; for Democritus, references are generally by only Ax, Bx, or Cx.

D

Writings of Leucippus and Democritus (D1–D9)
Titles Attested for Leucippus (D1)

D1

a (67 B2) Aët. 1.25.4 (Stob.) [περὶ ἀνάγκης]

Λεύκιππος [. . .] λέγει [. . .] ἐν τῷ Περὶ νοῦ [. . . cf. **D73**].

b (≠ DK) Ps.-Arist. *MXG* 980a7

[. . .] καθάπερ ἐν τοῖς Λευκίππου καλουμένοις λόγοις γέγραπται [. . . cf. **GORG. D26a[16]**].

ATOMISTS
(LEUCIPPUS, DEMOCRITUS)

D

Writings of Leucippus and Democritus (D1–D9)
Titles Attested for Leucippus (D1)

D1

a (67 B2) Aëtius

Leucippus [. . .] says in his *On Mind:* [. . . cf. **D73**].

b (≠ DK) Ps.-Aristotle, *On Melissus, Xenophanes, and Gorgias*

[. . .] as is written in what are called the arguments of Leucippus [. . .].

See also **D2b** (III.1)

Ancient Lists of the Writings of
Democritus (D2–D3)

D2 Diog. Laert.

a (< A1) 9.41

[. . .] ὡς δὲ Θράσυλλος ἐν τῷ ἐπιγραφομένῳ Τὰ πρὸ τῆς ἀναγνώσεως τῶν Δημοκρίτου βιβλίων [. . .].

b (A33) 9.45–49

τὰ δὲ βιβλία αὐτοῦ καὶ Θράσυλλος ἀναγέγραφε κατὰ τάξιν οὕτως ὡσπερεὶ καὶ τὰ Πλάτωνος κατὰ τετρα-λογίαν.
[46] ἔστι δὲ ἠθικὰ μὲν τάδε·

[I] 1. Πυθαγόρης 2. Περὶ τῆς τοῦ σοφοῦ διαθέσεως
3. Περὶ τῶν ἐν Ἅιδου[1] 4. Τριτογένεια (τοῦτο δέ
ἐστιν ὅτι τρία γίνεται ἐξ αὐτῆς, ἃ πάντα ἀνθρώ-
πινα συνέχει)

[1] Ἅιδου Suda T.1019: ἅ*δη vel ἅδη mss.

[II] 1. Περὶ ἀνδραγαθίας ἢ περὶ ἀρετῆς 2. Ἀμαλ-
θείης κέρας 3. Περὶ εὐθυμίης 4. Ὑπομνημάτων
ἠθικῶν·[1] ἢ γὰρ Εὐεστὼ οὐχ εὑρίσκεται.

καὶ ταῦτα μὲν τὰ ἠθικά.

[1] ἢ οἴκων mss., corr. Steph. Monachius ap. Menagium: post
ἠθικῶν lac. numerum librorum continens pos. Diels

ATOMISTS (LEUCIPPUS, DEMOCRITUS)

Ancient Lists of the Writings of
Democritus (D2–D3)

D2 Diogenes Laertius

a (< A1)

[. . .] according to Thrasyllus, in his book entitled *Preliminaries to Reading Democritus' Books* [. . .].

b (A33)

Thrasyllus has cataloged his books in order, just as he did for Plato's, in tetralogies.[1]
His ethical books are the following:

> [I] 1. *Pythagoras*   2. *On the Disposition of the Sage*
> 3. ***On those*** [scil. *People* or *Things*] ***in Hades***
> 4. *Tritogeneia* (that is because she produces the three things that comprise [or: preserve] all things human)

> [II] 1. *On Manly Excellence or On Virtue*   2. *The Horn of Amalthea*   3. *On Contentment*   4. *Ethical Treatises* (*hupomnêmata*) (for *Well-Being* is not to be found)

And these are the ethical ones.

---

[1] The titles attested elsewhere are in boldface. Many of the titles that figure in this catalog are certainly inauthentic. See the study by W. Leszl listed in the introduction to this chapter.

φυσικὰ δὲ τάδε·

[III] 1. **Μέγας διάκοσμος** (ὃν οἱ περὶ Θεόφραστον
Λεύκιππου φασὶν εἶναι)   2. **Μικρὸς διάκοσμος**
3. Κοσμογραφίη   4. Περὶ τῶν πλανήτων

[IV] 1. Περὶ φύσεως πρῶτον   2. Περὶ ἀνθρώπου
φύσιος (ἢ Περὶ σαρκός) δεύτερον   3. **Περὶ νοῦ**
4. Περὶ αἰσθησίων (ταῦτά τινες ὁμοῦ γράφοντες
Περὶ ψυχῆς ἐπιγράφουσι)

[V] 1. Περὶ χυμῶν   2. Περὶ χροῶν   [47] 3. Περὶ τῶν
διαφερόντων ῥυσμῶν   4. **Περὶ ἀμειψιρυσμιῶν**

[VI] 1. **Κρατυντήρια** (ὅπερ ἐστὶν ἐπικριτικὰ τῶν
προειρημένων)   2. Περὶ εἰδώλων[1] ἢ περὶ προ-
νοίας[2]   3. Περὶ λογικῶν[3] κανὼν α΄ β΄ γ΄   4. Ἀπορημάτων[4]

ταῦτα καὶ περὶ φύσεως.

[1] εἰδώλου mss., corr. Cobet   [2] ἀπορροίης Krische
[3] λογικῶν F, γρ. P[4]: λοιμῶν BP[1]: λογικῶν ⟨ἢ⟩ Cobet
[4] post Ἀπορημάτων lac. numerum librorum continens pos.
Diels

τὰ δὲ ἀσύντακτά ἐστι τάδε·

1. Αἰτίαι οὐράνιαι   2. Αἰτίαι ἀέριοι   3. Αἰτίαι
ἐπίπεδοι   4. Αἰτίαι περὶ πυρὸς καὶ τῶν ἐν πυρί
5. Αἰτίαι περὶ φωνῶν   6. Αἰτίαι περὶ σπερμάτων
καὶ φυτῶν καὶ καρπῶν   7. Αἰτίαι περὶ ζῴων α΄
β΄ γ΄   8. Αἰτίαι σύμμικτοι   9. Περὶ τῆς λίθου

ταῦτα καὶ τὰ ἀσύντακτα.

The physical ones are the following:

[III] 1. **The Great World System** (which Theophrastus attributes to Leucippus[1])   2. **The Small World System**   3. *Description of the world*   4. *On the Planets*

[IV] 1. *On Nature, first book*   2. *On the Nature of Man (or On Flesh), second book*   3. **On Mind**   4. *On the Sensations* (some people combine these books and entitle them *On the Soul*)

[V] 1. *On Flavors*   2. *On Colors*   3. *On the different Configurations*   4. **On Changes of Configuration**

[VI] 1. **Corroborations** (that is, confirmations of the preceding works)   2. *On Images or On Foreknowledge*   3. *Canon, On Logical Matters, Books 1, 2, 3*   4. *Difficulties*

These are the ones on nature.

[1] Cf. also *PHerc.* 1788 (67 B1a DK), where the name of Leucippus can probably be restored as the author of this work.

The unclassified ones are the following:

1. *Celestial Causes*   2. *Atmospheric Causes*   3. *Terrestrial Causes*   4. *Causes Relating to Fire and Fiery Phenomena*   5. *Causes Relating to Sounds*   6 *Causes Relating to Seeds, Plants, and Fruits*   7. *Causes Relating to Animals, Books 1, 2, 3.*   8. *Miscellaneous Causes*   9. *On the Magnet*

These are the unclassified ones.

μαθηματικὰ δὲ τάδε·

[VII] 1. Περὶ διαφορῆς γνώμης[1] ἢ Περὶ ψαύσιος κύκλου καὶ σφαίρης   2. Περὶ γεωμετρίης   3. Γεωμετρικῶν[2]   4. Ἀριθμοί

[1] γωνίης Heath: γνώμονος Cobet   [2] post Γεωμετρικῶν lac. numerum librorum continens pos. Diels

[VIII] 1. Περὶ ἀλόγων γραμμῶν καὶ ναστῶν α' β'   2. Ἐκπετάσματα   [48] 3. Μέγας ἐνιαυτὸς ἢ Ἀστρονομίη, παράπηγμα   4. Ἄμιλλα †κλεψύδρᾳ†[1]

[1] κλεψύδρας <καὶ οὐρανοῦ> Diels

[IX] 1. Οὐρανογραφίη   2. Γεωγραφίη   3. Πολογραφίη   4. Ἀκτινογραφίη

τοσαῦτα καὶ τὰ μαθηματικά.

μουσικὰ δὲ τάδε·

[X] 1. Περὶ ῥυθμῶν καὶ ἁρμονίης   2. Περὶ ποιήσιος   3. Περὶ καλλοσύνης ἐπέων   4. Περὶ εὐφώνων καὶ δυσφώνων γραμμάτων[1]

[1] γραμμάτων PF: πραγμάτων B

[XI] 1. Περὶ Ὁμήρου ἢ[1] ὀρθοεπείης καὶ γλωσσέων   2. Περὶ ἀοιδῆς   3. Περὶ ῥημάτων   4. Ὀνομαστικῶν[2]

τοσαῦτα καὶ τὰ μουσικά.

The mathematical ones are the following:

>   [VII] 1. *On a Difference of Opinion*[1] *or On the Contact of the Circle and Sphere* 2. *On Geometry* 3. *Geometrical Matters* 4. *Numbers*

>   [1] Or, emending the text: "On a Different Angle" (cf. **D60b**).

>   [VIII] 1. *On Irrational Lines and Solids, Books 1, 2* 2. *Projections* 3. *The Great Year, or* **Astronomy, an observation table** (*parapêgma*) 4. *Rivalry* †*for the Clepsydra*†
>   [IX] 1. *Description of the Heavens* 2. *Description of the Earth* 3. *Description of the Poles* 4. *Description of the Rays of Light*

These are the mathematical ones.

The ones on poetry and music are the following:

>   [X] 1. *On Rhythms and Harmony* 2. *On Poetry* 3. *On the Beauty of Verses* 4. *On Letters that Sound Good and Bad*
>   [XI] 1. *On Homer or Correct Diction and Unusual Terms* (*glôssai*) 2. *On Song* 3. *On Words* 4. *Onomastic Matters*

These are the ones on poetry and music.

---

[1] ἢ del. Friedel: περὶ Classen   [2] post Ὀνομαστικῶν lac. numerum librorum continens pos. Diels

τεχνικὰ δὲ τάδε·

[XII] 1. Πρόγνωσις   2. Περὶ διαίτης ἢ Διαιτητικόν
3. Ἡ[1] ἰητρικὴ γνώμη   4. Αἰτίαι περὶ ἀκαιριῶν
καὶ ἐπικαιριῶν

[1] ἡ nos: ἢ mss.: del. Diels

[XIII] 1. **Περὶ γεωργίης ἢ Γεωμετρικόν**[1]   2. Περὶ
ζωγραφίης   3. Τακτικὸν καὶ   4. Ὁπλομαχικόν

[1] Γεωργικὸν Menagius: -κῶν Wellmann: -κὰ Diels

τοσαῦτα καὶ τάδε.

[49] τάττουσι δέ τινες κατ᾿ ἰδίαν ἐκ τῶν ὑπομνημάτων
καὶ ταῦτα·

1. Περὶ τῶν ἐν Βαβυλῶνι ἱερῶν γραμμάτων
2. Περὶ τῶν ἐν Μερόῃ   3. Ὠκεανοῦ περίπλους
4. Περὶ ἱστορίης   5. Χαλδαικὸς λόγος   6. Φρύ-
γιος λόγος   7. Περὶ πυρετοῦ καὶ τῶν ἀπὸ νόσου
βησσόντων   8. Νομικὰ[1] αἴτια   9. †Χερνικὰ† ἢ[2]
προβλήματα

[1] Λοιμικὰ Reiske   [2] Χερνικὰ (vel Χερνιβὰ) ἢ mss.:
Χειρόκμητα Salmasius

τὰ δ᾿ ἄλλα ὅσα τινὲς ἀναφέρουσιν εἰς αὐτὸν τὰ μὲν
ἐκ τῶν αὐτοῦ διεσκεύασται, τὰ δ᾿ ὁμολογουμένως
ἐστὶν ἀλλότρια. ταῦτα καὶ περὶ τῶν βιβλίων αὐτοῦ
καὶ τοσαῦτα.

The ones on the crafts are the following:

[XII] 1. *Prognostication*   2. *On Diet or Dietetics*
     3. *The Medical Judgment*   4. *Causes of Inopportune*
     and Opportune Events
[XIII] 1. **On Agriculture or Land Measurement**
     2. *On Painting*   3. *Tactics* and   4. *Hoplite Combat*

This is the number of these books too.

Among his treatises (*hupomnêmata*), some people classify
the following separately:

1. *On the Sacred Writings of Babylon*   2. *On those*
[scil. *People* or *Things*] *in Meroe*   3. *Voyage around*
the Ocean   4. *On Research*   5. *Chaldean Dis-*
course   6. *Phrygian Discourse*   7. *On Fever and*
Coughing caused by Disease   8. *Causes Relating to*
Laws   9. †*Chernika*† *or Problems.*[1]

Among all the other works that some people attribute to
him, some derive from compilations of his writings, the
others are generally agreed not to be by him. So much for
his books and their number.

---

[1] Saumaise conjectured *Problems Relating to Works Fabri-*
cated Manually (*Kheirokmêta problêmata*).

D3 (A31) *Suda* Δ.447

γνήσια δὲ αὐτοῦ βιβλία εἰσὶ δύο, ὅ τε μέγας Διάκοσμος, καὶ τὸ Περὶ φύσεως κόσμου. ἔγραψε δὲ καὶ
ἐπιστολάς.

Titles Otherwise Attested (D4–D9)

D4 (< B9) Sext. Emp. *Adv. Math.* 7.136

ἐν δὲ τοῖς Κρατυντηρίοις [. . .] [cf. **D15**].

D5 (< B6) Sext. Emp. *Adv. Math.* 7.137

[. . .] ἐν δὲ τῷ Περὶ ἰδεῶν [. . .] [cf. **D17**].

D6 (< B11) Sext. Emp. *Adv. Math.* 7.138 (cf. 8.327)

[. . .] ἐν δὲ τοῖς Κανόσι [. . .] [cf. **D20**].

D7 (< B119) Dion. Alex. *Nat.* in Eus. *PE* 14.27.5 (cf. Stob.
2.8.16)

[. . .] τῶν γοῦν Ὑποθηκῶν ἀρχόμενος λέγει· [. . .] [cf.
D274].

D8 (< B1) Procl. *In Remp.* 2.113.8–9

[. . .] Δημόκριτος ὁ φυσικὸς ἐν τοῖς Περὶ τοῦ Ἅιδου
γράμμασιν [. . .] [cf. **D143**].

D3 (A31) *Suda*

There are two authentic books by him, *The Great World System* and *On the Nature of the World.* He also wrote letters[1] [cf. **R116**].

[1] The letters attributed to Democritus (68 C2–6) are certainly inauthentic.

Titles Otherwise Attested (D4–D9)[1]

[1] Cf. also perhaps **R3a.**

D4 (< B9) Sextus Empiricus, *Against the Logicians*
In the **Corroborations** [. . .].

D5 (< B6) Sextus Empiricus, *Against the Logicians*
[. . .] in **On the Forms** [. . .].

D6 (< B11) Sextus Empiricus, *Against the Logicians*
[. . .] in his **Criteria** [. . .].

D7 (< B119) Dionysius of Alexandria, *On Nature,* in Eusebius, *Evangelical Preparation*
[. . .] he says at the beginning of his **Precepts** [. . .].

D8 (< B1) Proclus, *Commentary on Plato's* Republic
[. . .] Democritus the natural philosopher in his writings **On Hades** [. . .].

D9 (B28) Colum. *Agric.* 11.3.2

Democritus in eo libro, quem Georgicon appellavit [. . .] [cf. **D402**].

Leucippus, the Founding Father (D10)

D10 (< 67 A1) Diog. Laert. 9.30

πρῶτός τε ἀτόμους ἀρχὰς ὑπεστήσατο.

Democritus, the Elaborator (D11)

D11 (67 A8) Cic. *Acad.* 2.36.118

Leucippus plenum et inane. Democritus huic in hoc similis, uberior in ceteris.

An Evolving Doctrine? (D12)

D12 (A35a) Plut. *Virt. moral.* 7 448A

[. . .] ἀλλ᾽ αὐτός τ᾽ Ἀριστοτέλης Δημόκριτός τε καὶ Χρύσιππος ἔνια τῶν πρόσθεν αὐτοῖς ἀρεσκόντων ἀθορύβως καὶ ἀδήκτως καὶ μεθ᾽ ἡδονῆς ἀφεῖσαν.

The General Summary in Diogenes Laertius (D13)

D13 (< A1) Diog. Laert. 9.44–45

[44] δοκεῖ δὲ αὐτῷ τάδε· ἀρχὰς εἶναι τῶν ὅλων ἀτόμους

D9 (B28) Columella, *On Agriculture*

Democritus, in the book that he entitled **Georgic** [*On Agriculture*] [. . .].

Leucippus, the Founding Father (D10)

D10 (< 67 A1) Diogenes Laertius

He was the first to posit the atoms as principles.

Democritus, the Elaborator (D11)

D11 (67 A8) Cicero, *Prior Academics*

Leucippus [scil. said that the principles] are the full and the void. Democritus is similar to him on this point but he is more elaborated in everything else.

An Evolving Doctrine? (D12)

D12 (A35a) Plutarch, *On Moral Virtue*

Aristotle himself, Democritus, and Chrysippus abandoned some of their earlier opinions, unperturbed, untroubled, and with pleasure.

The General Summary in Diogenes Laertius (D13)

D13 (< A1) Diogenes Laertius

[44] His opinions are as follows. The principles of the to-

καὶ κενόν, τὰ δ᾽ ἄλλα πάντα νενομίσθαι[1] ἀπείρους τε
εἶναι κόσμους καὶ γεννητοὺς καὶ φθαρτούς. μηδέν τε
ἐκ τοῦ μὴ ὄντος γίνεσθαι μηδὲ εἰς τὸ μὴ[2] ὂν φθείρεσθαι. καὶ τὰς ἀτόμους δὲ ἀπείρους εἶναι κατὰ μέγεθος
καὶ πλῆθος, φέρεσθαι δ᾽ ἐν τῷ ὅλῳ δινουμένας. καὶ
οὕτω πάντα τὰ συγκρίματα γεννᾶν, πῦρ, ὕδωρ, ἀέρα,
γῆν· εἶναι γὰρ καὶ ταῦτα ἐξ ἀτόμων τινῶν συστήματα·
ἅπερ εἶναι ἀπαθῆ καὶ ἀναλλοίωτα διὰ τὴν στερρό-
τητα. τόν τε ἥλιον καὶ τὴν σελήνην ἐκ τοιούτων λείων
καὶ περιφερῶν ὄγκων συγκεκρίσθαι, καὶ τὴν ψυχὴν
ὁμοίως· ἣν καὶ νοῦν ταὐτὸν εἶναι. ὁρᾶν δ᾽ ἡμᾶς κατ᾽
εἰδώλων ἐμπτώσεις. [45] πάντα τε κατ᾽ ἀνάγκην γίνεσθαι, τῆς δίνης αἰτίας οὔσης τῆς γενέσεως πάντων,
ἣν ἀνάγκην λέγει. [. . . = **D375**].

[1] post νενομίσθαι hab. δοξάζεσθαι BPF: om. φ
[2] μὴ F: μηδὲ BP[1]: μηδὲν φ

Knowledge (D14–D24)

D14 (B9, cf. B125) Sext. Emp. *Adv. Math.* 7.135

"νόμῳ," γάρ φησι, "γλυκὺ καὶ νόμῳ πικρόν, νόμῳ
θερμόν, νόμῳ ψυχρόν, νόμῳ χροιή· ἐτεῇ[1] δὲ ἄτομα
καὶ κενόν."

[1] αἰτίη mss., corr. Stephanus

tality of things are atoms and the void, everything else is
the object of convention. The worlds are unlimited and
they are subject to generation and destruction. Nothing
comes into being from what does not exist nor is it destroyed into what does not exist. And the atoms are unlimited in magnitude and number and they move in the
whole, whirling around. And this is how they generate all
the aggregates, fire, water, air, earth. For these too are
assemblages of atoms of a certain kind, which are impassible and inalterable because of their solidity. The sun and
the moon are the result of the aggregation of such smooth
and round masses, and so too the soul, which is the same
thing as the intellect. We see by virtue of the impact of
images. [45] Everything happens by necessity, the vortex,
which he calls **necessity,** being the cause of the generation of all things [. . .].

Knowledge (D14–D24)

D14 (B9, cf. B125) Sextus Empiricus, *Against the
Logicians*

**By convention sweet and by convention bitter, by
convention hot, by convention cold, by convention
color, but in reality (*eteê*) atoms and void.**

D15 (B9) Sext. Emp. *Adv. Math.* 7.136

ἐν δὲ τοῖς Κρατυντηρίοις [. . .] φησὶ γὰρ "ἡμεῖς δὲ τῷ
μὲν ἐόντι οὐδὲν ἀτρεκὲς συνίεμεν, μεταπίπτον δὲ
κατά τε σώματος διαθήκην[1] καὶ τῶν ἐπεισιόντων καὶ
τῶν ἀντιστηριζόντων."

   [1] διαθιγὴν Menzel

D16 (B10) Sext. Emp. *Adv. Math.* 7.136–137

καὶ πάλιν φησίν· "ἐτεῇ[1] μέν νυν ὅτι οἷον ἕκαστον
ἔστιν ‹ἢ›[2] οὐκ ἔστιν οὐ[3] συνίεμεν, πολλαχῇ δεδήλωται."

   [1] τίη vel τοίη mss., corr. Fabricius   [2] ‹ἢ› ed. Gen.
   [3] οὐ ed. Gen.: οὖ mss.

D17 (B6) Sext. Emp. *Adv. Math.* 7.137

ἐν δὲ τῷ Περὶ ἰδεῶν "γιγνώσκειν τε χρή," φησίν,
"ἄνθρωπον τῷδε τῷ κανόνι, ὅτι ἐτεῆς[1] ἀπήλλακται."

   [1] αἰτίας vel αἰτίης mss., corr. Menagius

D18 (B7) Sext. Emp. *Adv. Math.* 7.137

καὶ πάλιν· "δηλοῖ μὲν δὴ[1] καὶ οὗτος ὁ λόγος ὅτι
ἐτεῇ[2] οὐδὲν ἴσμεν περὶ οὐδενός, ἀλλ' ἐπιρυσμίη ἑκάστοισιν ἡ δόξις."

   [1] δὴ om. N⊊   [2] αἰτίη mss., corr. Menagius

D15 (B9) Sextus Empiricus, *Against the Logicians*

And in the **Corroborations** [. . .] he says, **"We grasp in actuality** (*eon*) **not anything that is certain, but something that changes according to the disposition** (*diathêkê*) **both of the body and of what penetrates and repels."**

D16 (B10) Sextus Empiricus, *Against the Logicians*

And again he says, **"That thus in reality** (*eteê*) **we do not grasp what each thing is ⟨or⟩ is not, has been made clear in a number of ways."**

D17 (B6) Sextus Empiricus, *Against the Logicians*

And in **On the Forms** he says, **"It is necessary to recognize that man by virtue of this criterion is separated from reality** (*eteê*)."

D18 (B7) Sextus Empiricus, *Against the Logicians*

And again: **"Certainly this argument too makes it clear that in reality** (*eteê*) **we know nothing about anything, but for each person opinion is a rhythmic afflux** (*epirhusmiê*)."

D19 (B8) Sext. Emp. *Adv. Math.* 7.137

καὶ ἔτι· "καίτοι δῆλον ἔσται ὅτι ἐτεῇ¹ οἷον ἕκαστον
γιγνώσκειν ἐν ἀπόρῳ ἐστί."

¹ αἰτίη mss., corr. Menagius

D20 (B11) Sext. Emp. *Adv. Math.*7.139

ἐν δὲ τοῖς Κανόσι [. . .] λέγει δὲ κατὰ λέξιν· "γνώμης
δὲ δύο εἰσὶν ἰδέαι, ἡ μὲν γνησίη, ἡ δὲ σκοτίη· καὶ
σκοτίης μὲν τάδε σύμπαντα, ὄψις ἀκοὴ ὀδμὴ γεῦσις
ψαῦσις· ἡ δὲ γνησίη,¹ ἀποκεκριμένη δὲ² ταύτης."

¹ post γνησίη lac. stat. Brieger   ² ἀποκεκριμένη δὲ VR:
ἀποκεκρυμμένη δὲ ceteri et VR i.m. (γρ.): ἀποκεκρυμμένη διὰ
Natorp

D21 (B11) Sext. Emp. *Adv. Math.* 7.139

εἶτα [. . .] ἐπιφέρει λέγων· "ὅταν ἡ σκοτίη μηκέτι
δύνηται μήτε ὁρῆν ἐπ' ἔλαττον μήτε ἀκούειν μήτε
ὀδμᾶσθαι μήτε γεύεσθαι μήτε ἐν τῇ ψαύσει αἰσθάνεσθαι, ἀλλ' ἐπὶ λεπτότερον ⟨. . .⟩?."¹

¹ post λεπτότερον lacunam pos. Diels ⟨δέῃ ζητεῖν, τότε ἐπι-
γίνεται ἡ γνησίη ἅτε ὄργανον ἔχουσα τοῦ νῶσαι λεπτότε-
ρον⟩, alii alia

D19 (B8) Sextus Empiricus, *Against the Logicians*

And again: **"And yet it will be clear that in reality** (*eteê*) **to recognize of what sort each thing is, belongs to what is impracticable** (*aporos*)**."**

D20 (B11) Sextus Empiricus, *Against the Logicians*

But in his ***Criteria*** [. . .] he says verbatim, **"There are two forms of knowledge** (*gnômê*), **the one genuine, the other obscure. And to the obscure one belong all of these: sight, hearing, smell, taste, touch. The other is genuine, and is separated from this one** [or: but, separated from this one . . .].**"**

D21 (B11) Sextus Empiricus, *Against the Logicians*

and then [. . .] he adds, saying, **"When the one** [scil. form of knowledge] **that is obscure is no longer able either to see what is smaller or to hear or to smell or to taste or to perceive by touching, but** [scil. one must have recourse (?)] **toward something that is finer** [. . . ?]**."**

D22 (≠ DK) Theophr. *Sens.* 71

[. . . cf. **R56**] ἐν οἷς φησι γίνεσθαι μὲν ἕκαστον καὶ εἶναι κατ᾽ ἀλήθειαν, ἰδίως δ᾽ ἐπὶ μικροῦ "μοῖραν ἔχειν συνέσεως."

Cf. app. ad **R56**

D23 Gal.

a (B125, cf. B9) *Exper. med.* 15.7.5, Frag. graec., p. 1259.10–14 Schöne 1901

τοῦτο καὶ Δημόκριτος εἰδὼς ὁπότε τὰ φαινόμενα δι-έβαλε "νόμῳ χροιή, νόμῳ γλυκύ, νόμῳ πικρόν," εἰ-πὼν "ἐτεῇ δ᾽ ἄτομα καὶ κενόν" [cf. **D14**] ἐποίησε τὰς αἰσθήσεις λεγούσας πρὸς τὴν διάνοιαν οὕτως· "τάλαινα φρήν, παρ᾽ ἡμέων λαβοῦσα τὰς πίστεις ἡμέας καταβάλλεις; πτῶμά τοι τὸ κατάβλημα."

b (A49) *Elem. Hipp.* 1.2 (p. 60.12–19 De Lacy)

[. . . = **D63**] τὸ γὰρ δὴ νόμῳ τοῦτ᾽ αὐτὸ βούλεται τὸ οἷον νομιστὶ καὶ πρὸς ἡμᾶς, οὐ κατ᾽ αὐτὴν τῶν πραγμάτων τὴν φύσιν· ὅπερ δ᾽ αὖ πάλιν ἐτεῇ καλεῖ, παρὰ τὸ ἐτεὸν, ὅπερ ἀληθὲς δηλοῖ, ποιήσας τοὔνομα. καὶ εἴη ἂν ὁ σύμπας αὐτοῦ νοῦς τοῦ λόγου τοιόσδε. νομίζεται μέν τι[1] παρὰ τοῖς ἀνθρώποις λευκόν τε εἶ-ναι, καὶ μέλαν καὶ γλυκὺ καὶ πικρὸν καὶ τἆλλα πάντα τὰ τοιαῦτα, κατὰ δὲ τὴν ἀλήθειαν δὲν καὶ μηδέν ἐστι

D22 (≠ DK) Theophrastus, *On Sensations*

[. . .] where he says that each thing becomes and exists according to truth, but, with regard to what is small, in a particular way, that it **"possesses a share of understanding."**

D23 Galen

a (B125, cf. B9) *On Medical Experience*

Democritus, knowing this [scil. that evidence (*enargeia*) is the basis of confidence], whenever he made his accusations against appearances, saying, **"by convention color, by convention sweet, by convention bitter, but in reality atoms and void,"** made the sensations reply to thought in this way: **"Poor mind** (*phrên*), **you receive from us all your certainties, and then you overthrow us? That overthrow is your downfall."**

b (A49) *On the Elements according to Hippocrates*

[. . .] The term **'by convention'** (*nomos*) signifies the same thing as 'conventionally' (*nomisti*) and 'relatively to us,' not according to the nature of the things themselves. This latter in turn he calls **"in reality"** (*eteê*), for 'real,' which signifies 'true,' inventing the word. And the whole meaning of what he says would be something like this: men think that white and black are something, as well as sweet and bitter and all the other qualities of this sort, but according to the truth all these things are **something** (*den*)

---

¹ μέντοι mss., corr. ed. Ald.

τὰ πάντα. καὶ γὰρ αὖ καὶ τοῦτ᾽ εἴρηκεν αὐτός, δὲν[2] μὲν τὰς ἀτόμους ὀνομάζων, μηδὲν δὲ τὸ κενόν. [. . .]

[2] ἓν . . . ἓν mss., corr. Mullach

D24 (B117) Diog. Laert. 9.72

[. . .] Δημόκριτος δὲ τὰς ποιότητας ἐκβάλλων, ἵνα φησί, "νόμῳ θερμόν, νόμῳ ψυχρόν, ἐτεῇ[1] δὲ ἄτομα καὶ κενόν" [cf. **D14**]· καὶ πάλιν, "ἐτεῇ[2] δὲ οὐδὲν ἴδμεν· ἐν βυθῷ γὰρ ἡ ἀλήθεια" [. . .].

[1–2] αἰτίη BPF, corr. Stephanus

Considerations of Method (D25–D28)
Definition (D25–D26)

D25 (A36) Arist.

a *PA* 1.1 642a25–27

[. . .] τὸ τί ἦν εἶναι καὶ τὸ ὁρίσασθαι τὴν οὐσίαν [. . .] ἥψατο μὲν Δημόκριτος πρῶτος [. . .].

b *Metaph.* M4 1078b19–21

τῶν μὲν γὰρ φυσικῶν ἐπὶ μικρὸν Δημόκριτος ἥψατο μόνον καὶ ὡρίσατό πως τὸ θερμὸν καὶ τὸ ψυχρόν [. . .].

and **nothing** (*mêden*). For again he has also said this, calling **"something"** (*den*) the atoms and **"nothing"** (*mêden*) the void [. . .].

D24 (B117) Diogenes Laertius

[. . .] Democritus, rejecting the qualities, where he says, **"by convention cold, by convention hot, but in reality** (*eteêi*) **atoms and void,"** and again, **"in reality** (*eteê*) **we know nothing. For truth is in an abyss"** [. . .].

Considerations of Method (D25–D28)
Definition (D25–D26)

D25 (A36) Aristotle

a *Parts of Animals*

[. . .] what a thing is and the definition of its essence [. . .] Democritus was the first to approach this question [. . .].[1]

[1] Cf. also *Physics* 2.2 194a20–21.

b *Metaphysics*

Among the natural philosophers, Democritus approached the question [scil. of definition] only to a small extent and defined in a certain way hot and cold [. . .].

D26 (< B165)

a Arist. *PA* 1.1 640b31–33

[. . . = **R24**] φησὶ γοῦν παντὶ δῆλον εἶναι οἷόν τι τὴν μορφήν ἐστιν ὁ[1] ἄνθρωπος, ὡς ὄντος αὐτοῦ τῷ τε σχήματι καὶ τῷ χρώματι γνωρίμου.

[1] ὁ om. ΕΠ

b Sext. Emp. *Adv. Math.* 7.265

Δημόκριτος [. . . = **P44b**] ἐπεχείρησε μὲν τὴν ἐπίνοιαν ἐκθέσθαι [. . . = **R105**] εἰπὼν "ἄνθρωπός ἐστιν ὃ πάντες ἴδμεν."

Argumentation (D27–D28)

D27 (B10b) Sext. Emp. *Adv. Math.* 8.327

οἱ δὲ ἐμπειρικοὶ ἀναιροῦσιν [scil. τὴν ἀπόδειξιν], τάχα δὲ καὶ Δημόκριτος (ἰσχυρῶς γὰρ αὐτῇ διὰ τῶν Κανόνων ἀντείρηκεν) [. . .].

D28 (B150) Plut. *Quaest. conv.* 1.1.5 614D

[. . .] ἐριδαντέων[1] δὲ κατὰ Δημόκριτον καὶ ἱμαντελικτέων[2] λόγους ἀφετέον [. . .].

[1-2] ἐριδανταίων et ἱμαντελικταίων T, corr. Stephanus

D26 (< B165)

a Aristotle, *Parts of Animals*

[. . .] He says that it is clear to everyone what kind of thing
a man is with regard to his form, on the idea that he is
recognizable by his shape and color [cf. **R24**].

b Sextus Empiricus, *Against the Logicians*

Democritus [. . .] tried to explain the concept [scil. of man]
[. . .] by saying, **"a man is what we all know."**

Argumentation (D27–D28)

D27 (B10b) Sextus Empiricus, *Against the Logicians*

The Empiricist [scil. doctors] suppress it [i.e. argumenta-
tion], and so too does Democritus, for he speaks strongly
against it in his *Criteria*.

D28 (B150) Plutarch, *Table Talk*

[. . .] one should dismiss the discourses of **quibblers** and
mountebanks according to Democritus [. . .].

Atoms and Void (D29–D69)
Four General Presentations by Aristotle, or
Going Back to Him (D29–D32)

D29 (A37) Simpl. *In Cael.*, pp. 294.33–295.22 (= Arist. *Dem.* Frag. 208 Rose)

ὀλίγα δὲ ἐκ τῶν Ἀριστοτέλους περὶ Δημοκρίτου
παραγραφέντα[1] δηλώσει τὴν τῶν ἀνδρῶν ἐκείνων διάνοιαν.

Δημόκριτος [295.1] ἡγεῖται τὴν τῶν ἀιδίων
φύσιν εἶναι μικρὰς οὐσίας πλῆθος ἀπείρους,
ταύταις δὲ τόπον ἄλλον ὑποτίθησιν ἄπειρον τῷ
μεγέθει· προσαγορεύει δὲ τὸν μὲν τόπον τοῖσδε
τοῖς ὀνόμασι τῷ τε κενῷ καὶ τῷ οὐδενὶ καὶ τῷ
ἀπείρῳ, τῶν δὲ οὐσιῶν ἑκάστην τῷ τε δὲν[2] καὶ
τῷ ναστῷ[3] καὶ τῷ[4] ὄντι. νομίζει [5] δὲ εἶναι οὕτω
μικρὰς τὰς οὐσίας ὥστε ἐκφυγεῖν τὰς ἡμετέρας
αἰσθήσεις, ὑπάρχειν δὲ αὐτοῖς παντοίας μορφὰς καὶ σχήματα παντοῖα καὶ κατὰ μέγεθος
διαφοράς· ἐκ τούτων οὖν ἤδη καθάπερ ἐκ[5] στοιχείων γεννᾶν καὶ συγκρίνειν τοὺς ὀφθαλμοφα-
νεῖς καὶ τοὺς αἰσθητοὺς ὄγκους· στασιάζειν δὲ
καὶ φέρεσθαι ἐν τῷ κενῷ διά τε τὴν ἀνομοι-
ότητα καὶ τὰς ἄλλας τὰς [10] εἰρημένας δια-
φοράς, φερομένας δὲ ἐμπίπτειν καὶ περιπλέκε-
σθαι περιπλοκὴν τοσαύτην, ἣ συμψαύειν μὲν
αὐτὰ καὶ πλησίον ἀλλήλων εἶναι ποιεῖ. φύσιν

Atoms and Void (D29–D69)
Four General Presentations by Aristotle, or
Going Back to Him (D29–D32)

D29 (A37) Aristotle in Simplicius, *Commentary on Aristotle's* On the Heavens

A few lines cited from Aristotle's *On Democritus* will indicate the thought of those men.

Democritus [295.1] thinks that the nature of eternal things consists of small substances (*ousiai*) unlimited in number; but he assumes a place for these that is unlimited in magnitude. He assigns to place the following terms: **void, nothing, the unlimited;** and to each of the substances (*ousiai*) **the something** (*den*), **the compact,** and **what is.** He thinks [5] that the substances are so small that they escape our senses. They possess all kinds of forms and all kinds of shapes and differences in magnitude. Out of these then, as though out of letters (*stoikheia*), they generate and combine the masses that appear to sight and are perceptible. They are at variance with one another and are borne along in the void because of both their dissimilarity and the other [10] differences mentioned, and as they are borne along they collide and become interlaced with so strong an interlacing that they adhere (*sumpsauei*) and become close to one another, but without in any

---

¹ παραγραφέντα A: -των DE   ² τῷ τε δὲν Heiberg: τῷ τε δὲ A: τῷ τε lac. VII litt. D: lac. VIII litt. E   ³ καὶ τῷ ναστῷ AD: om. E   ⁴ τῷ A: om. DE   ⁵ ἐκ A: εἰ DE

μέντοι μίαν ἐξ ἐκείνων κατ' ἀλήθειαν οὐδ' ἡντιναοῦν γεννᾷ· κομιδῇ γὰρ εὔηθες εἶναι τὸ[6] δύο ἢ
τὰ πλείονα γενέσθαι ἄν ποτε ἕν. τοῦ δὲ συμμένειν τὰς οὐσίας μετ' ἀλλήλων μέχρι τινὸς αἰτιᾶται τὰς ἐπαλλαγὰς καὶ τὰς [15] ἀντιλήψεις
τῶν σωμάτων· τὰ μὲν γὰρ αὐτῶν εἶναι σκα-
ληνά, τὰ δὲ ἀγκιστρώδη, τὰ δὲ κοῖλα, τὰ δὲ
κυρτά,[7] τὰ δὲ ἄλλας[8] ἀναρίθμους ἔχοντα δια-
φοράς· ἐπὶ τοσοῦτον οὖν χρόνον σφῶν αὐτῶν
ἀντέχεσθαι νομίζει καὶ συμμένειν, ἕως ἰσχυρο-
τέρα τις ἐκ τοῦ περιέχοντος ἀνάγκη παραγενο-
μένη διασείσῃ καὶ χωρὶς αὐτὰς διασπείρῃ.

λέγει δὲ τὴν γένεσιν καὶ τὴν ἐναντίαν [20] αὐτῇ[9] διά-
κρισιν οὐ μόνον περὶ ζῴων, ἀλλὰ καὶ περὶ φυτῶν καὶ
περὶ κόσμων καὶ συλλήβδην περὶ τῶν αἰσθητῶν σωμάτων ἁπάντων.

6 τὸ A: τὰ DE   7 τὰ δὲ κοῖλα, τὰ δὲ κυρτά Heiberg ex
vers. lat. (Moerbeke): lac. A: om. DE   8 ἄλλας D: ἄλλα AE
9 αὐτῶν A

D30 (67 A7) Arist. *GC* 1.8 324b35–325a3, 325a23–b5

ὁδῷ δὲ μάλιστα καὶ περὶ πάντων ἑνὶ λόγῳ[1] διωρίκασι
Λεύκιππος καὶ Δημόκριτος [325a] ἀρχὴν ποιησάμενοι
κατὰ φύσιν ᾗπερ[2] ἐστίν. ἐνίοις γὰρ τῶν ἀρχαίων
ἔδοξε τὸ ὂν ἐξ ἀνάγκης ἓν εἶναι καὶ ἀκίνητον· [. . . cf.
PARM. R44] [325a23] Λεύκιππος δ' ἔχειν ᾠήθη λό-

case engendering a single nature out of them. For it is absolutely simpleminded [scil. to think] that two or more things could ever become one. As for the fact that the substances remain with one another for a certain time, he attributes the cause of this to the bodies' interlacings (*epallagai*) and [15] adherences (*antilêpseis*). For some of them are irregular, others hook-shaped, others concave, others convex, others provided with innumerable other differences. So he thinks that they hold on to one another and remain together for a length of time until some stronger necessity arising from their surroundings shakes and disperses them.

He also speaks of generation, and of the dissociation [20] that is opposed to it, with regard not only to animals but also to plants and worlds, and in short to all perceptible bodies.

D30 (67 A7) Aristotle, *On Generation and Corruption*

It is by a very methodical procedure and by a single argument about the totality of things that Leucippus and Democritus [325a] have established their definitions (*diorizein*), taking a starting point in conformity with nature as it is. For some of the ancients were of the opinion that what is is necessarily one and unmovable [. . .]. [325a23] But Leucippus thought he possessed assertions

---

1 ἑνὶ λόγῳ om. E¹MJ²

2 ἥπερ mss., corr. Joachim

γους οἵτινες πρὸς τὴν αἴσθησιν ὁμολογούμενα λέγοντες οὐκ ἀναιρήσουσιν οὔτε γένεσιν οὔτε φθορὰν οὔτε
κίνησιν καὶ τὸ πλῆθος τῶν ὄντων. ὁμολογήσας δὲ
ταῦτα μὲν τοῖς φαινομένοις, τοῖς δὲ τὸ ἓν κατασκευ-
άζουσιν ὡς οὐκ³ ἂν κίνησιν οὖσαν ἄνευ κενοῦ τό τε
κενὸν μὴ ὂν καὶ τοῦ ὄντος οὐθὲν μὴ ὄν, φησὶν εἶναι
τὸ⁴ κυρίως ὂν⁵ παμπλῆρες ὄν, ἀλλ᾽ εἶναι τὸ τοιοῦτον
οὐχ ἕν, ἀλλ᾽ ἄπειρα τὸ πλῆθος καὶ ἀόρατα διὰ σμικρότητα τῶν ὄγκων. ταῦτα δ᾽ ἐν τῷ κενῷ φέρεσθαι
(κενὸν γὰρ εἶναι), καὶ συνιστάμενα μὲν γένεσιν ποιεῖν, διαλυόμενα δὲ φθοράν. ποιεῖν δὲ καὶ πάσχειν ᾗ
τυγχάνουσιν ἁπτόμενα (ταύτῃ γὰρ οὐχ ἓν εἶναι) καὶ
συντιθέμενα δὲ καὶ περιπλεκόμενα γεννᾶν· ἐκ δὲ τοῦ
κατ᾽ ἀλήθειαν ἑνὸς οὐκ ἂν γενέσθαι πλῆθος, οὐδ᾽ ἐκ
τῶν ἀληθῶς πολλῶν ἕν, ἀλλ᾽ εἶναι τοῦτ᾽ ἀδύνατον·
ἀλλ᾽ ὥσπερ Ἐμπεδοκλῆς καὶ τῶν ἄλλων τινές φασι
πάσχειν [325b] διὰ πόρων, οὕτω πᾶσαν ἀλλοίωσιν καὶ
πᾶν τὸ πάσχειν τοῦτον γίνεσθαι τὸν τρόπον, διὰ τοῦ
κενοῦ γινομένης τῆς διαλύσεως καὶ τῆς φθορᾶς,
ὁμοίως δὲ καὶ τῆς αὐξήσεως, εἰσδυομένων ἑτέρων.

³ οὐκ] οὔτ᾽ FHJVLW   ⁴ τὸ γὰρ FHL
⁵ ὄν] ἓν EJ¹V Hunayn

D31 (67 A6) Arist. *Metaph.* A4 985b4–20

Λεύκιππος δὲ καὶ ὁ ἑταῖρος αὐτοῦ Δημόκριτος στοιχεῖα μὲν τὸ πλῆρες καὶ τὸ κενὸν εἶναί φασι, λέγοντες
οἷον τὸ μὲν ὂν τὸ δὲ μὴ ὄν, τούτων δὲ τὸ μὲν πλῆρες

that, in agreement with sensation, would not abolish either generation or destruction or motion and the multiplicity of the things that are. Having thus granted these points to appearances and also to the defenders of the one, that there could not be motion without a void, that the void is what does not exist, and that nothing that is not belongs to being, he says that what is in the proper sense is being that is completely full, but that such a being is not one, but that they are unlimited in number and invisible because of the smallness of their masses. These are borne along in the void (because the void exists) and when they gather together they produce generation, and when they are dissociated, destruction. They act and are affected according to the way in which they happen to be in contact; for in this way they are not one. And it is by combining and interlacing that they generate. But neither could a multiplicity come to be out of what is in truth one nor one out of what are in truth multiple, but this is impossible. But just as Empedocles and some of the others say that there is affection [325b] by means of passages [cf. **EMP. D210**], in the same way all change and all affection are produced in this way, dissociation and destruction coming about by means of the void, and similarly growth, when other [scil. bodies] penetrate.

D31 (67 A6) Aristotle, *Metaphysics*

Leucippus and his companion Democritus say that the elements are the full and the void, saying something like this: that the one exists and that the other does not, and

καὶ στερεὸν τὸ ὄν, τὸ δὲ κενόν τε καὶ μανὸν[1] τὸ μὴ ὄν
(διὸ καὶ οὐθὲν μᾶλλον τὸ ὂν τοῦ μὴ ὄντος εἶναί φασιν, ὅτι οὐδὲ τὸ κενὸν τοῦ σώματος),[2] αἴτια δὲ τῶν
ὄντων ταῦτα ὡς ὕλην. καὶ καθάπερ οἱ ἓν ποιοῦντες
τὴν ὑποκειμένην οὐσίαν τἆλλα τοῖς πάθεσιν αὐτῆς
γεννῶσι, τὸ μανὸν καὶ τὸ πυκνὸν ἀρχὰς τιθέμενοι τῶν
παθημάτων, τὸν αὐτὸν τρόπον καὶ οὗτοι τὰς διαφορὰς
αἰτίας τῶν ἄλλων εἶναί φασιν. ταύτας μέντοι τρεῖς
εἶναι λέγουσι, σχῆμά τε καὶ τάξιν καὶ θέσιν· διαφέρειν γάρ φασι[3] τὸ ὂν ῥυσμῷ καὶ διαθηγῇ[4] καὶ
τροπῇ μόνον· τούτων δὲ ὁ μὲν ῥυσμὸς σχῆμά ἐστιν,
ἡ δὲ διαθηγὴ[5] τάξις, ἡ δὲ τροπὴ θέσις· διαφέρει γὰρ
τὸ μὲν Α τοῦ Ν σχήματι, τὸ δὲ ΑΝ τοῦ ΝΑ τάξει, τὸ
δὲ Ζ τοῦ Ν θέσει. περὶ δὲ κινήσεως, ὅθεν ἢ πῶς ὑπάρχει τοῖς οὖσι, καὶ οὗτοι παραπλησίως τοῖς ἄλλοις
ῥαθύμως ἀφεῖσαν.

[1] τε καὶ μανὸν E: om. A[b]
[2] τοῦ κενοῦ τὸ σῶμα Schwegler: τὸ κενὸν ἔλαττον τοῦ
σώματος Zeller
[3] διαφέρειν . . . φασι A[b]: διαφέρει . . . φησι E
[4,5] (bis) διαθηγῇ E: διαθιγῇ A[b]

D32 (67 A8, 68 A38) Simpl. In Phys., p. 28.4–27

Λεύκιππος [. . . = **P1b**] κοινωνήσας Παρμενίδῃ τῆς
φιλοσοφίας, οὐ τὴν αὐτὴν ἐβάδισε Παρμενίδῃ καὶ
Ξενοφάνει περὶ τῶν ὄντων ὁδόν, ἀλλ᾽ ὡς δοκεῖ τὴν
ἐναντίαν. ἐκείνων γὰρ ἓν καὶ ἀκίνητον καὶ ἀγένητον

that of these the one that is full and solid is the one that exists, and the other that is empty and rarefied is the one that does not exist (and that is why they say that being does not exist more than nonbeing, because neither does the void [scil. exist more] than the body[1]), and that these are the causes of the things that are as matter. And just as those who posit a single substance as substrate generate all the other things by means of its affections, positing the rarefied and the dense as principles of the affections, so too in the same way these too say that the differences are causes of all the other things. But they say that these are three in number: shape, order, and position. For they say that what is differs only by **configuration** (*rhusmos*), **disposition** (*diathêgê*), and **turning** (*tropê*). Of these, **configuration** is the shape, **disposition** is the order, and **turning** is the position. For A differs from N by form, AN from NA by order, and Z from N by position. As for motion, where it comes from or how it comes about for the things that are, they too, just like the others, have carelessly neglected these questions.

[1] This phrase is usually emended into its contrary: "because neither does the body exist more than the void."

D32 (67 A8, 68 A38) Simplicius, *Commentary on Aristotle's* Physics

Leucippus [. . .], who had made common cause with Parmenides in philosophy, did not continue along the same path as Parmenides and Xenophanes regarding the things that are, but rather, as it seems, the opposite one. For whereas these latter asserted that the whole is one, un-

καὶ πεπερασμένον ποιούντων τὸ πᾶν, καὶ τὸ μὴ ὂν
μηδὲ ζητεῖν συγχωρούντων, οὗτος ἄπειρα καὶ ἀεὶ κινούμενα ὑπέθετο στοιχεῖα τὰς ἀτόμους καὶ τῶν ἐν
αὐτοῖς σχημάτων ἄπειρον τὸ πλῆθος διὰ τὸ μηδὲν
μᾶλλον τοιοῦτον ἢ τοιοῦτον εἶναι[1] καὶ γένεσιν καὶ
μεταβολὴν ἀδιάλειπτον ἐν τοῖς οὖσι θεωρῶν. ἔτι δὲ
οὐδὲν μᾶλλον τὸ ὂν ἢ τὸ μὴ ὂν ὑπάρχειν, καὶ αἴτια
ὁμοίως εἶναι τοῖς γινομένοις ἄμφω. τὴν γὰρ τῶν ἀτόμων οὐσίαν ναστὴν καὶ πλήρη ὑποτιθέμενος ὂν ἔλεγεν εἶναι καὶ ἐν τῷ κενῷ φέρεσθαι, ὅπερ[2] μὴ ὂν ἐκάλει
καὶ οὐκ ἔλαττον τοῦ ὄντος εἶναί φησι.

παραπλησίως δὲ καὶ ὁ ἑταῖρος αὐτοῦ Δημόκριτος
ὁ Ἀβδηρίτης ἀρχὰς ἔθετο τὸ πλῆρες καὶ τὸ κενόν, ὧν
τὸ μὲν ὄν, τὸ δὲ μὴ ὂν ἐκάλει· ὡς <γὰρ>[3] ὕλην τοῖς
οὖσι τὰς ἀτόμους ὑποτιθέντες τὰ λοιπὰ γεννῶσι ταῖς
διαφοραῖς αὐτῶν. τρεῖς δέ εἰσιν αὗται ῥυσμὸς τροπὴ
διαθηγή,[4] ταὐτὸν δὲ εἰπεῖν σχῆμα καὶ θέσις καὶ τάξις. πεφυκέναι γὰρ τὸ ὅμοιον ὑπὸ τοῦ ὁμοίου κινεῖσθαι καὶ φέρεσθαι τὰ συγγενῆ πρὸς ἄλληλα καὶ τῶν
σχημάτων ἕκαστον εἰς ἑτέραν ἐγκοσμούμενον[5] σύγκρισιν ἄλλην ποιεῖν διάθεσιν· ὥστε εὐλόγως ἀπείρων
οὐσῶν τῶν ἀρχῶν πάντα τὰ πάθη καὶ τὰς οὐσίας
ἀποδώσειν ἐπηγγέλλοντο, ὑφ᾽ οὗ τέ τι γίνεται καὶ
πῶς. διὸ καί φασι μόνοις τοῖς ἄπειρα ποιοῦσι τὰ

---

[1] ταύτην γὰρ post εἶναι del. Diels   [2] φέρεσθει καὶ ὅπερ
EᵃF   [3] <γὰρ> ed. Ald.   [4] διαθιγή mss., corr. nos, cf.
app. ad **D31,** n.4   [5] ἐκκοσμούμενον mss., corr. Usener

movable, ungenerated, and limited, and accept that what is not cannot even be the object of research, he posited elements that are unlimited and always in motion, the indivisible [scil. natures] (*atomoi*), and the unlimited number of the shapes that are in them, for the reason that nothing is more of this sort than of that sort, and because he observed incessant generation and change among the things that are. Moreover, what exists does not exist at all more than what does not exist, and both are causes in a similar way for the things that come about. For positing that the substance of the indivisible [scil. natures] is **compact** and full, he said that it is what is and that it moves in the void, which he called 'what is not' and about which he says that it does not exist less than what is.

In the same way, his companion Democritus of Abdera posited as principles the full and the void, of which he called the one 'what is,' the other 'what is not.' ⟨For⟩ positing the indivisible [scil. natures] as matter for beings, they generate everything else by means of their differences. These are three in number: **configuration, turning,** and **disposition** (*diathêgê*); these are equivalent to shape, position, and order. For by its nature the similar is moved by the similar and things that are akin move toward each other, and each of the shapes, arranged in a different aggregate, produces a different disposition. So that, the principles being unlimited, it was reasonable for them to announce that they would explain all the properties and substances, from what something comes about and in what way. And that is why they say that it is only for those who make the elements unlimited that everything comes

στοιχεῖα πάντα συμβαίνειν κατὰ λόγον. καὶ τῶν ἐν ταῖς ἀτόμοις σχημάτων ἄπειρον τὸ πλῆθός φασι διὰ τὸ μηδὲν μᾶλλον τοιοῦτον ἢ τοιοῦτον εἶναι. ταύτην γὰρ αὐτοὶ τῆς ἀπειρίας αἰτίαν ἀποδιδόασι.

Some Terms Specific to Democritus (D33–D38)

D33 (< B156) Plut. *Adv. Col.* 4 1109A

[. . .] μὴ μᾶλλον τὸ δὲν ἢ τὸ μηδὲν εἶναι, 'δέν' μὲν ὀνομάζων τὸ σῶμα, 'μηδέν' δὲ τὸ κενόν, ὡς καὶ τούτου φύσιν τινὰ καὶ ὑπόστασιν ἰδίαν ἔχοντος.

D34

a (< A57) Plut. *Adv. Col.* 8 1111A

[. . .] τὰς ἀτόμους, 'ἰδέας' ὑπ' αὐτοῦ καλουμένας [. . .].

b (B141) Hesych. *Lex.* I.171

ἰδέα· ἡ ὁμοιότης, μορφή, εἶδος. καὶ τὸ ἐλάχιστον σῶμα.

D35 (≠ DK) Simpl. *In Cael.*, p. 609.24–25

τὴν δὲ συμπλοκὴν Ἀβδηρῖται ἐπάλλαξιν[1] ἐκάλουν, ὥσπερ Δημόκριτος.

---

[1] ἐπάλλαξιν A: παράλλαξιν C: περιπάλλαξιν DE: περιπάλ-ξιν F

about according to reason. And they say that the number of shapes that are in the indivisible [scil. natures] is unlimited, since nothing is more of this sort than of that sort. For that is the cause of the infinity that they assert.

Some Terms Specific to Democritus (D33–D38)

D33 (< B156) Plutarch, *Against Colotes*

[. . .] the **something** (*den*) does not exist more than the **nothing** (*mêden*). He calls the body 'something,' the void 'nothing,' on the idea that this too possesses a certain nature and its own existence.

D34

a (< A57) Plutarch, *Against Colotes*

[. . .] the indivisible [scil. natures], which he calls **'forms'** (*ideai*) [. . .].

b (B141) Hesychius, *Lexicon*

Form (*idea*): similarity, shape, form (*eidos*), and the smallest body.

D35 (≠ DK) Simplicius, *Commentary on Aristotle's* On the Heavens

The Abderites called the interlacing (*sumplokê*) **'intertwining'** (*epallaxis*), like Democritus.

D36 (A58, B168) Simpl. *In Phys.*, pp. 1318.31–1319.2

καὶ οἱ ποιητικοῦ δὲ μὴ μνησθέντες αἰτίου, περὶ δὲ
κινήσεως λέγοντες, ὡς οἱ περὶ Δημόκριτον, διὰ τὸ
κενὸν καὶ οὗτοι τὴν κατὰ τόπον κίνησιν κινεῖσθαι λέγουσι τὴν φύσιν, τουτέστι τὰ φυσικὰ καὶ πρῶτα καὶ
ἄτομα σώματα. ταῦτα γὰρ ἐκεῖνοι 'φύσιν' ἐκάλουν καὶ
ἔλεγον κατὰ τὴν ἐν αὐτοῖς βαρύτητα κινούμενα ταῦτα
διὰ τοῦ κενοῦ εἴκοντος καὶ μὴ ἀντιτυποῦντος κατὰ
τόπον κινεῖσθαι· 'περιπαλάσσεσθαι'[1] γὰρ ἔλεγον
αὐτά.

[1] περιπαλάσσεσθαι Diels: περιπαλαίσεσθαι mss.

D37 (< A47) Aët. 1.12.6 (Stob.) [περὶ σωμάτων]

Δημόκριτος τὰ πρῶτά φησι σώματα (ταῦτα δ᾽ ἦν τὰ[1]
ναστά) [. . .] [cf. **D53**].

[1] ἦν τὰ F: ἂν τὰ P: ὄντα Heeren

D38 (B139) Hesych. A.3563

ἀμειψιρυσμεῖν· ἀλλάσσειν τὴν σύγκρισιν ἢ μεταμορ-
φοῦσθαι. [cf. **D2** V.4]

D36 (A58, B168) Simplicius, *Commentary on Aristotle's Physics*

Those who have not mentioned the efficient cause but speak about motion, like Democritus, also say that nature, i.e. the natural bodies, which are the first and indivisible ones, are moved through the void by a locomotion. For they called these **'nature'** and said that, moved by virtue of their weight, they move locally through the void, which yields and does not resist. For they said that they **"are sprinkled about"** (?).

D37 (< A47) Aëtius

Democritus says that the first bodies (these are [scil. what he called] **'the compact'** ones) [. . .].

D38 (B139) Hesychius, *Lexicon*

'To change the configuration' (*ameipsirusmein*): to modify the aggregate or to change the form.

Void and Atoms (D39–D69)
Arguments in Favor of the
Existence of the Void (D39–D40)

D39 (< 67 A19) Arist. *Phys.* 4.6 213b3–b7; 213b15–16;
213b18–19; 213b 21–22

λέγουσιν δ' ἓν μὲν ὅτι κίνησις ἡ κατὰ τόπον οὐκ ἂν
εἴη (αὕτη δ' ἐστὶ φορὰ καὶ αὔξησις)· οὐ γὰρ ἂν δοκεῖν
εἶναι κίνησιν, εἰ μὴ εἴη κενόν· τὸ γὰρ πλῆρες ἀδύνατον εἶναι δέξασθαί τι. [. . .] ἄλλον δ' ὅτι φαίνεται ἔνια
συνιόντα καὶ πιλούμενα [. . .]. ἔτι δὲ καὶ ἡ αὔξησις
δοκεῖ πᾶσι γίγνεσθαι διὰ κενοῦ· [. . .]. μαρτύριον δὲ
καὶ τὸ περὶ τῆς τέφρας ποιοῦνται, ἣ δέχεται ἴσον
ὕδωρ ὅσον τὸ ἀγγεῖον τὸ κενόν.

D40 (cf. A60) Arist. *Cael.* 4.2 308b30–32, 309a2–11

[308b30] [. . .] ἀλλὰ καίπερ ὄντες ἀρχαιότεροι ταῖς
ἡλικίαις καινοτέρως ἐνόησαν περὶ τῶν νῦν λεχθέντων.
[. . . cf. **D68**] [309a2] τῶν δὲ συνθέτων, ἐπειδήπερ [. . .]
πολλὰ βαρύτερα ὁρῶμεν ἐλάττω τὸν ὄγκον ὄντα,
καθάπερ ἐρίου χαλκόν [. . .], ἕτερον τὸ αἴτιον οἴονταί
τε καὶ λέγουσιν ἔνιοι· τὸ γὰρ κενὸν ἐμπεριλαμβανό-
μενον κουφίζειν τὰ σώματά φασι καὶ ποιεῖν ἔστιν ὅτε
τὰ μείζω κουφότερα· πλεῖον γὰρ ἔχειν κενόν. διὰ
τοῦτο γὰρ καὶ τὸν ὄγκον εἶναι μείζω συγκείμενα πολλάκις ἐξ ἴσων στερεῶν ἢ καὶ ἐλαττόνων. ὅλως δὲ καὶ
παντὸς αἴτιον εἶναι τοῦ κουφοτέρου τὸ πλεῖον ἐνυπάρ-
χειν κενόν [. . . = **R44**].

ATOMISTS (LEUCIPPUS, DEMOCRITUS)

Void and Atoms (D39–D69)
Arguments in Favor of the
Existence of the Void (D39–D40)

D39 (< 67 A19) Aristotle, *Physics*

They [i.e. those who state that the void exists] say as one
[scil. argument] that [scil. otherwise] local motion (that is,
locomotion and growth) would not exist: for there would
not seem to be motion if there were no void, for what is
full is incapable of receiving anything. [. . .] Another [scil.
argument] is that certain things are seen to retract and
compress themselves [. . .]. Again, all people believe that
growth comes about thanks to the void; [. . .]. They also
use as evidence what happens with ash, which absorbs as
much water as an empty container.

D40 (cf. A60) Aristotle, *On the Heavens*

[. . .] [308b30] although they were more ancient in terms
of chronology [scil. than Plato], they thought in a more
modern way about the subjects mentioned just now [scil.
heavy and light in Plato's *Timaeus*]. [. . .] [309a2] Among
composite bodies, since [. . .] we see that many things that
are smaller in volume are heavier, like bronze compared
to wool [. . .], some people think and say that the reason is
different [scil. from the size of the constituents]; for they
say that the void contained in the interior makes the bodies light and sometimes has the effect of making bigger
things lighter; for they contain more void. For this is the
reason why the volume is often superior while the bodies
are composed of solids in the same number or even fewer.
And generally speaking, the cause of any body being
lighter is that there is more void in it [. . .].

The Atoms (D41–D62)
The Ultimate Indivisibility (D41–D44)

D41 (< A48b) Arist. *GC* 1.2 316a13–17

Δημόκριτος δ' ἂν φανείη οἰκείοις καὶ φυσικοῖς λόγοις
πεπεῖσθαι. [. . .] ἔχει γὰρ ἀπορίαν, εἴ τις θήσει[1] σῶμά
τι εἶναι καὶ μέγεθος πάντῃ διαιρετόν, καὶ τοῦτο δυνατόν. τί γὰρ ἔσται ὅπερ τὴν διαίρεσιν διαφεύγει; [. . .]

[1] θήσει Philoponus *In Phys.*, p. 27 (in lemmate): φήσει EM:
θείη cett.

D42 (A48) Aët. 1.16.2 (Ps.-Plut.; cf. Stob.) [περὶ τομῆς
σωμάτων]

οἱ τὰς ἀτόμους[1] περὶ[2] τὰ ἀμερῆ ἵστασθαι καὶ μὴ εἰς
ἄπειρον εἶναι τὴν τομήν.

[1] λέγοντες audiendum Diels, ‹εἰσάγοντες› Mau
[2] περὶ Diels ex Stob.: ἢ Plut. mss.

D43 (< A49) Galen. *Elem. Hipp.* 1.2 (p. 62.6–7 De Lacy)

ἀπαθῆ δ' ὑποτίθενται τὰ σώματα εἶναι τὰ πρῶτα·
[. . .] ἔνιοι δὲ ὑπὸ σμικρότητος ἀδιαίρετα, καθάπερ οἱ
περὶ[1] τὸν Λεύκιππον [. . .].

[1] περὶ ‹τὸν Διόδωρον καὶ› De Lacy ex Arab.

The Atoms (D41–D62)
The Ultimate Indivisibility (D41–D44)

D41 (< A48b) Aristotle, *On Generation and Corruption*

But Democritus seems to have been convinced by arguments that were appropriate and physical [scil. in contrast with the Platonists, who on the basis of purely logical arguments posit the existence of an indivisible 'triangle in itself']. [. . .] For there is a difficulty if someone posits that a body exists and that a magnitude is divisible everywhere and that this is possible: for what will there be that will escape division? [. . .][1]

1 What follows develops a series of arguments in favor of ultimate indivisibility (there will not remain any magnitude, and it is not possible that there subsist only points), which Philoponus in his commentary ad loc. (24.5 Leszl) attributes to Democritus; but this is doubtless a reconstruction.

D42 (A48) Aëtius

Those who [scil. posit] the indivisible [scil. natures]: the division [scil. of bodies] stops at what has no parts and it does not go on to infinity.

D43 (< A49) Galen, *On the Elements according to Hippocrates*

They [scil. Leucippus and his followers] assume that the first bodies are impassible [. . .], some because they are indivisible due to their smallness, like Leucippus and his disciples [. . .].

D44 (≠ DK) Simpl. *In Cael.*, p. 609.17–18

[. . .] τοὺς περὶ Λεύκιππον καὶ Δημόκριτον στοιχεῖα
λέγοντας τὰς διὰ σμικρότητα καὶ ναστότητα ἀτόμους
[. . .].

Number (D45–D47)

D45 (67 A15, 68 A120) Arist. *Cael.* 3.4 303a5–8, 10–12

[. . . cf. **R33**] φασὶ γὰρ εἶναι τὰ πρῶτα μεγέθη πλήθει
μὲν ἄπειρα, μεγέθει δὲ ἀδιαίρετα, καὶ οὔτ᾽ ἐξ ἑνὸς
πολλὰ γίγνεσθαι οὔτε ἐκ πολλῶν ἕν, ἀλλὰ τῇ τούτων
συμπλοκῇ καὶ ἐπαλλάξει[1] πάντα γεννᾶσθαι. [. . . cf.
R13] καὶ πρὸς τούτοις, ἐπεὶ διαφέρει τὰ σώματα
σχήμασιν, ἄπειρα δὲ τὰ σχήματα, ἄπειρα καὶ τὰ
ἁπλᾶ σώματά φασιν εἶναι.

[1] ἐπαλλάξει JHE[4]: περιπλέξει E: περιπαλάξει Diels (cf. app.
ad **D35, D36**)

D46 (59A45) Arist. *Phys.* 3.4 203a19–23

ὅσοι δ᾽ ἄπειρα ποιοῦσι τὰ στοιχεῖα, καθάπερ Ἀναξαγόρας καὶ Δημόκριτος, ὁ μὲν ἐκ τῶν ὁμοιομερῶν, ὁ δ᾽
ἐκ τῆς πανσπερμίας τῶν σχημάτων, τῇ ἁφῇ συνεχὲς
τὸ ἄπειρον εἶναί φασιν [. . . cf. **R15**].

D44 (≠ DK) Simplicius, *Commentary on Aristotle's* On the Heavens

[. . .] Leucippus and Democritus [. . .] say that the elements are [scil. natures] indivisible by virtue of their smallness and compactness [. . .].

Number (D45–D47)

D45 (67 A15, 68A120) Aristotle, *On the Heavens*

[. . .] For they [i.e. Leucippus and Democritus] say that the first magnitudes are unlimited in number, but indivisible in magnitude, and that neither does a plurality come about out of one nor one out of a plurality, but that it is by the interlacing and **intertwining** (*epallaxis*) of these things that all things are generated. [. . .] And furthermore, since the bodies differ by their shapes, and since the shapes are unlimited, they say that the simple bodies too are unlimited.

D46 (59A45) Aristotle, *Physics*

Those who posit that the elements are unlimited [scil. in number], like Anaxagoras and Democritus, constituted for the former out of the homoeomers [cf. e.g. **ANAXAG. D18**], for the latter out of the 'universal seminal reserve' (*panspermia*) of the shapes, say that the unlimited [scil. in magnitude] exists as continuous by virtue of contact [. . .].

D47 (67 A15) Aët. 1.18.3 (Ps.-Plut.) [περὶ κενοῦ]

Λεύκιππος Δημόκριτος [. . .] τὰ μὲν ἄτομα ἄπειρα τῷ πλήθει, τὸ δὲ κενὸν ἄπειρον τῷ μεγέθει.

Weight: Contradictory Reports (D48–D51)
The Atoms Have Weight (D48–D49)

D48 (A60) Arist. *GC* 1.8 326a9–10

καίτοι βαρύτερόν γε κατὰ τὴν ὑπεροχήν φησιν εἶναι Δημόκριτος ἕκαστον τῶν ἀδιαιρέτων [. . .].

D49 (A61) Simpl. *In Cael.*, p. 569.5–9

οἱ γὰρ περὶ Δημόκριτον καὶ ὕστερον Ἐπίκουρος τὰς ἀτόμους πάσας ὁμοφυεῖς οὔσας βάρος ἔχειν φασί, τῷ δὲ εἶναί τινα βαρύτερα ἐξωθούμενα τὰ κουφότερα ὑπ᾽ αὐτῶν ὑφιζανόντων ἐπὶ τὸ ἄνω φέρεται, καὶ οὕτω λέγουσιν οὗτοι δοκεῖν τὰ μὲν κοῦφα εἶναι τὰ δὲ βαρέα.

The Atoms Have No Weight (D50–D51)

D50 (< A47) Aët. 1.12.6 (Stob.) [περὶ σωμάτων]

Δημόκριτος τὰ πρῶτά φησι σώματα [. . . = **D37**] βάρος μὲν οὐκ ἔχειν [. . . = **D53**].

D47 (67 A15) Aëtius

Leucippus, Democritus [. . .]: the atoms are unlimited in number, the void unlimited in magnitude.

Weight: Contradictory Reports (D48–D51)
The Atoms Have Weight (D48–D49)

D48 (A60) Aristotle, *On Generation and Corruption*

And yet Democritus says that each of the indivisibles is at least heavier as a function of the preponderance [scil. of its mass] [. . .].

D49 (A61) Simplicius, *Commentary on Aristotle's* On the Heavens

Democritus and his disciples and later Epicurus say that the indivisible [scil. natures], which all have a similar nature, have weight, but because some are heavier, the lighter ones are expelled by these (which remain below) and are borne upward, and it is in this way, they say, that it seems that some things are light and others heavy.

The Atoms Have No Weight (D50–D51)

D50 (< A47) Aëtius

Democritus says that the first bodies [. . .] do not have weight [. . .].

D51 (< A47) Aët. 1.3.18 (Ps.-Plut.) [περὶ ἀρχῶν τί εἰσιν]

Δημόκριτος μὲν γὰρ ἔλεγε δύο, μέγεθός τε καὶ σχῆμα, ὁ δ᾽ Ἐπίκουρος τούτοις καὶ τρίτον, τὸ βάρος, ἐπέθηκεν.[1] [. . .].

[1] ἐπέθηκεν Plut.: προσέθηκεν Diels ex Eus. *PE* 14.14.5

The Motion of the Atoms (D52–D54)

D52 (A47) Aët. 1.23.3 (Stob.) [περὶ κινήσεως]

Δημόκριτος ἓν γένος κινήσεως τὸ κατὰ **παλμὸν** ἀπεφαίνετο.

D53 (A47) Aët. 1.12.6 (Stob.) [περὶ σωμάτων]

Δημόκριτος [. . . = **D50**] κινεῖσθαι δὲ κατ᾽ ἀλληλοτυπίαν ἐν τῷ ἀπείρῳ [. . . = **D62**].

D54 (A47) Simpl. *In Phys.*, p. 42.10–11

τοιγαροῦν καὶ Δημόκριτος φύσει ἀκίνητα λέγων τὰ ἄτομα **πληγῇ** κινεῖσθαί φησιν.

The Principle of Similarity (D55)

D55 (< B164) Sext. Emp. *Adv. Math.* 7.117–118

[117] ἀλλ᾽ ὁ μὲν Δημόκριτος ἐπί τε τῶν ἐμψύχων καὶ

D51 (< A47) Aëtius

Democritus said [scil. that the properties of the atoms are in number] two, magnitude and shape, but Epicurus added to these a third one, weight [. . .].

The Motion of the Atoms (D52–D54)

D52 (A47) Aëtius

Democritus declared that one kind of motion is by **vibration.**

D53 (A47) Aëtius

Democritus says [. . .] that they [scil. the first bodies] move because of collision with one another (*allêlotupia*) in the unlimited [. . .].

D54 (A47) Simplicius, *Commentary on Aristotle's* Physics

Democritus, who says that the atoms are immobile by nature, states that they are set in motion by **impact.**

The Principle of Similarity (D55)

D55 (< B164) Sextus Empiricus, *Against the Logicians*

[117] Democritus establishes this proposition [i.e. that the similar knows the similar] for both animate beings and

ἀψύχων ἵστησι τὸν λόγον. "καὶ γὰρ ζῷα, φησίν, ὁμο-
γενέσι ζῴοις συναγελάζεται, ὡς περιστεραὶ περι-
στεραῖς καὶ γέρανοι γεράνοις, καὶ ἐπὶ τῶν ἄλλων
ἀλόγων ⟨ὡσαύτως⟩· ὡσαύτως¹ δὲ καὶ ἐπὶ τῶν ἀψύχων, καθάπερ ὁρᾶν πάρεστιν ἐπί τε τῶν κοσκινευο-
μένων σπερμάτων καὶ ἐπὶ τῶν παρὰ ταῖς κυματω-
γαῖς ψηφίδων· ὅπου μὲν γὰρ κατὰ τὸν τοῦ κοσκίνου
δῖνον διακριτικῶς φακοὶ μετὰ φακῶν τάσσονται καὶ
κριθαὶ μετὰ κριθῶν καὶ πυροὶ μετὰ πυρῶν, [118]
ὅπου δὲ κατὰ τὴν τοῦ κύματος κίνησιν αἱ μὲν ἐπι-
μήκεις ψηφῖδες εἰς τὸν αὐτὸν τόπον ταῖς ἐπιμήκεσιν
ὠθοῦνται, αἱ δὲ περιφερεῖς ταῖς περιφερέσιν, ὡς ἂν
συναγωγόν τι ἐχούσης τῶν πραγμάτων τῆς ἐν τούτοις ὁμοιότητος." ἀλλ' ὁ μὲν Δημόκριτος οὕτως [. . .].

¹ ⟨ὡσαύτως⟩· ὡσαύτως Kochalsky: ὡσαύτως· ⟨ὡς⟩ Diels

The Shapes of the Atoms (D56–D61)

D56 (67 A9) Arist. GC 1.2 315b6–15

[. . . cf. **D71**] Δημόκριτος δὲ καὶ Λεύκιππος ποιήσαντες τὰ σχήματα τὴν ἀλλοίωσιν καὶ τὴν γένεσιν ἐκ
τούτων ποιοῦσι, διακρίσει μὲν καὶ συγκρίσει γένεσιν
καὶ φθοράν, τάξει δὲ καὶ θέσει ἀλλοίωσιν. ἐπεὶ δ'
ᾦοντο τἀληθὲς ἐν τῷ φαίνεσθαι, ἐναντία δὲ καὶ ἄπειρα
τὰ φαινόμενα, τὰ σχήματα ἄπειρα ἐποίησαν, ὥστε
ταῖς μεταβολαῖς τοῦ συγκειμένου τὸ αὐτὸ ἐναντίον

inanimate ones: **"For animals,"** he says, **"flock together with animals of the same species, like pigeons with pigeons, and cranes with cranes, and ‹so too› for the other irrational beings. So too for inanimate things, as can be seen in seeds that are sifted and in pebbles on beaches. For in the first case, because of the circular motion of the sieve, lentils separate out and are ordered together with lentils, and barleycorns with barleycorns, and grains of wheat with grains of wheat;** [118] **while in the latter one, because of the motion of the wave, oblong pebbles are pushed into the same place as oblong ones, and round ones as round ones, as though the similarity that exists in them had the capacity to bring things together."**[1] So much for Democritus [. . .].

---

[1] "For animals . . . bring things together" is generally considered to be a literal citation; but it could also be a summary.

The Shapes of the Atoms (D56–D61)

D56 (67 A9) Aristotle, *On Generation and Corruption*

[. . .] Democritus and Leucippus, by positing shapes, explain alteration and generation on the basis of these: generation and destruction by dissociation and association, alteration by order and position. But because they thought that truth is in appearance, and that appearances are contrary and unlimited [scil. in number], they posited shapes unlimited [scil. in number], so that the same thing would appear contrary to different people because of changes in the aggregate, that it be modified when a small element is

δοκεῖν ἄλλῳ καὶ ἄλλῳ,[1] καὶ μετακινεῖσθαι μικροῦ ἐμ-
μιγνυμένου καὶ ὅλως ἕτερον φαίνεσθαι ἑνὸς μετακι-
νηθέντος· ἐκ τῶν αὐτῶν γὰρ 'τραγῳδία' καὶ 'τρυγῳδία'[2] γίνεται γραμμάτων.

[1] ἄλλο καὶ ἄλλο W: καὶ ἄλλῳ om. L
[2] τρυγῳδία West: κωμῳδία mss.

D57 Theophr.

a (A120) in Simpl. *In Cael.*, p. 564.24–29

Δημόκριτος δέ, ὡς Θεόφραστος ἐν τοῖς Φυσικοῖς
ἱστορεῖ [Frag. 238 FSH&G], ὡς ἰδιωτικῶς ἀποδιδόντων
τῶν κατὰ τὸ θερμὸν καὶ τὸ ψυχρὸν καὶ τὰ τοιαῦτα
αἰτιολογούντων ἐπὶ τὰς ἀτόμους ἀνέβη, [. . .] νομίζον-
τες τὰ σχήματα αἴτια καὶ τὰ μεγέθη τῆς θερμότητος
καὶ τῆς ψύξεως· τὰ μὲν γὰρ διακριτικὰ καὶ διαιρετικὰ
θερμότητος συναίσθησιν παρέχεσθαι, τὰ δὲ συγκρι-
τικὰ καὶ πιλητικὰ ψύξεως.

b (≠ DK) *Metaph.* 11b20–23

εἰ γὰρ καὶ μὴ πᾶν ἀλλ' ἐν τούτοις πλέον τὸ τεταγμέ-
νον, πλὴν εἴ τις τοιαύτας λαμβάνοι τὰς μορφὰς οἵας
Δημόκριτος ὑποτίθεται τῶν ἀτόμων.

D58 (67 A11) Cic. *Nat. deor.* 1.24.66

ista enim flagitia Democriti sive etiam ante Leucippi, esse

added to the mixture, and in general that it appear different when a single [scil. element] is modified. For [scil. the words] 'tragedy' (*tragôidia*) and 'comedy' (*trugôidia*) are composed out of the same letters.[1]

[1] Or: "For a tragedy and a comedy are composed out of the same letters."

D57 Theophrastus

a (A120) in Simplicius, *Commentary on Aristotle's* On the Heavens

Because Democritus, as Theophrastus reports in his *Physics,* thought that those people who consider heat and cold and other things of this sort to be causes, are giving explanations in an idiosyncratic way, he had recourse to indivisible [scil. natures] [. . .], for they [i.e. Democritus and the Pythagoreans] thought that the shapes and magnitudes are the causes of heat and cold. For those that dissociate and divide produce the sensation of heat, those that assemble and condense that of cold.

b (≠ DK) *Metaphysics*

Even if the order is not total [scil. in the mathematical objects], at least it is greater in this domain, unless one conceives the forms as Democritus supposes them to be for the atoms.

D58 (67 A11) Cicero, *On the Nature of the Gods*

These disgraceful ideas of Democritus, or of Leucippus

113

corpuscula quaedam levia, alia aspera, rotunda alia, partim autem angulata et hamata, curvata quaedam et quasi adunca, ex iis effectum esse caelum atque terram nulla cogente natura, sed concursu quodam fortuito [. . .].

D59 (< 67 A15) Arist. *Cael.* 3.4 303a12–16

ποῖον δὲ καὶ τί ἑκάστου τὸ σχῆμα τῶν στοιχείων, οὐθὲν ἐπιδιώρισαν, ἀλλὰ μόνον τῷ πυρὶ τὴν σφαῖραν ἀπέδωκαν· ἀέρα δὲ καὶ ὕδωρ καὶ τἆλλα μεγέθει καὶ μικρότητι διεῖλον, ὡς οὖσαν αὐτῶν τὴν φύσιν οἷον πανσπερμίαν πάντων τῶν στοιχείων.

D60 (> B155a) Arist. *Cael.* 3.8

a 306b32–307a3

οἷον ἐπεὶ τὸ πῦρ εὐκίνητόν ἐστι καὶ θερμαντικὸν καὶ καυστικόν, οἱ μὲν ἐποίησαν αὐτὸ σφαῖραν, οἱ δὲ πυραμίδα· ταῦτα γὰρ εὐκινητότατα μὲν διὰ τὸ ἐλαχίστων ἅπτεσθαι καὶ ἥκιστα βεβηκέναι, θερμανικώτατα δὲ καὶ καυστικώτατα, διότι τὸ μὲν ὅλον ἐστὶ γωνία, τὸ δὲ ὀξυγωνιώτατον, καίει δὲ καὶ θερμαίνει ταῖς γωνίαις, ὥς φασιν.

b 307a16–17

Δημοκρίτῳ δὲ καὶ ἡ σφαῖρα, ὡς γωνία τις οὖσα, τέμνει ὡς εὐκίνητον.

114

even before him, that there are certain smooth corpuscles, others rough, others round, some angular or hooked, certain ones curved and almost bent[1] and that the heavens and the earth have been produced out of these without any compulsion by nature but by some chance encounter [. . .].

[1] But cf. **R94**.

D59 (< 67 A15) Aristotle, *On the Heavens*

Of what sort and what is [scil. exactly] the shape of each of the elements, they have not defined, but have only attributed the sphere to fire. As for air, water, and the others, they have distinguished them by largeness and smallness, on the idea that their nature is like the 'universal seminal reserve' (*panspermia*) of all the elements.

D60 (> B155a) Aristotle, *On the Heavens*

a

So, since fire is very mobile, and heats and burns, the ones made it a sphere, the others a pyramid [cf. Plato, *Timaeus* 56b]. For these are most mobile since the contact takes place between the smallest parts and they are least stable, and they are the hottest and burn the most because the one is entirely an angle while the other has extremely acute angles, and it is by means of its angles that something burns and heats, as they say.

b

For Democritus the sphere too, inasmuch as it is a kind of angle, cuts since it is very mobile.

D61 (67 A14) Simpl. *In Phys.*, p. 36.1–7

οἱ δὲ περὶ Λεύκιππον καὶ Δημόκριτον τὰ ἐλάχιστα
πρῶτα σώματα 'ἄτομα' καλοῦντες κατὰ τὴν τῶν σχημάτων αὐτῶν καὶ τῆς θέσεως καὶ τῆς τάξεως διαφορὰν τὰ μὲν θερμὰ γίνεσθαι καὶ πύρια τῶν σωμάτων, ὅσα ἐξ ὀξυτέρων καὶ λεπτομερεστέρων καὶ κατὰ
ὁμοίαν θέσιν κειμένων σύγκειται τῶν πρώτων σωμάτων, τὰ δὲ ψυχρὰ καὶ ὑδατώδη, ὅσα ἐκ τῶν ἐναντίων, καὶ τὰ μὲν λαμπρὰ καὶ φωτεινά, τὰ δὲ ἀμυδρὰ
καὶ σκοτεινά.

A Singular Report on the Size of the Atom (D62)

D62 (< A47) Aët. 1.12.6 (Stob.) [περὶ σωμάτων]

Δημόκριτος [. . . = **D37, D53**] δυνατὸν ⟨δ'⟩[1] εἶναι
κοσμιαίαν ὑπάρχειν ἄτομον.

[1] ⟨δ'⟩ Heeren

The Perceptible Qualities (D63–D69)
The Atoms Do Not Have Perceptible
Qualities (D63–D64)

D63 (< A49) Galen. *Elem. Hipp.* 1.2 (p. 60 De Lacy)

ὑπόκειται γὰρ ἅπασι τούτοις ἄποιον εἶναι τὸ πρῶτον
στοιχεῖον οὔτε λευκότητα σύμφυτον ἔχον ἢ μελανό-
τητα ἢ ὅλως ἡντιναοῦν χροιὰν οὔτε γλυκύτητα ἢ πι-

D61 (67 A14) Simplicius, *Commentary on Aristotle's Physics*

Leucippus and Democritus, who called the smallest first bodies 'atoms' [or: 'indivisible'], [scil. said that] as a function of their shapes, position, and order, certain bodies are warm and fiery, those that are composed of first bodies that are sharper and thinner and occupy a similar position, while others are cold and watery, those [scil. that are composed] of the contraries, and that the ones are clear and luminous, the others dark and obscure.

A Singular Report on the Size of the Atom (D62)

D62 (< A47) Aëtius

Democritus says [. . .] and that it is possible that there exists an atom of the size of a world.[1]

[1] This statement might represent not Democritus' position but a criticism: if there is an infinity of shapes and a lower limit to division, then there must also be atoms that are visible, indeed ones possessing the size of a world.

See also **R96**

The Perceptible Qualities (D63–D69)
The Atoms Do Not Have Perceptible
Qualities (D63–D64)

D63 (< A49) Galen, *On the Elements according to Hippocrates*

All of these authors [scil. Epicurus, Democritus, and their disciples] have in common that they posit that the first element is without quality, possessing by nature neither

κρότητα ἢ θερμότητα ἢ ψυχρότητα οὔθ᾽ ὅλως ἡντιναοῦν ἑτέραν ποιότητα. "νόμῳ γὰρ χροιή, νόμῳ γλυκύ, **νόμῳ πικρόν, ἐτεῇ δὲ ἄτομα καὶ κενόν**" [cf. **D14**], ὁ Δημόκριτός φησιν, ἐκ τῆς συνόδου τῶν ἀτόμων γίγνεσθαι νομίζων ἁπάσας τὰς αἰσθητὰς ποιότητας ὡς πρὸς ἡμᾶς τοὺς αἰσθανομένους αὐτῶν, φύσει δ᾽ οὐδὲν εἶναι λευκὸν ἢ μέλαν ἢ ξανθὸν ἢ ἐρυθρὸν ἢ πικρὸν ἢ γλυκύ [. . . = **D23b**].

D64 (< A135) Theophr. *Sens.* 63–64

[. . . = **D69**] [63] τῶν δὲ ἄλλων αἰσθητῶν οὐδενὸς εἶναι φύσιν, ἀλλὰ πάντα πάθη τῆς αἰσθήσεως ἀλλοιουμένης, ἐξ ἧς γίνεσθαι τὴν φαντασίαν. οὐδὲ γὰρ τοῦ ψυχροῦ καὶ τοῦ θερμοῦ φύσιν ὑπάρχειν, ἀλλὰ τὸ σχῆμα μεταπῖπτον ἐργάζεσθαι καὶ τὴν ἡμετέραν ἀλλοίωσιν· ὅ τι γὰρ ἂν ἄθρουν ᾖ, τοῦτ᾽[1] ἐνισχύειν ἑκάστῳ, τὸ δ᾽ εἰς μακρὰ διανενεμημένον ἀναίσθητον εἶναι. σημεῖον δ᾽ ὡς οὐκ εἰσὶ φύσει τὸ μὴ ταὐτὰ[2] πᾶσι φαίνεσθαι τοῖς ζῴοις, ἀλλ᾽ ὃ ἡμῖν γλυκύ, τοῦτ᾽ ἄλλοις πικρὸν καὶ ἑτέροις ὀξὺ καὶ ἄλλοις δριμὺ τοῖς δὲ στρυφνὸν καὶ τὰ ἄλλα δ᾽ ὡσαύτως. [64] ἔτι δ᾽ αὐτοὺς μεταβάλλειν τῇ κρίσει[3] κατὰ[4] τὰ πάθη καὶ τὰς ἡλικίας· ᾗ[5] καὶ φανερόν, ὡς ἡ διάθεσις αἰτία τῆς φαντασίας. ἁπλῶς μὲν οὖν περὶ τῶν αἰσθητῶν οὕτω δεῖν

---

[1] τοῦτ᾽ Stephanus: τοῦ mss.   [2] ταῦτα mss., corr. Vossianus   [3] κρίσει mss.: κράσει Schneider   [4] καὶ mss., corr. Papencordt   [5] ἢ mss., corr. Stephanus

whiteness nor blackness nor in general any color whatsoever, nor sweetness nor bitterness nor warmth nor coldness nor in general any other quality whatsoever. For **"by convention color, by convention sweet, by convention bitter, but in reality atoms and void"** [= **D14**], says Democritus, who thinks that it is from the encounter of the atoms that all the sensible qualities come about, since they are in relation to us who have the sensation of them, while by nature nothing is white or black or yellow or red or sweet or bitter [. . .].

D64 (< A135) Theophrastus, *On Sensations*

[. . .] [63] As for the other perceptibles [scil. besides heavy and light, hard and soft, cf. **D69**], [scil. according to Democritus] none of them possesses a nature, but they are all affections of sensation that is altered, and out of this arises the representation (*phantasia*). For there does not exist a nature of the cold or the hot either, but the shape **"that shifts"** [scil. place] produces our alteration too: for whatever is present in concentration prevails upon each person, while what is widely dispersed is imperceptible. Evidence that these qualities do not exist by nature is found in the fact that they do not appear as identical to all living beings, but what appears sweet to us appears bitter to others, acidic for others, pungent for others, sour for others, and similarly for the other qualities. [64] Furthermore, people themselves change in their judgment according to their affections and ages; by which it is manifest that the disposition is the cause of the representation. In general, therefore, it is in this way that one must think about the perceptibles [scil. according to Democritus].

ὑπολαμβάνειν. οὐ μὴν ἀλλ᾽ ὥσπερ καὶ τὰ ἄλλα καὶ
ταῦτα ἀνατίθησι⁶ τοῖς σχήμασι· πλὴν οὐχ ἁπάντων
ἀποδίδωσι τὰς μορφάς, ἀλλὰ μᾶλλον τῶν χυλῶν καὶ
τῶν χρωμάτων καὶ τούτων ἀκριβέστερον διορίζει τὰ
περὶ τοὺς χυλοὺς ἀναφέρων τὴν φαντασίαν πρὸς ἄνθρωπον [. . . = **D65**].

⁶ ἀντίθησι mss. (ἀντιτί- F²), corr. Stephanus

Flavors (D65)

D65 (< A135) Theophr. *Sens.* 65–68

[. . . = **D64**] [65] τὸν μὲν οὖν ὀξὺν εἶναι τῷ σχήματι
γωνοειδῆ τε καὶ πολυκαμπῆ καὶ μικρὸν καὶ λεπτόν.
διὰ γὰρ τὴν δριμύτητα ταχὺ καὶ πάντη διαδύεσθαι,¹
τραχὺν δ᾽ ὄντα καὶ γωνοειδῆ συνάγειν καὶ συσπᾶν,
διὸ καὶ θερμαίνειν τὸ σῶμα κενότητας ἐμποιοῦντα·
μάλιστα γὰρ θερμαίνεσθαι τὸ πλεῖστον ἔχον κενόν.
τὸν δὲ γλυκὺν ἐκ περιφερῶν συγκεῖσθαι σχημάτων²
οὐκ ἄγαν μικρῶν, διὸ καὶ διαχεῖν ὅλως³ τὸ σῶμα, καὶ
οὐ βιαίως καὶ οὐ ταχὺ πάντα περαίνειν· τοὺς ⟨δ᾽⟩⁴
ἄλλους ταράττειν, ὅτι διαδύνων πλανᾷ τὰ ἄλλα καὶ
ὑγραίνει· ὑγραινόμενα δὲ καὶ ἐκ τῆς τάξεως κινούμενα συρρεῖν εἰς τὴν κοιλίαν· ταύτην γὰρ εὐπορώτα-
τον εἶναι διὰ τὸ πλεῖστον ἐνεῖναι⁵ κενόν.

¹ διαδύεσθαι F²: διαδύνεσθαι PF¹
² σχημάτων ⟨καὶ⟩ Diels   ³ λείως prop. Diels
⁴ ⟨δ᾽⟩ Schneider   ⁵ διὰ τοῦτο πλεῖστον εἶναι mss.,
corr. Diels: an διὰ τοῦτο, τὸ πλεῖστον εἶναι?

And yet, just like all the others, he attributes these too to the shapes; except that he does not indicate the forms of all of them, but instead those of flavors and colors [cf. **D65**, **D66**], and that among these he distinguishes more precisely what regards flavors, referring their representation to man [. . .].

Flavors (D65)

D65 (< A135) Theophrastus, *On Sensations*

[. . .] [65] Thus what is acidic is in its form angular, sinuous, small, and thin. For thanks to its pungency it penetrates rapidly and everywhere, while, being rough and angular, it compresses and contracts. That is also why it warms the body, by producing voids within it. For whatever possesses the most void is warmed the most. But what is sweet is composed of round shapes, not too small: and that is why it liquefies the body completely, and accomplishes everything without violence and without haste. It disturbs the other [scil. flavors] because by penetrating it disorients the other [scil. forms] and makes them moist. And when they are moistened and disordered, they flow down into the intestines, for these offer the best passage, since there is the most void in them.

[66] τὸν δὲ στρυφνὸν ἐκ μεγάλων σχημάτων καὶ πο-
λυγωνίων καὶ περιφερὲς ἥκιστ᾽ ἐχόντων· ταῦτα γὰρ
ὅταν εἰς τὰ σώματα ἔλθῃ, ἐπιτυφλοῦν ἐμπλάττοντα
τὰ φλεβία καὶ κωλύειν συρρεῖν, διὸ καὶ τὰς κοιλίας
ἱστάναι. τὸν δὲ πικρὸν ἐκ μικρῶν καὶ λείων καὶ περιφερῶν, τὴν περιφέρειαν εἰληχότα¹ καὶ καμπὰς ἔχου-
σαν· διὸ καὶ γλισχρὸν² εἶναι καὶ³ κολλώδη. ἁλμυρὸν
δὲ τὸν⁴ ἐκ μεγάλων καὶ οὐ περιφερῶν, ἀλλ᾽ ἐπ᾽ ἐνίων
καὶ⁵ σκαληνῶν, διὸ οὐδὲ πολυκαμπῶν (βούλεται δὲ
σκαληνὰ λέγειν, ἅπερ παράλλαξιν ἔχει πρὸς ἄλληλα
καὶ συμπλοκήν)· μεγάλων μέν, ὅτι ἡ ἁλμυρὶς ἐπιπο-
λάζει· μικρὰ γὰρ ὄντα καὶ τυπτόμενα τοῖς περιέχουσι
μίγνυσθαι ἂν τῷ παντί· οὐ περιφερῶν δ᾽, ὅτι τὸ μὲν
ἁλμυρὸν τραχύ, τὸ δὲ περιφερὲς λεῖον· σκαληνῶν⁶ δὲ
διὰ τὸ μὴ περιπλάττεσθαι, διὸ ψαφαρὸν εἶναι.

¹ εἰληχότα Diels: εἰληκότα P: εἰλημμένα F   ² γλί-
σχρων P, -ῶν F, corr. Burchard   ³ καὶ om. P   ⁴ ἁλμυ-
ροὶ δὲ τῶ mss., corr. Burchard   ⁵ καὶ Diels: μὲν mss.
    ⁶ οὐ ante σκαληνῶν mss., del. Philippson

[67] τὸν δὲ δριμὺν μικρὸν¹ καὶ περιφερῆ καὶ γωνιοειδῆ, σκαληνὸν δὲ οὐκ ἔχειν. τὸν μὲν γὰρ δριμὺν πολυγώνιον ποιεῖν τῇ τραχύτητι θερμαίνειν καὶ διαχεῖν
διὰ τὸ μικρὸν εἶναι καὶ περιφερῆ καὶ γωνιοειδῆ·² καὶ
γὰρ τὸ γωνιοειδὲς εἶναι τοιοῦτον. ὡσαύτως δὲ καὶ τὰς
ἄλλας ἑκάστου δυνάμεις ἀποδίδωσιν ἀνάγων εἰς τὰ
σχήματα. ἁπάντων δὲ τῶν σχημάτων οὐδὲν ἀκέραιον
εἶναι καὶ ἀμιγὲς³ τοῖς ἄλλοις, ἀλλ᾽ ἐν ἑκάστῳ πολλὰ⁴
εἶναι καὶ τὸν αὐτὸν ἔχειν λείου καὶ τραχέος καὶ περι-

[66] The sour one [scil. is composed] of large shapes with many angles, possessing very little roundness. For when these enter into bodies, they obstruct the veins by blocking them and prevent the flowing; and this is also why they block the intestines. The bitter one [scil. is composed] of small, smooth, and round ones, and possesses a surface that has curvatures; and that is why it is viscous and adhesive. Salty is the one [scil. that is composed] of ones that are big and not round, and in some cases also irregular, and for this reason without many curvatures either (by 'irregular' he means those that can **intertwine** (*parallaxis*) and interlace with each other); big, because what is saline resides on the surface (for if they were small and were struck by those that surround them, they would mix with the whole); not round, because what is salty is rough while what is round is smooth; irregular, because they cannot be molded, and that is why they are friable.

[67] Pungent is small, round, and angular but does not have irregularity. For the pungent, having many angles, causes warming by its roughness and it liquefies because it is small, round, and angular (?); for what is angular is like this too. In the same way, he explains the other powers of each one [i.e. flavor], referring them to the shapes. But of all the shapes, none is unblended and unmixed with the others, but in each one there are many, and the same one has some that are smooth, rough, round, sharp, and the

---

¹ μικρὰ coni. Usener   ² ἀγωνιοειδῆ mss., corr. Diels (DK): διὰ . . . †ἀγωνιοειδῆ† del. Diels (Dox.)   ³ ἀμιγὲς Vossianus: ἀμιγῆ mss.   ⁴ πολλοὺς mss., corr. Wimmer

123

φερούς καὶ ὀξέος καὶ τῶν λοιπῶν. οὗ⁵ δ' ἂν ἐνῇ⁶ πλεῖστον, τοῦτο μάλιστα ἐνισχύειν πρός τε τὴν αἴσθησιν
καὶ τὴν δύναμιν. ἔτι δὲ εἰς ὁποίαν ἕξιν ἂν εἰσέλθῃ,⁷
διαφέρειν γὰρ⁸ οὐκ ὀλίγον. καὶ τοῦτο διὰ⁹ τὸ αὐτὸ
τἀναντία καὶ τἀναντία τὸ αὐτὸ πάθος ποιεῖν ἐνίοτε.
[68] καὶ περὶ μὲν τῶν χυλῶν οὕτως ἀφώρικεν. [. . . =
R46]

⁵ οὗ Wimmer: οὐ F¹: ὧ PF²   ⁶ ἔνι mss., corr. Wimer
⁷ εἰσέλθῃ F²: εἰσέλθοι P   ⁸ γὰρ secl. Schneider
⁹ τοῦτο διὰ mss.: διὰ τοῦτο Schneider

Colors (D66)

D66 (< A135) Theophr. *Sens.* 73–78

[. . . = **R62**] [73] τῶν δὲ χρωμάτων ἁπλᾶ μὲν λέγει
τέτταρα. λευκὸν μὲν οὖν εἶναι τὸ λεῖον· ὃ γὰρ ἂν μὴ
τραχὺ μηδ' ἀποσκιάζῃ¹ μηδὲ δυσδίοδόν τι,² τοιοῦτον
πᾶν λαμπρὸν εἶναι. δεῖ δὲ καὶ εὐρύτρυπα³ καὶ διαυγῆ
τὰ λαμπρὰ εἶναι. τὰ μὲν οὖν σκληρὰ τῶν λευκῶν ἐκ
τοιούτων σχημάτων συγκεῖσθαι οἷον ἡ ἐντὸς πλὰξ
τῶν κογχυλίων· οὕτω γὰρ ἂν ἄσκια καὶ εὐαγῆ καὶ
εὐθύπορα εἶναι. τὰ <δὲ>⁴ ψαθυρὰ καὶ εὔθρυπτα ἐκ περιφερῶν μὲν λοξῶν δὲ τῇ θέσει πρὸς ἄλληλα καὶ
κατὰ⁵ δύο συζεύξει,⁶ τὴν δ' ὅλην τάξιν ἔχειν ὅτι μάλιστα ὁμοίαν. τοιούτων δ' ὄντων ψαθυρὰ μὲν εἶναι, διότι κατὰ μικρὸν ἡ σύναψις· εὔθρυπτα δ', ὅτι ὁμοίως

¹ ἐπισκιάζῃ Schneider   ² ᾗ Burchard

others. That of which there is the most is what most prevails with regard to both sensation and power, but also the kind of condition [scil. matters] into which it [i.e. the flavor] penetrates, for the difference is not negligible, and this is because sometimes the same thing produces contrary [scil. affections], and contrary things the same affection. [68] It is in this way that he has made his definitions with regard to flavors. [. . .]

See also **D159**

Colors (D66)

D66 (< A135) Theophrastus, *On Sensations*

[. . .] [73] Of colors, he says that there are four simple ones. White is what is smooth [scil. according to him]; for whatever is not rough, does not cast a shadow, and is not hard to pass through, everything of this kind is bright. Bright things must also have wide perforations and be translucent. White things that are hard are composed of the same kinds of shapes, for example the inner surface of shells; for in this way they are without shadow and luminous, and are provided with straight perforations. Those that are friable and crumble easily are composed of shapes that are round, but oblique in their position with regard to each other combined in pairs, but their total order is the most regular possible. Being like this, they are friable, because there is little contact; they crumble easily, because they are arranged in a regular fashion; they are without shadow, be-

---

³ εὐθύτρυπα Schneider   ⁴ ‹δὲ› Schneider
⁵ κατὰ Usener: τὰ mss.   ⁶ συζεύξεις mss., corr. Diels

κεῖνται· ἄσκια δέ, διότι λεῖα καὶ πλατέα· λευκότερα δ'
ἀλλήλων[7] τῷ τὰ σχήματα τὰ εἰρημένα καὶ ἀκριβέ-
στερα καὶ ἀμιγέστερα εἶναι καὶ τὴν τάξιν καὶ τὴν
θέσιν ἔχειν μᾶλλον τὴν εἰρημένην. [74] τὸ μὲν οὖν
λευκὸν ἐκ τοιούτων εἶναι σχημάτων. τὸ δὲ μέλαν ἐκ
τῶν ἐναντίων, ἐκ τραχέων καὶ σκαληνῶν καὶ ἀνο-
μοίων· οὕτω γὰρ ἂν σκιάζειν καὶ οὐκ εὐθεῖς εἶναι τοὺς
πόρους οὐδ' εὐδιόδους.[8] ἔτι δὲ τὰς ἀπορροίας νωθεῖς
καὶ ταραχώδεις· διαφέρειν γάρ τι καὶ τὴν ἀπορροὴν
τῷ[9] ποιὰν εἶναι πρὸς τὴν φαντασίαν, ἣν γίνεσθαι διὰ
τὴν ἐναπόληψιν τοῦ ἀέρος ἀλλοίαν.

7 ἀλλήλοις mss., corr. Diels   8 εὐδιόδους Vossianus:
εὐδι cum lacuna mss.   9 τὸ mss., corr. Stephanus

[75] ἐρυθρὸν δ' ἐξ οἵωνπερ καὶ[1] τὸ θερμόν, πλὴν ἐκ
μειζόνων. ἐὰν γὰρ αἱ συγκρίσεις ὦσι μείζους ὁμοίων
ὄντων τῶν σχημάτων μᾶλλον ἐρυθρὸν εἶναι. σημεῖον
δ' ὅτι ἐκ τοιούτων τὸ ἐρυθρόν· ἡμᾶς τε γὰρ θερμαινο-
μένους ἐρυθραίνεσθαι καὶ τὰ ἄλλα τὰ πυρούμενα,
μέχρις ἂν οὗ ἔχῃ τὸ τοῦ πυροειδοῦς.[2] ἐρυθρότερα δὲ
τὰ ἐκ μεγάλων ὄντα σχημάτων οἷον τὴν φλόγα καὶ
τὸν ἄνθρακα τῶν χλωρῶν ξύλων ἢ τῶν αὔων, καὶ τὸν
σίδηρον δὲ καὶ τὰ ἄλλα τὰ πυρούμενα· λαμπρότατα
μὲν γὰρ εἶναι τὰ πλεῖστον ἔχοντα καὶ λεπτότατον
πῦρ, ἐρυθρότερα δὲ τὰ παχύτερον[3] καὶ ἔλαττον. διὸ
καὶ ἧττον εἶναι θερμὰ τὰ ἐρυθρότερα· θερμὸν[4] γὰρ τὸ
λεπτόν. τὸ δὲ χλωρὸν ἐκ τοῦ στερεοῦ καὶ τοῦ κενοῦ

cause they are smooth and flat. Some are whiter than others because the shapes mentioned are more exact and less mixed, and because they possess to a greater degree the order and the position mentioned. [74] What is white is composed of shapes of this sort. Black [scil. is composed] of the contrary ones, rough, irregular, and dissimilar; for in this way they cast a shadow and the perforations are not straight nor easy to pass through. Furthermore, the effluxes are sluggish and turbulent. For the efflux also differs to some extent according to its kind with regard to the representation—it becomes different as air is contained.

[75] Red [scil. is composed] out of ones of the same kind as what is warm, except that they [i.e. the red ones] are larger. For whenever the aggregates are larger, the shapes being similar, the result is redder. Evidence for red being composed of shapes of this sort: we become red when we are warm, and so too does everything else that is set ablaze, until it becomes incandescent. Redder are the substances made of large shapes, like flame and charcoal of green wood compared with dry wood, and also iron and other things set ablaze; for the brightest things are the ones that possess the most abundant and thinnest fire, while the redder ones possess thicker fire and less of it. And that is why redder things are less warm, for what is thin is warm. Greenish-yellow is composed of solid and

---

1 οἵωνπερ καὶ Diels: οἵωνπερ ὃ F: οἵων περὶ P   2 μέχρι
ἂν συνέχῃ τὸ τοῦ πυρὸς εἶδος coni. Diels   3 παχύτερα
mss., corr. Stephanus   4 μὲν post θερμὸν hab. mss., del.
Camotius

127

συνεστάναι⁵ μεγάλων ἐξ ἀμφοῖν,⁶ τῇ θέσει δὲ καὶ τάξει αὐτῶν τὴν χρόαν.⁷

⁵ post συνεστάναι lacunam posuit Wimmer   ⁶ ἐκ με-
γάλως δ᾽ ἀμφοῖν Mullach   ⁷ μεμιγμένων δὲ ἀμφοῖν τῇ
θέσει καὶ τάξει αὐτῶν τὴν χρόαν coni. Diels: τὴν χρόαν ‹γίγνεσθαι› Mullach

[76] τὰ μὲν οὖν ἁπλᾶ χρώματα τούτοις κεχρῆσθαι
τοῖς σχήμασιν· ἕκαστον δὲ καθαρώτερον, ὅσῳ ἂν ἐξ
ἀμιγεστέρων ᾖ. τὰ δὲ ἄλλα κατὰ τὴν τούτων μῖξιν·
οἷον τὸ μὲν χρυσοειδὲς καὶ τὸ τοῦ χαλκοῦ καὶ πᾶν τὸ
τοιοῦτον ἐκ τοῦ λευκοῦ καὶ τοῦ ἐρυθροῦ· τὸ μὲν γὰρ
λαμπρὸν ἔχειν¹ ἐκ τοῦ λευκοῦ, τὸ δὲ ὑπέρυθρον ἀπὸ
τοῦ θερμοῦ·² πίπτειν γὰρ εἰς τὰ κενὰ τοῦ λευκοῦ τῇ
μίξει τὸ ἐρυθρόν. ἐὰν δὲ προστεθῇ τούτοις τὸ χλωρόν,
γίνεσθαι τὸ κάλλιστον χρῶμα, δεῖν³ δὲ μικρὰς τοῦ
χλωροῦ τὰς συγκρίσεις εἶναι· μεγάλας γὰρ οὐχ οἷόν
τε συγκειμένων οὕτω τοῦ λευκοῦ καὶ τοῦ ἐρυθροῦ. δια-
φόρους⁴ δὲ ἔσεσθαι τὰς χρόας τῷ πλέον καὶ ἔλαττον
λαμβάνειν. [77] τὸ δὲ πορφυροῦν ἐκ λευκοῦ καὶ μέλανος καὶ ἐρυθροῦ, πλείστην μὲν μοῖραν ἔχοντος τοῦ
ἐρυθροῦ, μακρὰν⁵ δὲ τοῦ μέλανος, μέσην⁶ δὲ τοῦ λευ-
κοῦ· διὸ καὶ ἡδὺ φαίνεσθαι πρὸς τὴν αἴσθησιν. ὅτι
μὲν οὖν τὸ μέλαν καὶ τὸ ἐρυθρὸν αὐτῷ⁷ ἐνυπάρχει,
φανερὸν εἶναι τῇ ὄψει, διότι δὲ τὸ λευκόν, τὸ λαμπρὸν
καὶ διαυγὲς σημαίνειν· ταῦτα γὰρ ποιεῖν τὸ λευκόν.
τὴν δ᾽ ἴσατιν ἐκ μέλανος σφόδρα καὶ χλωροῦ, πλείονα
δὲ μοῖραν ἔχειν τοῦ μέλανος· τὸ δὲ πράσινον ἐκ πορ-

128

void, both big, the color resulting from their position and order.

[76] Thus the simple colors depend on these shapes, each one being more pure to the degree that it is composed of less mixed ones. The other [scil. colors] are in accordance with the mixture of these. Thus the gold-colored, that of bronze, and everything like this comes from white and red. They owe their brightness to what is white, their reddish hue to what is warm. For the red falls into the voids of the white when they mix. If greenish-yellow is added to these, the most beautiful color comes about, but the aggregates of the greenish-yellow must be small, for they should not be large, given that the white and the red are arranged in this way. The hues will be different depending on their accepting a greater or smaller quantity. [77] Purple comes from white, black, and red, with red having the greatest portion, black a large one, white an intermediate one. And this is why it appears agreeable to sensation. That there is black and red in it is clear to the eye; and that there is white is indicated by its brightness and transparency, for these are produced by the white. Indigo comes from extreme black and greenish-yellow, but it has a greater portion of black. Leek-green [scil. comes] from purple and

---

1 ἔχειν Camotius: ἔχει mss.   2 ἐρυθροῦ Burchard

3 δεῖν Schneider: δεῖ mss.   4 διαφοραῖς mss., corr. Stephanus   5 μακρὰν P[1] F: μικρὰν (ι ss.)P[2]   6 μέσην F: μέσον P   7 αὐτῶ F paene evanidum: om. P

φυροῦ καὶ τῆς ἰσάτιδος, ἢ ἐκ χλωροῦ καὶ πορφυροει-
δοῦς. τὸ γὰρ θεῖον[8] εἶναι τοιοῦτον καὶ μετέχειν τοῦ
λαμπροῦ. τὸ δὲ κυανοῦν ἐξ ἰσάτιδος καὶ πυρώδους,
σχημάτων δὲ περιφερῶν καὶ βελονοειδῶν, ὅπως τὸ
στίλβον τῷ μέλανι ἐνῇ. [78] τὸ δὲ καρύινον ἐκ χλωροῦ
καὶ κυανοειδοῦς. ἐὰν δὲ †χλωρὸν†[9] μιχθῇ, φλογοειδὲς
γίνεσθαι, τὸ γὰρ ἄσκιον[10] καὶ μελανόχρων ἐξείργεσθαι.[11] σχεδὸν δὲ καὶ τὸ ἐρυθρὸν τῷ λευκῷ μιχθὲν
<τὸ>[12] χλωρὸν ποιεῖν εὐαγὲς καὶ οὐ μέλαν· διὸ καὶ τὰ
φυόμενα χλωρὰ τὸ πρῶτον εἶναι πρὸ τοῦ θερμανθῆ-
ναι καὶ †διαχεῖσθαι†.[13]

καὶ πλήθει μὲν τοσούτων ἐπιμέμνηται[14] χρωμάτων,
ἄπειρα δὲ εἶναι καὶ[15] τὰ χρώματα καὶ τοὺς χυλοὺς
κατὰ τὰς μίξεις, ἐάν τις τὰ μὲν ἀφαιρῇ, τὰ δὲ προσ-
τιθῇ, καὶ τῶν μὲν ἔλαττον μίσγῃ,[16] τῶν δὲ πλεῖον.
οὐθὲν γὰρ ὅμοιον ἔσεσθαι θάτερον θατέρῳ.[17] [. . . =
R59]

8 τὸν γὰρ ἰὸν coni. Diels   9 χλωρὸν <πλέον> Schneider
10 κατάσκιον Mullach   11 ἐὰν δὲ καὶ λαμπρὸν μιχθῇ,
φλογοειδὲς γίνεσθαι (τοῦτο γὰρ ἄσκιον) καὶ τὸ μελανόχρων
ἐξείργεσθαι uel τῷ γὰρ ἀσκίῳ μελ. ἐξείργεσθαι coni. Diels
12 <τὸ> Burchard   13 διακαίεσθαι coni. Diels
14 τοσοῦτον ἐπιμέμικται mss., corr. Schneider
15 καὶ om. F   16 μίσγειν mss., corr. Schneider
17 θατέρου mss., corr. Schneider

indigo, or from greenish-yellow and purplish; for sulfur
(?)[1] too is like this and has a share in what is bright. Dark
blue [scil. comes] from indigo and what is fiery in color,
the shapes being round and pointed, so that there is glit-
tering in the black. [78] Nut-brown [scil. comes] from
greenish-yellow and dark blue; but if greenish-yellow (?)
is mixed, it becomes flame-colored; for in this way the
absence of shadow and the presence of black are excluded.[2] Red mixed with white can also produce a clear
green, without black; and this is why plant buds at first are
clear green, before becoming warm and spreading out (?).

And with regard to number, this is as many colors as he
mentions; but the colors and flavors are unlimited, in accordance with their mixtures, if one removes these and
adds those, and some are mixed in a smaller quantity, and
others in a larger one. For none will be similar to each
other. [. . .]

---

[1] Or, with Diels' correction: "the violet."

[2] Or, adopting Diels' further correction of the text: "for if what
is bright is mixed, it becomes flame-colored (for this does not have
a shadow) and what is black is excluded."

Odors (D67)

D67 (< A135) Theophr. *Sens.* 82

[. . . = **R59**] περὶ δὲ ὀσμῆς [. . .] τὸ λεπτὸν ἀπορρέον
ἀπὸ τῶν βαρέων[1] ποιεῖ τὴν ὀδμήν. [. . . cf. **R25**]

[1] θερμῶν Usener: παχέων Mullach

Heavy and Light, Hard and Soft (D68–D69)

D68 (< A60) Arist. *Cael.* 4.2 309a1–2

[. . . cf. **D40**] τοῖς δὲ στερεὰ μᾶλλον ἐνδέχεται λέγειν
τὸ μεῖζον εἶναι βαρύτερον αὐτῶν.

D69 (< A135) Theophr. *Sens.* 61–62

[. . . = **R21**] [61] βαρὺ μὲν οὖν καὶ κοῦφον τῷ μεγέθει
διαιρεῖ[1] Δημόκριτος. εἰ γὰρ διακριθείη[2] ἔνθεν ἕκαστον,[3] εἰ καὶ κατὰ σχῆμα διαφέροι, διαφέρει,[4] σταθ-
μοῦ[5] ἂν ἐπὶ μεγέθει τὴν φύσιν[6] ἔχειν. οὐ μὴν ἀλλ᾽ ἔν
γε τοῖς μικτοῖς κουφότερον μὲν[7] εἶναι τὸ πλέον ἔχον
κενόν, βαρύτερον δὲ τὸ ἔλαττον. ἐν ἐνίοις μὲν οὕτως
εἴρηκεν. [62] ἐν ἄλλοις δὲ κοῦφον εἶναί φησιν ἁπλῶς
τὸ λεπτόν. παραπλησίως δὲ καὶ περὶ σκληροῦ καὶ
μαλακοῦ. σκληρὸν μὲν γὰρ εἶναι τὸ πυκνόν, μαλακὸν
δὲ τὸ μανόν, καὶ τὸ μᾶλλον δὲ καὶ ἧττον καὶ μάλιστα

[1] διαιρεῖν mss., corr. Stephanus
[2] διακριθῇ mss., corr. Diels

ATOMISTS (LEUCIPPUS, DEMOCRITUS)

Odors (D67)

D67 (< A135) Theophrastus, *On Sensations*

[. . .] As for odor [. . .] it is the thin emanating from heavy bodies that makes odor [. . .].

Heavy and Light, Hard and Soft (D68–D69)

D68 (< A60) Aristotle, *On the Heavens*

[. . .] For the others [scil. who, unlike Plato, say that the principles are] solid [i.e. the Atomists], it is easier to say that the larger ones among them are heavier.

D69 (< A135) Theophrastus, *On Sensations*

[. . .] [61] Heavy and light Democritus distinguishes by magnitude. For if one analyzed from what source each thing, though differing in its shape too, differs, nature would have in magnitude its unit of weight. But as it is, among mixed bodies at least, the one possessing more void is lighter, the one with less is heavier. In some passages this is what he has said. [62] In others, he says simply that what is thin is light. He speaks similarly about hard and soft: hard is what is dense, soft what is loose; and what is more, less, and most of all [scil. dense and rarefied] varies in proportion. But there is a certain difference in the posi-

---

³ ἔνθεν ἕκαστον mss.: καθ' ἓν ἕκαστον Diels: ἓν ἕκαστον Mullach: ἓν μὲν ἕκαστον Burchard   ⁴ διαφέρει del. Vossianus   ⁵ σταθμὸν mss., corr. Papencordt   ⁶ τὴν φύσιν mss.: τὴν κρίσιν Preller: τὴν διαφοράν coni. Usener: τινὰ φύσιν coni. Diels   ⁷ ἂν mss., corr. Usener

κατὰ λόγον.[8] διαφέρειν δέ τι[9] τὴν θέσιν καὶ τὴν ἐναπόληψιν[10] τῶν κενῶν τοῦ[11] σκληροῦ καὶ μαλακοῦ καὶ
βαρέος καὶ κούφου. διὸ σκληρότερον μὲν εἶναι σίδηρον, βαρύτερον δὲ μόλυβδον· τὸν μὲν γὰρ σίδηρον
ἀνωμάλως συγκεῖσθαι καὶ τὸ κενὸν ἔχειν πολλαχῇ
καὶ κατὰ μεγάλα, πεπυκνῶσθαι δὲ[12] κατὰ ἔνια, ἁπλῶς
δὲ πλέον ἔχειν κενόν. τὸν δὲ μόλυβδον ἔλαττον ἔχοντα κενὸν ὁμαλῶς συγκεῖσθαι ⟨καὶ⟩[13] κατὰ πᾶν
ὁμοίως, διὸ βαρύτερον μέν, μαλακώτερον δ' εἶναι τοῦ
σιδήρου. [. . . = **D64**]

8 μάλιστα ⟨καὶ ἥκιστα⟩ κενὸν ἔχον coni. Burchard
9 δ' ἔτι Schneider   10 ἐναπόλειψιν mss., corr. Papencordt
11 τοῦ susp. Diels   12 καὶ mss., corr. Diels
13 ⟨καὶ⟩ Diels qui coni. καὶ κατὰ πᾶν ὁμοίως πεπυκνῶσθαι

The Process of Becoming (D70–D72)
Acting and Being Acted Upon (D70)

D70 (A63) Arist. *GC* 1.7 323b10–15

Δημόκριτος δὲ παρὰ τοὺς ἄλλους ἰδίως ἔλεξε μόνος·
φησὶ γὰρ τὸ αὐτὸ καὶ ὅμοιον εἶναι τό τε ποιοῦν καὶ
τὸ πάσχον· οὐ γὰρ ἐγχωρεῖ τὰ ἕτερα καὶ διαφέροντα
πάσχειν ὑπ' ἀλλήλων, ἀλλὰ κἂν ἕτερα ὄντα ποιῇ τι
ἄλληλα, οὐχ ᾗ ἕτερα ἀλλ' ᾗ ταὐτόν τι ὑπάρχει, ταύτῃ
τοῦτο συμβαίνειν αὐτοῖς.

tion [scil. of the shapes] and in the inclusion of voids between hard and soft on the one hand, and heavy and light
on the other. That is why iron is harder but lead is heavier:
for iron has an irregular composition and contains void in
many places and in large areas; it is condensed in some
places, but, speaking generally, it contains more void. But
lead, which possesses less void, has everywhere the same
regular composition. And that is why it is heavier, even
though it is softer than iron. [. . .]

The Process of Becoming (D70–D72)
Acting and Being Acted Upon (D70)

D70 (A63) Aristotle, *On Generation and Corruption*

Democritus is the only one, compared with the others, to
have spoken in his own way. For he says that what acts and
what is acted upon are the same and similar. For he does
not admit that things that are other and different can be
acted upon by each other, but if, even though they are
other, they do act in some way upon each other, this happens to them not by virtue of their being other, but by
virtue of their possessing something identical.

*Generation, Corruption, Alteration and
Other Processes (D71–D72)*

D71 (A35, < 67 A9) Arist. *GC* 1.2 315a34–b9

ὅλως δὲ παρὰ τὰ ἐπιπολῆς περὶ οὐδενὸς οὐδεὶς ἐπ-
έστησεν ἔξω Δημοκρίτου. οὗτος δ' ἔοικε μὲν περὶ
ἁπάντων φροντίσαι, ἤδη δὲ ἐν τῷ πῶς διαφέρειν. οὔτε
γὰρ περὶ αὐξήσεως οὐδεὶς οὐδὲν διώρικεν, ὥσπερ λέγομεν, ὅ τι μὴ κἂν ὁ τυχὼν εἴπειεν [. . .] οὐδὲ περὶ
μίξεως, οὐδὲ περὶ τῶν ἄλλων ὡς εἰπεῖν οὐδενός, οἷον
τοῦ ποιεῖν ἢ τοῦ πάσχειν, τίνα τρόπον τὸ μὲν ποιεῖ
τὸ δὲ πάσχει τὰς φυσικὰς ποιήσεις. Δημόκριτος δὲ
καὶ Λεύκιππος ποιήσαντες τὰ σχήματα τὴν ἀλλοίωσιν καὶ τὴν γένεσιν ἐκ τούτων ποιοῦσι, διακρίσει μὲν
καὶ συγκρίσει γένεσιν καὶ φθοράν, τάξει δὲ καὶ θέσει
ἀλλοίωσιν [. . . cf. **D56**].

D72 (> A123) Arist. *GC* 1.2 315b33–316a2

[. . .] ὅμως[1] δὲ τούτοις ἀλλοίωσιν καὶ γένεσιν ἐνδέχεται ποιεῖν [. . .], *τροπῇ* καὶ *διαθηγῇ*[2] μετακινοῦντα τὸ
αὐτὸ καὶ ταῖς τῶν σχημάτων διαφοραῖς, ὅπερ ποιεῖ
Δημόκριτος· διὸ καὶ χροιὰν οὔ φησιν εἶναι, τροπῇ
γὰρ χρωματίζεσθαι.

[1] ὅμως] ὁμοίως E[1]J[1]   [2] διαθηγῇ JL: διαθειγῇ E[1] ut vid.:
διαθιγῇ cett.

ATOMISTS (LEUCIPPUS, DEMOCRITUS)

Generation, Corruption, Alteration, and
Other Processes (D71–D72)

D71 (A35, < 67 A9) Aristotle, *On Generation and Corruption*

In general, setting aside superficial considerations, no one has paused to think about any [scil. of these processes] except for Democritus. He seems to have thought about all of them, already asking himself how they differ. For no one, as we say, has asserted anything about growth that any chance person might not have said [...] nor about mixture, nor about practically any of the other ones [i.e. processes], like acting and being acted upon—in what way one thing acts and another is acted upon in natural actions. But Democritus and Leucippus, by positing shapes, explain alteration and generation on the basis of these: generation and destruction by dissociation and association, alteration by order and position [...].

D72 (> A123) Aristotle, *On Generation and Corruption*

[...] All the same [scil. despite the absurdities arising from their doctrine] these [scil. Democritus and Leucippus] are able to explain alteration and generation [...] by transforming the same thing by **turning** and **disposition,** as well as by the differences in shapes, which is what Democritus does. And that is why he says that color does not exist: for coloration happens by virtue of **turning.**

Necessity and Chance (D73–D76)

D73 (67 B2) Aët. 1.25.4 (Stob.) [περὶ ἀνάγκης]

Λεύκιππος πάντα κατ᾿ ἀνάγκην, τὴν δ᾿ αὐτὴν ὑπάρχειν εἱμαρμένην· λέγει γὰρ ἐν τῷ Περὶ νοῦ· "οὐδὲν
χρῆμα μάτην γίγνεται, ἀλλὰ πάντα ἐκ λόγου τε καὶ
ὑπ᾿ ἀνάγκης."

D74 (A66) Arist. *GA* 5.8 789b2–4

Δημόκριτος δὲ τὸ οὗ ἕνεκα ἀφεὶς λέγειν, πάντα ἀνάγει εἰς ἀνάγκην οἷς χρῆται ἡ φύσις [. . . = **R30**].

D75 (A66) Aët. 1.26.2 (Ps.-Plut.; cf. Ps.-Gal.) [περὶ τῆς
οὐσίας ἀνάγκης]

Δημόκριτος τὴν ἀντιτυπίαν καὶ φορὰν[1] καὶ πληγὴν
τῆς ὕλης.

---

[1] φορὰν Ps.-Gal. *Hist. phil.* 41: φθορὰν vel τὴν φθορὰν mss.

D76

a (A68) Arist. *Phys.* 2.4 195b36–196a3

ἔνιοι γὰρ καὶ εἰ ἔστιν ἢ μὴ ἀποροῦσιν· οὐδὲν γὰρ δὴ
γίνεσθαι ἀπὸ τύχης φασίν, ἀλλὰ πάντων εἶναί τι
αἴτιον ὡρισμένον ὅσα λέγομεν ἀπὸ αὐτομάτου γίγνεσθαι ἢ τύχης [. . .].

ATOMISTS (LEUCIPPUS, DEMOCRITUS)

Necessity and Chance (D73–D76)

D73 (67 B2) Aëtius

Leucippus: everything [scil. happens] according to necessity, and this is the same as destiny (*heimarmenê*). For he says in his *On Mind,* **"nothing happens at random, but everything for a reason and as the effect of necessity."**

D74 (A66) Aristotle, *Generation of Animals*

Democritus, neglecting to speak of the final cause, refers to necessity everything of which nature makes use [. . .].

D75 (A66) Aëtius

Democritus: it [scil. necessity] is resistance (*antitupia*), locomotion, and the collision of matter.

D76

a (A68) Aristotle, *Physics*

For some people raise the difficulty whether it [i.e. chance, *tukhê*] exists or not. For they say that nothing happens by chance, but that there is a determinate cause for all the things about which we say that they happen spontaneously or by chance [. . .].

b (≠ DK) Arist. *Phys.* 2.4 196a11–16

πολλὰ γὰρ καὶ γίγνεται καὶ ἔστιν ἀπὸ τύχης καὶ ἀπὸ
ταὐτομάτου, ἃ οὐκ ἀγνοοῦντες ὅτι ἔστιν ἐπανενεγκεῖν
ἕκαστον ἐπί τι αἴτιον τῶν γιγνομένων, καθάπερ ὁ παλαιὸς λόγος εἶπεν ὁ ἀναιρῶν τὴν τύχην, ὅμως τούτων
τὰ μὲν εἶναί φασι πάντες ἀπὸ τύχης τὰ δ' οὐκ ἀπὸ
τύχης.

c (A68) Simpl. *In Phys.*, p. 330.14–20

τὸ δὲ "καθάπερ ὁ παλαιὸς λόγος ὁ ἀναιρῶν τὴν τύχην" [cf. **D76b**] πρὸς Δημόκριτον ἔοικεν εἰρῆσθαι·
ἐκεῖνος γὰρ κἂν ἐν τῇ κοσμοποιίᾳ ἐδόκει τῇ τύχῃ
κεχρῆσθαι, ἀλλ' ἐν τοῖς μερικωτέροις οὐδενός φησιν
εἶναι τὴν τύχην αἰτίαν ἀναφέρων εἰς ἄλλας αἰτίας,
οἷον τοῦ θησαυρὸν εὑρεῖν τὸ σκάπτειν ἢ τὴν φυτείαν
τῆς ἐλαίας, τοῦ δὲ καταγῆναι τοῦ φαλακροῦ τὸ
κρανίον τὸν ἀετὸν ῥίψαντα τὴν χελώνην, ὅπως τὸ
χελώνιον ῥαγῇ. οὕτως γὰρ ὁ Εὔδημος ἱστορεῖ [Frag.
54a Wehrli].

The Universe (D77–D127)
The Whole and Time Are Unlimited (D77–D79)

D77 (< A39) Ps.-Plut. *Strom.* 7 in Eus. *PE* 1.8.7

Δημόκριτος ὁ Ἀβδηρίτης ὑπεστήσατο τὸ πᾶν ἄπειρον διὰ τὸ μηδαμῶς ὑπό τινος αὐτὸ δεδημιουργῆ-
σθαι· ἔτι δὲ καὶ ἀμετάβλητον αὐτὸ λέγει· καὶ καθό-

b (≠ DK) Aristotle, *Physics*

For many things both happen and exist by chance and spontaneously, about which all people, although they are not unaware that it is possible to refer each of these things that happens to some cause (like the ancient argument that abolishes chance), nonetheless say that some of them are produced by chance and others not by chance.

c (A68) Simplicius, *Commentary on Aristotle's* Physics

The phrase "like the ancient argument that abolishes chance" seems to be said with reference to Democritus. For even if he seemed to have recourse to chance in the course of the formation of the world, nonetheless in his particular explanations he states that chance is not the cause of anything, referring to other causes, for example that digging or planting an olive tree [scil. was the cause] of the discovery of the treasure, or that the eagle dropping the tortoise in order that its shell be broken [scil. was that] of shattering the bald man's [i.e. Aeschylus'] skull. This is what Eudemus reports.

The Universe (D77–D127)
The Whole and Time Are Unlimited (D77–D79)

D77 (< A39) Ps.-Plutarch, *Stromata*

Democritus of Abdera supposed that the whole is unlimited because it has not been fashioned in any way at all by someone. He also says that it is immutable; and in general,

λου, οἷον πᾶν ἐστιν, ῥητῶς ἐκτίθεται μηδεμίαν ἀρχὴν
ἔχειν τὰς αἰτίας τῶν νῦν γιγνομένων, ἄνωθεν δ' ὅλως
ἐξ ἀπείρου χρόνου προκατέχεσθαι τῇ ἀνάγκῃ πάνθ'
ἁπλῶς τὰ γεγονότα καὶ ἐόντα καὶ ἐσόμενα [. . .].

D78 (< A71) Arist. *Phys.* 8.1 251b14–17

ἀγένητον γὰρ εἶναι λέγουσιν. καὶ διὰ τούτου Δημόκριτός γε δείκνυσιν ὡς ἀδύνατον ἅπαντα γεγονέναι·
τὸν γὰρ χρόνον ἀγένητον εἶναι.

D79 (< 42.1 Leszl) Arist. *GA* 2.6 742b20–23

[. . . cf. **R27**] Δημόκριτος ὁ Ἀβδηρίτης, ὅτι τοῦ μὲν ἀεὶ
καὶ ἀπείρου οὐκ ἔστιν ἀρχή, τὸ δὲ διὰ τί ἀρχή, τὸ δ'
ἀεὶ ἄπειρον, ὥστε τὸ ἐρωτᾶν τὸ διὰ τί περὶ τῶν
τοιούτων τινὸς τὸ ζητεῖν εἶναί φησι τοῦ ἀπείρου ἀρ-
χήν.

Cosmogony (D80–D89)
Two Summaries (D80–D81)

D80 (< 67 A1) Diog. Laert.

a 9.30

ἤρεσκε δὲ αὐτῷ ἄπειρα εἶναι τὰ πάντα καὶ εἰς ἄλληλα
μεταβάλλειν, τό τε πᾶν εἶναι κενὸν καὶ πλῆρες σωμάτων.[1] τούς τε κόσμους γίνεσθαι σωμάτων εἰς τὸ

[1] σωμάτων del. Rohde

according to what is a whole, he explicitly states that the causes of the things that exist now do not have any beginning, and that simply everything that has been, is, and will be is determined beforehand by necessity, from the earliest beginning, since unlimited time [. . .].

D78 (< A71) Aristotle, *Physics*

For they [i.e. everyone except Plato] say that it [i.e. time] is ungenerated. And this is how Democritus, for one, demonstrates that it is impossible for all things to have been generated: for time is ungenerated.

D79 (≠ DK) Aristotle, *Generation of Animals*

[. . .] Democritus of Abdera says that there is no beginning (*arkhê*) of the always and of the unlimited, that a cause is a beginning, and that the always is unlimited; so that to ask for the cause of this kind of thing is, he says, to seek a beginning of the unlimited.

Cosmogony (D80–D89)
Two Summaries (D80–D81)

D80 (< 67 A1) Diogenes Laertius

a

[30] He [scil. Leucippus] had the opinions that the totality of things is unlimited and they are transformed into one another, and the whole is empty and full of bodies. The worlds come to be when bodies fall in the void and be-

κενὸν ἐμπιπτόντων καὶ ἀλλήλοις περιπλεκομένων· ἔκ
τε τῆς κινήσεως κατὰ τὴν αὔξησιν αὐτῶν γίνεσθαι
τὴν τῶν ἀστέρων φύσιν. [. . . = **D93**] κεφαλαιωδῶς μὲν
ταῦτα.

b 9.30–33

[30] ἐπὶ μέρους δ' ὧδε ἔχει· [31] τὸ μὲν πᾶν ἄπειρόν
φησιν, ὡς προείρηται· τούτου δὲ τὸ μὲν πλῆρες εἶναι,
τὸ δὲ κενόν, ⟨ἃ⟩¹ καὶ στοιχεῖά φησι. κόσμους τε ἐκ
τούτων ἀπείρους εἶναι καὶ διαλύεσθαι εἰς ταῦτα. γίνεσθαι δὲ τοὺς κόσμους οὕτω· φέρεσθαι κατὰ ἀπο-
τομὴν ἐκ τῆς ἀπείρου πολλὰ σώματα παντοῖα τοῖς
σχήμασιν εἰς μέγα κενόν, ἅπερ ἀθροισθέντα δίνην
ἀπεργάζεσθαι μίαν, καθ' ἣν προσκρούοντα² καὶ παν-
τοδαπῶς κυκλούμενα διακρίνεσθαι χωρὶς τὰ ὅμοια
πρὸς τὰ ὅμοια. ἰσορρόπων δὲ διὰ τὸ πλῆθος μηκέτι
δυναμένων περιφέρεσθαι, τὰ μὲν λεπτὰ χωρεῖν εἰς τὸ
ἔξω κενόν, ὥσπερ διαττώμενα· τὰ δὲ λοιπὰ συμμένειν
καὶ περιπλεκόμενα συγκατατρέχειν ἀλλήλοις³ καὶ
ποιεῖν πρῶτόν τι σύστημα σφαιροειδές. [32] τοῦτο⁴ δὲ
οἷον ὑμένα ἀφίστασθαι⁵ περιέχοντα ἐν ἑαυτῷ παντοῖα
σώματα· ὧν κατὰ τὴν τοῦ μέσου ἀντέρεισιν περιδι-
νουμένων λεπτὸν γενέσθαι τὸν πέριξ ὑμένα, συρρεόν-
των ἀεὶ τῶν συνεχῶν κατ' ἐπίψαυσιν τῆς δίνης. καὶ
οὕτω γενέσθαι τὴν γῆν, συμμενόντων τῶν ἐνεχθέντων

¹ ⟨ἃ⟩ Hoelk   ² προσκρούοντα ⟨ἀλλήλοις⟩ Rohde

come interlaced with one another. From the motion that accompanies their growth, the nature of the heavenly bodies comes about. [. . .] So much for the general summary.

b

[30] For the details, it is as follows. [31] He says that the whole is unlimited, as I have just said. Of this, one part is full, the other empty, and he says that these are elements. The worlds that come from these are unlimited and they dissolve into these. The worlds come to be in the following way. Within a section originating from the unlimited, many bodies of all kinds of shapes are borne along toward a great void; when they have gathered together, they form a single vortex, by virtue of which, striking against [scil. one another] and moving circularly in various directions, similar things separate apart [scil. moving] toward similar ones. Since bodies of the same weight are no longer able to revolve because of their number, the light ones go toward the external void, as though they were being winnowed; while the others remain, become interlaced, and rush down to encounter each other and to produce a first stable ensemble (*sustêma*) in the form of a sphere. [32] This becomes detached like a membrane containing within itself bodies of all sorts; and as these revolve around by virtue of the vortex while the center exercises an opposing resistance, the surrounding membrane becomes thinner, while the adjacent bodies continue to flow together by the contact of the vortex. And this is how the

---

³ ἀλλήλοις Cobet: ἄλληλα mss.   ⁴ τούτου Kerschensteiner   ⁵ ἀφίστασθαι BPF: ὑφίστασθαι Φh

ἐπὶ τὸ μέσον. αὐτόν τε πάλιν τὸν περιέχοντα οἷον
ὑμένα αὔξεσθαι κατὰ τὴν ἐπέκρυσιν⁶ τῶν ἔξωθεν σω-
μάτων· δίνῃ τε φερόμενον αὐτόν, ὧν ἂν ἐπιψαύσῃ,
ταῦτα ἐπικτᾶσθαι. τούτων δέ τινα συμπλεκόμενα ποιεῖν σύστημα, τὸ μὲν πρῶτον κάθυγρον καὶ πηλῶδες,
ξηρανθέντα δὲ⁷ καὶ περιφερόμενα σὺν τῇ τοῦ ὅλου
δίνῃ, εἶτ᾽ ἐκπυρωθέντα τὴν τῶν ἀστέρων ἀποτελέσαι
φύσιν. [33] [. . . = **D94**] εἶναί τε ὥσπερ γενέσεις κόσμου,⁸ οὕτω καὶ αὐξήσεις καὶ φθίσεις καὶ φθοράς,
κατά τινα ἀνάγκην, ἣν ὁποία ἐστὶν ⟨οὐ⟩⁹ διασαφεῖ.

⁶ ἐπέκρυσιν BPF: ἐπικράτησιν Φh: ἐπέκκρισιν Arsenius,
coni. Heidel: ἐπείσρυσιν Rohde, alii alia   ⁷ δὲ Φh: om. BPF
⁸ κόσμων Rohde   ⁹ ⟨οὐ⟩ Stephanus

D81 (67 A10, 68 A40) (Ps.-?) Hippol. *Ref.* 1.12 et 13.2–4

[12] Λεύκιππος [. . .] κόσμους δὲ ⟨ὧδε⟩¹ γενέσθαι²
λέγει· ὅταν εἰς μέγα κενὸν³ ἐκ τοῦ περιέχοντος ἀθροι-
σθῇ πολλὰ σώματα καὶ συρρυῇ, προσκρούοντα
ἀλλήλοις συμπλέκεσθαι τὰ ὁμοιοσχήμονα καὶ παρα-
πλήσια τὰς μορφάς, καὶ περιπλεχθέντων⁴ ἄστρα⁵ γίνεσθαι, αὔξειν δὲ καὶ φθίνειν διὰ τὴν⁶ ἀνάγκην. τίς δ᾽
ἂν εἴη ἡ ἀνάγκη, οὐ διώρισεν. [. . .] [13.2] λέγει [. . .]
ἀπείρους δὲ εἶναι κόσμους καὶ μεγέθει διαφέροντας·
ἔν τισι δὲ μὴ εἶναι ἥλιον μηδὲ σελήνην, ἔν τισι δὲ

¹ ⟨ὧδε⟩ Usener   ² γενέσθαι mss.: γίνεσθαι Roeper
³ μετάκοινον mss., corr. Roeper   ⁴ περιπλεχθέντων
⟨αὐτῶν κατ᾽ αὔξησιν⟩ Marcovich conl. DL 9.32

earth was formed, since the bodies that are borne inward toward the center remain together there. But in turn the envelope, which is like a membrane, itself grows because of the afflux of bodies coming from outside. And since it is carried along by the vortex, it acquires additionally whatever bodies it comes into contact with. Of these, some become interlaced together and form a stable ensemble (*sustêma*), at first liquid and muddy, but then, drying out and revolving with the vortex of the whole and afterward being set on fire, they produce the nature of the heavenly bodies. [. . .] [33] And just as the generations of a world are, so too are its growth, decline, and destruction, by virtue of a certain necessity; he does ‹not› say of what sort this is.

D81 (67 A10, 68 A40) (Ps.-?) Hippolytus, *Refutation of All Heresies*

[12] Leucippus [. . .] says that worlds have come about ‹in the following way›: when many bodies coming from the periphery are gathered together and rush together into a great void, they collide against one another and those whose shapes are similar and which resemble one another in their forms become interlaced; and from their interlacing arise the heavenly bodies, and they increase and decline by virtue of necessity; but he has not defined what this necessity is. [. . .] [13.2] He [i.e. Democritus] says [. . .] that there exist unlimited worlds and that they are different in magnitude. In some of them there is neither a sun nor moon, in others they are larger than ours, and

---

⁵ εἰς ἕτερα mss., corr. Diels   ⁶ τὴν] τινα Roeper

μείζω τῶν παρ᾽ ἡμῖν καὶ ἔν τισι πλείω. [3] εἶναι δὲ τῶν
κόσμων ἄνισα τὰ διαστήματα, καὶ τῇ μὲν πλείους, τῇ
δὲ ἐλάττους, καὶ τοὺς μὲν αὔξεσθαι, τοὺς δὲ ἀκμάζειν,
τοὺς δὲ φθίνειν, καὶ τῇ μὲν γίνεσθαι, τῇ δ᾽ ‹ἐκ›λεί-
πειν·[7] φθείρεσθαι δὲ αὐτοὺς ὑπ᾽ ἀλλήλων προσπίπτον-
τας. εἶναι δὲ ἐνίους κόσμους ἐρήμους ζῴων καὶ φυτῶν
καὶ παντὸς ὑγροῦ. [. . . = **D92**] [4] ἀκμάζειν δὲ κόσμον
ἕως ἂν μηκέτι δύνηται ἔξωθέν τι προσλαμβάνειν.

[7] λείπειν mss., corr. Ritter

Some Parallels (D82–D85)

D82 (< A67, B167) Simpl. *In Phys.*, p. 327.24–25

δεῖνον ἀπὸ τοῦ παντὸς ἀποκριθῆναι[1] παντοίων εἰδέων.

[1] ἀποκριθῆναι E: ἀποκρίνεσθαι DF

D83

a (< A82) Simpl. *In Cael.*, p. 310.15–17

[. . .] οἱ δὲ Δημοκρίτου κόσμοι εἰς ἑτέρους κόσμους
μεταβάλλοντες ἐκ τῶν αὐτῶν ἀτόμων ὄντας οἱ αὐτοὶ
τῷ εἴδει γίνονται, εἰ καὶ μὴ τῷ ἀριθμῷ.

b (B138) Hesych. A.3562

ἀμειψικοσμίη: μετακόσμησις.

148

in some there are more than one. [3] The distances between the worlds are unequal, and there are more here
and fewer there; some grow, others reach their high point,
others decline; and here they come to be and there they
pass away. They are destroyed by one another by colliding
against each other. Some worlds are devoid of animals and
plants and of all humidity. [. . .] [4] The world remains at
its high point until it is no longer capable of accepting
something additional that comes from outside.

Some Parallels (D82–D85)

D82 (< A67, B167) Simplicius, *Commentary on Aristotle's* Physics

**A vortex of all kinds of forms became detached from
the whole.**

D83

a (< A82) Simplicius, *Commentary on Aristotle's* On the
Heavens

The worlds of Democritus that are transformed into other
worlds come from the same atoms and are identical in
species, even if not individually.

b (B138) Hesychius, *Lexicon*

Change of a world *(ameipsikosmiê)*: the transformation
of a world.

D84 (A84) Aët. 2.4.9 (Stob.) [εἰ ἄφθαρτος ὁ κόσμος]

Δημόκριτος φθείρεσθαι τὸν κόσμον τοῦ μείζονος τὸν μικρότερον νικῶντος.

D85 (< A81) Cic. *Acad.* 2.17.55

[. . .] et ais Democritum dicere innumerabiles esse mundos, et quidem sic quosdam inter sese non solum similes, sed undique perfecte et absolute ita[1] pares, ut inter eos nihil prorsus intersit et eo quidem innumerabiles,[2] itemque homines.

  [1] ita *del. Christ*   [2] *post* innumerabiles *ind. Plasberg lacunam, e.g.* <etiam soles lunas maria terras, singulas denique res>

The Genesis of Our World (D86–D89)

D86 (67 A23) Aët. 2.7.2 (Stob.) [περὶ τάξεως τοῦ κόσμου]

Λεύκιππος καὶ Δημόκριτος χιτῶνα κύκλῳ καὶ ὑμένα περιτείνουσι τῷ κόσμῳ διὰ τῶν ἀγκιστροειδῶν ἀτόμων συμπεπλεγμένον.

D87 (< A39) Ps.-Plut. *Strom.* 7 in Eus. *PE* 1.8.7

[. . . = **D77**] ἡλίου δὲ καὶ σελήνης γένεσίν φησιν· κατ᾽ ἰδίαν φέρεσθαι ταῦτα μηδέπω τὸ παράπαν ἔχοντα θερμὴν φύσιν μηδὲ μὴν καθόλου λαμπρότητα,[1] τοὐναντίον δὲ ἐξωμοιωμένην τῇ περὶ τὴν γῆν φύσει· γε-

D84 (A84) Aëtius

Democritus: a world is destroyed when a larger one gains victory over a smaller one.

D85 (< A81) Cicero, *Prior Academics*

[Lucullus:] [. . .] you [scil. Cicero] say that Democritus asserts that there exist innumerable worlds, and indeed some of them not only so similar to one another, but so perfectly and absolutely equal in all regards, that there is no difference whatsoever between them, and that for that very reason [scil. they are] innumerable, and the same for people.[1]

---

[1] The end of this passage is uncertain. See also **R70b.**

The Genesis of Our World (D86–D89)

D86 (67 A23) Aëtius

Leucippus and Democritus surround the world circularly with a mantle (*khitôn*) and a membrane, resulting from interlacing due to hook-shaped atoms.

D87 (< A39) Ps.-Plutarch, *Stromata*

[. . .] He [i.e. Democritus] speaks of the generation of the sun and moon. They moved along their own trajectory, not yet possessing a nature that was at all warm nor brilliance in general, but on the contrary their nature was entirely similar to that of the terrestrial region. For each

---

[1] λαμπροτάτην mss., corr. Diels

γονέναι γὰρ ἑκάτερον τούτων πρότερον ἔτι κατ' ἰδίαν
ὑποβολήν τινα κόσμου, ὕστερον δὲ μεγεθοποιουμένου
τοῦ περὶ τὸν ἥλιον κύκλου ἐναποληφθῆναι ἐν αὐτῷ τὸ
πῦρ.

D88 (A95) Aët. 3.13.4 (Ps.-Plut.) [περὶ κινήσεως γῆς]

κατ' ἀρχὰς μὲν πλάζεσθαι τὴν γῆν φησιν ὁ Δημόκριτος διά τε μικρότητα καὶ κουφότητα, πυκνωθεῖσαν δὲ
τῷ χρόνῳ καὶ βαρυνθεῖσαν καταστῆναι.

D89 (67 A27, 68 A96) Aët. 3.12.1–2 (Ps.-Plut.) [περὶ
ἐγκλίσεως γῆς]

[1] Λεύκιππος παρεκπεσεῖν τὴν γῆν εἰς τὰ μεσημ-
βρινὰ μέρη διὰ τὴν ἐν τοῖς μεσημβρινοῖς ἀραιότητα,
ἅτε δὴ πεπηγότων τῶν βορείων διὰ τὸ κατεψῦχθαι
τοῖς κρυμοῖς, τῶν δὲ ἀντιθέτων πεπυρωμένων.
[2] Δημόκριτος διὰ τὸ ἀσθενέστερον εἶναι τὸ μεσημ-
βρινὸν τοῦ περιέχοντος αὐξομένην τὴν γῆν κατὰ
τοῦτο ἐγκλιθῆναι· τὰ γὰρ βόρεια ἄκρατα, τὰ δὲ με-
σημβρινὰ κέκραται· ὅθεν κατὰ τοῦτο βεβάρηται,
ὅπου περισσή ἐστι τοῖς καρποῖς καὶ τῇ αὔξῃ.

of these two [scil. heavenly bodies] came into being even
earlier, because of a certain characteristic depositing (*hu-
pobolê*) deriving from the world, and it was later that, as
the circle of the sun became larger, fire came to be contained within it.

D88 (A95) Aëtius

Democritus says that at the beginning the earth wandered
because of its smallness and lightness, but with time, as it
became denser and heavier, it came to rest.

D89 (67 A27, 68 A96) Aëtius

[1] Leucippus: the earth subsided toward its southern
parts because of the rarefaction in these southern regions,
since the northern ones had been solidified by being frozen by the frosts, while the opposing ones were burned.
[2] Democritus: because the southern part of the periphery was weaker, the earth inclined in this direction as it
grew. For the northern parts are not tempered, while the
southern ones are tempered. And that is why it is weighted
in this direction, where it is overabundant because of
fruits and its growth.

Cosmology (D90–D123)
Nature and Position of the
Heavenly Bodies (D90–D95)

D90 (67 B1) Ach. Tat. *Introd. Arat.* 1.13

τοὺς ἀστέρας δὲ ζῷα εἶναι οὔτε Ἀναξαγόρᾳ οὔτε Δημοκρίτῳ ἐν[1] τῷ Μεγάλῳ ‹δια›κόσμῳ[2] δοκεῖ [. . .].

  [1] ἐν Maass: σὺν V: om. M   [2] ‹δια›κόσμῳ Maass: κόσμῳ
V: om. M

D91 (A85) Aët. 2.13.4 (Stob.) [περὶ οὐσίας ἄστρων]

Δημόκριτος πέτρους.

D92 (< 67 A10, 68 A40) (Ps.-?) Hippol. *Ref.* 1.13.4

[. . . cf. **D81**] τοῦ δὲ παρ᾽ ἡμῖν κόσμου πρότερον τὴν
γῆν τῶν ἄστρων γενέσθαι. εἶναι δὲ τὴν μὲν σελήνην
κάτω, ἔπειτα τὸν ἥλιον, εἶτα τοὺς ἀπλανεῖς ἀστέρας·
τοὺς δὲ πλανήτας οὐδ᾽ αὐτοὺς ἔχειν ἴσον ὕψος [. . .].

D93 (< 67 A1) Diog. Laert. 9.30

[. . . cf. **D80a**] φέρεσθαι δὲ τὸν ἥλιον ἐν μείζονι κύκλῳ
περὶ[1] τὴν σελήνην· τὴν γῆν ὀχεῖσθαι περὶ τὸ μέσον
δινουμένην· σχῆμά τε αὐτῆς τυμπανῶδες εἶναι [. . .].

  [1] περὶ BΡΦh: παρὰ F: ἢ Lapini

Cosmology (D90–D123)
Nature and Position of the
Heavenly Bodies (D90–D95)

D90 (67 B1) Achilles Tatius, *Introduction to Aratus'*
Phaenomena

That the heavenly bodies are living beings, neither Anaxagoras [**ANAXAG. D48**] thinks nor does Democritus in
his *Great World System* [. . .].

D91 (A85) Aëtius

Democritus: [scil. the heavenly bodies are] stones.

D92 (< 67 A10, 68 A40) (Ps.-?) Hippolytus, *Refutation of*
All Heresies

[. . .] In our world, the earth came into being before the
heavenly bodies. The moon is lowest, then comes the sun,
and then the fixed stars. The planets are not at the same
height either [. . .].

D93 (< 67 A1) Diogenes Laertius [Doxography of Leu-
cippus]

[. . .] The sun moves in a larger circle around the moon.
The earth is maintained in the central region because it is
whirled around by the vortex. Its shape is like that of a
drum [. . .].

D94 (< 67 A1) Diog. Laert. 9.33

[. . . = **D80b**] εἶναι δὲ τὸν τοῦ ἡλίου κύκλον ἐξώτατον, τὸν δὲ τῆς σελήνης προσγειότατον, τῶν ἄλλων μεταξὺ τούτων ὄντων.¹ καὶ πάντα μὲν τὰ ἄστρα πυροῦσθαι διὰ τὸ τάχος τῆς φορᾶς, τὸν δὲ ἥλιον καὶ ὑπὸ τῶν ἀστέρων ἐκπυροῦσθαι· τὴν δὲ σελήνην τοῦ πυρὸς ὀλίγον μεταλαμβάνειν.

¹ ὄντων Φh: om. BPF

D95 (A86) Aët. 2.15.3 (Stob., Ps.-Plut.) [περὶ τάξεως ἀστέρων]

Δημόκριτος πρῶτα¹ μὲν τὰ ἀπλανῆ, μετὰ δὲ ταῦτα τοὺς πλανήτας.²

¹ ante πρῶτα hab. mss. καὶ, del. Diels   ² post πλανήτας hab. Plut. ἐφ᾽ οἷς ἥλιον φωσφόρον σελήνην.

The Cosmic Year (D96)

D96 (B12) Cens. *Die nat.* 18.8

[. . .] et Democriti ex annis LXXXII¹ cum intercalariis perinde viginti octo.

¹ LXXII Tannery

D94 (< 67 A1) Diogenes Laertius [Doxography of Leucippus]

[. . .] The circle of the sun is the farthest out, that of the moon is the closest to earth, the others are located between these. All of the heavenly bodies are set ablaze by the rapidity of their motion, while the sun is set completely ablaze by the heavenly bodies too. The moon receives only a small share of fire.

D95 (A86) Aëtius

Democritus: the fixed stars come first, and after these the planets.[1]

> [1] The manuscripts of Ps.-Plutarch have, after "planets," a difficult phrase: "after which [scil. come] the sun, the morning star, the moon." But Venus is a planet, and the sun and moon are also sometimes considered to be planets by the Greeks. Perhaps one expression is a gloss on the other one.

The Cosmic Year (D96)

D96 (B12) Censorinus, *The Birthday*

[. . .] and Democritus' [scil. world-year consists] of eighty-two years with twenty-eight intercalary months.

Milky Way (D97–D98)

D97 (A91) Arist. *Meteor.* 1.8 345a25–31.

οἱ δὲ περὶ [. . . cf. **ANAXAG. D49**] Δημόκριτον φῶς
εἶναι τὸ γάλα λέγουσιν ἄστρων τινῶν· τὸν γὰρ ἥλιον
ὑπὸ τὴν γῆν φερόμενον οὐχ ὁρᾶν ἔνια τῶν ἄστρων.
ὅσα μὲν οὖν περιορᾶται ὑπ᾽ αὐτοῦ, τούτων μὲν οὐ
φαίνεσθαι τὸ φῶς (κωλύεσθαι γὰρ ὑπὸ τῶν τοῦ ἡλίου
ἀκτίνων)· ὅσοις δ᾽ ἀντιφράττει ἡ γῆ ὥστε μὴ ὁρᾶσθαι
ὑπὸ τοῦ ἡλίου, τὸ τούτων οἰκεῖον φῶς εἶναί φασι τὸ
γάλα.

D98 (A91)

a Aët. 3.1.6 (Ps.-Plut.) [περὶ τοῦ γαλαξίου κύκλου]

Δημόκριτος πολλῶν καὶ μικρῶν καὶ συνεχῶν ἀστέρων συμφωτιζομένων ἀλλήλοις συναυγασμὸν διὰ τὴν
πύκνωσιν.

b Ach. Tat. *Introd. Arat.* 24

ἄλλοι δὲ ἐκ μικρῶν πάνυ καὶ πεπυκνωμένων καὶ ἡμῖν
δοκούντων ἡνῶσθαι διὰ τὸ διάστημα τὸ ἀπὸ τοῦ
οὐρανοῦ ἐπὶ τὴν γῆν ἀστέρων αὐτὸν εἶναί φασιν, ὡς
εἴ τις ἁλάσι λεπτοῖς καὶ πολλοῖς καταπάσειέ τι.

Milky Way (D97–D98)

D97 (A91) Aristotle, *Meteorology*

The followers of [. . .] Democritus say that the Milky Way is the light of certain heavenly bodies; for the sun does not see some of the heavenly bodies when it moves below the earth. The light of those that are seen by it does not manifest itself (for it is prevented by the sun's rays); but those in front of which the earth interposes itself in such a way that they are not seen by the sun, the light belonging to these is, they say, the Milky Way.

D98 (A91)

a Aëtius

Democritus: [scil. the Milky Way is] the combined shining of many small and contiguous heavenly bodies that illuminate each other by reason of their density.

b Achilles Tatius, *Introduction to Aratus'* Phaenomena

Others say that it [i.e. the Milky Way] is made of extremely small and condensed heavenly bodies that seem to us to be unified by reason of the distance from the heavens to the earth, as if someone made a sprinkling of many fine salt crystals.

Comets (D99–D100)

D99 (59 A81) Arist. *Meteor.* 1.6 342b27–29

[. . . cf. **ANAXAG. D50**] καὶ Δημόκριτός φασιν εἶναι τοὺς κομήτας σύμφασιν τῶν πλανήτων ἀστέρων, ὅταν διὰ τὸ πλησίον ἐλθεῖν δόξωσι θιγγάνειν ἀλλήλων.

D100 (< A92) Sen. *Quaest. nat.* 7.3.2

Democritus [. . . = **P29**] suspicari se ait plures stellas esse, quae currant, sed nec numerum illarum posuit nec nomina, nondum comprehensis quinque siderum cursibus.

Sun and Moon (D101–D107)

D101 (A87) Aët. 2.20.7 (Theod.) [περὶ οὐσίας ἡλίου]

[. . .] Δημόκριτος [. . .] μύδρον ἢ πέτρον διάπυρον.

D102 (A87) Cic. *Fin.* 1.6.20

sol Democrito magnus videtur [. . .].

D103 (< 67 A1) Diog. Laert. 9.33

[. . .] ἐκλείπειν δὲ ἥλιον καὶ σελήνην <. . .>[1] [. . .]. καὶ

---

[1] lac. indic. Orelli

Comets (D99–D100)

D99 (59 A81) Aristotle, *Meteorology*

[. . .] and Democritus say that comets are the conjunction of planets, when by coming close together they seem to touch one another.

D100 (< A92) Seneca, *Natural Questions*

Democritus [. . .] says that he suspects that there are many shooting stars, but he has attributed to them neither a number nor a name, since the revolutions of the five heavenly bodies have not yet been understood.[1]

---

[1] For Democritus (and Anaxagoras), the comets depend on the conjunction of planets (cf. **D99**).

Sun and Moon (D101–D107)

D101 (A87) Aëtius

[. . .] Democritus [. . .]: [scil. the sun is] a blazing mass or stone.

D102 (A87) Cicero, *On Ends*

For Democritus, the sun seems large [. . .].

D103 (< 67 A1) Diogenes Laertius

The sun and the moon are eclipsed ⟨. . .⟩[1] [. . .]. Solar

---

[1] At this point the text continues with a phrase about an entirely different subject: "because the earth is inclined toward the south; the regions of the north are always snowing, extremely cold, and frozen" [cf. **D89[2]**]. Part of the sentence must have been lost.

τὸν μὲν ἥλιον ἐκλείπειν σπανίως, τὴν δὲ σελήνην συνεχῶς, διὰ τὸ ἀνίσους εἶναι τοὺς κύκλους αὐτῶν.

D104 (A89) Aët. 2.23.7 (Stob.) [περὶ τροπῶν ἡλίου]

Δημόκριτος [. . .] τροπὴν δὲ γίνεσθαι[1] ἐκ τῆς περιφε-
ρούσης αὐτὸν δινήσεως.

¹ τροπὴν δὲ γίνεσθαι ut additamentum secl. Diels

D105 (< A88) Lucr. 5.620–24

non, inquam, simplex his rebus reddita causast.
nam fieri vel cum primis id posse videtur,
Democriti quod sancta viri sententia ponit,
quanto quaeque magis sint terram sidera propter,
tanto posse minus cum caeli turbine ferri.

D106 (A89a) Plut. *Fac. orb. lun.* 16 929C

[. . .] ἀλλὰ κατὰ στάθμην, φησὶ Δημόκριτος, ἱσταμένη
τοῦ φωτίζοντος ὑπολαμβάνει καὶ δέχεται τὸν ἥλιον,
ὥστ' αὐτήν τε φαίνεσθαι καὶ διαφαίνειν ἐκεῖνον εἰκὸς
ἦν.

eclipses happen rarely, lunar ones continually, because of the inequality of their circles.

D104 (A89) Aëtius

Democritus: [. . .] the return (*tropê*) [scil. of the sun] is due to the vortex that carries it around.

D105 (< A88) Lucretius, *On the Nature of Things*

> No simple cause, I say, has been assigned to these
>   things [i.e. the turnings of the sun].
> For it seems that first of all those things could
>   happen
> As the holy opinion of that great man Democritus
>   posited:
> That the closer that each of the heavenly bodies is to
>   the earth,
> The less it can be borne along by the vortex of the
>   heavens.[1]

---

[1] What follows (v. 625–36) provides a detailed explanation in terms that could either go back to Democritus or reflect an Epicurean elaboration.

D106 (A89a) Plutarch, *On The Face in the Moon*

[. . .] but when it [scil. the moon] stands aligned with what illuminates it, says Democritus, it takes up and receives the [scil. light of the] sun. So that it is plausible that it itself [i.e. the moon] shines and that it [i.e. the sun] shines through it.

163

D107 (A90) Aët. 2.30.3 (Stob.) [περὶ ἐμφάσεως αὐτῆς καὶ διὰ τί γεώδης φαίνεται]

Δημόκριτος ἀποσκιάσματα¹ τῶν ὑψηλῶν ἐν αὐτῇ μερῶν· ἄγκη² γὰρ αὐτὴν ἔχειν καὶ νάπας.

¹ ἀποσκίασμά τι Canter   ² ἀνάγκη mss., corr. Canter

Democritean Calendars and
Ephemerides (D108–D109)
Democritus, Author of Ephemerides (D108)

D108 (< B14.6) Clod. Tusc. *Calend.* in Io. Lyd. *Ost.*, pp. 157.18–158.1

[. . .] καὶ ταῦτα μὲν ὁ Κλώδιος [. . .]· καὶ οὐκ αὐτὸς μόνος, ἀλλὰ μὴν καὶ Εὔδοξός τε ὁ πολύς, Δημόκριτος πρῶτος αὐτῶν [. . .].

An Example (D109)

D109 (B14.3) Gemin. *Isag.*, p. 218.14–17

ἐν δὲ τῇ δ΄ ἡμέρᾳ Δημοκρίτῳ Πλειάδες δύνουσιν ἅμα ἠοῖ· ἄνεμοι χειμέριοι, ὡς τὰ πολλὰ καὶ ψύχη ἤδη καὶ πάχνη, ἐπιπνεῖν φιλεῖ· φυλλορροεῖν ἄρχεται τὰ δένδρα μάλιστα.

D107 (A90) Aëtius

Democritus: [scil. the reason why the moon seems earth-like is] the shadows of the high places in it; for it has valleys and dales.

Democritean Calendars and Ephemerides (D108–D109)[1]
Democritus, Author of Ephemerides (D108)

[1] Ephemerides associate meteorological and celestial phenomena with the days of the year. DK edit as B14 eight testimonia (taken from Vitruvius, Eudoxus, Geminus, Pliny the Elder, the scholia to Apollonius Rhodius, Clodius Tuscus, Ptolemy, and John Lydus) including many examples, of which we present only one, as **D109**.

D108 (< B14.6) Clodius Tuscus, *Calendar*, in John Lydus, *On Prodigies*

[. . .] and this is what Clodius [scil. says in his collection of ephemerides] [. . .]; and not only he, but so too the celebrated Eudoxus, and Democritus the first of them all [. . .].

An Example (D109)

D109 (B14.3) Geminus, *Introduction to the Phenomena*

[Scorpion] On the fourth day, for Democritus, the Pleiades set at dawn; stormy winds tend to blow, and for the most part [scil. there is] already cold weather and frost; trees start to lose their leaves in great quantity.

165

The Shape and Position of the Earth (D110–D112)

D110 (13 A20) Arist. *Cael.* 2.13 294b13–23

[. . . cf. **ANAXIMEN. D19; ANAXAG. D58**] καὶ Δημόκριτος τὸ πλάτος αἴτιον εἶναί φασι τοῦ μένειν αὐτήν.
οὐ γὰρ τέμνειν ἀλλ᾽ ἐπιπωμάζειν τὸν ἀέρα τὸν κάτωθεν, ὅπερ φαίνεται τὰ πλάτος ἔχοντα τῶν σωμάτων
ποιεῖν· ταῦτα γὰρ καὶ πρὸς τοὺς ἀνέμους ἔχει δυσκι-
νήτως διὰ τὴν ἀντέρεισιν. ταὐτὸ δὴ τοῦτο ποιεῖν τῷ
πλάτει φασὶ τὴν γῆν πρὸς τὸν ὑποκείμενον ἀέρα (τὸν
δ᾽ οὐκ ἔχοντα[1] μεταστῆναι τόπον ἱκανὸν[2] ἀθρόως[3] κάτωθεν ἠρεμεῖν), ὥσπερ τὸ ἐν ταῖς κλεψύδραις ὕδωρ.
ὅτι δὲ δύναται πολὺ βάρος φέρειν ἀπολαμβανόμενος
καὶ μένων ὁ ἀήρ, τεκμήρια πολλὰ λέγουσιν.

[1] ἔχοντα ‹τοῦ› Diels   [2] an τόπον ἱκανὸν μεταστῆναι?
[3] τῷ post ἀθρόως utrum delendum an ante ἀθρόως ponendum
dub. Moraux

D111 (67 A26, 68 A94) Aët. 3.10.4–5 (Ps.-Plut.) [περὶ
σχήματος γῆς]

[4] Λεύκιππος τυμπανοειδῆ.
[5] Δημόκριτος δισκοειδῆ μὲν τῷ πλάτει, κοίλην δὲ τῷ
μέσῳ.[1]

[1] τῷ μέσῳ Eus. *PE* 15.56.5: τὸ μέσον Plut.

The Shape and Position of the Earth (D110–D112)

D110 (13 A20) Aristotle, *On the Heavens*

[. . .] and Democritus say that its [i.e. the earth's] flatness is the cause for its stationary position. For it does not cut the air beneath it but covers it like a lid, which is what one sees bodies possessing flatness to do; for winds have difficulty moving these bodies too, because of their resistance. And they say that it is in exactly the same way that the earth acts with regard to the air underlying it, because of its flatness, and that since it [i.e. the air] does not have sufficient room to move, it remains motionless below [scil. the earth] in a dense mass, just like the water in clepsydras. And for the fact that air that is enclosed and stationary can bear a great weight, they provide many proofs.

D111 (67 A26, 68 A94) Aëtius

[4] Leucippus: [scil. the earth is] drum-shaped.
[5] Democritus: [scil. it is] disk-shaped in its breadth, and sunken in the middle.

D112 (< B15) Agathem. *Geogr.* 1.1.2 (*GGM* 2.471.12–14)

πρῶτος δὲ Δημόρκιτος [. . . = **P30**] συνεῖδεν ὅτι προμήκης ἐστὶν ἡ γῆ, ἡμιόλιον τὸ μῆκος τοῦ πλάτους ἔχουσα.

Geography of the Earth (D113–D115)

D113 (< B15) Agathem. *Geogr.* 1.1.2 (*GGM* 2.471.7–9)

ἑξῆς [. . .] Δημόκριτος καὶ Εὔδοξος καὶ ἄλλοι τινὲς γῆς περιόδους καὶ περίπλους ἐπραγματεύσαντο.

D114 (187.1.1 Leszl) Eustath. *In Dion. Perieg.* (*GGM* 2.208.14–17)

οὗ δὴ τολμήματος κατάρξαι μὲν ἱστόρηται Ἀναξίμανδρος [. . .], Ἑκαταῖος δὲ μετ᾿ αὐτὸν τῇ αὐτῇ τόλμῃ ἐπιβαλεῖν, μετὰ δὲ Δημόκριτος, καὶ τέταρτος Εὔδοξος.

D115 (< A12) Strab. 15, p. 703

ἐν δὲ τῇ ὀρεινῇ Σίλαν ποταμὸν εἶναι, ᾧ μηδὲν ἐπιπλεῖ. Δημόκριτον μὲν οὖν ἀπιστεῖν ἅτε πολλὴν τῆς Ἀσίας πεπλανημένον [. . .].

D112 (< B15) Agathemerus, *A Sketch of Geography in Epitome*

Democritus [. . .] was the first to understand that the earth is oblong, with a length one and a half times its breadth.

See also **D89**

Geography of the Earth (D113–D115)

D113 (< B15) Agathemerus, *A Sketch of Geography in Epitome*

Afterward [scil. after Damastes of Sigeum] [. . .] Democritus, Eudoxus, and some others elaborated accounts of travels around the earth and sea.

D114 (≠ DK) Eustathius, *Commentary on Dionysius Periegetes*

Of this bold undertaking [i.e. geography], it is reported that Anaximander [. . .] began it; and after him, Hecataeus dedicated himself to the same bold undertaking; after him, Democritus; and fourth, Eudoxus.

D115 (A12) Strabo, *Geography*

In the mountainous region [scil. of India] there is a river, the Sila, on which nothing floats. Democritus, who had traveled through much of Asia, disbelieves this [. . .].

Atmospheric Phenomena (D116–D118)

D116 (B152) Plut. *Quaest. conv.* 4.2.4 665F

"διόβλητον μὲν οὐδέν," ὥς φησι Δημόκριτος "<. . .>¹
παρ'² αἰθρίης στέγειν <εὐαγὲς>³ σέλας."

¹ lac. V-VI lit. ms., <οἷον μὴ τὸ> Bernardakis, <γήινον οἷον
τὸ> Pohlenz: an ὥστε?   ² παρ' ed. Ald.: περ ms.

³ <εὐαγὲς> Diels: lac. IV-V litt. ms.

D117 (67 A25, 68 A93) Aët. 3.3.10–11 (Stob.) [περὶ
βροντῶν, ἀστραπῶν, κεραυνῶν, πρηστήρων τε καὶ
τυφώνων]

[10] Λεύκιππος πυρὸς ἐναποληφθέντος¹ νέφεσι παχυ-
τάτοις ἔκπτωσιν ἰσχυρὰν βροντὴν ἀποτελεῖν ἀποφαί-
νεται.
[11] Δημόκριτος βροντὴν μὲν ἐκ συγκρίματος ἀνω-
μάλου τὸ περιειληφὸς αὐτὸ νέφος πρὸς τὴν κάτω φορὰν ἐκβιαζομένου· ἀστραπὴν δὲ σύγκρασιν² νεφῶν,
ὑφ' ἧς τὰ γεννητικὰ τοῦ πυρὸς διὰ τῶν πολυκένων
ἀραιωμάτων ταῖς παρατρίψεσιν εἰς τὸ αὐτὸ συναλι-
ζόμενα³ διηθεῖται· κεραυνὸν δέ, ὅταν ἐκ καθαρωτέρων
καὶ λεπτοτέρων⁴ ὁμαλωτέρων τε καὶ πυκναρμόνων,
καθάπερ αὐτὸς γράφει, γεννητικῶν τοῦ πυρὸς ἡ φορὰ
βιάσηται·⁵ πρηστῆρα δέ, ὅταν πολυκενώτερα συγκρίματα πυρὸς ἐν πολυκένοις κατασχεθέντα χώραις
καὶ περιοχαῖς ὑμένων ἰδίων σωματοποιούμενα τῷ
πολυμιγεῖ τὴν ἐπὶ τὸ βάρος⁶ ὁρμὴν λάβῃ.

ATOMISTS (LEUCIPPUS, DEMOCRITUS)

Atmospheric Phenomena (D116–D118)

D116 (B152) Plutarch, *Table Talk*

"Nothing sent by Zeus," as Democritus says, **"⟨such as
(?)⟩ to protect the ⟨pure⟩ gleam coming from the
aether."**

D117 (67 A25, 68 A93) Aëtius

[10] Leucippus asserts that the powerful expulsion of fire
enclosed in very dense clouds causes thunder.
[11] Democritus: thunder [scil. comes] from a nonhomo-
geneous aggregate that violently forces the cloud surrounding it to move downward. Lightning is the fusion of
clouds, by the effect of which the seeds of fire, converging
toward the same place through the interstices that contain
much void because of friction, are filtered. The thunder-
bolt [scil. occurs] whenever the motion violently forces a
passage because of seeds of fire that are purer and thinner,
more homogeneous and, as he himself writes, **"dense-
fitted."** The lightning storm (*prêstêr*) [scil. occurs] whenever aggregates of fire containing more void, confined in
places with abundant void and acquiring the consistency
of bodies thanks to their own envelopes of membranes,
assume an impulse following their weight as an effect of
the mass of the mixture.

---

¹ ἐναπολειφθέντος mss., corr. Canter   ² σύγκρουσιν
Diels: σύγκρισιν Schneider   ³ συναυλιζόμενα mss., corr.
Meineke   ⁴ λεπτοπόρων Usener   ⁵ βιώσηται mss.,
corr. Gaisford: βιάζηται Diels   ⁶ βάρος mss.: βάθος Diels

D118 (A93a) Sen. *Quaest. nat.* 5.2.1

Democritus ait, cum in angusto inani multa sint corpuscula, quae ille atomos vocat, sequi ventum; at contra
quietum et placidum aëris statum esse cum in multo inani
pauca sint corpora. nam quemadmodum in foro aut vico,
quamdiu paucitas est, sine tumultu ambulatur, ubi turba
in angustum concurrit aliorum in alios incidentium rixa fit,
sic in hoc quo circumdati sumus spatio, cum exiguum
locum multa corpora impleverint, necesse est alia aliis
incidant et impellent ac repellantur, implicenturque et
comprimantur; ex quibus nascitur ventus, cum illa quae
colluctabantur incubuere, et diu fluctuata ac dubia in-
clinavere se. at ubi in magna laxitate corpora pauca versan-
tur, nec aretari possunt nec impelli.

Earthquakes (D119)

D119

a (A97) Arist. *Meteor.* 2.7 365b1–6

Δημόκριτος δέ φησι πλήρη τὴν γῆν ὕδατος οὖσαν,
καὶ πολὺ δεχομένην ἕτερον ὄμβριον ὕδωρ, ὑπὸ τούτου
κινεῖσθαι· πλείονός τε γὰρ γιγνομένου διὰ τὸ μὴ δύνασθαι δέχεσθαι τὰς κοιλίας ἀποβιαζόμενον ποιεῖν
τὸν σεισμόν, καὶ ξηραινομένην[1] ἕλκουσαν[2] εἰς τοὺς

1 ⟨καὶ⟩ post ξηραινομένην F^{pc} HN: ξηραινομένης Thurot
2 ἑλκούσης Thurot

D118 (A93a) Seneca *Natural Questions*

Democritus says that when there are many tiny bodies (which he calls atoms) in a narrow void, a wind follows; but that on the other hand there is a quiet and peaceful condition of the air when there are few bodies in a large void. For just as in a public square or street, as long as there are few people, one can walk about without trouble, but where a crowd comes together in a narrow place a scuffle is caused when people collide with one another: so too in the space that surrounds us, when many bodies have filled up a small space, of necessity they collide with each other, strike, and are repelled, they become intertwined and pressed together; out of these a wind comes about, when those that were struggling with one another press down and change direction after they have fluctuated for a long time and were uncertain. But where few bodies are situated in a large area, they can be neither butted nor struck.

Earthquakes (D119)

D119

a (A97) Aristotle, *Meteorology*

Democritus says that when the earth is full of water and receives a great quantity of additional water from rain, it is thereby set in motion: both because its cavities cannot receive any more [scil. water], since there is too much of it, so that it is violently forced back and causes an earthquake, and because when it [scil. the earth] dries out and attracts it [scil. the water] out of fuller places to empty

κενοὺς τόπους ἐκ τῶν πληρεστέρων τὸ μεταβάλλον
ἐμπῖπτον κινεῖν.

b (< A98) Sen. *Quaest. nat.* 6.20.1, 4

[1] Democritus plura putat. ait enim motum aliquando
spiritu fieri aliquando aqua aliquando utroque, et id hoc
modo prosequitur: "aliqua pars terrae concava est; in hanc
aquae magna vis confluit. ex hac est aliquid tenue et
ceteris liquidius. hoc cum superveniente gravitate[1] reiectum[2] est, illiditur terris et illas movet, nec enim fluctuari
potest sine motu eius, in quod impingitur. [2] [. . .] ubi in
unum locum congesta est et capere se desiit, aliquo
incumbit et primo viam pondere aperit deinde impetu. nec
enim exire nisi per devexum potest diu inclusa nec in
directum cadere moderate aut sine concussione eorum,
per quae vel in quae cadit. [3] si vero, cum iam rapi coepit,
aliquo loco substitit et illa vis fluminis in se revoluta est,
in continentem terram repellitur et illam, qua parte
maxime pendet, exagitat. praeterea aliquando madefacta
tellus liquore penitus accepto altius sedit et fundus ipse
vitiatur: tunc ea pars premitur, in quam maxime aquarum
vergentium pondus inclinat. [4] spiritus vero nonnum-
quam impellit undas et si vehementius institit, eam scilicet
partem terrae movet, in quam coactas aquas intulit; non-

---

[1] <densioris aquae gravitate> *Hine*
[2] reiectum Z^c θυ: -tus ρ: rectum δ: deiectum *Gercke*

ones, it [scil. the water] pours down when it moves and causes the earth to shake.

b (< A98) Seneca, *Natural Questions*

[1] Democritus thinks that there are several [scil. causes of earthquakes]. For he says that sometimes the motion is caused by wind, sometimes by water, sometimes by both, and he develops this point as follows: "A certain portion of the earth is hollow; into this a great abundance of water flows. Some of this water is rarefied and more liquid than the rest. When this part is repelled by a heavy mass that falls upon it, it strikes the earth and shakes it; for it cannot be agitated without causing what it collides with to shake. [2] [. . .] When it has accumulated in one place and can no longer be contained, it presses down somewhere and opens up a passageway, first by means of its weight, then by its impetus. For, having been enclosed for a long time, it cannot escape except in a downward direction, and it cannot fall vertically in a moderate manner or without shaking those things through which or against which it falls. [3] If then, when it has already begun to move rapidly, it stops somewhere and its abundant stream turns back upon itself, it is pushed back against the earth that surrounds it and shakes that part upon which it weighs most heavily. Moreover, sometimes the earth, moistened by liquid that has penetrated to its depths, subsides more deeply and its very foundation is damaged: when that happens, the part upon which the weight of the falling waters presses most heavily crashes down. [4] But as for wind, sometimes it strikes the waves, and if it propels them violently, it evidently shakes that part of the earth toward

numquam in terrena itinera coniectus et exitum quaerens
movet omnia; et[3] terra autem penetrabilis ventis est, et[4]
spiritus subtilior est quam ut possit excludi, vehementior,
quam ut sustineri concitatus ac rapidus."

3 et ZVθP: e U: ‹nam› et *Gercke:* ut *Diels*   4 et] ita *Diels*

Two Different Explanations for the
Floods of the Nile (D120–D121)

D120

a (A99) Aët. 4.1.4 (Ps.-Plut.) [περὶ Νείλου ἀναβάσεως]

Δημόκριτος τῆς χιόνος τῆς ἐν τοῖς πρὸς ἄρκτον μέρε-
σιν ὑπὸ θερινὰς τροπὰς ἀναλυομένης τε καὶ διαχεο-
μένης νέφη μὲν ἐκ τῶν ἀτμῶν πιλοῦσθαι· τούτων δ'
ἀνελαυνομένων[1] πρὸς μεσημβρίαν καὶ τὴν Αἴγυπτον
ὑπὸ τῶν ἐτησίων ἀνέμων, ἀποτελεῖσθαι ῥαγδαίους
ὄμβρους, ὑφ' ὧν ἀναπίμπλασθαι τάς τε λίμνας καὶ
τὸν Νεῖλον ποταμόν.

1 ἀνελαυνομένων Mm: ἀπε- Π

b (> A99) Diod. Sic. 1.39.1–4

[1] Δημόκριτος δ' ὁ Ἀβδηρίτης φησὶν οὐ τὸν περὶ τὴν
μεσημβρίαν τόπον χιονίζεσθαι, καθάπερ εἴρηκεν Εὐ-
ριπίδης καὶ Ἀναξαγόρας, ἀλλὰ τὸν περὶ τὰς ἄρκτους,
καὶ τοῦτο ἐμφανὲς εἶναι πᾶσι. [2] τὸ δὲ πλῆθος τῆς

which it impels the accumulated waters; at other times, collected in pathways in the earth and seeking an exit, it shakes everything. Moreover, the earth can be penetrated by winds, and the wind is also too rarefied to be kept out and too violent to be resisted when it is agitated and rapid."

Two Different Explanations for the
Floods of the Nile (D120–D121)

D120

a (A99) Aëtius

Democritus: when the snow in the northern regions melts at the summer solstice and spreads out, clouds form by condensation from the evaporations. These are driven toward the south and toward Egypt by the Etesian winds and cause torrential rains, which fill the marshes and the river Nile.

b (> A99) Diodorus Siculus

[1] Democritus of Abdera says that it does not snow around the southern region, as Euripides and Anaxagoras have said [cf. **DRAM. T76; ANAXAG. D66**], but around the northern one, and that this is clear to everybody. [2] Most of the snow that gets heaped up in the northern re-

σωρευομένης χιόνος ἐν τοῖς βορείοις μέρεσι περὶ μὲν
τὰς τροπὰς μένειν πεπηγός, ἐν δὲ τῷ θέρει διαλυομέ-
νων ὑπὸ τῆς θερμασίας τῶν πάγων πολλὴν τηκεδόνα
γίνεσθαι, καὶ διὰ τοῦτο πολλὰ γεννᾶσθαι καὶ παχέα
νέφη περὶ τοὺς μετεωροτέρους τῶν τόπων, δαψιλοῦς
τῆς ἀναθυμιάσεως πρὸς τὸ ὕψος αἰρομένης. [3] ταῦτα
δ᾽ ὑπὸ τῶν ἐτησίων ἐλαύνεσθαι, μέχρι ἂν ὅτου προσ-
πέσῃ τοῖς μεγίστοις ὄρεσι τῶν κατὰ τὴν οἰκουμένην,
ἅ φησιν εἶναι περὶ τὴν Αἰθιοπίαν· ἔπειτα πρὸς τούτοις οὖσιν ὑψηλοῖς βιαίως θραυόμενα παμμεγέθεις
ὄμβρους γεννᾶν, ἐξ ὧν πληροῦσθαι τὸν ποταμὸν μάλιστα κατὰ τὴν τῶν ἐτησίων ὥραν.

D121 (A99) Schol. in Apoll. Rhod. 4.269–71a

Δημόκριτος δὲ ὁ φυσικὸς ἀπὸ τοῦ κατὰ μεσημβρίαν
ὑπερκειμένου πελάγους λαμβάνειν τὸν Νεῖλον τὴν
ἐπίχυσιν, ἀπογλυκαίνεσθαι δὲ τὸ ὕδωρ διὰ τὸ διάστημα καὶ τὸ μῆκος τοῦ πόρου καὶ ὑπὸ τοῦ καύματος
ἀφεψόμενον· διὸ καὶ ἐναντίαν φησὶν ἔχειν τὴν γεῦσιν.

The Sea (D122–D123)

D122 (< A100) Arist. *Meteor.* 2.3 356b9–11

τὸ δὲ νομίζειν ἐλάττω τε γίγνεσθαι τὸ πλῆθος, ὥσπερ
φησὶ Δημόκριτος, καὶ τέλος ὑπολείψειν[1] [. . . cf. **R49**].

[1] ἀπολείψειν cod. Matritensis Bibliothecae Regiae 41

gions remains frozen around the [scil. winter] solstice, but during the summer, when the frost is thawed by the heat, there is a great melting, and for this reason many thick clouds form around the loftier regions, as an abundance of evaporation rises up toward the heights. [3] These are driven along by the Etesian winds until they encounter the highest mountains of the inhabited region, which he says are in Ethiopia. Then they are shattered by striking violently against these (they are extremely high), and they thereby produce enormous rainstorms by which the river is filled up during the season of the Etesian winds [i.e. the summer].

D121 (A99) Scholia on Apollonius Rhodius

Democritus, the natural philosopher, says that the Nile receives an influx from the sea that lies beyond it to the south and that this water is rendered sweet by the distance and the length of its route, and by being boiled down by the heat. And it is for this reason, he says, that it has the opposite taste.

The Sea (D122–D123)

D122 (< A100) Aristotle, *Meteorology*

To think that it [i.e. the sea] decreases in volume, as Democritus says, and at the end will cease to exist [. . .].

D123 (A99a) Theophr. (?) *Aqua* (?) in P. Hib. 16 Col. 1.9–16, 2.1–22, 3.1 (ed. FHS&G vol. 1, App. 4, pp. 462–65)

[Col. 1] [. . .] Δη]μόκριτος δὲ | [. . .]ι ποιεῖν | [. . .] τρων. . . | . . . desunt 5 versus . . .

[Col. 2] [. . .]πεσθαι φησ[ὶ]ν¹ ἐν τῶι ὑγρῶι τὰ ὅμοια | πρὸς τὰ ὅμοια καθάπερ ἐν τῶι παντί, | καὶ οὕτως [γ]ενέσθαι² θάλατταν καὶ | τᾶλλα τὰ ἁ[λμῶν]τα πάντα συνενε|χθέντων τ[ῶ]ν³ ὁμοφύλων. ὅτι δὲ | ἐκ τῶν ὁμο-γενῶν ἐστιν θάλαττα | καὶ ἐξ ἄλλων εἶναι φανερόν· οὔτε γὰρ | λιβανωτὸν οὔτε θεῖον οὔτε σίλφιον | οὔτε νίτρον οὔτε στυπτηρίαν οὔτε ἄσφαλτον οὔτε ὅσα με-γάλα καὶ θαυμασ|τὰ πολλαχοῦ γίνεσθαι τῆς γῆς. τού|τωι μὲν οὖν πρόχειρον εἰ καὶ μηθὲν | ἄλλο σκέψα-σθαι διότι μέρος ποιῶν | τὴν θάλατταν τοῦ κόσμου τὸν αὐ|τὸν τρ[ό]πον⁴ φησὶ γενέσθαι καὶ τὰ | θαυμαστὰ καὶ τὰ παραλογώτατα | τῆς φύσεως ὥσπερ οὐ πολλὰς οὔσας | ἐν τῆι γῆι διαφοράς, ἐπεὶ ποιοῦντί | [γε] τοὺ[ς]⁵ χυλοὺς διὰ τὰ σχήματα, καὶ | [τὸ] ἁ[λ]μυρὸν⁶ ἐκ με-γάλων καὶ γωνιο|[ει]δῶν,⁷ οὐκ [ἄ]λογόν πως περὶ τὴν [. . .].

1–7 rest. Grenfell-Hunt, cetera Diels

D123 (A99a) Theophrastus (?), *On Water* (?) in Hibeh Papyrus

[Col. 1] ‹De›mocritus ‹. . .› produces ‹. . . five lines missing›

[Col. 2] he says that similar things ‹. . .› to similar ones in the liquid, just as in the universe, and that in this way were produced the sea and the other s‹alt›y substances, by things that are akin coming together. It is manifest from other things too that the sea is composed of things akin: for neither frankincense nor sulfur nor silphium nor soda nor alum nor bitumen nor all the other great and wonderful things are produced in many places in the earth. So in this way it is easy to see, if nothing else, that when he makes the sea a part of the world he is saying that it is produced in the same way as the wonderful and most astounding things in nature, given that there are not many differences in the earth, since for someone who explains flavors by means of shapes, and saltiness from large and angular ones, it is not unreasonable regarding ‹. . .›.

Explanations of Various Natural
Phenomena (D124–D127)
Why Does a Flame Have Its Shape? (D124)

D124 (A73) Theophr. *Ign.* 52

ἀπορεῖται δὲ τοῦτο, διὰ τί[1] τὸ τῆς φλογὸς σχῆμα
πυραμοειδές ἐστι· καί φησι Δημόκριτος μὲν περιψυ-
χομένων αὐτῶν[2] τῶν ἄκρων εἰς μικρὸν[3] συνάγεσθαι
καὶ τέλος ἀποξύνεσθαι.

[1] τί ποτε Ψ   [2] αὐτῆς Münzel   [3] μικρὸν Ψ: μέσον Φ

Why Do Bodies Float? (D125)

D125 (< A62) Arist. *Cael.* 4.6 313a22–b5

[. . .] ἐκεῖνος γάρ φησι τὰ ἀναφερόμενα θερμὰ ἐκ τοῦ
ὕδατος ἀνακωχεύειν τὰ πλατέα τῶν ἐχόντων βάρος,
τὰ δὲ στενὰ διαπίπτειν· ὀλίγα γὰρ εἶναι τὰ ἀντι-
κρούοντα αὐτοῖς. ἔδει δ᾽ ἐν τῷ ἀέρι ἔτι μᾶλλον τοῦτο
ποιεῖν, ὥσπερ ἐνίσταται κἀκεῖνος αὐτός. ἀλλ᾽ ἐνστὰς
λύει μαλακῶς· φησὶ γὰρ οὐκ εἰς ἓν ὁρμᾶν τὸν σοῦν,
λέγων τὸν σοῦν τὴν κίνησιν τῶν ἄνω φερομένων σωμάτων.

Explanations of Various Natural Phenomena (D124–D127)
Why Does a Flame Have Its Shape? (D124)

D124 (A73) Theophrastus, *On Fire*

This is a difficulty: for what reason the shape of a flame is pyramidal. Democritus says that when their extremities are cooled they gather into a small space and end up being sharpened.

Why Do Bodies Float? (D125)

D125 (< A62) Aristotle, *On the Heavens*

[. . .] For he says that the warmth carried upward out of the water sustains those heavy objects that are flat, while narrow ones fall down, for there are only a few bumpings against them. And yet this ought to happen even more in the air, as he himself objects. But his reply to this objection is feeble: for he says that **the impulse** (*sous*) is not directed toward a single point, **'impulse'** being the name he gives to the motion of bodies moving upward.

Why Does the Magnet Attract Iron? (D126)

D126 (< A165) Alex. (?) *Quaest.* 2.23, pp. 72.28–73.7

ὁ Δημόκριτος δὲ καὶ αὐτὸς ἀπορροίας τε γίνεσθαι
τίθεται καὶ τὰ ὅμοια φέρεσθαι πρὸς τὰ ὅμοια, ἀλλὰ
καὶ εἰς τὸ κενὸν[1] πάντα φέρεσθαι. ταῦθ᾽ ὑποθέμενος
λαμβάνει[2] τὸ τὴν λίθον καὶ τὸν σίδηρον ἐξ ὁμοίων
ἀτόμων συγκεῖσθαι, λεπτοτέρων[3] δὲ τὴν λίθον, καὶ
ἐκείνου[4] ἀραιοτέραν τε καὶ πολυκενωτέραν αὐτὴν εἶναι, καὶ διὰ τοῦτ᾽ εὐκινητότερα[5] θᾶττον[6] ἐπὶ τὸν σίδηρον φέρεσθαι (πρὸς γὰρ τὰ ὅμοια ἡ φορά), καὶ ἐνδυ-
όμενα εἰς τοὺς πόρους τοῦ σιδήρου κινεῖν[7] τὰ ἐν ἐκείνῳ
σώματα διαδυόμενα δι᾽ αὐτῶν διὰ λεπτότητα, τὰ δὲ
κινηθέντα ἔξω τε φέρεσθαι ἀπορρέοντα καὶ πρὸς τὴν
λίθον διά τε ὁμοιότητα καὶ διὰ τὸ κενὰ ἔχειν πλείω,
οἷς ἑπόμενον τὸν σίδηρον διὰ τὴν ἀθρόαν ἔκκρισίν τε
καὶ φορὰν φέρεσθαι καὶ αὐτὸν πρὸς τὴν [5] λίθον.
οὐκέτι δὲ ἡ λίθος πρὸς τὸν σίδηρον φέρεται, ὅτι μὴ
ἔχει τοσαῦτα ὁ σίδηρος κενὰ ὅσα ἡ λίθος.

[1] κοινὸν mss., corr. Diels   [2] λαμβάνειν mss., corr.
Spengel   [3] λεπτοτέραν coni. Spengel   [4] καὶ ἐκείνου
Diels: καὶ ὅτι (τῷ B², τὸ S²a) εἶναι VS¹B¹: εἶναι καὶ coni.
Spengel   [5] εὐκινητοτέραν mss., corr. Bruns   [6] εὐκινη-
τότερ᾽ ὄντα τὰ ἄτομα Diels   [7] κινεῖ mss., corr. Spengel

Why Does the Magnet Attract Iron? (D126)

D126 (< A165) Alexander of Aphrodisias, *Problems and Solutions (Questions) on Nature*

Democritus too [scil. like Empedocles, **D148**] posits that effluxes are produced and that similar things move toward similar ones, but also that all things move toward the void. Having assumed this, he supposes that the magnet and iron are composed of similar atoms, but that the magnet's are thinner, and that it has a more rarefied consistency and possesses more void than the other and that this is why, being more mobile, they move more quickly toward the iron (for motion is toward what is similar), and penetrating into the passages of the iron they set in motion the bodies in it that penetrate through them [i.e. the passages] because of their lightness and, once they have been set in motion, move as effluxes outward and toward the magnet, both because of their similarity and because it contains more void, and the iron follows these because of the massive outflow and itself moves in a motion toward the [5] magnet. The magnet does not move toward the iron because the iron does not have as many void places as the magnet does.

Why Do Different Materials React to
Heat Differently? (D127)

D127 (90.1 Leszl) Sen. *Quaest. nat.* 4b.9

accedit his ratio Democriti: "omne corpus quo solidius est, hoc calorem citius concipit, diutius servat. itaque si in sole posueris aeneum vas et vitreum et argenteum,[1] aeneo calor citius accedet, diutius haerebit." adicit deinde, quare hoc existimet fieri. "his," inquit, "corporibus, quae duriora et pressiora sunt, necesse est minora foramina esse et tenuiorem in singulis spiritum: sequitur ut, quemadmodum minora balnearia et minora miliaria citius calefiunt, sic haec foramina occulta et oculos effugientia et celerius fervorem sentiant et propter easdem angustias, quicquid receperunt, tardius reddant."

[1] et argenteum *del. Gercke*: aut argenteum *Koeler*

Life and Vital Functions (D128–D201)
Origin of Life (D128–D129)

D128 (A139) Cens. *Die nat.* 4.9

Democrito vero Abderitae ex aqua limoque primum visum esse homines procreatos.

Why Do Different Materials React to
Heat Differently? (D127)

D127 (≠ DK), Seneca, *Natural Questions*

To these [scil. other explanations for the fact that the portion of the atmosphere closest to the earth is the warmest] is added Democritus' explanation: "The more solid every body is, the more quickly does it absorb heat and the longer does it conserve it. That is why if you expose a vessel of bronze, one of glass, and one of silver to the sun, the heat will go more quickly to the bronze one and will remain there longer." He goes on to add the reason why he thinks this happens: "Those bodies," he says, "that are harder and more compact must necessarily have smaller passages and thinner air in each of them; it follows that, just as smaller bathing rooms and smaller water heaters become warm more quickly, in the same way these invisible passages, which escape our vision, both feel heat more quickly and because of the narrowness of the same passageways give back more slowly what they have received."

Life and Vital Functions (D128–D201)
Origin of Life (D128–D129)

D128 (A139) Censorinus, *The Birthday*

Democritus of Abdera thought that humans were created at first from water and mud.

D129 (< B5) Diod. Sic. 1.7.2–6

[2] εἰλούμενον δ᾽ ἐν ἑαυτῷ συνεχῶς καὶ συστρεφόμενον ἐκ μὲν τῶν ὑγρῶν τὴν θάλασσαν, ἐκ δὲ τῶν στερεμνιωτέρων ποιῆσαι τὴν γῆν πηλώδη καὶ παντελῶς ἁπαλήν. [3] ταύτην δὲ τὸ μὲν πρῶτον τοῦ περὶ τὸν ἥλιον πυρὸς καταλάμψαντος πῆξιν λαβεῖν, ἔπειτα διὰ τὴν θερμασίαν ἀναζυμουμένης τῆς ἐπιφανείας συνοιδῆσαί τινα τῶν ὑγρῶν κατὰ πολλοὺς τόπους, καὶ γενέσθαι περὶ αὐτὰ σηπεδόνας ὑμέσι λεπτοῖς περιεχομένας· ὅπερ ἐν τοῖς ἕλεσι καὶ τοῖς λιμνάζουσι τῶν τόπων ἔτι καὶ νῦν ὁρᾶσθαι γινόμενον, ἐπειδὰν τῆς χώρας κατεψυγμένης ἄφνω διάπυρος ὁ ἀὴρ γένηται μὴ λαβὼν τὴν μεταβολὴν ἐκ τοῦ κατ᾽ ὀλίγον. [4] ζωογονουμένων δὲ τῶν ὑγρῶν διὰ τῆς θερμασίας τὸν εἰρημένον τρόπον τὰς μὲν νύκτας λαμβάνειν αὐτίκα τὴν τροφὴν ἐκ τῆς πιπτούσης ἀπὸ τοῦ περιέχοντος ὀμίχλης, τὰς δ᾽ ἡμέρας ὑπὸ τοῦ καύματος στερεοῦσθαι· τὸ δ᾽ ἔσχατον τῶν κυοφορουμένων τὴν τελείαν αὔξησιν λαμβανόντων καὶ τῶν ὑμένων διακαυθέντων τε καὶ περιρραγέντων ἀναφυῆναι παντοδαποὺς τύπους ζῴων· [5] τούτων δὲ τὰ μὲν πλείστης θερμασίας κεκοινωνηκότα πρὸς τοὺς μετεώρους τόπους ἀπελθεῖν γενόμενα πτηνά, τὰ δὲ γεώδους ἀντεχόμενα συγκρίσεως ἐν τῇ τῶν ἑρπετῶν καὶ τῶν ἄλλων τῶν ἐπιγείων τάξει καταριθμηθῆναι, τὰ δὲ φύσεως ὑγρᾶς μάλιστα μετειληφότα πρὸς τὸν ὁμογενῆ τόπον συνδραμεῖν, ὀνομασθέντα πλωτά. [6] τὴν δὲ γῆν ἀεὶ μᾶλλον στε-

D129 (< B5) Diodorus Siculus

[2] As this [scil. the muddy and turbid matter] turned around continually upon itself and contracted, it made the sea out of the wet parts, and out of the more solid ones the earth, which was muddy and completely soft. [3] This solidified, at first when the fire of the sun blazed down on it, and then, since it surface was fermenting because of the warmth, some of the wet parts swelled up in many places, and around these putrid humors formed, covered by thin membranes. This can be seen to happen even now in marshes and swampy areas, when the ground has become cold and the air suddenly becomes very warm without having gone through a gradual change. [4] And while the wet parts were generating animals because of the heat in the way I have described, they received their nourishment at night from the mist that fell from the atmosphere, and during the day they were solidified by the heat; and finally, when the embryos had attained their complete growth and the membranes had been completely heated and had broken apart, all kinds of animals emerged. [5] Of these, those that had received the largest share of heat rose up toward the higher regions and became winged, while those whose aggregate contained earth were counted in the class of reptiles and other terrestrial animals, while those that had received most of all a share of the moist nature went to the region that was akin to them and were called fish. [6] And since the earth became continually more solid because of

ρεουμένην ὑπό τε τοῦ περὶ τὸν ἥλιον πυρὸς καὶ τῶν
πνευμάτων τὸ τελευταῖον μηκέτι δύνασθαι μηδὲν τῶν
μειζόνων ζῳογονεῖν, ἀλλ' ἐκ τῆς πρὸς ἄλληλα μίξεως
ἕκαστα γεννᾶσθαι τῶν ἐμψύχων [. . . cf. **D202**].

The Soul and Thought (D130–D135)

D130 (< A101) Arist. *An.* 1.2 405a8–13

Δημόκριτος δὲ καὶ γλαφυρωτέρως εἴρηκεν ἀποφαινό-
μενος διὰ τί τούτων ἑκάτερον· ψυχὴν μὲν γὰρ εἶναι
ταὐτὸ καὶ νοῦν, τοῦτο δ' εἶναι τῶν πρώτων καὶ ἀδιαιρέτων σωμάτων, κινητικὸν δὲ διὰ μικρομέρειαν[1] καὶ
τὸ σχῆμα· τῶν δὲ σχημάτων εὐκινητότατον τὸ σφαιροειδὲς λέγει· τοιοῦτον δ' εἶναι τόν τε νοῦν καὶ τὸ πῦρ.

[1] λεπτομέρειαν C

D131 (< A104) Arist. *An.* 1.3 406b19–22

ὁμοίως δὲ καὶ Δημόκριτος λέγει· κινουμένας γὰρ
φησι τὰς ἀδιαιρέτους σφαίρας διὰ τὸ πεφυκέναι μηδέποτε μένειν συνεφέλκειν καὶ κινεῖν τὸ σῶμα πᾶν.
[. . . = **R51**]

the fire of the sun and the winds, in the end it was no longer capable of generating any of the larger animals, but it is out of sexual intercourse with each other that every living being is generated.[1]

[1] Diodorus does not name the text from whom he derives this account (perhaps the *Aegyptica* of Hecataeus of Abdera [73 DK]), but it contains a number of Democritean elements that permit it to be included among his testimonia.

The Soul and Thought (D130–D135)

D130 (< A101) Aristotle, *On the Soul*

Democritus expressed himself more precisely [scil. than those who simply identify the soul with fire] when he explains why it [scil. the soul possesses] each of these two [scil. subtlety and mobility]: for the soul is the same thing as the mind, and this [scil. mind] belongs to the first and indivisible bodies, while it is mobile because of the smallness of its parts and because of their shape. And he says that the most mobile of the shapes is the spherical one, and that mind and fire are [scil. composed of atoms] of this sort.

D131 (< A104) Aristotle, *On the Soul*

Democritus speaks similarly to him [i.e. Philip the comic playwright, who said that Daedalus made wooden statues mobile by pouring quicksilver into them]. For he says that the indivisible spheres in motion (because by nature they never rest) drag the whole body along and set it in motion.

D132 (< 67 A28) Arist. *An.* 1.2 403b31–404a10

ὅθεν Δημόκριτος μὲν πῦρ τι καὶ θερμόν φησιν αὐτὴν
εἶναι· ἀπείρων γὰρ ὄντων σχημάτων καὶ ἀτόμων τὰ
σφαιροειδῆ πῦρ καὶ ψυχὴν λέγει (οἷον ἐν τῷ ἀέρι τὰ
καλούμενα ξύσματα, ἃ φαίνεται ἐν ταῖς διὰ τῶν θυ-
ρίδων ἀκτῖσιν), ὧν[1] τὴν μὲν πανσπερμίαν στοιχεῖα
λέγει τῆς ὅλης φύσεως (ὁμοίως δὲ καὶ Λεύκιππος),
τούτων δὲ τὰ σφαιροειδῆ ψυχήν, διὰ τὸ μάλιστα διὰ
παντὸς δύνασθαι διαδύνειν τοὺς τοιούτους ῥυσμοὺς
καὶ κινεῖν τὰ λοιπά, κινούμενα καὶ αὐτά, ὑπολαμβά-
νοντες τὴν ψυχὴν εἶναι τὸ παρέχον τοῖς ζῴοις τὴν
κίνησιν. διὸ καὶ τοῦ ζῆν ὅρον εἶναι τὴν ἀναπνοήν [. . .
= **D136**].

[1] τὰ σφαιροειδῆ . . . ὧν ut gloss. del. Diels

D133 (< A101) Arist. *An.* 1.2 404a27–30

ἐκεῖνος μὲν γὰρ ἁπλῶς ταὐτὸν ψυχὴν καὶ νοῦν· τὸ
γὰρ ἀληθὲς εἶναι τὸ φαινόμενον, διὸ καλῶς ποιῆσαι
τὸν Ὅμηρον ὡς "Ἕκτωρ κεῖτ᾿ ἀλλοφρονέων."

D134 (< A135) Theophr. *Sens.* 58

[. . . = **D158**] περὶ δὲ τοῦ φρονεῖν ἐπὶ τοσοῦτον εἴρηκεν, ὅτι γίνεται συμμέτρως ἐχούσης τῆς ψυχῆς μετὰ
τὴν κίνησιν·[1] ἐὰν δὲ περίθερμός τις ἢ περίψυχρος
γένηται, μεταλλάττειν φησί. διὸ[2] καὶ τοὺς παλαιοὺς

[1] κατὰ τὴν κρᾶσιν Schneider   [2] διὸ Diels: διότι mss.

D132 (< 67 A28) Aristotle, *On the Soul*

whence Democritus says that it [i.e. the soul] is a certain kind of fire and heat. For the shapes and atoms being unlimited, he says that the spherical ones are fire and the soul (like the so-called motes (*xusmata*) that are visible in the air in sunbeams that pass through windows), of which he says that the 'universal seminal reserve' (*panspermia*) is the elements of the whole of nature (just like Leucippus), and that among these, the spherical ones are the soul because such **configurations** (*rhusmoi*) can penetrate best through everything and set everything else in motion by their own motion, since they think that the soul is what supplies motion to living beings. And that is why what limits life is respiration [. . .].

D133 (< A101) Aristotle, *On the Soul*

He [i.e. Democritus says] simply that soul and mind are the same thing. For what is true is what appears. And that is why Homer was right to say, "Hector lay there, his thoughts being other."[1]

> [1] This phrase does not occur in our texts of Homer's epics.

D134 (< A135) Theophrastus, *On Sensations*

[. . .] Concerning thinking he has said only that it happens when the soul is in equilibrium after motion. But if someone becomes too warm or too cold, he says that it [i.e. thinking] changes. And that is why the ancients were right

καλῶς τοῦθ' ὑπολαβεῖν, ὅτι ἐστὶν 'ἀλλοφρονεῖν'. ὥστε φανερόν, ὅτι τῇ κράσει τοῦ σώματος ποιεῖ τὸ φρονεῖν, ὅπερ ἴσως αὐτῷ καὶ κατὰ λόγον ἐστὶ σῶμα ποιοῦντι τὴν ψυχήν.

D135 (A105) Aët. 4.5.1 (Ps.-Plut.) [περὶ τοῦ ἡγεμονικοῦ]

[. . .] Δημόκριτος ἐν ὅλῃ τῇ κεφαλῇ.

Respiration (D136)

D136 (< 67 A28) Arist. *An.* 1.2 404a10–15

[. . . = **D132**] συνάγοντος γὰρ τοῦ περιέχοντος τὰ σώματα καὶ ἐκθλίβοντος τῶν σχημάτων τὰ παρέχοντα τοῖς ζῴοις τὴν κίνησιν διὰ τὸ μηδ' αὐτὰ ἠρεμεῖν μηδέποτε, βοήθειαν γίνεσθαι θύραθεν ἐπεισιόντων ἄλλων τοιούτων ἐν τῷ ἀναπνεῖν· κωλύειν γὰρ αὐτὰ καὶ τὰ ἐνυπάρχοντα ἐν τοῖς ζῴοις ἐκκρίνεσθαι, συνανείργοντα τὸ συνάγον καὶ πηγνύον.

Sleep and Death (D137–D143)

D137 (A136) Tert. *An.* 43

Democritus indigentiam spiritus.

to suppose that this is 'to have thoughts that are other' [cf. **D133**]. So that it is evident that he explains thinking by the mixture of the body, which is surely in accordance with his reasoning, since he makes the soul a body.

D135 (A105) Aëtius

[. . .] Democritus: it [i.e. the directive center is located] in the whole head.

Respiration (D136)

D136 (< 67 A28) Aristotle, *On the Soul*

[. . .] For since what surrounds bodies [i.e. the ambient atmosphere] compresses them and expels those shapes that supply motion to living beings (because they [i.e. the shapes] are never at rest), help comes about from outside, when other [scil. shapes] of the same kind enter during the course of respiration; for these prevent those that are present within the living beings from being expelled, by helping to counteract what contracts and solidifies.[1]

[1] The process is described in very similar terms in *On Respiration,* 4 471b30 (68 A106 DK).

Sleep and Death (D137–D143)

D137 (A136) Tertullian, *On the Soul*

Democritus [scil. says that sleep is] a lack of breath.

D138 (67 A34) Aët. 5.25.3 (Ps.-Plut.) [ὁποτέρου ἐστὶν ὕπνος καὶ θάνατος, ψυχῆς ἢ σώματος]

Λεύκιππος οὐ μόνον[1] σώματος γίνεσθαι, ἀλλὰ κράσει[2] τοῦ λεπτομεροῦς πλείονι τῆς ἐκκρίσεως[3] τοῦ ψυχικοῦ θερμοῦ, τὸν <δὲ>[4] πλεονασμὸν αἴτιον[5] θανάτου· [. . .].

---

[1] οὐ μόνον mss.: οὐ κόπῳ Reiske: τὸν ὕπνον Diels
[2] ἀλλὰ κράσει mss.: ἀλλ' ἐκκρίσει Heimsoeth: ἅμ' ἐκκρίσει Bernardakis   [3] ἐκκρίσεως nos: ἐκκράσεως mss.: εἰσκρίσεως Diels   [4] τὸν <δ'> Diels (Dox.): <ἧς> τὸν Diels (DK): τὸν mss.   [5] αἴτιον mM: αἰτίαν Π

D139 (A109) Aët. 4.7.4 (Ps.-Plut.) [περὶ ἀφθαρσίας ψυχῆς]

Δημόκριτος [. . .] φθαρτὴν τῷ σώματι συνδιαφθειρομένην.

D140 (A117) Aët. 4.4.7 (Ps.-Plut.) [περὶ μερῶν τῆς ψυχῆς]

ὁ δὲ Δημόκριτος πάντα μετέχειν φησὶ ψυχῆς ποιᾶς, καὶ τὰ νεκρὰ τῶν σωμάτων, διότι ἀεὶ διαφανῶς τινος θερμοῦ καὶ αἰσθητικοῦ μετέχει τοῦ πλείονος διαπνεομένου.

D141 (A160) Cels. *Medic.* 2.6

quin etiam vir iure magni nominis Democritus ne finitae

D138 (67 A34) Aëtius

Leucippus: it [i.e. sleep] belongs not only to the body, but occurs because of a mixture of the thin part that is greater in quantity than the expulsion of the heat of the soul; an excess causes death [. . .].

D139 (A109) Aëtius

Democritus [. . .]: it [scil. the soul is] destructible and is destroyed together with the body.

D140 (A117) Aëtius

But Democritus says [scil. unlike Epicurus] that all things have a share in a certain kind of soul, even including those bodies that are corpses, since they manifestly always have some share in heat and sensation, even if most of it has been exhaled.

D141 (A160) Celsus, *On Medicine*

Indeed, Democritus, a man of a justly great renown, maintained that there are not even sufficiently certain signs of

quidem vitae satis certas notas esse proposuit, quibus
medici credidissent: adeo illud non reliquit, ut certa aliqua
signa futurae mortis essent.

D142 (A160) Tert. *An.* 51

ad hoc et Democritus crementa unguium et comarum in
sepulturis aliquanti temporis denotat.

D143 (< B1) Procl. *In Remp.* 2.113.6–9

τὴν μὲν περὶ τῶν ἀποθανεῖν δοξάντων, ἔπειτα ἀνα-
βιούντων ἱστορίαν ἄλλοι τε πολλοὶ τῶν παλαιῶν
ἤθροισαν καὶ Δημόκριτος ὁ φυσικὸς ἐν τοῖς Περὶ τοῦ
Ἄιδου γράμμασιν.

Sensations and Their Objects (D144–D161)
The Number of Senses (D144)

D144 (A116) Aët. 4.10.4 (Stob.) [πόσαι εἰσὶν αἱ αἰσθή-
σεις]

Δημόκριτος πλείους εἶναι αἰσθήσεις περὶ τὰ ἄλογα
ζῷα καὶ περὶ τοὺς σοφοὺς καὶ περὶ τοὺς θεούς.

the ending of life on which doctors could rely; and even less did he accept that there might be any certain signs of a future death.

D142 (A160) Tertullian, *On the Soul*

On this point [scil. the continuing signs of some vitality after death], Democritus too notes that the nails and hair grow for a certain time on bodies that have been buried.

D143 (< B1) Proclus, *Commentary on Plato's* Republic

Many of the ancients, including Democritus the natural philosopher in his writings ***About Hades,*** have collected reports about people who were thought to have died but then came to life again.

Sensations and Their Objects (D144–D161)
The Number of Senses (D144)

D144 (A116) Aëtius

Democritus: there are more senses [scil. than the five], if one considers irrational animals, the sages, and the gods.

Sight (D145–D154)
Ordinary Sight (D145–D150)

D145 (67 A29) Aët. 4.13.1 (Stob.) [περὶ ὁράσεως]

Λεύκιππος Δημόκριτος [. . .] κατὰ εἰδώλων εἴσκρισιν
τὸ ὁρατικὸν συμβαίνειν πάθος.

D146 (B123) *Etym. Gen.*

δείκελον· [. . .] παρὰ δὲ Δημοκρίτῳ, κατ᾽ εἶδος ὅμοια
τοῖς πράγμασιν ἀπόρροια.

D147 (< A135) Theophr. *Sens.* 50

[. . . = **R55**] ὁρᾶν μὲν οὖν ποιεῖ τῇ ἐμφάσει· ταύτην δὲ
ἰδίως λέγει· τὴν γὰρ ἔμφασιν οὐκ εὐθὺς ἐν τῇ κόρῃ
γίνεσθαι, ἀλλὰ τὸν ἀέρα τὸν μεταξὺ τῆς ὄψεως καὶ
τοῦ ὁρωμένου τυποῦσθαι συστελλόμενον ὑπὸ τοῦ
ὁρωμένου καὶ τοῦ ὁρῶντος· ἅπαντος γὰρ ἀεὶ γίνεσθαί
τινα ἀπορροήν· ἔπειτα τοῦτον στερεὸν ὄντα καὶ ἀλλό-
χρων ἐμφαίνεσθαι τοῖς ὄμμασιν ὑγροῖς. καὶ τὸ μὲν
πυκνὸν οὐ δέχεσθαι, τὸ δὲ ὑγρὸν διιέναι. διὸ καὶ τοὺς
ὑγροὺς τῶν σκληρῶν ὀφθαλμῶν ἀμείνους εἶναι πρὸς
τὸ ὁρᾶν, εἰ ὁ μὲν ἔξω χιτὼν ὡς λεπτότατος καὶ πυκνό-
τατος εἴη, τὰ δ᾽ ἐντὸς ὡς μάλιστα σομφὰ καὶ κενὰ
πυκνῆς καὶ ἰσχυρᾶς[1] σαρκός, ἔτι δὲ ἰκμάδος παχείας
τε καὶ λιπαρᾶς, καὶ αἱ φλέβες ⟨αἱ⟩[2] κατὰ τοὺς ὀφθαλ-

---

[1] στιφρᾶς Usener   [2] ⟨αἱ⟩ Diels

200

Sight (D145–D154)
Ordinary Sight (D145–D150)

D145 (67 A29) Aëtius

Leucippus, Democritus [. . .]: the affection of vision comes about because of the penetration of images.

D146 (B123) *Etymologicum genuinum*

Portrait (*deikelon*): [. . .] in Democritus, an efflux that is similar in species to things.

D147 (< A135) Theophrastus, *On Sensations*

[. . .] He explains vision by impression (*emphasis*); but he provides a particular description of this. For the impression (*emphasis*) is not produced directly in the pupil, but the air located between the organ of vision and what is seen receives an impression (*tupousthai*), since it is compressed by the action of what is seen and of what sees; for from everything some efflux is always being detached. Then this [scil. air], which is solid and of a different color, is reflected in moist eyes: what is dense does not receive it, while what is moist offers it a passage. And that is why moist eyes are better at seeing than dry ones, so long as the external membrane is as thin and as dense as possible, the interior is as spongy as possible and is free of dense and strong flesh, and furthermore of thick and fatty liquid, and the blood vessels near the eyes are straight and free

μοὺς εὐθεῖαι καὶ ἄνικμοι, †καὶ μὴ εὐσχημονεῖν†[3] τοῖς
ἀποτυπουμένοις. τὰ γὰρ ὁμόφυλα μάλιστα ἕκαστον
γνωρίζειν [. . . = **R57**].

[3] ὡς ὁμοιοσχημονεῖν Diels: καὶ ὁμοιοσχημονοῖεν Schneider: καὶ μὴ ἐνοχλοῖεν coni. Burchard

D148 (< A121) Arist. *Sens.* 2 438a5–7

Δημόκριτος δ᾿ ὅτι μὲν ὕδωρ εἶναί φησι, λέγει καλῶς,
ὅτι δ᾿ οἴεται τὸ ὁρᾶν εἶναι τὴν ἔμφασιν, οὐ καλῶς.

D149 (< A122) Arist. *An.* 2.7 419a15–17

[. . .] Δημόκριτος, οἰόμενος, εἰ γένοιτο κενὸν τὸ μεταξύ,
ὁρᾶσθαι ἂν ἀκριβῶς καὶ εἰ μύρμηξ ἐν τῷ οὐρανῷ εἴη
[. . . = **R58**].

D150 (67 A31) Aët. 4.14.2 (Stob.; cf. Ps.-Plut., Ps.-Gal.)
[περὶ κατοπτρικῶν ἐμφάσεων]

Λεύκιππος,[1] Δημόκριτος [. . .] τὰς κατοπτρικὰς ἐμφάσεις γίνεσθαι κατ᾿ εἰδώλων ἐνστάσεις,[2] ἅ τινα φέρεσθαι μὲν ἀφ᾿ ἡμῶν, συνίστασθαι δὲ ἐπὶ τοῦ κατ-
όπτρου κατ᾿ ἀντιπεριστροφήν.

[1] Λεύκιππος non hab. Plut.   [2] ἐνστάσεις Meineke: ἐμφάσεις Stob.: ὑποστάσεις Plut.: ἐπιστάσεις Gal.: ἀποστάσεις
Usener

of liquid, and †. . .† to the objects that are impressed (*apotupoumenois*) on them; for it is things that are akin that each one recognizes best [. . .].

D148 (< A121) Aristotle, *On Sensation*

When Democritus says that it is water [scil. by which we see], he speaks correctly, but when he thinks that seeing is the impression (*emphasis*) he speaks incorrectly.

D149 (< A122) Aristotle, *On the Soul*

[. . .] Democritus, thinking that if the intermediate [scil. space] were void, one would see exactly even if an ant were in the sky [. . .].

D150 (67 A31) Aëtius

Leucippus, Democritus [. . .]: the reflections (*emphaseis*) in mirrors are produced by the interference (*enstaseis*) of the images that come from us but then are arranged on the mirror in order to go in the inverse direction.

Dreams and Visions of Gods (D151–D154)

D151 (A136) Aët. 5.2.1 (Ps.-Plut.) [πῶς ὄνειροι γίνον-
ται]

Δημόκριτος τοὺς ὀνείρους γίνεσθαι κατὰ τὰς τῶν εἰδώλων παραστάσεις.

D152 (< A77) Plut. *Quaest. conv.* 8.10.2 735A–B

[. . .] φησὶν Δημόκριτος ἐγκαταβυσσοῦσθαι τὰ εἴδωλα διὰ τῶν πόρων εἰς τὰ σώματα καὶ ποιεῖν τὰς
κατὰ ὕπνον ὄψεις ἐπαναφερόμενα· φοιτᾶν δὲ ταῦτα
πανταχόθεν ἀπιόντα καὶ σκευῶν καὶ ἱματίων καὶ φυτῶν, μάλιστα δὲ ζῴων ὑπὸ σάλου πολλοῦ καὶ θερμότητος οὐ μόνον ἔχοντα μορφοειδεῖς τοῦ σώματος
ἐκμεμαγμένας ὁμοιότητας [. . .], ἀλλὰ καὶ τῶν κατὰ
ψυχὴν κινημάτων καὶ βουλευμάτων ἑκάστῳ καὶ ἠθῶν
καὶ παθῶν ἐμφάσεις ἀναλαμβάνοντα συνεφέλκεσθαι,
καὶ προσπίπτοντα μετὰ τούτων ὥσπερ ἔμψυχα φρά-
ζειν καὶ διαγγέλλειν[1] τοῖς ὑποδεχομένοις τὰς τῶν μεθ-
ιέντων αὐτὰ δόξας καὶ διαλογισμοὺς καὶ ὁρμάς [. . .].

[1] διαγγέλλειν Wyttenbach: διαστέλλειν ms.

D153 (< A77) Plut. *Quaest. conv.* 5.7.6 682F–683A

[. . .] ἅ φησιν ἐκεῖνος ἐξιέναι τοὺς φθονοῦντας, οὔτ᾽
αἰσθήσεως ἄμοιρα παντάπασιν οὔθ᾽ ὁρμῆς ἀνάπλεά
τε τῆς ἀπὸ τῶν προιεμένων μοχθηρίας καὶ βασκανίας,

Dreams and Visions of Gods (D151–D154)

D151 (A136) Aëtius

Democritus: dreams are produced by the manifestations (*parastaseis*) of images.

D152 (< A77) Plutarch, *Table Talk*

[. . .] Democritus says that the images **penetrate deeply into bodies by means of their passages** and produce visions during sleep **when they rise up again.** These roam about, coming from everywhere, from equipment, clothes, plants, but especially from living beings, by the effect of intense agitation and heat; they possess not only similarities of form modeled upon the body [. . .] but they also receive impressions (*emphaseis*) of the motions and desires of each person's soul, of his character traits and passions, which they carry along with them; when they encounter people, accompanied by these things, they speak like living beings and announce to those who receive them the opinions of those who sent them, their considerations, and their impulses [. . .].

D153 (< A77) Plutarch, *Table Talk*

[. . .] That man [scil. Democritus] says that they [scil. the images] are emitted by envious people; they are not at all deprived of a share of sensation nor of impulse, but are filled with the wickedness and malice of those people who

μεθ᾽ ἧς ἐμπλασσόμενα καὶ παραμένοντα καὶ συνοι-
κοῦντα τοῖς βασκαινομένοις ἐπιταράττειν καὶ κακοῦν
αὐτῶν τό τε σῶμα καὶ τὴν διάνοιαν.

D154 (B166) Sext. Emp. Adv. Math. 9.19

Δημόκριτος δὲ εἴδωλά τινά φησιν ἐμπελάζειν τοῖς
ἀνθρώποις, καὶ τούτων τὰ μὲν εἶναι ἀγαθοποιά, τὰ δὲ
κακοποιά (ἔνθεν καὶ εὔχετο εὐλόγχων τυχεῖν εἰδώλων), εἶναι δὲ ταῦτα μεγάλα τε καὶ ὑπερμεγέθη,[1] καὶ
δύσφθαρτα μέν, οὐκ ἄφθαρτα δέ, προσημαίνειν τε τὰ
μέλλοντα τοῖς ἀνθρώποις, θεωρούμενα καὶ φωνὰς ἀφ-
ιέντα. ὅθεν τούτων αὐτῶν φαντασίαν λαβόντες οἱ παλαιοὶ ὑπενόησαν εἶναι θεόν, μηδενὸς ἄλλου παρὰ
ταῦτα ὄντος θεοῦ τοῦ[2] ἄφθαρτον φύσιν ἔχοντος.

[1] ὑπερφυῆ Papencordt   [2] τοῦ del. Kayser

Hearing and Sound (D155–D157)

D155 (< A126a) Porph. In Ptol. Harm., p. 32.9–11

[. . .] ἀλλ᾽ ὥς φησιν Δημόκριτος, ἐκδοχεῖον μύθων
οὖσα μένει τὴν φωνὴν ἀγγείου δίκην· ἡ δὲ γὰρ εἰσ-
κρίνεται καὶ ἐνρεῖ [. . .].

D156 (< A128) Aët. 4.19.3 (Ps.-Plut.) [περὶ φωνῆς]

Δημόκριτος καὶ τὸν ἀέρα φησὶν εἰς ὁμοιοσχήμονα

emitted them; modeled upon this and staying and dwelling with those who are bewitched by malice, they agitate them and inflict damage on their body and thought.

D154 (B166) Sextus Empiricus, *Against the Natural Philosophers*

Democritus says that certain images **approach people** and that of these some do good and others do evil. That is why he expressed the wish **to obtain propitious images.** These are large and of greater size than normal, and hard to destroy but not indestructible, and they indicate beforehand the future for people when they are observed and utter words. It is on this basis that the ancients, having a representation (*phantasia*) of these very images, came to suppose that there is a god, given that no other god exists that has an indestructible nature besides these.

Hearing and Sound (D155–D157)

D155 (< A126a) Porphyry, *Commentary on Ptolemy's* Harmonics

[. . .] but as Democritus says, it [i.e. hearing], being **a receptacle for words,** waits for a sound in the manner of a vessel; and this latter penetrates inside and flows into it [. . .].

D156 (< A128) Aëtius

Democritus says that the air too **is shattered into** bodies

θρύπτεσθαι σώματα καὶ συγκαλινδεῖσθαι τοῖς ἐκ τῆς
φωνῆς θραύσμασι. 'κολοιὸς' γάρ 'παρὰ κολοιὸν ἱζά-
νει' καὶ 'ὡς αἰεὶ τὸν ὁμοῖον ἄγει θεὸς ὡς τὸν ὁμοῖον.'
καὶ γὰρ ἐν τοῖς αἰγιαλοῖς αἱ ὅμοιαι ψῆφοι κατὰ τοὺς
αὐτοὺς τόπους ὁρῶνται κατ' ἄλλο μὲν αἱ σφαιροει-
δεῖς, κατ' ἄλλο δὲ αἱ ἐπιμήκεις· καὶ ἐπὶ τῶν κοσκινευ-
όντων δὲ ἐπὶ τὸ αὐτὸ συναλίζεται τὰ ὁμοιοσχήμονα,
ὥστε χωρὶς εἶναι τοὺς κυάμους καὶ ἐρεβίνθους [. . . =
R61].

D157 (< A135) Theophr. *Sens.* 55–56

[. . . = **R57**] [55] τὴν δ' ἀκοὴν παραπλησίως ποιεῖ τοῖς
ἄλλοις. εἰς γὰρ τὸ κενὸν ἐμπίπτοντα τὸν ἀέρα κίνησιν
ἐμποιεῖν· πλὴν ὅτι κατὰ πᾶν μὲν ὁμοίως τὸ σῶμα εἰσιέναι, μάλιστα δὲ καὶ πλεῖστον διὰ τῶν ὤτων, ὅτι
διὰ πλείστου τε κενοῦ διέρχεται καὶ ἥκιστα διαμί-
μνει. διὸ καὶ κατὰ μὲν τὸ ἄλλο σῶμα οὐκ αἰσθάνεσθαι, ταύτῃ δὲ μόνον. ὅταν δὲ ἐντὸς γένηται, σκίδνα-
σθαι διὰ τὸ τάχος· τὴν γὰρ φωνὴν εἶναι πυκνουμένου[1]
τοῦ ἀέρος καὶ μετὰ βίας εἰσιόντος. ὥσπερ οὖν ἐκτὸς
ποιεῖ τῇ ἀφῇ τὴν αἴσθησιν, οὕτω καὶ ἐντός. [56]
ὀξύτατα[2] δ' ἀκούειν, εἰ ὁ μὲν ἔξω χιτὼν εἴη πυκνός, τὰ
δὲ φλεβία κενὰ καὶ ὡς μάλιστα ἄνικμα καὶ εὔτρητα
κατά τε[3] τὸ ἄλλο σῶμα καὶ τὴν κεφαλὴν καὶ τὰς
ἀκοάς, ἔτι δὲ τὰ ὀστᾶ πυκνὰ καὶ ὁ ἐγκέφαλος εὔκρα-

---

[1] τυπτομένου Burchard: θρυπτομένου Papencordt
[2] ὀξύτατον mss., corr. Diels   [3] δὲ mss., corr. Diels

of a similar shape and **rolls about** together with the fragments that come from sound. For "jackdaw sits next to jackdaw"[1] and "a god always leads a similar man toward a similar one" [*Odyssey* 17.218]. For on beaches too similar pebbles are seen gathered together in the same places, spherical ones here, oblong ones there. And when people use sieves, those [scil. seeds] of a similar shape gather in the same place, so that beans and chickpeas are separated [. . .].

[1] A proverb.

D157 (< A135) Theophrastus, *On Sensations*

[. . .] [55] But he explains hearing in a way similar to the other [scil. philosophers]: air falling into the void causes a motion, except that it penetrates in the same way into the whole surface of the body, but especially and most of all through the ears, for there it passes through the most void and **remains** there least. And that is why it [i.e. the air] is not perceived on the rest of the body, but only in this place. Once it has passed inside, it **is dispersed** by its speed; for a sound comes from air that has been condensed and that penetrates violently. So that just as he explains sensation by contact on the exterior, so he does too on the interior. [56] Hearing is sharpest if the external membrane is dense, the blood vessels empty and as free of liquid as possible and well pierced, in the rest of the body as well as in the head and ears, and furthermore the bones are dense, the brain well tempered, and what sur-

τος καὶ τὸ περὶ αὐτὸν ὡς ξηρότατον· ἀθρόον γὰρ ἂν
οὕτως εἰσιέναι τὴν φωνὴν ἄτε διὰ πολλοῦ κενοῦ καὶ
ἀνίκμου καὶ εὐτρήτου εἰσιοῦσαν καὶ ταχὺ σκίδνα-
σθαι καὶ ὁμαλῶς κατὰ τὸ σῶμα καὶ οὐ διεκπίπτειν⁴
ἔξω. [. . . = **R60**]

⁴ οὐδὲ ἐκπίπτειν mss., corr. Diels

Other Senses (D158–D161)

D158 (< A135) Theophr. *Sens.* 57

[. . . = **R60**] καὶ περὶ μὲν ὄψεως καὶ ἀκοῆς οὕτως ἀποδίδωσι, τὰς δὲ ἄλλας αἰσθήσεις σχεδὸν ὁμοίως ποιεῖ
τοῖς πλείστοις [. . . = **D134**].

D159 Theophr.

a (< A135) *Sens.* 72

[. . . = **R56b**] τῶν δὲ χυλῶν ἑκάστῳ τὸ σχῆμα ἀποδίδωσι πρὸς τὴν δύναμιν ἀφομοιῶν τὴν ἐν τοῖς πάθεσιν
[. . . cf. **R62**].

cf. app. ad **R62**

b (A119) *CP* 6.1.2.1–10

αὐτὸ γὰρ τοῦτο πρῶτον ἔχει τινὰ σκέψιν, πότερον¹
τοῖς πάθεσιν τοῖς κατὰ τὰς αἰσθήσεις ἀποδοτέον ἢ
ὥσπερ Δημόκριτος τοῖς σχήμασιν ἐξ ὧν ἕκαστοι.²

rounds this as dry as possible. For in this way sound penetrates all together, since it passes through many empty
places that are free of liquid and are well pierced, and it **is
dispersed** quickly and evenly throughout the body, without escaping outward [. . .].

Other Senses (D158–D161)

D158 (< A135) Theophrastus, *On Sensations*

[. . .] This is how he explains vision and hearing; the other
senses he discusses more or less in the same way as most
people [. . .].

D159 Theophrastus

a (< A135) *On Sensations*

[. . .] As for the flavors, he [i.e. Democritus] attributes to
each one its shape, making it similar to the property manifested in the affections [. . .].

b (A119) *Causes of Plants*

For first of all one has to examine whether one must give
an account [scil. of the various kinds of flavors] in terms of
the affections of the senses or, like Democritus, in terms
of the shapes which are at the origin of each one.

---

[1] γὰρ post πότερον del. Scaliger   [2] ἕκαστοι Heinsius
(*singuli* Gaza): ἑκάστοις mss.

D160 (A129) Theophr. *CP* 6.1.6.1–11

Δημόκριτος δὲ σχῆμα περιτιθεὶς ἑκάστῳ γλυκὺν μὲν
τὸν στρογγύλον καὶ εὐμεγέθη ποιεῖ. στρυφνὸν δὲ τὸν
μεγαλόσχημον τραχύν τε καὶ[1] πολυγώνιον καὶ ἀπεριφερῆ. ὀξὺν δὲ κατὰ τοὔνομα τὸν ὀξὺν τῷ ὄγκῳ καὶ
γωνοειδῆ[2] καὶ καμπύλον καὶ λεπτὸν καὶ ἀπεριφερῆ.
δριμὺν δὲ τὸν περιφερῆ καὶ λεπτὸν καὶ γωνοειδῆ καὶ
καμπύλον. ἁλμυρὸν δὲ τὸν γωνοειδῆ καὶ εὐμεγέθη καὶ
σκολιὸν καὶ ἰσοσκελῆ.[3] πικρὸν δὲ τὸν περιφερῆ καὶ
λεῖον ἔχοντα σκολιότητα μέγεθος δὲ μικρόν. λιπαρὸν
δὲ τὸν λεπτὸν καὶ στρογγύλον καὶ μικρόν.

[1] δὲ τὸν mss., corr. Schneider   [2] γωνοειδῆ Diels: κωνο-
ειδῆ mss.: γωνιοειδῆ Schneider   [3] οὐ σκαληνῆ Einarson-
Link

D161 (< A130) Theophr. *CP* 6.2.1

αὐτῶν γὰρ τῶν δυνάμεων οὕτως ἀποδιδοὺς[1] οἴεται τὰς
αἰτίας ἀποδιδόναι, δι' ἃς ὁ μὲν στύφει καὶ ξηραίνει
καὶ πήγνυσιν, ὁ δὲ λεαίνει καὶ ὁμαλύνει καὶ καθίστη-
σιν, ὁ δὲ ἐκκρίνει καὶ διαχεῖ καὶ ἄλλο τι τοιοῦτο δρᾷ
[. . . = **R63**].

[1] ἀποδιδοὺς ‹τὰς διαφορὰς› Diels

D160 (A129) Theophrastus, *Causes of Plants*

Democritus, who attributes a shape to each one [scil. of the flavors], makes sweet the round and good-sized flavor; sour, the one that is large-shaped, rough, polygonal, and devoid of roundness; acidic (*oxu*), as its name indicates, the one that is sharp (*oxu*) in its mass, angular, crooked, thin, and devoid of roundness; pungent, the one that is round, light, angular, and crooked; salty, the one that is angular, good-sized, twisted, and equal-sided; bitter, the one that is round and smooth, possessing crookedness and a small size; fatty, the one that is thin, round, and small.

D161 (< A130) Theophrastus, *Causes of Plants*

Having provided an explanation in this way [scil. by the shapes], he thinks that he has provided an explanation of the causes of the faculties themselves whereby the one [scil. flavor] is sour, dries out, and rigidifies, another smooths out, equalizes, and regularizes, and another expels, diffuses, and causes some other effect of this sort [. . .].

Reproduction (D162–D179)
Seed (D162–D168)

D162 (67 A35, 68 A140) Aët. 5.4.1 et 3 (Ps.-Plut.) [εἰ σῶμα τὸ σπέρμα]

[1] Λεύκιππος [. . .] σῶμα· ψυχῆς γὰρ εἶναι ἀπόσπασμα.
[3] [. . .] Δημόκριτος καὶ τὴν δύναμιν σῶμα· πνευματικὴ γάρ.

D163 (B32)

a Stob. 3.6.28

ξυνουσίη ἀποπληξίη σμικρή· ἐξέσσυται γὰρ ἄνθρωπος ἐξ ἀνθρώπου.

b Clem. Alex. *Paed.* 2.10.94.3–4

"μικρὰν ἐπιληψίαν" τὴν συνουσίαν ὁ Ἀβδηρίτης ἔλεγεν σοφιστής, νόσον ἀνίατον ἡγούμενος. ἢ γὰρ οὐχὶ καὶ ἐκλύσεις παρέπονται τῷ μεγέθει τῆς ἀπουσίας ἀνατιθέμεναι; "ἄνθρωπος γὰρ ἐξ ἀνθρώπου ἐκφύεταί τε καὶ ἀποσπᾶται."

c Ps.-Gal. *An animal sit* 5 (vol. 19, p. 176 Kühn)

φησὶ δὲ καὶ Δημόκριτος ἄνθρωπον ἐξ ἀνθρώπου ἐξέσσυσθαι καὶ κύνα ἐκ κυνὸς καὶ βοῦν ἐκ βοός.

Reproduction (D162–D179)
Seed (D162–D168)

D162 (67 A35, 68 A140) Aëtius

[1] Leucippus [. . .]: [scil. the seed is] a body; for it is a fragment of the soul.

[3] [. . .] Democritus: also the power [scil. of the seed and not only its matter is] a body; for it is of the nature of air.

D163 (B32)[1]

> [1] We give four versions of a passage that was well known and often paraphrased in antiquity (see, besides the apparatus of DK, the texts collected by Leszl as 93.2.1–10).

a Stobaeus, *Anthology*

Sexual intercourse is a small attack of apoplexy (*apoplêxiê*): **for a human bursts out of a human.**

b Clement of Alexandria, *Pedagogue*

The sophist of Abdera called sexual intercourse **a small attack of epilepsy** (*epilêpsiê*), considering it to be an incurable disease. For indeed is it not accompanied by feelings of faintness comparable to the magnitude of what is lost [i.e. the semen]? **For a human** is born **out of a human and is torn away from him.**

c Ps.-Galen, *Is What is in the Uterus Alive?*

And for his part Democritus says that **a human bursts out of a human,** and a dog out of a dog, and a bull out of a bull.

d (Ps.-?) Hippol. *Ref.* 8.14.4

"ἄνθρωπος ἐξ ἀνθρώπου ἐξέσσυται," φησίν, "καὶ
ἀποσπᾶται πληγῇ τινι μεριζόμενος."

D164 (B124) Ps.-Galen. *Def. med.* 439

[. . .] καὶ Δημόκριτος [. . .] ἐξ ὅλου τοῦ σώματος, ὁ μὲν
Δημόκριτος λέγων "ἄνθρωποι εἷς ἔσται καὶ ἄνθρωπος πάντες."

D165 (A141) Aët. 5.3.6 (Ps.-Plut.) [τίς ἡ οὐσία τοῦ
σπέρματος]

Δημόκριτος ἀφ᾽ ὅλων τῶν σωμάτων καὶ τῶν κυριω-
τάτων μερῶν οἷον ὀστῶν σαρκῶν καὶ ἰνῶν.[1]

[1] ὁ γόνος τῶν σαρκῶν καὶ ἰνῶν m, ὁ γόνος τῶν σαρκικῶν
ἰνῶν MΠ, corr. Diels

D166 (< A142) Aët. 5.5.1 (Ps.-Plut.) [εἰ καὶ αἱ θήλειαι
προίενται σπέρμα]

[. . .] Δημόκριτος καὶ τὸ θῆλυ προίεσθαι σπέρμα· ἔχει
γὰρ παραστάτας ἀπεστραμμένους· διὰ τοῦτο καὶ ὄρε-
ξιν ἔχει περὶ τὰς χρήσεις.

D167 (B122a) *Etym. Gen.*

γυνή· [. . .] ἤ, ὡς Δημόκριτος, γονή τις οὖσα, ἡ γονῆς
δεκτική.

d (Ps.-?) Hippolytus, *Refutation of All Heresies*

"A human bursts out of a human," he says, **"and is torn away from him** (*apospatai*)**, being divided off by a kind of blow** (*plêgê*)**."**

D164 (B124) Ps.-Galen, *Medical Definitions*

[. . .] and Democritus [. . .] [scil. say that the seed separates out] from the whole body; Democritus says, **"One will be humans and a human will be all."**

D165 (A141) Aëtius

Democritus: [scil. the seed comes] from the whole of bodies and from their principal parts, like the bones, flesh, and muscles.

D166 (< A142) Aëtius

[. . .] Democritus: the female too emits a seed; for she has the [scil. spermatic] ducts inverted. And that is why she too has desire for sexual activities.

D167 (B122a) *Etymologicum Genuinum*

Woman (*gunê*): [. . .] or, as Democritus, **because she is a kind of seed** (*gonê*)**, she who receives the seed** (*gonê*).

D168 (A146) Arist. *GA* 4.4 769b30–36.

Δημόκριτος μὲν οὖν ἔφησε γίγνεσθαι τὰ τέρατα διὰ τὸ δύο γονὰς συμπίπτειν, τὴν μὲν πρότερον ὁρμήσασαν τὴν δ᾽ ὕστερον, καὶ ταύτην ἐξελθοῦσαν ἐλθεῖν εἰς τὴν ὑστέραν ὥστε συμφύεσθαι καὶ ἐπαλλάττειν τὰ μόρια. ταῖς δ᾽ ὄρνισιν ἐπεὶ συμβαίνει ταχεῖαν γίνεσθαι τὴν ὀχείαν, ἀεὶ τά τ᾽ ᾠὰ καὶ τὴν χρόαν αὐτῶν ἐπαλλάττειν φησίν.

Embryology (D169–D176)

D169 (A144) Arist. *GA* 2.4 740a35–37

[. . .] Δημόκριτός φησιν, ἵνα διαπλάττηται τὰ μόρια κατὰ τὰ μόρια τῆς ἐχούσης.

D170 (A145) Arist. *GA* 2.4 740a13–15

[. . .] Δημόκριτος, τὰ ἔξω πρῶτον διακρίνεσθαι τῶν ζῴων, ὕστερον δὲ τὰ ἐντός [. . .].

D171 (A145) Censor. *Die nat.* 6.1

Democritus alvum cum capite, quae plurumum habent ex inani.

D172 (< B148) Plut. *Am. prol.* 3 495E

ὁ γὰρ ὀμφαλὸς πρῶτον ἐν μήτρῃσιν, ὥς φησι Δημόκριτος, ἀγκυρηβόλιον σάλου καὶ πλάνης ἐμφύεται,

D168 (A146) Aristotle, *Generation of Animals*

Democritus said that monstrous births were caused by two seeds meeting, the one impelled first, the other later. This one too enters into the womb after it is emitted, so that the parts grow together and become intermingled. And he says that in birds, since their copulation takes place rapidly, both the eggs and their colors are always intermingled.

Embryology (D169–D176)

D169 (A144) Aristotle, *Generation of Animals*

[. . .] Democritus says [scil. that the animal remains in the womb] so that its parts can be fashioned according to the parts of the female that bears it.

D170 (A145) Aristotle, *Generation of Animals*

[. . .] Democritus [scil. says] that the external parts of animals are the first ones to be differentiated, and the internal ones later [. . .].

D171 (A145) Censorinus, *The Birthday*

Democritus [scil. says that what is formed first in the embryo is] the belly at the same time as the head: they have the most void.

D172 (< B148) Plutarch, *On Affection for Offspring*

The umbilical cord is the first thing, says Democritus, that develops in the womb, as an anchorage against fluctuation

πεῖσμα καὶ κλῆμα τῷ γεννωμένῳ[1] καρπῷ καὶ μέλλοντι.

[1] γενομένῳ mss., corr. Xylander

D173 (A143) Arist. GA 4.1 764a6–10

Δημόκριτος δὲ ὁ Ἀβδηρίτης ἐν μὲν τῇ μητρὶ γίνεσθαί φησι τὴν διαφορὰν τοῦ θήλεος καὶ τοῦ ἄρρενος, οὐ μέντοι διὰ θερμότητά γε καὶ ψυχρότητα τὸ μὲν γίγνεσθαι θῆλυ τὸ δ' ἄρρεν, ἀλλ' ὁποτέρου ἂν κρατήσῃ τὸ σπέρμα τὸ ἀπὸ τοῦ μορίου ἐλθὸν ᾧ διαφέρουσιν ἀλλήλων τὸ θῆλυ καὶ τὸ ἄρρεν.

D174 (67 A36, 68 A143) Aët. 5.7.5 et 6 (Ps.-Plut.) [πῶς ἄρρενα γεννᾶται καὶ θήλεα]

[5] Λεύκιππος διὰ τὴν παραλλαγὴν τῶν μορίων καθ' ἣν ὁ μὲν καυλόν, ἡ δὲ μήτραν ἔχει· τοσοῦτον γὰρ μόνον λέγει.
[6] Δημόκριτος τὰ μὲν κοινὰ μέρη ἐξ ὁποτέρου ἂν τύχῃ, τὰ δ' ἰδιάζοντα καὶ[1] κατ' ἐπικράτειαν.

[1] καὶ del. Reiske

D175 (< A144) Aët. 5.16.1 (Ps.-Plut.) [πῶς τρέφεται τὰ ἔμβρυα]

Δημόκριτος [. . .] τὸ ἔμβρυον ἐν τῇ μήτρᾳ διὰ τοῦ στόματος τρέφεσθαι, ὅθεν εὐθέως γεννηθὲν ἐπὶ τὸν

and wandering, a cable and stem for the fruit that is being generated and will go on to live.

D173 (A143) Aristotle, *Generation of Animals*

Democritus of Abdera says that it is in the mother that the difference between female and male is produced, but that it is not because of heat or cold that the one becomes a female and the other male, but depending on whether the seed of the one or of the other dominates that comes from that part by which female and male are differentiated from one another.

D174 (67 A36, 68 A143) Aëtius

[5] Leucippus: [scil. males and females are generated] by a modification of the parts, by virtue of which the male acquires a penis, the female a vagina. For that is all he says. [6] Democritus: the parts in common [scil. to both sexes] come from either the one [scil. parent] or the other, by chance, while the parts that are peculiar to each are also due to the dominance [scil. of one parent].

D175 (< A144) Aëtius

Democritus [. . .]: the embryo is nourished in the womb through its mouth. That is why, as soon as it is born, it

μαστὸν φέρεται τῷ στόματι· εἶναι γὰρ καὶ ἐν τῇ μήτρᾳ θηλάς τινας καὶ στόματα, δι᾽ ὧν τρέφεται.

D176 (A152) Ael. *Nat. anim.* 12.17

ἐν τοῖς νοτίοις μᾶλλον ἐκπίπτειν τὰ ἔμβρυα Δημόκριτος λέγει ἢ ἐν τοῖς βορείοις, καὶ εἰκότως· χαυνοῦσθαι
γὰρ ὑπὸ τοῦ νότου τὰ σώματα ταῖς κυούσαις καὶ δι-
ίστασθαι. ἅτε τοίνυν τοῦ σκήνους διακεχυμένου καὶ
οὐχ ἡρμοσμένου, πλανᾶσθαι καὶ¹ τὰ κυόμενα² καὶ
θερμαινόμενα δεῦρο καὶ ἐκεῖσε διολισθάνειν καὶ ἐκπίπτειν ῥᾷον· εἰ δὲ εἴη πάγος καὶ βορρᾶς καταπνέοι,
συμπέπηγε μὲν τὸ ἔμβρυον, δυσκίνητον δέ ἐστι καὶ
οὐ ταράττεται ὡς ὑπὸ κλύδωνος, ἅτε δὲ ἄκλυστον καὶ
ἐν γαλήνῃ ὄν, ἔρρωταί τε καί ἐστι σύντονον καὶ δι-
αρκεῖ πρὸς τὸν κατὰ φύσιν χρόνον τῆς ζῳογονίας.
οὐκοῦν "ἐν κρυμῷ μέν" φησὶν ὁ Ἀβδηρίτης, "συμμέ-
νει, ἐν ἀλέᾳ δὲ ὡς τὰ πολλὰ ἐκπτύεται." ἀνάγκην δὲ
εἶναι λέγει τῆς θέρμης πλεοναζούσης δίστασθαι καὶ
τὰς φλέβας καὶ τὰ ἄρθρα.

¹ καὶ del. Hercher   ² κυούμενα mss., corr. Hercher

Resemblances (D177)

D177 (A143) Censor. *Die nat.* 6.5

utrius vero parentis principium sedem prius occupaverit,
eius reddi naturam Democritus rettulit.

moves toward the breast with its mouth. For in the womb too there are certain nipples and orifices by which it is nourished.

D176 (A152) Aelian, *On the Nature of Animals*

Democritus says that embryos are born more in the south than in the north, and this is plausible. For the bodies of pregnant females are made porous and distended by the south wind. Since then **the body** (*skênos*) becomes relaxed and is not closely fitted, the embryos too wander here and there and, being heated, slip out and are born more easily. But if there is frost and the north wind blows, the embryo solidifies and, being less mobile, it is not agitated as though by waves but, being unsubmerged and in a sea-calm, it remains strong and is vigorous and can endure until the natural time of birth. And so, says the Abderite, **"in the cold it stays where it is, while in the heat it is most often spat out."** And he says that necessarily, when it is very warm, the veins and joints too are distended.

Resemblances (D177)

D177 (A143) Censorinus, *The Birthday*

Democritus reports that the nature of that parent is reproduced whose principle was the first to occupy the place.

Fertility and Sterility (D178–D179)

D178 (A149) Arist. *GA* 2.8 747a29–31

Δημόκριτος μὲν γάρ φησι διεφθάρθαι τοὺς πόρους
τῶν ἡμιόνων ἐν ταῖς ὑστέραις διὰ τὸ μὴ ἐκ συγγενῶν
γίνεσθαι τὴν ἀρχὴν τῶν ζῴων [. . . cf. **EMP. R22**].

D179 (A151) Ael. *Nat. anim.* 12.16

λέγει Δημόκριτος πολύγονα εἶναι ὗν καὶ κύνα, καὶ
τὴν αἰτίαν προστίθησι λέγων ὅτι πολλὰς ἔχει τὰς
μήτρας καὶ τοὺς τόπους τοὺς δεκτικοὺς τοῦ σπέρμα-
τος. ὁ τοίνυν θορὸς οὐκ ἐκ μιᾶς ὁρμῆς ἁπάσας αὐτὰς
ἐκπληροῖ, ἀλλὰ δίς τε καὶ τρὶς ταῦτα τὰ ζῷα ἐπιθόρ-
νυται, ἵνα ἡ συνέχεια πληρώσῃ τὰ τοῦ γόνου δεκτικά.
ἡμιόνους δὲ λέγει μὴ τίκτειν· μὴ γὰρ ἔχειν ὁμοίας
μήτρας τοῖς ἄλλοις ζῴοις, ἑτερομόρφους δέ, ἥκιστα
δυναμένας γονὴν δέξασθαι· μὴ γὰρ εἶναι φύσεως
ποίημα τὴν ἡμίονον, ἀλλὰ ἐπινοίας ἀνθρωπίνης καὶ
τόλμης ὡς ἂν εἴποις μοιχιδίου[1] ἐπιτέχνημα τοῦτο καὶ
κλέμμα. "δοκεῖ δέ μοι," ἦ δ᾽ ὅς, "ὄνου ἵππον βιασαμένου[2] κατὰ τύχην κυῆσαι, μαθητὰς δὲ ἀνθρώπους τῆς βίας ταύτης γεγενημένους εἶτα μέντοι
προελθεῖν ἐπὶ τὴν τῆς γονῆς αὐτῶν συνήθειαν." καὶ
μάλιστά γε τοὺς τῶν Λιβύων ὄνους μεγίστους ὄντας
ἐπιβαίνειν ταῖς ἵπποις οὐ κομώσαις ἀλλὰ κεκαρμέ-
ναις· ἔχουσα γὰρ τὴν ἑαυτῆς ἀγλαΐαν τὴν διὰ τῆς

ATOMISTS (LEUCIPPUS, DEMOCRITUS)

Fertility and Sterility (D178–D179)

D178 (A149) Aristotle, *Generation of Animals*

For Democritus says that the passages in the wombs of
mules have been destroyed because at the beginning they
were not born from animals of the same species.

D179 (A151) Aelian, *On the Nature of Animals*

Democritus says that the pig and dog are prolific and he
adds the cause, saying that they have many wombs and
places receptive of seed. So a single copulation is not sufficient to fill them all up in only one impetus, but these
animals copulate additionally two and three times so that
the sequence fills up the receptacles of the seed. As for
mules, he says that they do not give birth. For they do not
have wombs similar to other animals', but ones of a different form, not at all capable of receiving seed. For the mule
is not a product of nature, but rather an artificial supple-
ment and theft deriving from a human inspiration and
audacity one might call adulterous. **"It seems to me,"** he
said, **"that after an ass had violated a mare she became pregnant by chance, and that humans learned
from this violence and then progressed to the point
of making their procreation a habit."** And indeed most
of all the Libyans' mules, which are the largest in size,
mount mares that are not long-maned but that have been
shorn; for if she [i.e. the mare] possessed the splendor
belonging to her that derives from her mane, she would

---

¹ μοιχίδιον (μοσχ- A) mss., corr. Reiske
² ὄνου . . . βιασαμένου Diels: ὄνος . . . βιασαμένος mss.

225

κόμης οὐκ ἂν ὑπομείναι³ τὸν τοιόνδε γαμέτην, οἱ σοφοὶ τοὺς τούτων γάμους φασίν.

³ ὑπομείναι Lᵖᶜ: ὑπομεῖναι cett.

Medicine (D180–D183)

D180 (A159) Soran. *Gyn.* 3.17

ἡ 'φλεγμονὴ' κέκληται μὲν ἀπὸ τοῦ φλέγειν καὶ οὐχ
ὡς ὁ Δημόκριτος εἴρηκεν ἀπὸ τοῦ αἴτιον εἶναι τὸ
φλέγμα.

D181 (< B120) Erot. *Lex. Hipp.*, p. 90.18

καὶ ὁ Δημόκριτος δὲ 'φλεβοπαλίην' καλεῖ τὴν τῶν
ἀρτηριῶν κίνησιν.

D182 (B135) Hesych.

δεξαμεναί· ὑδάτων δοχεῖα, καὶ ἐν τῶι σώματι φλέβες.
Δημοκρίτου.

D183 (B212) Stob. 3.6.27

ἡμερήσιοι ὕπνοι σώματος ὄχλησιν ἢ ψυχῆς ἀδημο-
σύνην ἢ ἀργίην ἢ ἀπαιδευσίην σημαίνουσι.

not tolerate this kind of spouse, say the experts in their espousals.

Medicine (D180–D183)

D180 (A159) Soranus, *Gynecology*

'Phlegmonê' ('inflamed tumor') received its name from *phlegein* ('to inflame') and not, as Democritus said, from the fact that its cause is phlegm.

D181 (< B120) Erotian, *Hippocratic Lexicon*

Democritus calls the movement of the arteries **'the beating of the pulse.'**

D182 (B135) Hesychius, *Lexicon*

dexamenai (literally, "receivers," feminine): containers for fluids, and the veins in the body. From Democritus.

D183 (B212) Stobaeus, *Anthology*

Sleeping during the day indicates a disturbance in the body, or distress or indolence or lack of education in the soul.

Animals (D184–D198)
The Intelligence of Animals (D184)

D184 (≠ DK) Porph. *Abst.* 3.6.7

[. . .] Δημόκριτός τε καὶ [. . .] ἔγνωσαν τὸ μετέχον τοῦ λόγου.

Animal Physiology (D185–D198)
Dentition (D185–D186)

D185 (A147) Arist. *GA* 5.8 788b9 et 12–14

εἴρηκε μὲν οὖν περὶ αὐτῶν καὶ Δημόκριτος [. . .]. φησὶ γὰρ ἐκπίπτειν μὲν διὰ τὸ πρὸ ὥρας γίνεσθαι τοῖς ζῴοις· ἀκμαζόντων γὰρ ὡς εἰπεῖν φύεσθαι κατά γε φύσιν· τοῦ δὲ πρὸ ὥρας γίνεσθαι τὸ θηλάζειν αἰτιᾶται.

D186 (< 98.3 Leszl) Arist. *GA* 5.8 788b24–25 et 28

a

εἰ οὖν συνέβαινεν, ὡς ἐκεῖνος λέγει, πρὸς ἥβην [. . . = **R67b**].

b

βίᾳ δέ φησι συμβαίνειν τὴν γένεσιν τῶν ὀδόντων.

Animals (D184–D198)
The Intelligence of Animals (D184)

D184 (≠ DK) Porphyry, *On Abstinence*

[. . .] Democritus and [. . .] recognized that they [i.e. animals] have a share in reason.

Animal Physiology (D185–D198)
Dentition (D185–D186)

D185 (A147) Aristotle, *Generation of Animals*

Democritus too has spoken about these [i.e. milk teeth] [. . .]. For he says that they fall out because they appear prematurely in animals. For when these have attained their full vigor, they [i.e. the teeth] grow as it were according to nature. Their premature appearance, he says, is caused by suckling.

D186 (≠ DK) Aristotle, *Generation of Animals*

a

If it [scil. the eruption of the permanent teeth] occurred, as he [i.e. Democritus] says, at puberty [. . .].

b

He says that the generation of the teeth occurs by force.

Viscera (D187)

D187 (< A148) Arist. *PA* 3.4 665a28–33

Δημόκριτος [. . .] ᾠήθη διὰ μικρότητα τῶν ἀναίμων ζῴων ἄδηλα εἶναι ταῦτα.

Visual Organs (D188–D189)

D188

a (A156) Ael. *Nat. anim.* 5.39

λέγει Δημόκριτος τῶν ζῴων μόνον τὸν λέοντα ἐκπεπταμένοις τίκτεσθαι τοῖς ὀφθαλμοῖς ἤδη τρόπον τινὰ τεθυμωμένον καὶ ἐξ ὠδίνων δρασείοντά τι γεννικόν.

b (< 99.4.2 Leszl) Eust. *In Il.* 11.554, vol. 3, p. 252.7–8

[. . .] οὐδὲ μύει κοιμώμενος, ὡς δὲ Δημόκριτός φησι, οὐδὲ τικτόμενος [. . .].

D189 (< A157) *Etym. Mag.* s.v. γλαύξ (p. 233.12–18 Gaisford)

Δημόκριτος δὲ ἱστορεῖ ὅτι μόνον τῶν γαμψωνύχων καὶ σαρκοφάγων μὴ τυφλὰ τίκτει, ὅτι πολὺ τὸ πυρῶδες καὶ θερμὸν περὶ τοὺς ὀφθαλμοὺς ἔχει, ὃ σφοδρῶς ὀξὺ καὶ τμητικὸν ὑπάρχον διαιρεῖ καὶ ἀναμίγνυσι τὴν ὅρασιν· διὸ καὶ ἐν ταῖς σκοτομήνησιν ὁρᾷ διὰ τὸ πυρῶδες τῶν ὄψεων.

Viscera (D187)

D187 (< A148) Aristotle, *Parts of Animals*

Democritus [. . .] thought that these [i.e. the viscera] are not visible because of the smallness of the bloodless animals.

Visual Organs (D188–D189)

D188

a (A156) Aelian, *On the Nature of Animals*

Democritus says that the lion, alone among animals, is born with its eyes wide open, since already at its birth it is in a certain way full of ferocity and wants to accomplish something noble.

b (≠ DK) Eustathius, *Commentary on Homer's* Iliad

[. . .] it [i.e. the lion] does not close its eyes when it sleeps, nor, as Democritus says, when it is born [. . .].

D189 (< A157) *Etymologicum Magnum*

Democritus reports that, alone among the taloned and carnivorous ones [i.e. birds], it [i.e. the owl] does not give birth to young that are blind, because in its eyes it has much fire and heat which, being very sharp and cutting, divides [scil. the object of their vision] and blends their vision [scil. with this object].[1] And this is why it sees even in moonless nights, because of the fieriness of its eyes.

[1] The expression of this last phrase is elliptical and its meaning uncertain.

Horns and Other Secretions (D190–D193)

D190 (A153) Ael. *Nat. anim.* 12.18

αἰτίαν δὲ ὁ αὐτὸς λέγει τοῖς ἐλάφοις τῆς τῶν κεράτων
ἀναφύσεως ἐκείνην εἶναι. ἡ γαστὴρ αὐτοῖς ὡς ἐστι
θερμοτάτη ὁμολογεῖ, καὶ τὰς φλέβας δὲ αὐτῶν τὰς
διὰ τοῦ σώματος πεφυκυίας παντὸς ἀραιοτάτας λέγει,
καὶ τὸ ὀστέον τὸ κατειληφὸς τὸν ἐγκέφαλον λεπτότατον εἶναι καὶ ὑμενῶδες καὶ ἀραιόν, φλέβας τε ἐντεῦθεν
καὶ ἐς ἄκραν τὴν κεφαλὴν ὑπανίσχειν παχυτάτας.
τὴν γοῦν τροφὴν καὶ ταύτης γε τὸ γονιμώτατον ὤκισ-
στα ἀναδίδοσθαι καὶ ἡ μὲν πιμελὴ αὐτοῖς ἔξωθέν
φησι περιχεῖται, ἡ δὲ ἰσχὺς τῆς τροφῆς ἐς τὴν κεφαλὴν διὰ τῶν φλεβῶν ἀναθόρνυται. ἔνθεν οὖν τὰ
κέρατα ἐκφύεσθαι διὰ πολλῆς ἐπαρδόμενα τῆς ἰκμάδος. συνεχὴς οὖν οὖσα ἐπιρρέουσά τε ἐξωθεῖ τὰ
πρότερα. καὶ τὸ μὲν ὑπερίσχον ὑγρὸν ἔξω τοῦ σώματος σκληρὸν γίνεται, πηγνύντος αὐτὸ καὶ κερατοῦν-
τος τοῦ ἀέρος, τὸ δὲ ἔνδον ἔτι μεμυκὸς ἁπαλόν ἐστι.
καὶ τὸ μὲν σκληρύνεται ὑπὸ τῆς ἔξωθεν ψύξεως, τὸ δὲ
ἁπαλὸν μένει ὑπὸ τῆς ἔνδον ἀλέας. οὐκοῦν ἡ ἐπίφυσις
τοῦ νέου κέρατος τὸ πρεσβύτερον[1] ὡς ἀλλότριον
ἐξωθεῖ, θλίβοντος τοῦ ἔνδοθεν καὶ ἀνωθεῖν τοῦτο ἐθέ-
λοντος καὶ ὀδυνῶντος καὶ σφύζοντος, ὥσπερ οὖν ἐπει-
γομένου τεχθῆναι καὶ προελθεῖν. ἡ γάρ τοι ἰκμὰς
πηγνυμένη καὶ ὑπανατέλλουσα ἀτρεμεῖν ἀδύνατός
ἐστι· γίνεται γὰρ καὶ αὐτὴ σκληρὰ καὶ ἐπωθεῖται τοῖς

Horns and Other Secretions (D190–D193)

D190 (A153) Aelian, *On the Nature of Animals*

The same man [i.e. Democritus] says that the cause for the growth of horns on deer is this: he accepts that their stomach is very warm, and he says that the blood vessels that extend throughout their whole body are very fine and that the bone that contains their brain is very thin, like a veil and porous, and that very thick blood vessels arise from there and go to the top of the head. Their food, and of this the most productive part, is diffused very rapidly, and, he says, the soft fat spreads outward in them while the strength of the food leaps up into the head through the blood vessels. So it is from there that the horns grow, since they are irrigated by abundant liquid. Now, since this is continuous and keeps flowing, it extrudes the earlier parts. And the excess liquid becomes hard on the outside of the body, as the air solidifies it and turns it into horn, while the part remaining hidden inside is soft. And the one part becomes hard by the effect of the external cold, while the other remains soft by that of the internal warmth. The further growth of the new horn extrudes the older one as though it were a foreign body, while the interior exerts pressure and tends to make this rise up, causes pain, and throbs as though it desired to be born and leave. For the liquid, solidifying and rising up from below, is not able to remain immobile; for it too becomes hard and is extruded by the earlier parts. And most often they are expelled by

---

1 πρεσβύτατον mss., corr. Hercher

προτέροις. καὶ τὰ μὲν πλείω ἐκθλίβεται ὑπὸ τῆς
ἰσχύος τῆς ἔνδον, ἤδη δέ τινα καὶ κλάδοις περισχε-
θέντα καὶ ἐμποδίζοντα ἐς τὸν ὠκὺν δρόμον ὑπὸ ῥύμης[2]
τὸ θηρίον ὠθούμενον ἀπήραξε. καὶ τὰ μὲν ἐξώλισθε,
τὰ δὲ ἕτοιμα ἐκκύπτειν ἡ φύσις προάγει.

2 ῥώμης mss., corr. Gesner

D191 (A154) Ael. *Nat. anim.* 12.19

οἱ τομίαι βόες, Δημόκριτος λέγει, σκολιὰ καὶ λεπτὰ
καὶ μακρὰ φύεται τὰ κέρατα αὐτοῖς, τοῖς δὲ ἐνόρχοις
παχέα τὰ πρὸς τῇ ῥίζῃ καὶ ὀρθὰ καὶ πρὸς μῆκος
προήκοντα ἧττον. καὶ πλατυμετώπους εἶναι λέγει τούτους τῶν ἑτέρων πολὺ μᾶλλον· τῶν γὰρ φλεβῶν πολλῶν ἐνταῦθα οὐσῶν, εὐρύνεσθαι τὰ ὀστέα ὑπ' αὐτῶν.
καὶ ἡ ἔκφυσις δὲ τῶν κεράτων παχυτέρα οὖσα ἐς πλάτος τὸ αὐτὸ τῷ ζῴῳ μέρος προάγει καὶ ἐκείνη· οἱ δὲ
τομίαι μικρὸν ἔχοντες τὸν κύκλον τῆς ἕδρας τῆς τῶν
κεράτων πλατύνονται ἧττόν φησιν.

D192 (A155) Ael. *Nat. anim.* 12.20

οἱ δὲ ἄκερῳ ταῦροι τὸ τενθρηνιῶδες[1] (οὕτω δὲ ὀνομάζει Δημόκριτος) ἐπὶ τοῦ βρέγματος οὐκ ἔχοντες (εἴη
δ' ἂν τὸ σηραγγῶδες λέγων) ἀντιτύπου τοῦ παντὸς
ὄντος ὀστέου καὶ τὰς συρροίας τῶν χυμῶν οὐ δεχο-
μένου γυμνοί τε καὶ ἄμοιροι γίνονται τῶν ἀμυντη-
ρίων. καὶ αἱ φλέβες δὲ αἱ κατὰ τοῦ ὀστέου τοῦδε

the internal strength, but sometimes the animal, driven by its own impetus, breaks them off when they are caught in branches and prevent it from running quickly. And some slip out, while nature brings out those that are ready to peep out.

D191 (A154) Aelian, *On the Nature of Animals*

With regard to castrated bulls, says Democritus, their horns grow curved, thin, and long, while those of uncastrated ones are thick at the base, straight, and shorter. And he says that the latter have a much broader forehead than the former. For since there are many vessels in this place, the bones become wider because of them. And the outgrowth of the horns too, being thicker, makes this part of the animal grow broader too; while the castrated ones, since the circle of the emplacement of their horns is smaller, become less broad, he says.

D192 (A155) Aelian, *On the Nature of Animals*

Bulls without horns, since they do not have the front part of their head **honeycombed** (this is what Democritus calls it, presumably referring to its porosity), and so the whole bone being resistant and not receptive of the combined flow of fluids, are defenseless and deprived of protection. And the vessels leading to this bone, being less

---

¹ θρηνιῶδες vel θρινῶδες mss., corr. J. G. Schneider

ἀτροφώτεραι οὖσαι λεπτότεραί τε καὶ ἀσθενέστεραι
γίνονται. ἀνάγκη δὲ καὶ ξηρότερον τὸν αὐχένα τῶν
ἀκεράτων εἶναι. λεπτότεραι γὰρ καὶ αἱ τούτου φλέβες.
ταύτῃ τοι καὶ ἐρρωμέναι ἧττον. ὅσαι δὲ Ἀράβιοι βόες
θήλειαι μέν εἰσι τὸ γένος, εὐφυεῖς δὲ τὰ κέρατα, καὶ
ταύταις ἥ γε² πολλὴ ἐπίρροια τῶν χυμῶν, φησί,
τροφὴ τῆς εὐγενοῦς βλάστης τοῖς κέρασίν ἐστιν.
ἀκέρῳ δὲ καὶ αὗται ὅσαι τὸ δεκτικὸν τῆς ἰκμάδος
ὀστέον στερεώτερόν τε ἔχουσι καὶ δέχεσθαι τοὺς χυμοὺς ἥκιστον. καὶ συνελόντι εἰπεῖν αὔξης ἡ ἐπιρροὴ
αἰτία τοῖς κέρασι· ταύτην δὲ ἄρα ἐποχετεύουσι φλέβες πλεῖσταί τε καὶ παχύταται καὶ ὑγρὸν κύουσαι
ὅσον καὶ δύνανται στέγειν.

² ἥ γε Hercher: ἥ τε P: τις LA: τῇ H

D193 (< A150)

a Arist. *HA* 9.39 623a30–33

δύνανται δ᾽ ἀφιέναι οἱ ἀράχναι τὸ ἀράχνιον [. . .], οὐκ
ἔσωθεν ὡς ὂν περίττωμα, καθάπερ φησὶ Δημόκριτος
[. . .].

b Plin. *Nat. hist.* 11.80

[. . .] tantique operis materiae uterus ipsius sufficit, sive
ita corrupta alvi natura stato tempore, ut Democrito
placet, sive [. . .].

nourished, are thinner and weaker. Necessarily, too, the neck of hornless animals is drier. For the vessels of this kind of animal are thinner, and hence less robust. But all the bovids of Arabia are female in sex but are supplied with fine horns by nature; and among these it is the abundant afflux of fluids, he says, that nourishes a majestic growth of horns. But all those are hornless whose liquid-receiving bone is too hard and less able to receive fluids. And summarizing, the cause of the growth of horns is the afflux. And this is caused by irrigation by the most numerous and thickest vessels, which become impregnated with as much moisture as they are able to contain.

D193 (< A150)

a Aristotle, *History of Animals*

Spiders are capable of producing their web [. . .], not from inside as though it were a residue, as Democritus says [. . .].

b Pliny, *Natural History*

[. . .] its [i.e. a third kind of spider's] own abdomen supplies enough material for such a large-scale work, whether because, as Democritus supposes, at a certain moment the natural matter within its bowels is corrupted in this way, or [. . .].

237

Birds (D194–D195)

D194 (A158) Cic. *Div.* 2.26.57

Democritus quidem optumis verbis causam explicat cur ante lucem galli canant: depulso enim de pectore et in omne corpus diviso et mitificato cibo cantus edere quiete satiatos.

D195 (< B22) Porph. *Quaest. Hom.* 1.274.9–12 ad *Il.* 21.252

[. . .] Δημόκριτον ἱστορεῖν ἐπὶ τοῦ ἀετοῦ τὰ ὀστᾶ μέλανα εἶναι [. . .].

Invertebrates (D196)

D196 (< B126) Gal. *Diff. puls.* 1.25

[. . .] καθάπερ καὶ Δημόκριτος λέγει που περὶ τῶν τοιούτων διαλεγόμενος τῶν "ὅσα κυματοειδῶς ἀνὰ τὴν πορείαν πλάζεται."

Fish (D197–D198)

D197 (< A155a) Ael. *Nat. anim.* 9.64

λέγει [. . .] Δημόκριτος [. . .] μὴ τῷ ἁλμυρῷ τρέφεσθαι τοὺς ἰχθῦς, ἀλλὰ τῷ παρακειμένῳ[1] τῇ θαλάττῃ γλυκεῖ ὕδατι.

Birds (D194–D195)

D194 (A158) Cicero, *On Divination*

Democritus provides an excellent explanation for why roosters crow before daybreak: for when their food has left the stomach and has been distributed through the whole body and has been well digested, they are satiated and serene, and they emit songs.

D195 (< B22) Porphyry, *Homeric Questions*

[. . .] Democritus reports about the eagle that its bones are black [. . .].

Invertebrates (D196)

D196 (< B126) Galen, *On the Difference in Pulses*

[. . .] as Democritus says when discussing [scil. animals] of this sort [scil. worms] , **"all those that wander about proceeding with a wave-like motion."**

Fish (D197–D198)

D197 (< A155a) Aelian, *On the Nature of Animals*

[. . .] Democritus [. . .] says that fish are nourished not by salty water but by the sweet water that exists next to it in the sea.

---

¹ παραμεμιγμένῳ Hercher

D198 (< A155b) Theophr. *Pisc.* 12

[. . .] εἰκὸς δὲ μᾶλλον καὶ τοῖς ὀρυκτοῖς καὶ τοῖς ἑτέροις, τοῖς μὲν ἁπλῶς,[1] τοῖς δ' ὡς ἀμφιβίοις κατὰ
Δημόκριτον, ὃ καὶ ἐπ' ἄλλων συμβαίνει [. . .].

[1] ἁπλοῖς ms., corr. Schneider

Plants (D199–D201)

D199 (< 59 A116) Plut. *Quaest. nat.* 911D

ζῷον γὰρ ἔγγαιον τὸ φυτὸν εἶναι οἱ περὶ [. . . cf.
ANAXAG. D93] καὶ Δημόκριτον οἴονται.

D200 (31 A70, cf. 68 A163) Nic. Dam. *Plant.* 1.10, p. 129
Drossaart Lulofs (cf. Ps.-Arist. *Plant.* 1.1 815b17–18)

فأما أنكساغورس و همفدوقلس وديمقراطيس فزعموا أن للنبات عقلا وفهما.

D201 (A162) Theophr. *CP*

a 2.11.7–8

[7] ὡς δὲ Δημόκριτος αἰτιᾶται τὰ εὐθέα τῶν σκολιῶν
βραχυβιώτερα καὶ πρωϊβλαστότερα διὰ τὰς αὐτὰς
ἀνάγκας εἶναι (τοῖς μὲν γὰρ ταχὺ διαπέμπεσθαι τὴν
τροφὴν ἀφ' ἧς ἡ βλάστησις καὶ οἱ καρποί, τοῖς δὲ
βραδέως διὰ τὸ μὴ εὔρουν εἶναι τὸ ὑπὲρ γῆς, ἀλλ'
αὐτὰς τὰς ῥίζας ἀπολαύειν· καὶ γὰρ μακρόρριζα
ταῦτα εἶναι καὶ παχύρριζα), δόξειεν ἂν οὐ καλῶς λέ-

D198 (< A155b) Theophrastus, *On Fishes*

This [i.e. that they live in their natural place] is more plausible in those [scil. fish] that dig themselves [scil. into the sand] and of the others [scil. that live on dry land]—for the former, purely and simply; for the latter, inasmuch as they are **'amphibious,'** according to Democritus, something that is also the case for others as well [. . .].

Plants (199–D201)

D199 (< 59 A116) Plutarch, *Natural Questions*

Democritus and [. . .] and their disciples think that a plant is an animal in the ground.

D200 (31 A70, cf. 68 A163) Nicolaus of Damascus, *On Plants*

Anaxagoras, Empedocles and Democritus maintained that plants possess reason and understanding.[1]

---

[1] Translated by H. J. Drossaart Lulofs.

D201 (A162) Theophrastus, *Causes of Plants*

a

[7] The way in which Democritus explains by the same necessities the cause of the fact that those [scil. trees of which the wood is] straight live less long and bud earlier than those [scil. of which the wood is] curved—namely that in the former the nourishment from which the foliage and fruits come passes through quickly, but slowly in the latter, since the part above the ground does not have **an easy passage,** but the roots themselves consume it (for these have roots that are long and thick)—does not seem

γειν. [8] καὶ γὰρ τὰς ῥίζας ἀσθενεῖς φησιν εἶναι τῶν
εὐθέων, ἐξ ὧν ἀμφοτέρων θᾶττον γίνεσθαι τὴν
φθοράν· ταχὺ γὰρ ἐκ τοῦ ἄνω διιέναι καὶ τὸ ψῦχος
καὶ τὴν ἀλέαν ἐπὶ τὰς ῥίζας διὰ τὴν εὐθυπορίαν,
ἀσθενεῖς δ' οὔσας οὐχ ὑπομένειν· ὅλως δὲ τὰ πολλὰ
τῶν τοιούτων κάτωθεν ἄρχεσθαι γηράσκειν διὰ τὴν
ἀσθένειαν τῶν ῥιζῶν. ἔτι δὲ τὰ ὑπὲρ γῆς διὰ τὴν
λεπτότητα καμπτόμενα ὑπὸ τῶν πνευμάτων κινεῖν τὰς
ῥίζας· τούτου δὲ συμβαίνοντος ἀπορρήγνυσθαι καὶ
πηροῦσθαι καὶ ἀπὸ τούτων τῷ ὅλῳ δένδρῳ γίγνεσθαι[1] τὴν φθοράν. ἃ μὲν οὖν λέγει ταῦτά ἐστιν.

[1] γίγνεσθαι Wimmer: πήγνυσθαι mss.: ῥήγνυσθαι ‹καὶ τῷ
δένδρῳ γίγνεσθαι› Diels

b 1.8.2

[. . .] πότερα κατὰ τὰς εὐθύτητας τῶν πόρων ληπτέον,
ὥσπερ Δημόκριτος (εὔρους γὰρ ἡ φορὰ καὶ ἀνεμπό-
διστος, ὥς φησιν) [. . .].

Mankind: Technology, Forms of Knowledge, and
Representations (D202–D224)
The Development of Civilization and
Technology (D202–D204)

D202 (< B5) Diod. Sic. 1.8.1–9

[. . . cf. **D129**] [1] τοὺς δὲ ἐξ ἀρχῆς γεννηθέντας τῶν
ἀνθρώπων φασὶν ἐν ἀτάκτῳ καὶ θηριώδει βίῳ καθε-

to be correct. [8] For he says that the roots of straight trees are weak too. For both of these reasons [scil. the easiness of the passage and the weakness of the roots] they are destroyed more rapidly. For both cold and heat pass rapidly from the upper part to the roots because of the straightness of the passage, and since they are weak they do not offer resistance. In general, most of these species begin to grow old from below because of the weakness of their roots. Furthermore, the parts above the ground, being bent by the winds because of their thinness, shake the roots, and when this happens these are broken off and mutilated, and starting from these destruction comes about for the whole tree. This then is what he says.

b

[. . .] whether one should take the straightness of the passages [scil. for determining whether trees grow quickly or slowly], like Democritus (for then the motion is **easy-flowing** and unobstructed, as he says) [. . .].

Mankind: Technology, Forms of Knowledge, and
Representations (D202–D224)
The Development of Civilization and
Technology (D202–D204)

D202 (< B5) Diodorus Siculus

[. . .] [1] they say that the first men to be born in the beginning, leading a disordered and bestial life, dispersed and

στῶτας σποράδην ἐπὶ τὰς νομὰς ἐξιέναι καὶ προσ-
φέρεσθαι τῆς τε βοτάνης τὴν προσηνεστάτην καὶ
τοὺς αὐτομάτους ἀπὸ τῶν δένδρων καρπούς. [2] καὶ
πολεμουμένους μὲν ὑπὸ τῶν θηρίων ἀλλήλοις βοη-
θεῖν ὑπὸ τοῦ συμφέροντος διδασκομένους, ἀθροιζομέ-
νους δὲ διὰ τὸν φόβον ἐπιγινώσκειν ἐκ τοῦ κατὰ μικρὸν τοὺς ἀλλήλων τύπους.

[3] τῆς φωνῆς δ᾽ ἀσήμου καὶ συγκεχυμένης οὔσης ἐκ
τοῦ κατ᾽ ὀλίγον διαρθροῦν τὰς λέξεις, καὶ πρὸς ἀλλήλους τιθέντας σύμβολα περὶ ἑκάστου τῶν ὑποκει-
μένων γνώριμον σφίσιν αὐτοῖς ποιῆσαι τὴν περὶ
ἁπάντων ἑρμηνείαν. [4] τοιούτων δὲ συστημάτων γι-
νομένων καθ᾽ ἅπασαν τὴν οἰκουμένην, οὐχ ὁμόφωνον
πάντας ἔχειν τὴν διάλεκτον, ἑκάστων ὡς ἔτυχε συν-
ταξάντων τὰς λέξεις· διὸ καὶ παντοίους τε ὑπάρξαι
χαρακτῆρας διαλέκτων καὶ τὰ πρῶτα γενόμενα συ-
στήματα τῶν ἁπάντων ἐθνῶν ἀρχέγονα γενέσθαι.

[5] τοὺς οὖν πρώτους τῶν ἀνθρώπων μηδενὸς τῶν
πρὸς βίον χρησίμων εὑρημένου ἐπιπόνως διάγειν,
γυμνοὺς μὲν ἐσθῆτος ὄντας, οἰκήσεώς τε καὶ πυρὸς
ἀήθεις, τροφῆς δ᾽ ἡμέρου παντελῶς ἀνεννοήτους. [6]
καὶ γὰρ τὴν συγκομιδὴν τῆς ἀγρίας τροφῆς ἀγνο-
οῦντας μηδεμίαν τῶν καρπῶν εἰς τὰς ἐνδείας ποιεῖσθαι παράθεσιν· διὸ καὶ πολλοὺς αὐτῶν ἀπόλλυσθαι
κατὰ τοὺς χειμῶνας διά τε τὸ ψῦχος καὶ τὴν σπάνιν
τῆς τροφῆς. [7] ἐκ δὲ τοῦ[1] κατ᾽ ὀλίγον ὑπὸ τῆς πείρας
διδασκομένους εἴς τε τὰ σπήλαια καταφεύγειν ἐν τῷ
χειμῶνι καὶ τῶν καρπῶν τοὺς φυλάττεσθαι δυναμέ-

went out to the pastures and nourished themselves with the healthiest herbs and the fruits that grew spontaneously on the trees. [2] When they were attacked by wild animals, they came to one another's help, being taught by utility, and, gathering together out of fear, they gradually came to recognize one another's features.

[3] Their voices being meaningless and confused, they gradually articulated their words, and establishing in accord with one another signs regarding each object, they made understandable to one another their way of expressing all things. [4] Since groups of this sort came into being throughout the whole of the inhabited world, they did not all have the same language, since each one organized the words according to the circumstances. And that is why the characters of the various languages are so different and how the first groups that came into being came to be the original ancestors of all the nations.

[5] Now the first men lived wretchedly, since none of the things useful for life had been discovered: they were bare of clothing, ignorant of dwellings and fire, completely unaware of domestic food. [6] Indeed, knowing nothing of the communal provision of wild food, they made no reserves of fruits against eventual need. And that is why many of them died during the winters, because of cold and scarcity of food. [7] But being taught gradually by experience, they took refuge in caves during the winter and stored away those fruits that could be conserved.

---

¹ τοῦ Schäfer: τούτου mss.

νους ἀποτίθεσθαι. [8] γνωσθέντος δὲ τοῦ πυρὸς καὶ
τῶν ἄλλων τῶν χρησίμων κατὰ μικρὸν καὶ τὰς τέ-
χνας εὑρεθῆναι καὶ τἆλλα τὰ δυνάμενα τὸν κοινὸν
βίον ὠφελῆσαι. [9] καθόλου γὰρ πάντων τὴν χρείαν
αὐτὴν διδάσκαλον γενέσθαι τοῖς ἀνθρώποις, ὑφηγου-
μένην οἰκείως τὴν ἑκάστου μάθησιν εὐφυεῖ ζῴῳ καὶ
συνεργοὺς ἔχοντι πρὸς ἅπαντα χεῖρας καὶ λόγον καὶ
ψυχῆς ἀγχίνοιαν.

D203 (< B154) Plut. *Soll. anim.* 20 974A

[. . .] τὰ ζῷα [. . .] ὧν ὁ Δημόκριτος ἀποφαίνει μαθητὰς
ἐν τοῖς μεγίστοις γεγονότας ἡμᾶς· ἀράχνης ⟨ἐν⟩[1]
ὑφαντικῇ καὶ ἀκεστικῇ, χελιδόνος ἐν οἰκοδομίᾳ, καὶ
τῶν λιγυρῶν, κύκνου καὶ ἀηδόνος, ἐν ᾠδῇ κατὰ μίμη-
σιν.

[1] ⟨ἐν⟩ Xylander

D204 (< B144) Philod. *Music.* 4.23 (Col. 150.29–39
Delattre)

Δημόκριτος [. . . = **P43**] μουσικήν | φησι νεωτέραν
εἶναι καὶ | τὴν αἰτίαν [ἀπ]οδίδωσι λέγων μὴ ἀπ᾽ ἐκεί-
νο[υ] τὰ|ναγκαῖον, [ἀ]λλὰ ἐκ τοῦ περιεῦντος ἤδη
[γ]ενέσθαι.

Language (D205–D206)

D205 (< B26) Procl. *In Crat.* 16, pp. 6.20–7.6

ὁ δὲ Δημόκριτος θέσει λέγων τὰ ὀνόματα διὰ τεσ-

[8] Once fire and other useful things came to be known, the crafts were gradually discovered, and everything else that can assist life in common. [9] For in general, it was need itself that taught humans all things, and that supplied instruction about everything in an appropriate way for a creature that was well endowed by nature and possessed hands, reason (*logos*), and subtlety of mind to assist in everything.[1]

 [1] Cf. **D129**, n. 1.

D203 (< B154) Plutarch, *On the Cleverness of Animals*

[. . .] animals [. . .] of which Democritus affirms that we have been the pupils in the most important matters: of the spider for weaving and mending; of the swallow for house building, of the singing birds, the swan and nightingale, for song, by imitation.

D204 (< B144) Philodemus, *On Music*

Democritus says that music is more recent and gives the reason for this, saying that **it was not necessity starting at that time** [scil. that caused it], **but it came into being when there was already overabundance.**

Language (D205–D206)[1]

 [1] Some scholars think that this and the following text are to be attributed to a different Democritus, a Platonist who lived in the third century AD.

D205 (< B26) Proclus, *Commentary on Plato's* Cratylus

Democritus, who said that names are arbitrary (*thesei*),

σάρων ἐπιχειρημάτων τοῦτο κατεσκεύαζεν· ἐκ τῆς
ὁμωνυμίας· τὰ γὰρ διάφορα πράγματα τῷ αὐτῷ κα-
λοῦνται ὀνόματι, οὐκ ἄρα φύσει τὸ ὄνομα· καὶ ἐκ τῆς
πολυωνυμίας· εἰ γὰρ τὰ διάφορα ὀνόματα ἐπὶ τὸ αὐτὸ
καὶ ἓν πρᾶγμα ἐφαρμόσουσιν, καὶ ἐπάλληλα, ὅπερ
ἀδύνατον· τρίτον ἐκ τῆς τῶν ὀνομάτων μεταθέσεως·
διὰ τί γὰρ τὸν Ἀριστοκλέα μὲν Πλάτωνα, τὸν δὲ Τύρ-
ταμον Θεόφραστον μετωνομάσαμεν, εἰ φύσει τὰ
ὀνόματα; ἐκ δὲ τῆς τῶν ὁμοίων ἐλλείψεως· διὰ τί ἀπὸ
μὲν τῆς φρονήσεως λέγομεν φρονεῖν, ἀπὸ δὲ τῆς δι-
καιοσύνης οὐκέτι παρονομάζομεν; τύχῃ ἄρα καὶ οὐ
φύσει τὰ ὀνόματα. καλεῖ δὲ ὁ αὐτὸς τὸ μὲν πρῶτον
ἐπιχείρημα **πολύσημον**, τὸ δὲ δεύτερον **ἰσόρροπον**,
⟨τὸ δὲ τρίτον **μετώνυμον**⟩,[1] τὸ δὲ τέταρτον **νώνυμον**.

---

[1] ⟨τὸ δὲ τρίτον μετώνυμον⟩ Diels

D206 (< B142) Damasc. *In Phil.* 22 (24 Westerink)

[. . .] τὰ τῶν θεῶν ὀνόματα [. . .] 'ἀγάλματα φωνήεντα'
καὶ ταῦτά ἐστι 'τῶν θεῶν,' ὡς Δημόκριτος.

The Origin of Belief in the Gods (D207–D210)

D207 (A75) Sext. Emp. *Adv. Math.* 9.24

εἰσὶ δὲ οἱ ἀπὸ τῶν γιγνομένων κατὰ τὸν κόσμον
παραδόξων ὑπονοήσαντες εἰς ἔννοιαν ἡμᾶς ἐληλυθέ-

established this by means of four arguments: from hom-
onymy (for different things are called by the same name,
hence the name is not by nature); from polyonymy (for if
different names are applied to one and the same thing,
[scil. they will be applied] mutually as well, which is impossible[1]); the third from the change of names (for why
did we change the name of Aristocles to Plato, and of
Tyrtamus to Theophrastus, if names are by nature?[2]); and
from the lack of similar [scil. forms] (why do we say *phronein* ('to think') derived from *phronêsis* ('thought'), but
we have no word derived from *dikaiosunê* ('justice')? So
names are by chance and not by nature. The same author
calls the first argument that **of multiple meanings,** the
second that of **equal tendency,** ‹the third that of name-
changing,› the fourth that of **the absence of a term.**

[1] The argument is unclear.   [2] Chronology would permit
Democritus to invoke Plato's name, but not Theophrastus'. So this
last example at least, and perhaps both of them, must be assigned
to Proclus or to his source if this Democritus is the ancient Atomist.

D206 (‹ B142) Damascius, *Commentary on Plato's
Philebus*

[. . .] the names of the gods [. . .] they too are **speaking
icons of the gods,** according to Democritus.

The Origin of Belief in the Gods (D207–D210)

D207 (A75) Sextus Empiricus, *Against the Natural Philosophers*

There are some people who think that it was on the basis
of the unexpected events that happen in the world that we

ναι θεῶν, ἀφ' ἧς φαίνεται εἶναι δόξης καὶ ὁ Δημόκρι-
τος· ὁρῶντες γάρ, φησί, τὰ ἐν τοῖς μετεώροις παθή-
ματα οἱ παλαιοὶ τῶν ἀνθρώπων, καθάπερ βροντὰς
καὶ ἀστραπάς, κεραυνούς τε καὶ ἄστρων συνόδους
ἡλίου τε καὶ σελήνης ἐκλείψεις, ἐδειματοῦντο, θεοὺς
οἰόμενοι τούτων αἰτίους εἶναι.

D208 (< A76) Plin. *Nat. hist.* 2.14

innumeros quidem credere [. . .] aut, ut Democrito
placuit, duos omnino, Poenam et Beneficium [. . .].

D209 (< A74) Cic. *Nat. deor.*

a 1.12.29

[. . .] Democritus [. . .] tum imagines eorumque circumitus
in deorum numero refert, tum illam naturam quae imagines fundat ac mittat, tum sententiam intellegentiamque
nostram [. . .].

b 1.43.120

[. . .] Democritus [. . .] nutare videtur in natura deorum.
tum enim censet imagines divinitate praeditas inesse in
universitate rerum, tum principia mentis quae sint in
eodem universo deos esse dicit, tum animantes imagines
quae vel prodesse nobis solent vel nocere, tum ingentis
quasdam imagines tantasque ut universum mundum
conplectantur extrinsecus [. . .].

have come to conceive of gods; Democritus too seems to be of this opinion. For, he says, when ancient men saw what happens in the sky, like thunder, lightning, lightning bolts, conjunctions of stars, eclipses of the sun and moon, they became frightened and thought that gods were the causes of these things.

D208 (< A76) Pliny, *Natural History*

To believe that there are innumerable [. . .] [scil. gods] [. . .] or, [. . .] as Democritus thought, just two, Punishment and Reward [. . .].

D209 (< A74) Cicero, *On the Nature of the Gods*

a

[. . .] Democritus [. . .] sometimes counts among the gods their images and wanderings, sometimes the nature that sends forth and emits images, sometimes our judgment and intelligence [. . .].

b

[. . .] Democritus [. . .] seems to waver in his opinion concerning the nature of the gods. For at one time he thinks that images endowed with divinity exist in the universe, at another he calls gods the principles of mind that exist in the same universe, at another images endowed with life that have the custom either of benefiting or of harming us, at another certain enormous images, so large that they encompass the whole world from outside [. . .].

D210 (> B30) Clem. Alex. *Protr.* 68.5 (et *Strom.* 5.102.1 = Eus. *PE* 13.13)

[. . .] οὐκ ἀπεικότως ὁ Δημόκριτος "τῶν λογίων ἀνθρώπων ὀλίγους" φησίν "ἀνατείναντας[1] τὰς χεῖρας ἐνταῦθα, ὃν[2] νῦν ἠέρα καλέομεν οἱ Ἕλληνες, ⟨εἰπεῖν⟩[3] 'πάντα[4] Ζεὺς ἐνθυμέεται[5] καὶ πάνθ'[6] οὗτος οἶδε καὶ διδοῖ[7] καὶ ἀφαιρέεται καὶ βασιλεὺς οὗτος τῶν πάντων.'"

---

[1] ἀνατείναντας Protr.: -οντες Strom.: -αντες Eus.   [2] ὃν Clem.: οὗ Eus.   [3] ⟨εἰπεῖν⟩ nos   [4] πάντα ⟨φασί⟩ Diels: πάντα ⟨εἶπαν⟩ Reinhardt   [5] Ζεὺς ἐνθυμέεται nos: Ζεὺς μυθέεται Strom. (μυθεῖται Eus.): διαμυθεῖσθαι Protr. (Δία μυθεῖσθαι corr. Heinsius)   [6] καὶ πάνθ' Strom.: καὶ πάντα Protr.: καὶ ⟨γὰρ⟩ πάντα Stählin   [7] οἱ Ἕλληνες . . . διδοῖ locus vexatus et aliis aliter temptatus

Divination (D211–D212)

D211 (< A138) Cic. *Div.* 1.3.5

[. . .] cum [. . .] plurumisque locis gravis auctor Democritus praesensionem rerum futurarum comprobaret [. . .].

D212 (A138) Cic. *Div.* 1.57.131

Democritus autem censet sapienter instituisse veteres ut hostiarum immolatarum inspicerentur exta; quorum ex habitu atque ex colore tum salubritatis tum pestilentiae signa percipi, non numquam etiam quae sit uel sterilitas agrorum vel fertilitas futura.

D210 (> B30) Clement of Alexandria, *Proptreptic* (and *Stromata*)

[. . .] Democritus said, not implausibly, that **"a few wise men** (*logioi*), **lifting their hands toward that place that we Greeks now call the air,** ⟨said⟩, **'Zeus meditates on all things, and he knows all things, gives them, and takes them away, and he is the king of all things.'"**

Divination (D211–D212)

D211 (< A138) Cicero, *On Divination*

[. . .] since [. . .] in many passages Democritus, a weighty authority, has assented to a presentiment of future things [. . .].

D212 (A138) Cicero, *On Divination*

Democritus thinks that the ancients acted wisely in establishing that the most important internal organs of sacrificial animals be examined, for their condition and color reveal signs of health and of pestilence, and sometimes even what will be the sterility or fertility of the fields.

EARLY GREEK PHILOSOPHY VII

Mathematics (D213–D216)

D213 (< B155) Plut. *Comm. not.* 39 1079E

[. . .] Δημοκρίτῳ διαποροῦντι φυσικῶς καὶ ἐμψύχως,[1] εἰ κῶνος τέμνοιτο παρὰ τὴν βάσιν ἐπιπέδῳ, τί χρὴ διανοεῖσθαι τὰς τῶν τμημάτων ἐπιφανείας, ἴσας ἢ ἀνίσους γιγνομένας. "ἄνισοι μὲν γὰρ οὖσαι τὸν κῶνον ἀνώμαλον παρέξουσι, πολλὰς ἀποχαράξεις λαμβάνοντα βαθμοειδεῖς καὶ τραχύτητας· ἴσων δ' οὐσῶν ἴσα τμήματα ἔσται καὶ φανεῖται τὸ τοῦ κυλίνδρου πεπονθὼς ὁ κῶνος, ἐξ ἴσων συγκείμενος καὶ οὐκ ἀνίσων κύκλων, ὅπερ ἐστὶν ἀτοπώτατον." [. . . = **R110**]

[1] ἐπιτυχῶς vel εὐφυῶς Wyttenbach

D214 (ad B155) Archim. *Meth. Mech. Theor.* 2.430.1–9

<. . . διόπερ καὶ τῶν θεωρη>μάτων τούτων <ὧν> Εὔδοξος ἐξηύρηκεν πρῶτος τὴν ἀπόδειξιν, ἐπὶ τοῦ κώνου καὶ τῆς πυραμίδος, ὅτι τρίτον μέρος ὁ μὲν κῶνος τοῦ κυλίνδρου ἡ δὲ πυραμὶς τοῦ πρίσματος τῶν βάσιν ἐχόντων τὴν αὐτὴν καὶ ὕψος ἴσον, οὐ μικρὰν ἀπονείμαι <ἄν> τις Δημοκρίτῳ μερίδα πρώτῳ τὴν ἀπόφασιν τὴν περὶ τοῦ εἰρημένου σχήματος χωρὶς ἀποδείξεως ἀποφηναμένῳ.

omnia add. Heiberg

D215 (B162) Schol. AB ad *Il.* 13.137b

Δημόκριτος δὲ τὸ κυλινδρικὸν σχῆμα ὀλοοίτροχον καλεῖ.

254

Mathematics (D213–D216)

D213 (< B155) Plutarch, *On Common Conceptions*

[. . .] Democritus poses the following difficulty in physical terms and very vividly: if a cone is cut by a surface parallel to its basis, how must one think of the surfaces of the sections? Will they be equal or unequal? If unequal, they will make the cone irregular, with a multitude of step-like incisions and asperities; but if equal, the sections will be equal and the cone, being composed of equal circles and not of unequal ones, will evidently be the same as a cylinder, which is completely absurd.

D214 (ad B155) Archimedes, *Method for Mechanical Theorems*

‹. . . wherefore of those theorems› of which Eudoxus was the first to discover the demonstration, on the cone and pyramid, viz. that the cone is the third part of the cylinder and the pyramid is the third part of the prism if these have the same basis and an equal height to theirs, a considerable part must be assigned to Democritus, who was the first person to make such an assertion regarding the above-mentioned shape [i.e. the cone in the cylinder], though without supplying a demonstration.

D215 (B162) Scholia on Homer's *Iliad*

Democritus calls the shape of a cylinder **'rolling mass.'**

D216 (< 59 A39) Vitruv. 7 *Praef.* 11

[. . .] Democritus et [. . . cf. **ANAXAG. D97**] de eadem
re scripserunt, quemadmodum oporteat ad aciem oculorum radiorumque extentionem certo loco centro consti-
tuto lineas[1] ratione naturali respondere, uti de incerta re
certae imagines aedificiorum in scaenarum picturis red-
derent speciem et quae in directis planisque frontibus sint
figurata, alia abscedentia alia prominentia esse videantur.

[1] adlineas *GH, corr. Schneider*

Poetics (D217–D224)
The Poet (D217–D221)

D217 (B18) Clem. Alex. *Strom.* 6.168.2

καὶ ὁ Δημόκριτος ὁμοίως· "ποιητὴς δὲ ἄσσα μὲν ἂν
γράφῃ μετ' ἐνθουσιασμοῦ καὶ ἱεροῦ πνεύματος,
καλὰ κάρτα ἐστίν."

D218 (< B129) *Etym. Gen.* s.v. νένωται ex Hdn. *Affect.*
(Frag. 120 Lentz)

Δημόκριτος· φρενὶ θείῃ[1] νοῦνται.

[1] φρενὶ θείῃ (vel φρενὶ θεῖα) Lobeck: φῆνι θεὰ ms.

D219 (< B17) Cic. *Div.* 1.38.80

negat enim sine furore Democritus quemquam poetam
magnum esse posse [. . .].

D216 (< 59 A39) Vitruvius, *On Architecture*

[. . .] Democritus and [. . .] wrote about the same subject [scil. as Agatharchus, viz. scene painting]: how, by taking a certain point as the center, to make the lines correspond by a natural ratio to the visual angle and the projection of the rays, in such a way that, in virtue of an object without reality, real images would produce the appearance of buildings on the scene painting, and so that what was represented on vertical and plane surfaces would seem in some cases to recede and in others to project outward.

Poetics (D217–D224)
The Poet (D217–D221)

D217 (B18) Clement of Alexandria, *Stromata*

And Democritus similarly [scil. as Plato, cf. *Ion* 534b]: **"On the one hand, whatever a poet writes with divine inspiration and sacred breath is extremely beautiful;** [scil. but on the other hand . . .]."

D218 (< B129) *Etymologicum Genuinum*

Democritus: **They** [scil. poetic creations?] **are thought of by a divine spirit.**[1]

[1] The text is uncertain and the context unknown.

D219 (< B17) Cicero, *On Divination*

Democritus says that no one can be a great poet without madness [. . .].

D220 (B16) Flav. Manl. Theod. *Metr.,* p. 19.13–14 Romanini

metrum dactylicum hexametrum inventum primitus [. . .] adserit Democritus a Musaeo [. . .].

D221 (B21) Dio *Homer.* 1 (*Oratio* 36 = 53 Arnim, vol. 2, p. 109.21–24)

Ὅμηρος φύσεως λαχὼν θεαζούσης ἐπέων κόσμον ἐτεκτήνατο παντοίων [. . .].

Exegeses of Homer (D222–D224)

D222 (< B23) Schol. A *in Il.* 7.390

τὸ 'ὡς πρὶν ὤφελλ' ἀπολέσθαι' [. . .] λέγει ὁ κῆρυξ [. . .] καθ' ἑαυτὸν καὶ ἠρέμα, ὡς Δημόκριτος ἀξιοῖ ἀπρεπὲς ἡγησάμενος τὸ φανερῶς λέγεσθαι [. . .].

D223 (< B24) Eust. *In Od.* 15.376, p. 1784.58–60

ἰστέον δὲ ὅτι ἐς τοσοῦτον ἠξιώθη λόγου τοῖς παλαιοῖς ὁ εὐνοϊκὸς οὗτος δοῦλος Εὔμαιος, ὥστε καὶ μητέρα αὐτοῦ ἐξευρίσκουσι. Δημόκριτος μὲν Πενίαν [. . .].

D220 (B16) Flavius Manlius Theodorus, *On Meters*

Democritus says [. . .] that the meter of the dactylic hexameter was first invented by Musaeus.

D221 (B21) Dio of Prusa, *On Homer*

Homer, who received as his share a nature that was divine, has constructed an ordered world (*kosmos*) **of all kinds of epic verses** [. . .].

Exegeses of Homer (D222–D224)

D222 (< B23) Scholia on Homer's *Iliad*

The herald says the phrase "if only he could have died earlier!" (*Il.* 7.390) [. . .] to himself and softly, as is thought by Democritus, who considers it inappropriate that it be spoken out clearly [. . .].

D223 (< B24) Eustathius, *Commentary on Homer's* Odyssey

One should know that this benevolent slave Eumaeus was estimated so highly by the ancients that they even invented a mother for him: for Democritus, it was Poverty [. . .].

D224 (B25) Eust. *In Od.* 12.65, p. 1713.14, 15–16

ἄλλοι δὲ Δία μὲν νοοῦσι τὸν ἥλιον [. . .], ἀμβροσίαν δὲ τὰς ἀτμίδας αἷς ὁ ἥλιος τρέφεται, καθὰ δοξάζει καὶ Δημόκριτος.

Mankind: Ethics and Politics (D225–D412)
What a Human Being Is (D225)

D225 (< B34) David. *Proleg.* 38.18

[. . .] ἐν τῷ ἀνθρώπῳ μικρῷ κόσμῳ ὄντι κατὰ τὸν Δημόκριτον [. . .].

The Goal of Life (D226–D232)

D226 (B191) Stob. 3.1.210

ἀνθρώποισι γὰρ εὐθυμίη γίνεται μετριότητι τέρψιος καὶ βίου συμμετρίῃ· τὰ δ᾿ ἐλλείποντα¹ καὶ ὑπερβάλ-λοντα μεταπίπτειν τε φιλεῖ καὶ μεγάλας κινήσιας ἐμποιεῖν τῇ ψυχῇ. αἱ δ᾿ ἐκ μεγάλων διαστημάτων

¹ δὲ λείποντα mss., corr. Hirschig

D224 (B25) Eustathius, *Commentary on Homer's* Odyssey

Other people think that Zeus is the sun [. . .] and ambrosia the vapors by which the sun is nourished, as Democritus too supposes.[1]

   [1] Some scholars think that Democritus is cited here only for the theory of the nourishment of the sun, and not for the exegesis of Homer.

Mankind: Ethics and Politics (D225–D412)
What a Human Being Is (D225)

D225 (< B34) David, *Prolegomena*

[. . .] in man, who is **a small world** according to Democritus [. . .].[1]

   [1] David invokes Democritus with regard to a triple analogy (of Platonic inspiration) between god and master, masters and slaves, and irrational animals and slaves. But the original context of the quotation could have been physical or medical.

The Goal of Life (D226–D232)

D226 (B191) Stobaeus, *Anthology*

For contentment (*euthumia*) **comes about for human beings from the moderation of enjoyment and pro-portion** (*summetria*) **in life. Lacks and excesses tend to change** [scil. into one another] **and to produce powerful movements in the soul. Among souls, those that move from large distances** [or: intervals] **are neither**

261

κινούμεναι τῶν ψυχέων οὔτε εὐσταθέες εἰσὶν οὔτε
εὔθυμοι· ἐπὶ τοῖς δυνατοῖς οὖν δεῖ ἔχειν τὴν γνώμην
καὶ τοῖς παρεοῦσιν ἀρκέεσθαι, τῶν μὲν ζηλουμένων
καὶ θαυμαζομένων ὀλίγην μνήμην ἔχοντα καὶ τῇ
διανοίᾳ μὴ προσεδρεύοντα, τῶν δὲ ταλαιπωρεόντων
τοὺς βίους θεωρέειν, ἐννοούμενον ἃ πάσχουσι
κάρτα,[2] ὅκως ἂν τὰ παρεόντα σοι καὶ ὑπάρχοντα
μεγάλα καὶ ζηλωτὰ φαίνηται, καὶ μηκέτι πλειόνων
ἐπιθυμέοντι συμβαίνῃ κακοπαθέειν τῇ ψυχῇ. ὁ γὰρ
θαυμάζων τοὺς ἔχοντας καὶ μακαριζομένους ὑπὸ
τῶν ἄλλων ἀνθρώπων, καὶ τῇ μνήμῃ πᾶσαν ὥραν
προσεδρεύων ἀεὶ ἐπικαινουργεῖν ἀναγκάζεται, καὶ
ἐπιβάλλεσθαι δι᾽ ἐπιθυμίην τοῦ τι πρήσσειν ἀνήκε-
στον ὧν[3] νόμοι κωλύουσιν. διόπερ τὰ μὲν μὴ δίζε-
σθαι χρεών, ἐπὶ δὲ τοῖς εὐθυμέεσθαι χρεὼν παρα-
βάλλοντα τὸν ἑαυτοῦ βίον πρὸς τὸν τῶν φαυλοτέρων
πρησσόντων καὶ μακαρίζειν ἑωυτὸν ἐνθυμεύμενον ἃ
πάσχουσιν, ὁκόσῳ[4] αὐτέων βέλτιον πρήσσει τε καὶ
διάγει. ταύτης γὰρ ἐχόμενος τῆς γνώμης εὐθυμό-
τερόν τε διάξεις καὶ οὐκ ὀλίγας κῆρας ἐν τῷ βίῳ
διώσεαι, φθόνον καὶ ζῆλον καὶ δυσμενίην.

[2] κακὰ coni. Iacobs   [3] ὧν A: ᾧ M^d: ὃ Gesner
[4] ὁκόσῳ Wachsmuth.: ὅκως mss.

D227 (B189) Stob. 3.1.47

ἄριστον ἀνθρώπῳ τὸν βίον διάγειν ὡς πλεῖστα εὐθυ-

well balanced (*eustathees*) nor contented. Therefore you must direct your thought (*gnômê*) to what is possible and be satisfied with what is present, maintaining only a small memory of the things that cause envy and admiration and not sitting and watching them (*prosedreuonta*) in thought (*dianoia*), and you must observe the lives of those who are distressed, thinking of their great sufferings, so that what is present to you and what belongs to you appears to be great and enviable, and so that it no longer happens to you that, because you desire more, you suffer in your soul. For when one admires those who have riches and are considered happy by other people, and sits and constantly watches them (*prosedreuôn*) at every hour in one's memory, one is obliged always to invent something new and to desire eagerly, because of the passion to do some irreparable deed, one of those things that the laws prohibit. That is why one must not seek certain things and must be contented with regard to other ones, comparing one's own life to that of those who are less successful, and must consider oneself happy, reflecting upon what they suffer, to what degree one succeeds and passes one's life better than they do. For if you hold fast to this thought (*gnômê*), you will pass your life with greater contentment and you will drive away quite a few sources of destruction in life, envy, rivalry, and hostility.

D227 (B189) Stobaeus, *Anthology*

The best thing for a man is to pass his life as far as possible

μηθέντι καὶ ἐλάχιστα ἀνιηθέντι. τοῦτο δ᾽ ἂν εἴη, εἴ τις
μὴ ἐπὶ τοῖς θνητοῖσι τὰς ἡδονὰς ποιοῖτο.

D228 (B3) Stob. 4.39.25

τὸν εὐθυμεῖσθαι μέλλοντα χρὴ μὴ πολλὰ πράσσειν,
μήτε ἰδίῃ μήτε ξυνῇ, μηδὲ ἄσσ᾽ ἂν πράσσῃ ὑπέρ τε
δύναμιν αἱρεῖσθαι τὴν ἑωυτοῦ καὶ φύσιν· ἀλλὰ τοσαύτην ἔχειν φυλακήν, ὥστε καὶ τῆς τύχης ἐπιβαλλού-
σης καὶ ἐς τὸ δέον[1] ὑπηγεομένης τῷ δοκεῖν κατατίθε-
σθαι, καὶ μὴ πλέω προσάπτεσθαι τῶν δυνατῶν· ἡ
γὰρ εὐογκίη ἀσφαλέστερον τῆς μεγαλογκίης.

[1] πλέον Orelli

D229 (< A1) Diog. Laert. 9.45

τέλος δ᾽ εἶναι τὴν εὐθυμίαν [. . . = **R99**] καθ᾽ ἣν γαλη-
νῶς καὶ εὐσταθῶς ἡ ψυχὴ διάγει, ὑπὸ μηδενὸς ταρατ-
τομένη φόβου ἢ δεισιδαιμονίας ἢ ἄλλου τινὸς πάθους.
καλεῖ δ᾽ αὐτὴν καὶ **εὐεστὼ** καὶ πολλοῖς ἄλλοις ὀνόμασι.

D230 (< A169) Cic. *Fin.* 5.29.87

ideo enim ille summum bonum εὐθυμίαν et saepe ἀθαμ-
βίαν appellat, id est animum terrore liberum.

in contentment (euthumêthenti) *and as little as possible in distress* (aniêthenti). *This will be the case if one does not set one's pleasures upon mortal things.*

D228 (B3) Stobaeus, *Anthology*

He who intends to live in contentment (euthumeisthai) *should not do many things, either on his own or in common with others, nor, whatever he does, should he choose what is beyond his own capability and nature; but he should be so much on his guard that even if fortune strikes and guides him toward what ought to be done, by means of his thinking he deposits it safely and does not try to grasp more than what is possible. For the right mass is safer than a large mass.*

D229 (< A1) Diogenes Laertius

The goal is **contentment** (*euthumia*) [. . .], the state by virtue of which the soul lives in serenity and equilibrium, without being disturbed by any fear, superstition, or other affection. He calls this **well-being** (*euestô*) and many other terms.

D230 (< A169) Cicero, *On Ends*

And that is why he calls the greatest good **contentment** (*euthumia*) and often **unastoundedness** (*athambia*), that is, a spirit free of terror.

D231 (A167) Stob. 2.7.3i

Δημόκριτος καὶ Πλάτων κοινῶς ἐν τῇ ψυχῇ τὴν εὐδαιμονίαν τίθενται. γέγραφε δ' ὁ μὲν οὕτως· [. . . =
D237, D238] · τὴν δ'[1] εὐθυμίαν καὶ εὐεστὼ καὶ ἁρμο-
νίαν, συμμετρίαν τε καὶ ἀταραξίαν καλεῖ· συνίστασθαι δ' αὐτὴν ἐκ τοῦ διορισμοῦ καὶ τῆς διακρίσεως
τῶν ἡδονῶν· καὶ τοῦτ' εἶναι τὸ κάλλιστόν τε καὶ συμ-
φορώτατον ἀνθρώποις.

[1] τὴν δ' ‹εὐδαιμονίαν καὶ› Meineke

D232 (B140) Hesych. E.6809

εὐεστώ· [. . .] εὐδαιμονία· ἀπὸ τοῦ εὖ ἑστάναι τὸν
οἶκον.

Body and Soul (D233–D240)

D233 Plut.

a (B159) *Libid. et aegrit.* 2

ἔοικε παλαιά τις αὕτη τῷ σώματι διαδικασία πρὸς
τὴν ψυχὴν περὶ τῶν παθῶν εἶναι. καὶ Δημόκριτος μὲν
ἐπὶ τὴν ψυχὴν ἀναφέρων ‹τὴν αἰτίαν τοῦ› κακοδαι-
μον‹εῖν›[1] φησίν, εἰ τοῦ σώματος αὐτῇ[2] δίκην λαχόν-
τος, παρὰ πάντα τὸν βίον ὧν ὠδύνηται ‹καὶ›[3] κακῶς
πέπονθεν αὐτὸς γένοιτο τοῦ ἐγκλήματος δι‹καστής›,[4]
ἡδέως ἂν καταψηφίσασθαι τῆς ψυχῆς, ἐφ' οἷς τὰ μὲν
ἀπώλεσε[5] τοῦ σώματος ταῖς ἀμελείαις καὶ ἐξέλυσε

D231 (A167) Stobaeus, *Anthology*

Democritus and Plato both locate happiness in the soul. The former writes, "[. . . = **D237, D238**]." This [scil. happiness] he also calls **contentment** (*euthumia*), **well-being** (*euestô*), and **harmony, equilibrium** and **imperturbability** (*ataraxia*). It comes from the delimitation and distinction of pleasures, and this is the finest and most useful thing for human beings.

D232 (B140) Hesychius, *Lexicon*

Well-being (*euestô*): [. . .] happiness, deriving from "the house is in good shape."

Body and Soul (D233–D240)

D233 Plutarch

a (B159) *On Desire and Grief*

This lawsuit of the body against the soul regarding the affections seems to be ancient. Democritus, ascribing ‹the cause of› unhappiness to the soul, says that if the body were permitted to file a lawsuit against it [i.e. the soul] because of what it had suffered ‹and› how it had been mistreated during the course of its whole life, and if he [i.e. apparently: the man in question] were himself made ‹judge› of the accusation, he would gladly condemn the soul for having destroyed some parts of the body by its

---

¹ κακοδαίμων mss., corr. Ziegler, alii alia   ² ἡ. . . αὕτη mss., corr. Wyttenbach   ³ ‹καὶ› Tyrrell   ⁴ δι‹καστής› Tyrrell: lac. 3–7 litt. mss.   ⁵ ἀπέλυσε mss., corr. Wyttenbach

ταῖς μέθαις, τὰ δὲ κατέφθειρε καὶ διέσπασε ταῖς φι-
ληδονίαις, ὥσπερ ὀργάνου τινὸς ἢ σκεύους κακῶς
ἔχοντος τὸν χρώμενον ἀφειδῶς αἰτιασάμενος.

b (< B159) *Sanit. praec.* 24 135E

πρὸς τούτους γὰρ οἶμαι μάλιστα τὸν Δημόκριτον εἰπεῖν, ὡς εἰ τὸ σῶμα δικάσαιτο τῇ ψυχῇ κακώσεως,
οὐκ ἂν αὐτὴν ἀποφυγεῖν.

D234 (B223) Stob. 3.10.65

ὧν τὸ σκῆνος χρῄζει, πᾶσι πάρεστιν εὐμαρέως ἄτερ
μόχθου καὶ ταλαιπωρίης· ὁκόσα δὲ μόχθου καὶ ταλαι-
πωρίης χρῄζει καὶ βίον ἀλγύνει, τούτων οὐκ ἱμείρεται
τὸ σκῆνος, ἀλλ᾽ ἡ τῆς γνώμης κακοηθίη.[1]

[1] κακοηθίη Gesner: κακοθηγία SA: καθοδιγίη Mᵈ: κακοθι-
γίη dub. Diels

D235 (B31) Clem. Alex. *Paed.* 1.2.6.2

ἰατρικὴ μὲν γὰρ κατὰ Δημόκριτον σώματος νόσους
ἀκέεται, σοφίη δὲ ψυχὴν παθῶν ἀφαιρεῖται.

D236 (B187) Stob. 3.1.27 (cf. Democrat. *Sent.* 2)

ἀνθρώποις ἁρμόδιον ψυχῆς μᾶλλον ἢ σώματος λόγον
ποιεῖσθαι. ψυχὴ μὲν γὰρ τελεωτάτη σκήνεος μοχθη-
ρίην ὀρθοῖ, σκήνεος δὲ ἰσχὺς ἄνευ λογισμοῦ ψυχὴν
οὐδέν τι ἀμείνω τίθησιν.

negligence and enfeebled it by drinking-bouts, and for having ruined and ripped to pieces other parts by its desire for pleasure, just as, if an instrument or tool were in bad shape, he would accuse the man who used it without taking proper care of it.

b (< B159) *Advice about Keeping Well*

[. . .] For it was with regard to these [i.e. various kinds of people harmful to society], I believe, that Democritus said that if the body filed a lawsuit against the soul for mistreatment the latter would not be acquitted.

D234 (B223) Stobaeus, *Anthology*

What the body requires is easily available to all without toil (mokhthos) or suffering (talaiporiê); but what requires toil and suffering and makes life painful, is desired not by the body but by a bad disposition of judgment.

D235 (B31) Clement of Alexandria, *Pedagogue*

Medicine, according to Democritus, cures the illnesses of the body, but wisdom removes the soul from its affections [or: sufferings].

D236 (B187) Stobaeus, *Anthology*

For humans it is fitting to take account of the soul more than of the body. For perfection of the soul corrects the bad condition of the bodily envelope (skênos), while strength of the body, devoid of reasoning, does not make the soul better at all.

269

D237 (B170) Stob. 2.7.3i

εὐδαιμονίη ψυχῆς καὶ κακοδαιμονίη.

D238 (B171) Stob. 2.7.3i

εὐδαιμονίη οὐκ ἐν βοσκήμασιν οἰκεῖ, οὐδὲ ἐν χρυσῷ·
ψυχὴ[1] οἰκητήριον δαίμονος.

[1] ψυχὴ ⟨δ'⟩ Heeren

D239 (B290) Stob. 4.44.67

λύπην ἀδέσποτον ψυχῆς ναρκώσης λογισμῷ ἔκκρουε.

D240 (B234) Stob. 3.18.30

ὑγιηίην εὐχῇσι[1] παρὰ θεῶν αἰτέονται ἄνθρωποι, τὴν
δὲ ταύτης δύναμιν ἐν ἑωυτοῖς ἔχοντες οὐκ ἴσασιν·
ἀκρασίη δὲ τἀναντία πρήσσοντες αὐτοὶ προδόται τῆς
ὑγιηίης τῇσιν ἐπιθυμίῃσι γίνονται.

[1] ὑγιηίην εὐχῇσι Meineke (ὑγιείην εὐχαῖς Gesner ex
Frobenio): ὑγιεινὴν εὐχὴν mss.

Pleasure (D241–D250)

D241 (B188) Stob. 3.1.46

ὅρος συμφόρων καὶ ἀσυμφόρων[1] τέρψις καὶ ἀτερπίη.

[1] συμφορέων καὶ ἀσυμφορέων mss., corr. Cobet

D237 (B170) Stobaeus, *Anthology*

Happiness belongs to the soul, and unhappiness too.

D238 (B171) Stobaeus, *Anthology*

Happiness (eudaimoniê) *does not reside in flocks nor in gold: the soul is the residence of a divinity* (daimôn).

D239 (B290) Stobaeus, *Anthology*

The unmastered pain of a numbed soul—repel it by reasoning.

D240 (B234) Stobaeus, *Anthology*

In their prayers, men ask for health from the gods, but they do not know that they possess the capacity for possessing this within themselves; doing the opposite because of their intemperance, they themselves betray their health by their desires.

Pleasure (D241–D250)

D241 (B188) Stobaeus, *Anthology*

The dividing line between what is useful and what is useless is satisfaction (terpsis) *and dissatisfaction.*

D242 (B207) Stob. 3.5.22

ἡδονὴν οὐ πᾶσαν, ἀλλὰ τὴν ἐπὶ τῷ καλῷ αἱρεῖσθαι χρεών.

D243 (B194) Stob. 3.3.46

αἱ μεγάλαι τέρψιες[1] ἀπὸ τοῦ θεᾶσθαι τὰ καλὰ τῶν ἔργων γίνονται.

[1] τέρψιες Orelli: θέρψεις ed. Trincav.: desunt mss.

D244 (B211) Stob. 3.5.27

σωφροσύνη τὰ τερπνὰ ἀέξει καὶ ἡδονὴν ἐπιμείζονα[1] ποιεῖ.

[1] ἔτι μείζονα Diels

D245 (B146) Plut. *Quis suos* 10 81A

[. . .] τὸν λόγον [. . .] κατὰ Δημόκριτον αὐτὸν ἐξ ἑαυτοῦ τὰς τέρψιας ἐθιζόμενον λαμβάνειν.

D246 (B233) Stob. 3.17.38

εἴ τις ὑπερβάλλοι τὸ μέτριον, τὰ ἐπιτερπέστατα ἀτερπέστατα ἂν γίγνοιτο.

D247 (B232) Stob. 3.17.37

τῶν ἡδέων τὰ σπανιώτατα γινόμενα μάλιστα τέρπει.

D242 (B207) Stobaeus, *Anthology*

It is necessary to choose not every pleasure, but that one which depends upon what is fine.

D243 (B194) Stobaeus, *Anthology*

Great satisfactions (terpsies) *come about from observing fine actions.*

D244 (B211) Stobaeus, *Anthology*

Temperance increases satisfactions (terpna) *and makes pleasure even greater.*

D245 (B146) Plutarch, *Progress in Virtue*

[. . .] reason [. . .] according to Democritus, is accustomed to derive satisfactions (*terpsies*) from itself.

D246 (B233) Stobaeus, *Anthology*

If someone exceeds the right measure, the greatest satisfactions become the greatest dissatisfactions.

D247 (B232) Stobaeus, *Anthology*

Among pleasures, the ones that happen most rarely satisfy the most.

D248 (B235) Stob. 3.18.35 (cf. 3.6.65)

ὅσοι ἀπὸ γαστρὸς τὰς ἡδονὰς ποιέονται ὑπερβεβλη-
κότες τὸν καιρὸν ἐπὶ βρώσεσιν ἢ πόσεσιν ἢ ἀφροδι-
σίοισιν, τούτοισι[1] πᾶσιν αἱ μὲν ἡδοναὶ βραχέαι τε καὶ
δι᾽ ὀλίγου γίνονται, ὁκόσον ἂν χρόνον ἐσθίωσιν ἢ
πίνωσιν, αἱ δὲ λῦπαι πολλαί. τοῦτο μὲν γὰρ τὸ ἐπι-
θυμεῖν ἀεὶ τῶν αὐτῶν πάρεστι, καὶ ὁκόταν γένηται
ὁκοίων ἐπιθυμέουσι, διὰ ταχέος τε ἡ ἡδονὴ παροίχε-
ται, καὶ οὐδὲν ἐν[2] αὐτοῖσι χρηστόν ἐστιν ἀλλ᾽ ἢ τέρψις βραχεῖα καὶ αὖθις τῶν αὐτῶν δέει.

[1] τούτοισι 3.6.65: τοῖσι ms.   [2] ἐν secl. Hense

D249 (B127) Hdn. *Prosod. cath.* in Eust. *In Od.* 11.428,
p. 1766.7–8

καὶ Δημόκριτος· ξυόμενοι ἄνθρωποι ἥδονται καὶ
σφιν γίνεται ἅπερ τοῖς ἀφροδισιάζουσιν.

D250 (B147) Clem. Alex. *Protr.* 92.4

ὕες [. . .] "ἐπὶ φορυτῷ μαργαίνουσιν" κατὰ Δημόκριτον.

Desires (D251–D266)
Self-Sufficiency (D251–D255)

D251 (B224) Stob. 3.10.68

⟨ἡ⟩[1] τοῦ πλέονος ἐπιθυμίη τὸ παρεὸν ἀπόλλυσι, τῇ
Αἰσωπίῃ κυνὶ ἰκέλη γιγνομένη.

D248 (B235) Stobaeus, *Anthology*

*For all those who derive their pleasures from the belly, exceeding the proper measure (*kairos*) in eating, drinking, or sex, their pleasures are small and short-lived, lasting as long a time as they eat or drink, but their sufferings are many. For this desire is always present for the same things, and whenever what they desire occurs, the pleasure departs quickly, and there is nothing of value in them except for a brief satisfaction, and once again a need for the same things arises.*

D249 (B127) Herodian, *General Prosody*, in Eustathius, *Commentary on Homer's* Odyssey

And Democritus: **When men scratch themselves they feel pleasure, and they feel like those who are having sex.**

D250 (B147) Clement of Alexandria, *Protreptic*

Pigs [. . .] **go mad for rubbish,** according to Democritus.[1]

[1] This fragment, a reprise of Heraclitus (cf. **HER. D80a**), is cited by many ancient authors.

Desires (D251–D266)
Self-Sufficiency (D251–D255)

D251 (B224) Stobaeus, *Anthology*

The desire for what is more destroys what is present, revealing itself to be like the dog in Aesop.[1]

[1] Cf. Fable 233 Halm, 185 Chambry.

---

[1] ⟨ἤ⟩ Br: om. cett.

D252 (B176) Stob. 2.9.5

τύχη μεγαλόδωρος, ἀλλ᾽ ἀβέβαιος, φύσις δὲ αὐτάρ-
κης· διόπερ νικᾷ τῷ ἥσσονι καὶ βεβαίῳ τὸ μεῖζον τῆς
ἐλπίδος.

D253 (B231) Stob. 3.17.25

εὐγνώμων ὁ μὴ λυπεόμενος ἐφ᾽ οἷσιν οὐκ ἔχει, ἀλλὰ
χαίρων ἐφ᾽ οἷσιν ἔχει.

D254 (B246) Stob. 3.40.6

ξενιτείη βίου αὐτάρκειαν διδάσκει· μᾶζα γὰρ καὶ στι-
βὰς λιμοῦ καὶ κόπου γλυκύτατα ἰάματα.

D255 (B209) Stob. 3.5.25 (et al.)

αὐταρκείη τροφῆς[1] σμικρὴ[2] νὺξ οὐδέποτε γίνεται.

[1] αὐταρκείη τροφῆς Max. Conf. 13.17: αὐτάρκει τροφῇ mss.
[2] σμικρὴ M (-ὰ A, μικ-L): μακρὴ Hense

Wealth and Poverty (D256–D264)

D256 (B285) Stob. 4.34.65

γιγνώσκειν χρεὼν ἀνθρωπίνην βιοτὴν ἀφαυρήν τε
ἐοῦσαν καὶ ὀλιγοχρόνιον, πολλῇσί τε κηρσὶ συμπε-
φυρμένην καὶ ἀμηχανίῃσιν, ὅκως ἄν τις[1] μετρίης τε
κτήσιος ἐπιμέληται καὶ μετρῆται[2] ἐπὶ τοῖς ἀναγκαίοις
ἡ ταλαιπωρίη.[3]

ATOMISTS (LEUCIPPUS, DEMOCRITUS)

D252 (B176) Stobaeus, *Anthology*

Fortune bestows big gifts but is instable; but nature is self-sufficient, which is why it gains the victory, by being less and stable, over what is bigger and belongs to hope.

D253 (B231) Stobaeus, *Anthology*

He has good judgment who does not suffer for what he does not have but rejoices at what he does have.

D254 (B246) Stobaeus, *Anthology*

Living abroad [scil. probably: as a mercenary] teaches self-sufficiency in life. For a loaf of barley bread and some straw are the most pleasant remedies for hunger and fatigue.

D255 (B209) Stobaeus, *Anthology*

For self-sufficiency in food, the night is never short (?).[1]

> [1] Meaning obscure, text uncertain.

Wealth and Poverty (D256–D264)

D256 (B285) Stobaeus, *Anthology*

It is necessary to recognize that human life is feeble and of short duration, and is mixed together with many sources of ruin and difficulties, so that one should care about moderate possessions and so that suffering should be measured in relation to necessities.

---

[1] πρὸς mss., corr. Mullach   [2] ἀμέτρητα Diels
[3] ἀναγκαίοις ἡ ταλαιπωρίη ut vid. S: ἀναγκαίοις ἡ ταλαιπωρέη MA: ἀναγκαίοισι ταλαιπωρέη Meineke

D257 (B219) Stob. 3.10. 43

χρημάτων ὄρεξις, ἢν μὴ ὁρίζηται κόρῳ,[1] πενίης ἐσχάτης πολλὸν χαλεπωτέρη· μέζονες γὰρ ὀρέξεις μέζονας ἐνδείας ποιεῦσιν.

[1] καίρῳ coni. Meineke, οὔρῳ Hirschig, λόγῳ Iacobs

D258 (B283) Stob. 4.33.23

πενίη πλοῦτος ὀνόματα ἐνδείης καὶ κόρου. οὔτε οὖν πλούσιος ‹ὁ›[1] ἐνδέων οὔτε πένης ὁ μὴ ἐνδέων.

[1] ‹ὁ› Orelli

D259 (B284) Stob. 4.33.24 et 25

ἢν μὴ πολλῶν ἐπιθυμέῃς, τὰ ὀλίγα τοι πολλὰ δόξει. σμικρὰ γὰρ ὄρεξις πενίην ἰσοσθενέα πλούτῳ ποιέει.

D260 (B198) Stob. 3.4.72

τὸ χρῇζον οἶδεν ὁκόσον χρῄζει, ὁ δὲ χρῄζων οὐ γινώσκει.

D261 (B78) Stob. 4.31.121 (= Democrat. Sent. 43)

χρήματα πορίζειν μὲν οὐκ ἀχρεῖον, ἐξ ἀδικίης δὲ πάντων[1] κάκιον.

[1] πάντων A: πάντως SM

D257 (B219) Stobaeus, *Anthology*

The appetite (orexis) for wealth, if it is not limited by satiety, is much harder to endure than extreme poverty. For greater appetites create greater needs.

D258 (B283) Stobaeus, *Anthology*

Poverty, wealth: names for need and satiety. So the man in need is not wealthy, nor poor the one not in need.

D259 (B284) Stobaeus, *Anthology*

If you do not desire many things, few will seem to you to be many; for a small appetite makes poverty as strong as wealth.

D260 (B198) Stobaeus, *Anthology*

That which needs knows how much it needs, but he who needs does not know.[1]

[1] The meaning is obscure, perhaps the sentence is incomplete. Scholars often suppose that the opposition between neuter and masculine refers to that between animal and human.

D261 (B78) Stobaeus, *Anthology* (attributed to Democrates)

To acquire wealth is not useless, but [scil. to do so] unjustly is the worst thing of all.

D262 (B282) Stob. 4.31.120

χρημάτων χρῆσις ξὺν νόῳ μὲν χρήσιμον εἰς τὸ ἐλευ-
θέριον εἶναι καὶ δημωφελέα, ξὺν ἀνοίῃ δὲ χορηγίη
ξυνή.[1]

   [1] ξυνή mss.: κενεή Gomperz

D263 (B218, cf. B302.194) Stob. 3.10.36

πλοῦτος ἀπὸ κακῆς ἐργασίης περιγινόμενος ἐπιφανέ-
στερον τὸ ὄνειδος κέκτηται.

D264 (B281) Stob. 4.31.49

ὥσπερ ἐν[1] τοῖς ἕλκεσι φαγέδαινα κάκιστον νόσημα,
οὕτως ἐν τοῖς χρήμασι τὸ †μὴ προσαρμόσαν καὶ τὸ
συνεχές†.[2]

   [1] ἐν Natorp: ἐν μὲν S: μὲν MA   [2] post τὸ lac. indic. et
μὴ προσαρμόσαν καὶ τὸ συνεχές ut gloss. secl. Philippson qui
μὴ λήγειν πλούτου ἐπιθυμέοντα prop.: μὴ προσαρμόσασθαι
τοῖς ἄν ἔχῃς ⟨τὴν δαπάνην⟩ prop. Diels

Love and Sex (D265–D266)

D265 (B271) Stob. 4.20.33

ἐρωτικὴν μέμψιν ἡ ἀγαπωμένη[1] λύει.

   [1] ἀγαπωμένη mss., corruptum iud. Hense: ἀγάπη (εὐνὴ
Meineke, στρωμνὴ Haupt, εὐεστὼ Mekler) μούνη Nauck:
ἀγαπῶ μόνη Diels

D262 (B282) Stobaeus, *Anthology*

*The use of wealth in conjunction with intelligence is useful
for being generous and beneficial for the common people,
but in conjunction with lack of intelligence it is a public
contribution shared in common (?).*[1]

[1] Meaning uncertain.

D263 (B218, cf. B302.194) Stobaeus, *Anthology*

*Wealth deriving from a sordid activity acquires blame
more visibly.*

D264 (B281) Stobaeus, *Anthology*

*Just as, among ulcers, cancer is the worst disease, so too
among kinds of wealth †that which is unadapted and con-
tinuous†.*

Love and Sex (D265–D266)

D265 (B271) Stobaeus, *Anthology*

*A woman regarded with affection dissolves the blame at-
taching to sexual desire (erôs).*

D266 (B73) Stob. 3.5.23 (= Democrat. *Sent.* 38)

δίκαιος ἔρως, ἀνυβρίστως ἐφίεσθαι τῶν καλῶν.

Good and Evil Things (D267–D273)

D267 (< B149) Plut. *Anim. an corp. aff.* 2 500D

ἂν δὲ σαυτὸν ἀνοίξῃς ἔνδοθεν, ποικίλον τι καὶ πολυπαθὲς κακῶν ταμιεῖον εὑρήσεις καὶ θησαύρισμα, ὥς φησι Δημόκριτος, οὐκ ἔξωθεν ἐπιρρεόντων [. . .].

D268 (B172) Stob. 2.9.1

ἀφ᾽ ὧν ἡμῖν τἀγαθὰ γίνεται, ἀπὸ τῶν αὐτῶν τούτων καὶ τὰ κακὰ ἐπαυρισκοίμεθ᾽ ἄν,[1] τῶν δὲ κακῶν ἐκτὸς εἴημεν.[2] αὐτίκα ὕδωρ βαθὺ εἰς πολλὰ χρήσιμον καὶ δῆτε κακόν, κίνδυνος γὰρ ἀποπνιγῆναι· μηχανὴ οὖν εὑρέθη, νήχεσθαι διδάσκειν.[3]

[1] ἐπαυρισκοίμεθα τῶν mss., corr. Meineke   [2] post εἴημεν lac. stat. Heeren: εἰδήμονες seu εἶναι εἰδήμονος coni. Wachsmuth   [3] νήχεσθαι διδάσκειν mss.: νήχεσθαι καὶ πλέειν Usener: νήχειν διδάσκεσθαι Meineke

D269 (B173) Stob. 2.9.2

ἀνθρώποισι κακὰ ἐξ ἀγαθῶν φύεται, ἐπήν τις τἀγαθὰ μὴ ᾽πιστῆται ποδηγετεῖν μηδὲ ὀχεῖν εὐπόρως. οὐ[1] δίκαιον <ὦν>[2] ἐν κακοῖσι τὰ τοιάδε κρίνειν, ἀλλ᾽ ἐν ἀγα-

D266 (B73) Stobaeus, *Anthology* (attributed to Demo-crates)

A just desire (erôs): to crave beautiful things without ar-rogant excess.

Good and Evil Things (D267–D273)

D267 (< B149) Plutarch, *Do the Passions Come from the Soul or the Body?*

If you open yourself up inside, you will find a kind of trea-sury and storeroom of evils, variegated and full of suf-ferings [or: passions], as Democritus says, which do not come from outside [. . .].

D268 (B172) Stobaeus, *Anthology*

The source of our good things is the same one from which we could derive evil ones too, but remaining outside of the evils. For example, deep water is useful for many things but also inversely it is evil: for there is a danger of drown-ing. So a resource was discovered: to teach people how to swim.

D269 (B173) Stobaeus, *Anthology*

For humans, evils are born by nature from good things, when someone does not know how to guide good things and ride them easily. It is not justified to count such things

---

1 οὐδὲ Heeren
2 ‹ὧν› Hense, ‹δὲ› Meineke

θοῖσι·[3] τοῖσι δὲ[4] ἀγαθοῖσι οἷόν τε χρῆσθαι καὶ πρὸς τὰ κακά, εἴ τινι βουλομένῳ, ἀλκῇ.[5]

[3] ὧν post ἀγαθοῖσιν del. Koen: ὧν Diels: χρεὼν Meineke
[4] τοῖς τε mss., corr. Wachsmuth   [5] εἴ τινι βουλομένῳ (βουλόμενον F) ἀλκὴν mss., corr. Diels: ᾧ τινι βουλομένῳ ἂν εἴη Usener cum Meineke, εἴ τινι βουλομένῳ ἂν ᾖ Koen

D270 (B221) Stob. 3.10.58

ἐλπὶς κακοῦ κέρδεος ἀρχὴ ζημίης.

D271 (B220) Stob. 3.10.44

κακὰ κέρδεα ζημίαν ἀρετῆς φέρει.

D272 (B196) Stob. 3.4.70

λήθη τῶν ἰδίων κακῶν θρασύτητα γεννᾷ.

D273 (B108) Stob. 4.34.58 (= Democrat. *Sent.* 75)

διζημένοισι τἀγαθὰ μόλις παραγίνεται, τὰ δὲ κακὰ καὶ μὴ διζημένοισι.

Fortune (D274–D279)

D274 (< B119) Dion. Alex. *Nat.* in Eus. *PE* 14.27.5 (cf. Stob. 2.8.16)

[. . .] τῶν γοῦν Ὑποθηκῶν ἀρχόμενος λέγει·[1]

ἄνθρωποι τύχης εἴδωλον ἐπλάσαντο πρόφασιν

among evils, but rather among good things. And it is pos-
sible to make use of good things, if one will, as a defense
against evils.

D270 (B221) Stobaeus, *Anthology*

The hope for evil gain is the beginning of loss [or: punish-
ment].

D271 (B220) Stobaeus, *Anthology*

Evil gains bring the loss [or: punishment] of virtue.

D272 (B196) Stobaeus, *Anthology*

Forgetfulness of one's own evils generates impudence.

D273 (B108) Stobaeus, *Anthology* (attributed to Democrates)

Good things come only with difficulty to those who seek
them, but evils [scil. come] even to those who do not seek
them.

Fortune (D274–D279)

D274 (< B119) Dionysius of Alexandria, *On Nature,* in
Eusebius, *Evangelical Preparation*

[. . .] he [scil. Democritus] says at the beginning of his
Precepts,

Humans have fabricated an image of fortune

---

[1] τῶν . . . λέγει hab. solus Dion. Alex., qui Democriti
sententiam paraphrasi ampliat

ἰδίης ἀβουλίης. βαιὰ γὰρ φρονήσει τύχη μά-
χεται, τὰ δὲ πλεῖστα ἐν βίῳ εὐξύνετος ὀξυδερ-
κείη κατιθύνει.

D275 (B269) Stob. 4.10.28

τόλμα πρήξιος ἀρχή, τύχη δὲ τέλεος κυρίη.

D276 (B288*) Stob. 4.41.59

οὐκ ἔστιν οὕτως ἀσφαλὴς πλούτου πυλεών, ὃν οὐκ
ἀνοίγει[1] τύχης καιρός.

  [1] ἀνοίγει S: ἐπανοίγει MA

D277 (B210) Stob. 3.5.26

τράπεζαν πολυτελέα μὲν τύχη παρατίθησιν, αὐταρ-
κέα δὲ σωφροσύνη.

D278 (B286) Stob. 4.39.17

εὐτυχὴς ὁ ἐπὶ μετρίοισι χρήμασιν εὐθυμεόμενος, δυσ-
τυχὴς δὲ ὁ ἐπὶ πολλοῖσι δυσθυμεόμενος.

D279 (B293) Stob. 4.48.10

οἷσιν ἡδονὴν ἔχουσιν αἱ τῶν πέλας ξυμφοραί, οὐ ξυν-
ιᾶσι μὲν ὡς τὰ τῆς τύχης κοινὰ πᾶσιν, ἀπορέουσι δὲ
οἰκηίης χαρᾶς.

as a screen for their own imprudence (*abouliê*). **For only rarely does fortune fight against prudence** (*phronêsis*), **and most of the things in life an intelligent sharp-sightedness straightens out.**

D275 (B269) Stobaeus, *Anthology*

Audacity begins an action, but fortune is in charge of its end.

D276 (B288*) Stobaeus, *Anthology*

There is no portal for wealth so secure that it cannot be opened by the opportunities of fortune.

D277 (B210) Stobaeus, *Anthology*

Fortune sets an abundant table, temperance a self-sufficient one.

D278 (B286) Stobaeus, *Anthology*

Fortunate is he who is contented with moderate wealth, unfortunate he who is discontented with much.

D279 (B293) Stobaeus, *Anthology*

Those who derive pleasure from the adversities of their neighbors not only do not understand that what belongs to fortune is shared by all people in common, but also they are deprived (aporeousi) *of their own joy.*

Life and Death (D280–D292)

D280 (B160) Porph. *Abst.* 4.21.6

τὸ γὰρ κακῶς ζῆν καὶ μὴ φρονίμως καὶ σωφρόνως
καὶ ὁσίως Δημόκριτος[1] ἔλεγεν οὐ κακῶς ζῆν εἶναι,
ἀλλὰ πολὺν χρόνον ἀποθνήσκειν.

[1] Δημόκριτος coni. Reiske ; Δημοκράτης mss.

D281 (B1a) Philod. *Mort.* 28.27–33

[27] τῆς δ᾽ αὐ[τῆς ἀλγη]δόνος ἔχετ[αι κατὰ] | Δημό-
κριτο[ν καὶ] τὸ δυσωπε[ῖσθαι . .] | διὰ τὴν οσο [.]
αντ[. . .]νιτουσ [. . . . . .] | [.]ας [. . .] καὶ [δ]υσμο[ρφ]
ίας· καταφέρονται γὰρ ἐπὶ [το]ιοῦτο πάθος ὡς [κ]αὶ
τῶ[ν] |μετὰ τ[ῆς εὐ]σαρκίας [κ]αὶ τοῦ κάλλου[ς | ἀπο-
θνη[σκόν]των καὶ τῶν ἐκ [. . . .

Rest. Mekler, Diels, Delattre   27 αὐ[τῆς ἀλγη]δόνος
Delattre, αὐ[τῆς φλε]δόνος Amstrong-Henry, αὖ σηπε]δόνος
Mekler   29–30 διὰ τὴν ὀσφ‹ρ›αντ‹ικ›ῶν τού‹των φαν›τα-
σ‹ίαν› καὶ δυσμορφίας Diels post Mekler

D282 (B1a) Philod. *Mort.* 39.9–15

[9] εἶθ᾽ ὅταν ἐναρ|γὴς αὐτοῦ γένηται θεωρία, παράδο|
ξος αὐτοῖς ὑποπίπτει, παρ᾽ ἣν αἰτίαν | οὐδὲ διαθήκας
ὑπομένοντες γράφεσ|θαι περικατάληπτοι γίνονται καὶ
δι|ξυμφορεῖν ἀναγκάζονται κατ[ὰ] Δη|μόκριτον.

ATOMISTS (LEUCIPPUS, DEMOCRITUS)

Life and Death (D280–D292)

D280 (B160) Porphyry, *On Abstinence*

To live badly and not wisely, temperately, and piously, Democritus (?),[1] said was not to live badly but **to die over the course of a long time**.

> [1] Democrates, according to the manuscripts.

D281 (B1a) Philodemus, *On Death*

To the same sense of pain (?) belongs, according to Democritus, the feeling of disgust on account of . . . and of ugliness. For they fall into an affection of this sort when those who die with their flesh in good condition and with beauty and those who . . .

D282 (B1a) Philodemus, *On Death*

Then, when the sight of it [i.e. death] becomes manifestly visible, it befalls them unexpected. That is the reason why, not even bearing to write their testament, they are taken by surprise and obliged **to undergo a double suffering** according to Democritus.

---

rest. Mekler, Diels   13–14 διξυμφορεῖν leg. Amstrong-Henry post Crönert (δισυμφορεῖν): δίσσ᾽ ἐμφορεῖν Diels post Gomperz (δὶς ἐμφορεῖν)

D283 (B200) Stob. 3.4.74

ἀνοήμονες βιοῦσιν οὐ τερπόμενοι βιοτῇ.

D284 (B201) Stob. 3.4.75

ἀνοήμονες δηναιότητος ὀρέγονται οὐ τερπόμενοι δη-
ναιότητι.[1]

  [1] δὴ νεότητος . . . δὴ νεότητι mss., corr. Bücheler

D285 (B205) Stob. 3.4.79

ἀνοήμονες ζωῆς ὀρέγονται[1] θάνατον δεδοικότες.

  [1] post ὀρέγονται hab. mss. γήραος, del. Friedländer,
Philippson: <ἀντὶ> γήραος Gomperz: γήρας ὡς θάνατον coni.
Schenkl, γήραος κάματον Hense

D286 (B199) Stob. 3.4.73

ἀνοήμονες τὸ ζῆν ὡς στυγέοντες ζῆν ἐθέλουσι δείματι
Ἅιδεω.

D287 (B206) Stob. 3.4.80

ἀνοήμονες θάνατον δεδοικότες γηράσκειν ἐθέλουσι.

D288 (B203) Stob. 3.4.77

ἄνθρωποι[1] τὸν θάνατον φεύγοντες διώκουσιν.

  [1] ἀνόητοι vel ἀνοήμονες coni. Meineke

D283 (B200) Stobaeus, *Anthology*

Thoughtless people live without enjoying life.

D284 (B201) Stobaeus, *Anthology*

Thoughtless people desire duration without deriving satisfaction (terpomenoi) *from duration.*

D285 (B205) Stobaeus, *Anthology*

Thoughtless people desire life because they are afraid of death.

D286 (B199) Stobaeus, *Anthology*

Thoughtless people want to exist as though hating to exist, out of fear of Hades.

D287 (B206) Stobaeus, *Anthology*

Thoughtless people, fearing death, want to grow old.

D288 (B203) Stobaeus, *Anthology*

People that flee death are pursuing it.

D289 (B297) Stob. 4.52.40 (cf. 4.34.62)

ἔνιοι θνητῆς φύσεως διάλυσιν οὐκ εἰδότες ἄνθρωποι,
συνειδήσει δὲ τῆς ἐν τῷ βίῳ κακοπραγμοσύνης, τὸν
τῆς βιοτῆς χρόνον ἐν ταραχαῖς καὶ φόβοις ταλαι-
πωροῦσι, ψεύδεα περὶ τοῦ μετὰ τὴν τελευτὴν μυθο-
πλαστέοντες χρόνου.

D290 (B295) Stob. 4.50.22

ὁ γέρων νέος ἐγένετο, ὁ δὲ νέος ἄδηλον εἰ ἐς γῆρας
ἀφίξεται· τὸ τέλειον οὖν ἀγαθὸν τοῦ μέλλοντος ἔτι[1]
καὶ ἀδήλου κρέσσον.

[1] ἔτι Diels: εἰ mss.

D291 (B296) Stob. 4.50.76

γῆρας ὁλόκληρός ἐστι πήρωσις· πάντ᾽ ἔχει καὶ πᾶσιν
ἐνδεῖ.

D292 (B230) Stob. 3.16.22

βίος ἀνεόρταστος μακρὴ ὁδὸς ἀπανδόκευτος.

Wisdom and Folly (D293–D310)

D293 (B2) *Tritogeneia* (cf. **D2b** I.4)

a *Etym. Orion.*, p. 153.5

Τριτογένεια. ἡ Ἀθηνᾶ. κατὰ Δημόκριτον, φρόνησις

292

D289 (B297) Stobaeus, *Anthology*

Some people, ignorant of the dissolution of mortal nature, but aware of the adversity that affects life, suffer during the time of their life in troubles and fears, fabricating false myths about the time after death.

D290 (B295) Stobaeus, *Anthology*

The old man used to be young, but as for the young man, it is unclear whether he will arrive at old age. So a fulfilled good is better than one that is still to come and is unclear.

D291 (B296) Stobaeus, *Anthology*

Old age is a mutilation intact in all its parts: it has all things and it lacks all things.

D292 (B230) Stobaeus, *Anthology*

A life without public holidays is a long road without hotels.

Wisdom and Folly (D293–D310)

D293 (B2) *Tritogeneia* (cf. **D2b** I.4)

a *Etymologicum Orionis*

Tritogeneia. Athena. According to Democritus, she is con-

νομίζεται. γίνεται δὲ ἐκ τοῦ φρονεῖν τρία ταῦτα· βου-
λεύεσθαι καλῶς, λέγειν ἀναμαρτήτως, καὶ πράττειν ἃ
δεῖ.

b *Schol. BT in Il.* 8.39

Δημόκριτος δὲ ἐτυμολογῶν τὸ ὄνομα, φησὶν ὅτι φρό-
νησίς ἐστιν, ἀφ᾽ ἧς τρία συμβαίνει, εὖ λογίζεσθαι,
λέγειν καλῶς, πράττειν ἃ δεῖ.

D294 (B289) Stob. 4.44.64

ἀλογιστίη μὴ ξυγχωρέειν ταῖσι κατὰ τὸν βίον ἀνάγ-
καις.

lemma δημοκρίτου A: δημητρίου M

D295 (B216) Stob. 3.7.74

σοφίη ἄθαμβος ἀξίη πάντων τιμιωτάτη οὖσα.[1]

[1] τιμιωτάτη οὖσα secl. H. Gomperz

D296 (B236) Stob. 3.20.56

θυμῷ μάχεσθαι μὲν χαλεπόν· ἀνδρὸς δὲ τὸ κρατέειν
εὐλογίστου.

sidered to be prudence (*phronêsis*). For out of prudent thinking (*phronein*) come about (*ginetai*) these three (*tria*) things: to deliberate well, to speak unerringly, and to do what ought to be done.

b Scholia on Homer's *Iliad*

Democritus, providing an etymology for the name [i.e. 'Tritogeneia'] says that from prudence these three things come about: to reason well, to speak well, and to do what ought to be done.

D294 (B289) Stobaeus, *Anthology*

It is a lack of intelligence not to submit to the necessities that life imposes.

D295 (B216) Stobaeus, *Anthology*

Wisdom that is unastounded is valuable, being the most honorable of all things.

D296 (B236) Stobaeus, *Anthology*

To fight against an ardor (thumos) is hard [cf. **HER. D116**]; *but it is the mark of a rational man to dominate over it.*

EARLY GREEK PHILOSOPHY VII

D297 (B197) Stob. 3.4.71

ἀνοήμονες ῥυσμοῦνται τοῖς τῆς τύχης[1] κέρδεσιν, οἱ δὲ
τῶν τοιῶνδε δαήμονες τοῖς τῆς σοφίης.

[1] τύχης Grotius: ψυχῆς ed. Trincav.

D298 (B202) Stob. 3.4.76

ἀνοήμονες τῶν ἀπεόντων ὀρέγονται, τὰ δὲ παρεόντα
καὶ παρῳχημένων κερδαλεώτερα ἐόντα ἀμαλδύνου-
σιν.

D299 (B204) Stob. 3.4.78

ἀνοήμονες οὐδὲν ἀνδάνουσιν[1] ἐν ὅλῃ τῇ βιοτῇ.

[1] ἀνδάνουσιν (ἀνδ- A) M^dA: μανθάνουσιν coni. Valckenaer,
κατάνουσι vel ἀνύουσι Meineke, λαγχάνουσιν Wachsmuth,
ἀλδαίνουσιν dub. Hense

D300 (B42) Stob. 4.44.68 (= Democrat. *Sent.* 8)

μέγα τὸ ἐν συμφορῇσι φρονεῖν ἃ δεῖ.

D301 (B58) Stob. 4.46.18 (= Democrat. *Sent.* 23a)

ἐλπίδες αἱ τῶν ὀρθὰ φρονεόντων ἐφικταί, αἱ δὲ τῶν
ἀξυνέτων ἀδύνατοι.

D302 (B292) Stob. 4.46.19

ἄλογοι τῶν ἀξυνέτων αἱ ἐλπίδες.

296

D297 (B197) Stobaeus, *Anthology*

Thoughtless people derive their bearing (rhusmountai) *from the advantages that come from fortune, those who are expert in such matters from those that come from wisdom.*

D298 (B202) Stobaeus, *Anthology*

Thoughtless people desire what is absent, while what is present, even if it is more advantageous than what has departed, they destroy.

D299 (B204) Stobaeus, *Anthology*

Thoughtless people cannot please at all during the course of their whole lifetime.

D300 (B42) Stobaeus, *Anthology* (attributed to Democrates)

It is a great thing to think as one ought to in adversities.

D301 (B58) Stobaeus, *Anthology* (attributed to Democrates)

The hopes of people who think correctly are attainable, those of people who do not understand are impossible.

D302 (B292) Stobaeus, *Anthology*

The hopes of people who do not understand are irrational.

D303 (B175) Stob. 2.9.4

οἱ θεοὶ τοῖσι ἀνθρώποισι διδοῦσι τἀγαθὰ[1] πάντα καὶ
πάλαι καὶ νῦν, πλὴν ὁκόσα κακὰ καὶ βλαβερὰ καὶ
ἀνωφελέα· τάδε δ' οὔτε[2] πάλαι οὔτε νῦν θεοὶ ἀνθρώποισι δωροῦνται, ἀλλ' αὐτοὶ τοῖσδεσι ἐμπελάζουσι[3]
διὰ νοῦ τυφλότητα καὶ ἀγνωμοσύνην.

[1] τἀγαθὰ del. Meineke: τἆλλα ἅπαντα coni. Wachsmuth
[2] οὔτε Meineke: οὐ mss.
[3] ἀμπελάζουσι mss, corr. Valckenaer

D304 (B61) Stob. 3.37.25 (= Democrat. *Sent.* 26)

οἷσιν ὁ τρόπος ἐστὶν εὔτακτος, τουτέοισι καὶ ⟨ὁ⟩[1]
βίος συντέτακται.[2]

[1] ὁ Democrat., om. mss.   [2] εὖ τέτακται Meineke

D305 (B57) Stob. 4.29.18 (= Democrat. *Sent.* 23)

κτηνέων μὲν εὐγένεια ἡ τοῦ σκήνεος[1] εὐσθένεια, ἀνθρώπων δὲ ἡ τοῦ ἤθεος εὐτροπίη.

[1] σκήνεος mss.: σώματος Democrat.

D306 (B193) Stob. 3.3.43

φρονήσιος ἔργον[1] μέλλουσαν ἀδικίην φυλάξασθαι,
ἀναλγησίης δὲ γενομένην[2] μὴ ἀμύνασθαι.

D303 (B175) Stobaeus, *Anthology*

The gods give to human beings all good things, both in ancient times and now. Except that everything that is evil, harmful, and useless—these things neither in ancient times nor now do gods bestow them upon human beings, but these themselves approach them by reason of the blindness of their mind and their lack of judgment.

D304 (B61) Stobaeus, *Anthology* (attributed to Democrates)

Those whose character (tropos) is well ordered have their life too in good order.

D305 (B57) Stobaeus, *Anthology* (attributed to Democrates)

For livestock, noble birth is a fine strength of body; for humans, it is the fine turning of their character.

D306 (B193) Stobaeus, *Anthology*

The function of prudence (phronêsis) is to protect against injustice that will occur, that of insensitivity to pain (analgêsiê) is not to take vengeance for that which has occurred.

---

[1] ἔργον ⟨τὸ⟩ Hense   [2] γενομένην Max. Conf. *Sent.* 2.41: τὸ γενομένην M^d, τὸ γενόμενον A

D307 (B64) Stob. 3.4.81 (= Democrat. *Sent.* 29)

πολλοὶ πολυμαθέες νόον οὐκ ἔχουσι.

D308 (B52) Stob. 3.10.42 (= Democrat. *Sent.* 18)

τὸν οἰόμενον νόον ἔχειν ὁ νουθετέων τι ματαιοπονέει.

D309 (B169) Stob. 2.1.12

μὴ πάντα ἐπίστασθαι προθύμεο, μὴ πάντων ἀμαθὴς
γένῃ.

D310 (B158) Plut. *Lat. viv.* 5 1129E (et al.)

[. . .] ὥς φησι Δημόκριτος νέα ἐφ᾽ ἡμέρῃ φρονέοντες[1]
ἄνθρωποι [. . .].

[1] τρέφοντες mss., corr. Pohlenz ex Plut. *Quaest. conv.* 655D
et 722D

Virtues and Vices (D311–D337)
The Influence of Other People (D311–D313)

D311 (B39) Stob. 3.37.22 (= Democrat. *Sent.* 15)

ἀγαθὸν ἢ εἶναι χρεὼν ἢ μιμέεσθαι.

D312 (B184) Stob. 2.31.90

φαύλων ὁμιλίη συνεχὴς ἕξιν κακίης συναύξει.

D307 (B64) Stobaeus, *Anthology* (attributed to Democrates)

Many people who possess much learning do not have intelligence [cf. **HER. R103**].

D308 (B52) Stobaeus, *Anthology* (attributed to Democrates)

He who admonishes (noutheteôn) someone who thinks he possesses intelligence (nous) labors in vain.

D309 (B169) Stobaeus, *Anthology*

Do not desire to know everything, do not be ignorant of everything.

D310 (B158) Plutarch, *Is the Saying 'Live in Obscurity' Right?*

[. . .] as Democritus says, humans, **"thinking new thoughts every day"** [. . .].

Virtues and Vices (D311–D337)
The Influence of Other People (D311–D313)

D311 (B39) Stobaeus, *Anthology* (attributed to Democrates)

One should either be a good man, or else imitate one.

D312 (B184) Stobaeus, *Anthology*

Spending time continually with worthless people helps increase the disposition to wickedness.

D313 (< B143) Philod. *Ira* 29.25–29 Indelli

. . . καὶ μικροῦ δεῖν ὅσα τις ἂν νώσαιτο κατὰ Δημόκριτον κακὰ πάντα παρακολουθεῖ διὰ τὰς ὑπερμέτρους ὀργάς.

Effort (D314–D316)

D314 (B240) Stob. 3.29.63

οἱ ἑκούσιοι πόνοι τὴν τῶν ἀκουσίων ὑπομονὴν ἐλαφροτέρην παρασκευάζουσι.

D315 (B241) Stob. 3.29.64

πόνος συνεχὴς ἐλαφρότερος ἑαυτοῦ συνηθίῃ γίνεται.

D316 (B243) Stob. 3.29.88

τῆς ἡσυχίης πάντες οἱ πόνοι ἡδίονες, ὅταν ὧν εἵνεκεν πονέουσι τυγχάνωσιν ἢ εἰδέωσι κύρσοντες· †ἐν δὲ ἄκος τῇ ἀποτυχίῃ τὸ πᾶν†[1] ὁμοίως ἀνιηρὸν καὶ ταλαίπωρον.

[1] loc. corruptum alii aliter emend., e.g.: ἐὰν δὲ ἀποστῇ Iacobs: ἐν δὲ ἑκάστῃ τῇ ἀποτυχίῃ τὸ πονεῖν dub. Diels: ἐν δὲ ἄκος ‹ἡ ἐπιτυχίη ἐν δὲ› τῇ ἀποτυχίῃ τὸ πᾶν Fränkel (ἐπιτυχίη pro ἀποτυχίη iam ed. Trincav.)

D313 (< B143) Philodemus, *On Anger*

It is almost the case that **all the evils one could think of,** as Democritus puts it, ensue from instances of excessive anger.

Effort (D314–D316)

D314 (B240) Stobaeus, *Anthology*

Voluntary efforts make it easier to endure involuntary ones.

D315 (B241) Stobaeus, *Anthology*

A continuous effort becomes easier because of habituation to it.

D316 (*B243*) Stobaeus, *Anthology*

All efforts are more pleasant than rest, when one obtains what one exerts effort for or knows that one will do so. †But one remedy in misfortune is entirely† vexatious and distressful in a similar way.

Temperance (D317–D318)

D317 (B294) Stob. 4.50.20

ἰσχὺς καὶ εὐμορφίη νεότητος ἀγαθά, γήραος[1] δὲ σω-
φροσύνης ἄνθος.

[1] γῆρας mss., corr. Halm

D318 (B291) Stob. 4.44.70

πενίην ἐπιεικέως φέρειν σωφρονέοντος.[1]

[1] σωφρονέοντος ed. Trincav.: -ντα mss.

Justice (D319–D324)

D319 (B256) Stob. 4.2.14

δίκη μέν ἐστιν ἔρδειν τὰ χρὴ ἐόντα, ἀδικίη δὲ μὴ
ἔρδειν τὰ χρὴ ἐόντα, ἀλλὰ παρατρέπεσθαι.

D320 (B174) Stob. 2.9.3

ὁ μὲν εὔθυμος εἰς ἔργα ἐπιφερόμενος δίκαια καὶ νόμιμα καὶ ὕπαρ καὶ ὄναρ χαίρει τε καὶ ἔρρωται καὶ
ἀνακηδής[1] ἐστιν· ὃς δ᾽ ἂν καὶ δίκης ἀλογῇ καὶ τὰ
χρέοντα[2] μὴ ἔρδῃ, τούτῳ πάντα τὰ τοιάδε ἀτερπέα[3]
ὅταν τευ[4] ἀναμνησθῇ, καὶ δέδοικε καὶ ἑωυτὸν[5] κακίζει.

[1] ἀνακύδης mss., corr. Mullach   [2] χρηέοντα mss., corr.
Heeren   [3] ἀτερπείη mss., corr. Usener

Temperance (D317–D318)

D317 (B294) Stobaeus, *Anthology*

Strength and beauty are the good things of youth, but of old age the flower is temperance.

D318 (B291) Stobaeus, *Anthology*

It is the mark of a temperate man to endure poverty equably.

Justice (D319–D324)

D319 (B256) Stobaeus, *Anthology*

Justice is to do what is necessary, injustice not to do what is necessary but to turn aside from it.

D320 (B174) Stobaeus, *Anthology*

The contented man, being inclined toward deeds that are just and lawful, is joyous day and night, strong and carefree. But for him who disregards justice and does not do what is necessary, all such things cause dissatisfaction whenever he recalls them, and he is frightened and upbraids himself.

---

⁴ τευ Diels: τεῦ mss.: τ᾿ εὖ Usener   ⁵ ὤυτον F, οὐτὸν P: corr. cod. Vatic.

D321 (B217) Stob. 3.9.30

μοῦνοι θεοφιλέες, ὅσοις ἐχθρὸν τὸ ἀδικέειν.

D322 (B215) Stob. 3.7.31

δίκης κῦδος γνώμης θάρσος καὶ ἀθαμβίη, ἀδικίης δὲ δεῖμα ξυμφορῆς τέρμα.

D323 (B216bis) Stob. 3.9.29 (= Democrat. *Sent.* 27)

ἀγαθὸν οὐ τὸ μὴ ἀδικέειν ἀλλὰ τὸ μηδὲ ἐθέλειν.

D324 (B263) Stob. 4.5.45

δίκης καὶ ἀρετῆς μεγίστην μετέχει μοῖραν ὁ[1] ἀξίας τὰς μεγίστας τάμνων.[2]

[1] τιμὰς post ὁ hab. mss., del. Meineke ut gloss.
[2] τάμνων ‹τοῖς ἀξιωτάτοις› dub. Diels: ὁ τιμὰς ἀξίως τὰς μεγίστας ταμιεύων prop. Gomperz

Courage (D325–D326)

D325 (B214) Stob. 3.7.25 (et al.)

ἀνδρεῖος οὐχ ὁ τῶν πολεμίων[1] μόνον ἀλλὰ καὶ ὁ τῶν ἡδονῶν κρέσσων. ἔνιοι δὲ πόλεων[2] μὲν δεσπόζουσι, γυναιξὶ δὲ δουλεύουσιν.[3]

[1] κρατῶν post πολεμίων hab. mss., om. Stob. 3.17.39, secl. Hense   [2] πόλεων A: πόνων Md Br   [3] duas sententias separatim praeb. Stob. 3.17.39 et 3.6.26

D321 (B217) Stobaeus, *Anthology*

Only those people are friends of the gods for whom it is hateful to commit injustice.

D322 (B215) Stobaeus, *Anthology*

The glory arising from justice is courage and unastoundedness (athambiê) of judgment, while the fear arising from injustice has an end consisting in misfortune.

D323 (B216bis) Stobaeus, *Anthology* (attributed to Democrates)

The good thing is not to not commit injustice, but to not even wish to do so.

D324 (B263) Stobaeus, *Anthology*

Of justice and virtue he has the greatest share who divides up the greatest rewards.

Courage (D325–D326)

D325 (B214) Stobaeus, *Anthology*

Courageous is he who is stronger not only than enemies but also than pleasures. Some men are masters over cities but slaves to women.

D326 (B213) Stob. 3.7.21

ἀνδρείη τὰς ἄτας μικρὰς ἔρδει.

Magnanimity (D327)

D327 (B46) Stob. 4.4.69 (= Democrat. *Sent.* 12)

μεγαλοψυχίη τὸ φέρειν πράως πλημμέλειαν.

Virtues and Vices of Women (D328–D329)

D328 (B273) Stob. 4.22.199

γυνὴ πολλὰ ἀνδρὸς ὀξυτέρη πρὸς κακοφραδμοσύνην.

D329 (B274) Stob. 4.23.38

κόσμος ὀλιγομυθίη γυναικί· καλὸν δὲ καὶ κόσμου λιτότης.

Avarice (D330–D333)

D330 (B222) Stob. 3.10.64

ἡ τέκνοις ἄγαν χρημάτων συναγωγὴ πρόφασίς ἐστι φιλαργυρίης τρόπον ἴδιον ἐλέγχουσα.

D331 (B227) Stob. 3.16.17

οἱ φειδωλοὶ τὸν τῆς μελίσσης οἶτον ἔχουσιν ἐργαζόμενοι ὡς ἀεὶ βιωσόμενοι.[1]

D326 (B213) Stobaeus, *Anthology*
Courage makes calamities small.

Magnanimity (D327)

D327 (B46) Stobaeus, *Anthology* (attributed to Democrates)
Great-spiritedness: to endure a blunder easily.

Virtues and Vices of Women (D328–D329)

D328 (B273) Stobaeus, *Anthology*
A woman is much keener for evil thoughts than a man.

D329 *(B274)* Stobaeus, *Anthology*
Adornment for a woman is to speak little; but simplicity of adornment is a fine thing too.

Avarice (D330–D333)

D330 (B222) Stobaeus, *Anthology*
Gathering much wealth for one's children is a pretext for avarice that reveals one's own character.

D331 (B227) Stobaeus, *Anthology*
Thrifty people have the fate of the bee: they work as though they were going to live forever.

---

¹ βλισσόμενοι Buecheler

D332 (B228) Stob. 3.16.18

οἱ τῶν φειδωλῶν παῖδες ἀμαθέες γινόμενοι, ὥσπερ οἱ
ὀρχησταὶ οἱ ἐς τὰς μαχαίρας ὀρούοντες, ἢν ἑνὸς μού-
νου ⟨μὴ⟩[1] τύχωσι καταφερόμενοι, ἔνθα δεῖ τοὺς πόδας
ἐρεῖσαι, ἀπόλλυνται· χαλεπὸν δὲ τυχεῖν ἑνός,[2] τὸ γὰρ
ἴχνιον μοῦνον λέλειπται τῶν ποδῶν· οὕτω δὲ καὶ οὗτοι, ἢν ἁμάρτωσι τοῦ πατρικοῦ τύπου τοῦ ἐπιμελέος
καὶ φειδωλοῦ, φιλέουσι διαφθείρεσθαι.

[1] ⟨μὴ⟩ Diels: τύχωσι ⟨μὴ⟩ Mullach   [2] χαλεπὸν δὲ τυχεῖν ἑνός ms.: ⟨οὐ⟩ χαλεπὸν δὲ μὴ τυχεῖν ἑνός coni. Salmasius:
χαλ. δὲ μὴ ἀτυχεῖν ἑνός Iacobs: χαλ. δὲ τυχέειν ⟨τοῦ⟩ ἑνός
Mullach

D333 (B229) Stob. 3.16.19

φειδώ τοι καὶ λιμὸς χρηστή, ἐν καιρῷ δὲ καὶ δαπάνη·
γινώσκειν δὲ ἀγαθοῦ.

Envy and Rivalry (D334–D335)

D334 (B88) Stob. 3.38.47 (= Democrat. *Sent.* 54)

ὁ φθονέων ἑωυτὸν ὡς ἐχθρὸν λυπέει.

D335 (B237) Stob. 3.20.62

φιλονεικίη πᾶσα ἀνόητος· τὸ γὰρ κατὰ τοῦ δυσμενέος
βλαβερὸν θεωρεῦσα τὸ ἴδιον συμφέρον οὐ βλέπει.

D332 (B228) Stobaeus, *Anthology*

Children of thrifty people, if they do not learn, die like dancers who leap among swords, if when they land they miss only one of the spots where they have to set their feet (and it is difficult to hit that one spot, since there is only enough space for their feet): in the same way, they too tend to perish, if they fall short of the paternal model of carefulness and thrift.

D333 (B229) Stobaeus, *Anthology*

Thrift and hunger are useful; but in the right circumstances so too is expense. To discern this is the mark of a good man.

Envy and Rivalry (D334–D335)

D334 (B88) Stobaeus, *Anthology* (attributed to Democrates)

He who envies inflicts suffering upon himself just as upon an enemy.

D335 (B237) Stobaeus, *Anthology*

Every contentiousness is thoughtless: for, watching only for what is harmful for the enemy, he does not see what is advantageous for himself.

Shame (D336–D337)

D336 (B244) Stob. 3.31.7

φαῦλον, κἂν μόνος ἦς, μήτε λέξης μήτ' ἐργάσῃ· μάθε
δὲ πολὺ μᾶλλον τῶν ἄλλων σεαυτὸν αἰσχύνεσθαι.

D337 (B60) Stob. 3.13.46 (= Democrat. *Sent.* 25)

κρέσσον τὰ οἰκήια ἁμαρτήματα ἐλέγχειν ἢ τὰ
ὀθνήια.[1]

[1] ὀθνήια Meineke: ὀθνεῖα mss. et Democrat.: ἀλλότρια Max.
Conf.

Words and Deeds (D338–D352)

D338 (B145) Plut. *De lib. ed.* 14 9F

λόγος γὰρ ἔργου σκιὴ κατὰ Δημόκριτον.

D339 (B53a) Stob. 2.15.33 (= Democrat. *Sent.* 19b)

πολλοὶ δρῶντες τὰ αἴσχιστα λόγους τοὺς[1] ἀρίστους
ἀσκέουσιν.

[1] τοὺς om. Democrat.

D340 (B55) Stob. 2.15.36 (= Democrat. *Sent.* 21)

ἔργα καὶ πρήξιας ἀρετῆς, οὐ λόγους ζηλοῦν[1] χρεών.

Shame (D336–D337)

D336 (B244) Stobaeus, *Anthology*

What is sordid, even if you are alone, you should neither say nor do: learn to feel shame much more before yourself than before others.

D337 (B60) Stobaeus, *Anthology* (attributed to Democrates)

It is a better thing to put to shame one's own errors than someone else's.

Words and Deeds (D338–D352)

D338 (B145) Plutarch, *On the Education of Children*

A word is the shadow of a deed, according to Democritus.

D339 (B53a) Stobaeus, *Anthology* (attributed to Democrates)

Many people who perform the most shameful deeds cultivate the best words.

D340 (B55) Stobaeus, *Anthology* (attributed to Democrates)

One must emulate the deeds and actions of virtue, not its words.[1]

---

[1] ζηλοῦν Democrat.: ζηλεύειν ms.

D341 (B177) Stob. 2.15.40

οὔτε λόγος ἐσθλὸς φαύλην πρῆξιν ἀμαυρίσκει, οὔτε πρῆξις ἀγαθὴ λόγου βλασφημίῃ λυμαίνεται.

D342 (B190) Stob. 3.1.91

φαύλων ἔργων καὶ τοὺς λόγους παραιτητέον.

D343 (B192) Stob. 3.2.36

ἔστι ῥᾴδιον μὲν ἐπαινεῖν ἃ μὴ χρὴ καὶ ψέγειν, ἑκάτερον δὲ πονηροῦ τινος ἤθους.

D344 (B226) Stob. 3.13.47

οἰκήιον ἐλευθερίης παρρησίη, κίνδυνος δὲ ἡ τοῦ καιροῦ διάγνωσις.

D345 (B226bis, B63) Stob. 3.14.8 (= Democrat. *Sent.* 28)

εὐλογέειν ἐπὶ καλοῖς ἔργμασι καλόν· τὸ γὰρ ἐπὶ φλαύροισι κίβδηλον καὶ ἀπατεῶνος ἔργον.

D346 (B51) Stob. 2.4.12 (= Democrat. *Sent.* 17)

ἰσχυρότερος[1] ἐς πειθὼ λόγος πολλαχῇ γίνεται χρυσοῦ.[2]

---

[1] ἰσχυρότερος Democrat.: ἰσχυρὸν mss.
[2] χρυσοῦ cum init. prox. sent. iunx. mss.

D341 (B177) Stobaeus, *Anthology*

Neither do noble words obscure a worthless action nor is a good action defiled by the defamation of words.

D342 (B190) Stobaeus, *Anthology*

About worthless deeds one should avoid even speaking.

D343 (B192) Stobaeus, *Anthology*

It is all too easy to praise and blame what one should not [scil. praise or blame]: both belong to a wicked character.

D344 (B226) Stobaeus, *Anthology*

It belongs to freedom to speak frankly, but the danger is in discerning the favorable opportunity.

D345 (B226bis, B63) Stobaeus, *Anthology* (attributed to Democrates)

It is a fine thing to speak well about fine deeds; for to do so about worthless ones is the deed of a liar and a cheat.

D346 *(B51)* Stobaeus, *Anthology* (attributed to Democrates)

Words are often stronger for persuading than gold.

D347

a (B225) Stob. 3.12.13

ἀληθομυθέειν χρεών, ὃ πολὺ λώιον.[1]

[1] οὐ πολυλογέειν Friedländer e Democrat. *Sent.* 10

b (B44) Democrat. *Sent.* 10

ἀληθόμυθον χρὴ εἶναι,[1] οὐ πολύλογον.

[1] χρὴ εἶναι P: εἶναι χρὴ B: χρὴ ALC

D348 (B85) Stob. 2.31.73 (= Democrat. *Sent.* 51)

ὁ ἀντιλογεόμενος καὶ πολλὰ λεσχηνευόμενος ἀφυὴς
ἐς μάθησιν ὧν χρή.[1]

[1] ὧν χρή Democrat., om. mss.

D349 (B86) Stob. 3.36.24 (= Democrat. *Sent.* 52)

πλεονεξίη τὸ πάντα λέγειν, μηδὲν δὲ ἐθέλειν ἀκούειν.

D350 (B239) Stob. 3.28.13

ὅρκους οὓς ποιέονται ἐν ἀνάγκῃσιν ἐόντες, οὐ τηρέου-
σιν οἱ φλαῦροι ἐπὴν διαφύγωσιν.

D351 (B81) Stob. 3.29.67 (= Democrat. *Sent.* 46)

τὸ αἰεὶ μέλλειν ἀτελέας ποιεῖ τὰς πρήξιας.

D347

a (B225) Stobaeus, *Anthology*

One should speak the truth—that is much better.

b (B44) attributed to Democrates

One should be someone who speaks the truth, not lots of words.

D348 (B85) Stobaeus, *Anthology* (attributed to Democrates)

He who retorts and chatters a lot is ill-suited by nature to learn what is necessary.

D349 (B86) Stobaeus, *Anthology* (attributed to Democrates)

It is greed to want to say everything but not to want to listen.

D350 (B239) Stobaeus, *Anthology*

Worthless people do not respect oaths that they made when they were under duress once they escape from it.

D351 (B81) Stobaeus, *Anthology* (attributed to Democrates)

Always to be about to do something results in actions remaining unaccomplished.

D352 (B48) Stob. 3.38.46 (= Democrat. *Sent.* 14)

μωμεομένων φλαύρων ὁ ἀγαθὸς οὐ ποιέεται λόγον.

Appearances (D353)

D353 (B195) Stob. 3.4.69

. . . εἴδωλα¹ ἐσθῆτι καὶ² κόσμῳ διαπρεπέα πρὸς θεω-
ρίην, ἀλλὰ καρδίης κενεά.

¹ ante εἴδωλα pos. lac. Diels   ² αἰσθητικὰ καὶ mss.,
corr. Meineke

The City and Social Life (D354–D374)

D354 (B247) Stob. 3.40.7

ἀνδρὶ σοφῷ πᾶσα γῆ βατή· ψυχῆς γὰρ ἀγαθῆς πα-
τρὶς ὁ ξύμπας κόσμος.

D355 (< B157) Plut. *Adv. Col.* 32 1126A

[. . .] ὧν Δημόκριτος μὲν παραινεῖ τήν τε πολιτικὴν¹
τέχνην μεγίστην οὖσαν ἐκδιδάσκεσθαι καὶ τοὺς πό-
νους διώκειν, ἀφ᾽ ὧν τὰ μεγάλα καὶ λαμπρὰ γίνεται
τοῖς ἀνθρώποις.

¹ πολεμικὴν mss., corr. Reiske

D352 (B48) Stobaeus, *Anthology* (attributed to Democrates)

The good man takes no account of the blame of worthless people.

Appearances (D353)

D353 (B195) Stobaeus, *Anthology*

. . . *images brilliant to look upon in their clothing and adornment, but devoid of a heart.*

The City and Social Life (D354–D374)

D354 (B247) Stobaeus, *Anthology*

A wise man can walk upon the whole earth. For the whole world is the fatherland of a good soul.

D355 (< B157) Plutarch, *Against Colotes*

[. . .] Democritus recommends that one learn thoroughly the art of politics, the greatest that there is, and to pursue those exertions from which the greatest and most brilliant things come about for people.

D356 (B 252) Stob. 4.1.43

τὰ κατὰ τὴν πόλιν χρεὼν τῶν λοιπῶν μέγιστα ἡγεῖσθαι, ὅκως ἄξεται[1] εὖ, μήτε φιλονεικέοντα παρὰ τὸ
ἐπιεικὲς μήτε ἰσχὺν ἑαυτῷ περιτιθέμενον παρὰ τὸ
χρηστὸν τὸ τοῦ ξυνοῦ.[2] πόλις γὰρ εὖ ἀγομένη μεγί-
στη ὄρθωσίς ἐστι, καὶ ἐν τούτῳ πάντα ἔνι, καὶ τούτου
σῳζομένου <τὰ>[3] πάντα σῴζεται καὶ τούτου διαφθει-
ρομένου τὰ πάντα διαφθείρεται.

[1] αὔξεται mss., corr. Koen   [2] ξένου mss., corr. Schaefer
[3] <τὰ> Meineke

D357 (B250) Stob. 4.1.40

ἀπὸ ὁμονοίης τὰ μεγάλα ἔργα καὶ ταῖς πόλεσι τοὺς
πολέμους δυνατὸν κατεργάζεσθαι, ἄλλως δ' οὔ.

D358 (B186) Stob. 2.33.9

ὁμοφροσύνη φιλίην[1] ποιεῖ.

[1] φίλην ms., corr. Wachsmuth

D359 (B151) Plut. *Quaest. Conv.* 2.10.2 643E

ἐν γὰρ ξυνῷ ἰχθύι ἄκανθαι οὐκ ἔνεισιν, ὥς φησιν ὁ
Δημόκριτος.

D356 (B252) Stobaeus, *Anthology*

*One should consider the affairs of the city to be the most
important of all, so that it will be well directed, neither
being contentious against what is equitable nor attributing
to oneself a power contrary to what is useful for the whole.
For a well-directed city is the greatest rectification, and it
contains everything; and as long as it is safe, everything is
safe, and if it is destroyed, everything is destroyed.*

D357 (B250) Stobaeus, *Anthology*

*It is from consensus that great deeds and, for cities, wars
can be brought to a successful conclusion, otherwise not.*

D358 (B186) Stobaeus, *Anthology*

Agreement in thought creates friendship.

D359 (B151) Plutarch, *Table Talk*

In fish [scil. eaten] **in common there are no fish bones,**
as Democritus says.

D360 (B249) Stob. 4.1.34

στάσις ἐμφύλιος ἐς ἑκάτερα κακόν· καὶ γὰρ νικέουσι
καὶ ἡσσωμένοις ὁμοίη φθορή.

D361 (B251) Stob. 4.1.42

ἡ ἐν δημοκρατίη πενίη τῆς παρὰ τοῖς δυνάστῃσι κα-
λεομένης εὐδαιμονίης τοσοῦτόν ἐστιν αἱρετωτέρη,
ὁκόσον ἐλευθερίη δουλείης.

D362 (B254) Stob. 4.1.45

οἱ κακοὶ ἰόντες ἐς τὰς τιμὰς ὁκόσῳ ἂν μᾶλλον ἀνάξιοι
ἐόντες ἴωσι, τοσούτῳ μᾶλλον ἀνακηδέες γίγνονται
καὶ ἀφροσύνης καὶ θράσεος πίμπλανται.

D363 (B266) Stob. 4.5.48

οὐδεμία μηχανὴ τῷ νῦν καθεστῶτι ῥυθμῷ μὴ οὐκ ἀδικέειν τοὺς ἄρχοντας, ἢν καὶ πάνυ ἀγαθοὶ ἔωσιν. οὐδενὶ γὰρ ἄλλῳ ἔοικεν ἢ ἑωυτῷ τὸν[1] αὐτὸν[2] ἐφ᾽[3] ἑτέροισι
γίγνεσθαι· δεῖ δέ κως οὕτω καὶ ταῦτα κοσμηθῆναι,
ὅκως ὁ μηδὲν ἀδικέων, ἢν καὶ πάνυ ἐτάζῃ τοὺς ἀδι-
κέοντας, μὴ ὑπ᾽ ἐκείνους[4] γενήσεται,[5] ἀλλά τις ἢ
θεσμὸς ἤ τι ἄλλο ἀμυνεῖ τῷ τὰ δίκαια ποιεῦντι.

[1] post τὸν lac. pos. Diels   [2] τὸν αὐτὸν S: τῶν αὐτῶν
MA   [3] ἐφ᾽] ὑφ᾽ Iacobs   [4] ἐκείνοις Diels   [5] γενήσεται Halm: γενέσθαι mss.

D360 (B249) Stobaeus, *Anthology*

Internal strife is evil for both sides: for the destruction is the same for the victors and the vanquished.

D361 (B251) Stobaeus, *Anthology*

Poverty in a democracy is just as preferable to what the powerful call happiness as liberty is to slavery.

D362 (B254) Stobaeus, *Anthology*

Bad people who occupy posts of honor become more negligent and more full of folly and impudence, the more unworthy they are of them.

D363 (B266) Stobaeus, *Anthology*

In the currently established [scil. political] configuration, there is no way to prevent the magistrates from committing injustice, even if they are entirely good men. For it does not seem right to anyone other than himself that the same man exercise power over others. But it is necessary to organize this too in such a way that he who commits no injustice, even when he examines thoroughly those who do commit injustice, not fall under their power, but that some regulation or something else protect the man who acts justly.

D364 (B255) Stob. 4.1.46

ὅταν οἱ δυνάμενοι τοῖς μὴ ἔχουσι καὶ προτελεῖν τολ-
μέωσι καὶ ὑπουργεῖν καὶ χαρίζεσθαι, ἐν τούτῳ ἤδη
καὶ τὸ οἰκτίρειν ἔνεστι καὶ ⟨τὸ⟩[1] μὴ ἐρήμους εἶναι καὶ
τὸ ἑταίρους γίγνεσθαι, καὶ τὸ ἀμύνειν ἀλλήλοισι καὶ
⟨τὸ⟩[2] τοὺς πολιήτας ὁμονόους εἶναι καὶ ἄλλα ἀγαθά,
ἄσσα οὐδεὶς ἂν δύναιτο καταλέξαι.

[1] ⟨τὸ⟩ Meineke   [2] ⟨τὸ⟩ Hense

D365 (B267) Stob. 4.6.19

φύσει τὸ ἄρχειν οἰκήιον τῷ κρέσσονι.

D366 (B47) Stob. 3.1.45 (= Democrat. *Sent.* 13)

νόμῳ καὶ ἄρχοντι καὶ[1] σοφωτέρῳ εἴκειν κόσμιον.

[1] καὶ ⟨τῷ⟩ Democrat.

D367 (B75) Stob. 4.2.13 (= Democrat. *Sent.* 40)

κρέσσον ἄρχεσθαι τοῖσιν ἀνοήτοισιν ἢ ἄρχειν.

D368 (B49) Stob. 4.4.27 (= Democrat. *Sent.* 15)

χαλεπὸν ἄρχεσθαι ὑπὸ χερείονος.

D369 (B253) Stob. 4.1.44

τοῖς χρηστοῖσιν οὐ συμφέρον ἀμελέοντας[1] τῶν ἑων-

D364 (B255) Stobaeus, *Anthology*

When powerful men have the courage to lend money to those who have none, and to help and gratify them, in this then are present compassion, freedom from solitude, companionship, mutual help, consensus among fellow citizens, and other good things, so many that no one could enumerate them all.

D365 (B267) Stobaeus, *Anthology*

By nature, ruling belongs to the stronger [or: better] one.

D366 (B47) Stobaeus, *Anthology* (attributed to Democrates)

To submit to law, to a magistrate, and to a wiser man is orderly (kosmion).

D367 (B75) Stobaeus, *Anthology* (attributed to Democrates)

It is better for thoughtless people to be governed than to govern.

D368 (B49) Stobaeus, *Anthology* (attributed to Democrates)

It is a hard thing to be governed by a lesser man.

D369 (B253) Stobaeus, *Anthology*

For good men, it is not advantageous to neglect their own

---

1 ἀμελέοντας ed. Trincav.: ἀμελαίνοντας mss.

τῶν ἄλλα πρήσσειν· τὰ γὰρ ἴδια κακῶς² ἔσχεν. εἰ δὲ
ἀμελέοι τις³ τῶν δημοσίων, κακῶς ἀκούειν γίγνεται,
καὶ ἢν μηδὲν μήτε κλέπτῃ μήτε ἀδικῇ. ἐπεὶ καὶ ⟨μὴ⟩⁴
ἀμελέοντι ἢ ἀδικέοντι κίνδυνος κακῶς ἀκούειν καὶ δὴ
καὶ παθεῖν τι· ἀνάγκη δὲ ἁμαρτάνειν, συγγιγνώσκε-
σθαι δὲ τοὺς ἀνθρώπους οὐκ εὐπετές.

  ² κακῶς ⟨ἂν⟩ Iacobs   ³ ἀμελέοιτο mss., corr. Meineke
  ⁴ ⟨μὴ⟩ Meineke

D370 (B265) Stob. 4.5.47

τῶν ἡμαρτημένων ἄνθρωποι μεμνέαται μᾶλλον ἢ τῶν
εὖ πεποιημένων. καὶ γὰρ δίκαιον οὕτως· ὥσπερ ⟨γὰρ
τὸν⟩¹ τὰς παρακαταθήκας ἀποδιδόντα οὐ χρὴ ἐπαινεῖ-
σθαι, τὸν δὲ μὴ ἀποδιδόντα κακῶς ἀκούειν καὶ πάσχειν, οὕτω καὶ τὸν ἄρχοντα. οὐ γὰρ ἐπὶ τούτῳ ᾑρέθη
ὡς κακῶς ποιήσων, ἀλλ' ὡς εὖ.

  ¹ ⟨γὰρ τὸν⟩ Hirschig

D371 (B287) Stob. 4.40.20

ἀπορίη ξυνὴ τῆς ἑκάστου χαλεπωτέρη· οὐ γὰρ ὑπο-
λείπεται ἐλπὶς ἐπικουρίης.

D372 (B238) Stob. 3.22.42

τελευτᾷ γὰρ ἐς κακοδοξίην¹ ὁ παρεκτεινόμενος τῷ
κρέσσονι.

affairs and to tend to other people's. For then their own affairs go badly. But if someone neglects public affairs, he acquires a bad reputation even if he steals nothing and commits no injustice. For even someone who neglects ⟨nothing⟩ and commits ⟨no⟩ injustice runs the risk of a bad reputation and even of ill-treatment. And it is unavoidable that one makes mistakes, but not easy that people forgive.

D370 (B265) Stobaeus, *Anthology*

People remember mistakes committed more than things done well. And it is right that they do so. ⟨For⟩ just as the man who pays back deposits should not be praised, but the one who does not pay them back should suffer a bad reputation and ill-treatment, so too the man in charge. For he was chosen for this: not to act badly, but to act well.

D371 (B287) Stobaeus, *Anthology*

A predicament shared in common is more onerous than an individual's: for no hope for assistance remains.

D372 (B238) Stobaeus, *Anthology*

The man who measures himself with someone stronger [or: better] than he is ends up with a bad reputation.

---

1 κακὴν post κακοδοξίην del. Meineke

D373 (B268) Stob. 4.7.13

φόβος κολακείην μὲν ἐργάζεται, εὔνοιαν δὲ οὐκ ἔχει.

D374 (< B153) Plut. *Praec.* 28 821A

[. . .] οὐδέ γε δόξαν ἀτιμάσει [scil. ὁ πολιτικὸς ἀνήρ] φεύγων τὸ τοῖς πέλας ἀνδάνειν, ὡς ἠξίου Δημόκριτος.

Laws and Judgments (D375–D387)

D375 (< A1) Diog. Laert. 9.45

[. . . = **D13**] ποιητὰ[1] δὲ <τὰ>[2] νόμιμα[3] εἶναι· φύσει δὲ ἄτομα καὶ κενόν.

[1] ποιότητας Menagius [2] <τὰ> Bignone [3] νόμῳ Zeller

D376 (< A166) Epiph. *Pan.* 3.2.9

Δημόκριτος [. . .] ἔφη [. . .] καὶ τὸ δοκοῦν δίκαιον οὐκ εἶναι δίκαιον, ἄδικον δὲ τὸ ἐναντίον τῆς φύσεως. ἐπίνοιαν γὰρ κακὴν τοὺς νόμους ἔλεγε καί 'οὐ χρὴ νόμοις πειθαρχεῖν τὸν σοφόν, ἀλλὰ ἐλευθερίως ζῆν.'

D377 (B261) Stob. 4.5.43

ἀδικουμένοισι τιμωρεῖν κατὰ δύναμιν χρὴ καὶ μὴ παριέναι· τὸ μὲν γὰρ τοιοῦτον δίκαιον καὶ ἀγαθόν, τὸ δὲ μὴ τοιοῦτον ἄδικον καὶ κακόν.

D373 (B268) Stobaeus, *Anthology*

Fear produces flattery but does not entail benevolence.

D374 (< B153) Plutarch, *Precepts*

[. . .] he [scil. the politician] will not disdain renown, refusing to please his neighbors, as Democritus thought.

Laws and Judgments (D375–D387)

D375 (< A1) Diogenes Laertius

[. . .] Legal usages are constructed; but by nature, atoms and void.

D376 (< A166) Epiphanius, *Against Heresies*

Democritus [. . .] said [. . .] also that what seems to be just is not just, but unjust is what is contrary to nature. For he said that laws are an evil notion and that "the wise man should not obey laws but live freely."

D377 (B261) Stobaeus, *Anthology*

One should take vengeance as far as possible for those who suffer injustice and not disregard them. For an action of this sort is just and good, while one that is not of this sort is unjust and bad.

D378 (B262) Stob. 4.5.44

καὶ οἱ φυγῆς ἄξια ἔρδουσιν ἢ δεσμῶν, ἢ θωιῆς[1]
ἄξιοι,[2] καταψηφιστέον,[3] καὶ μὴ ἀπολύειν· ὃς δ' ἂν
παρὰ νόμον[4] ἀπολύῃ κέρδει ὁρίζων ἢ ἡδονῇ, ἀδικεῖ,
καὶ οἱ τοῦτο ἐγκάρδιον ἀνάγκη εἶναι.

[1] θωιῆς Burchard: θοίνης ms.: ποινῆς Gesner   [2] ἄξιοι
secl. Hirschig, Natorp   [3] καταψηφισματέον ms., corr.
Mullach   [4] νόμον Iacobs: νοῦν ms.

D379 (B248) Stob. 4.1.33 (et al.)

ὁ νόμος βούλεται μὲν εὐεργετεῖν βίον ἀνθρώπων· δύναται δέ, ὅταν αὐτοὶ βούλωνται πάσχειν <εὖ>·[1] τοῖσι
γὰρ πειθομένοισι τὴν ἰδίην ἀρετὴν ἐνδείκνυται.

[1] <εὖ> Gnom. Palat. 58

D380 (B245) Stob. 3.38.53

οὐκ ἂν ἐκώλυον οἱ νόμοι ζῆν ἕκαστον κατ' ἰδίην ἐξ-
ουσίην, εἰ μὴ ἕτερος ἕτερον ἐλυμαίνετο. φθόνος γὰρ
στάσιος ἀρχὴν ἀπεργάζεται.

D381 (B257) Stob. 4.2.15

κατὰ δὲ ζῴων ἔστιν ὧν φόνου καὶ μὴ φόνου ὧδε ἔχει·
τὰ ἀδικέοντα καὶ θέλοντα ἀδικεῖν ἀθῷος ὁ κτείνων,
καὶ πρὸς εὐεστοῦν τοῦτο ἔρδειν μᾶλλον ἢ μή.

D378 (B262) Stobaeus, *Anthology*

Those who perform deeds deserving of exile or prison or who deserve a penalty should be condemned and not acquitted: whoever acquits against the law, deciding with a view toward gain or pleasure, commits injustice, and it is necessary that this be on his mind.

D379 (B248) Stobaeus, *Anthology*

The law wants to bestow a good life upon humans. And it can do this if they themselves wish to do well. For to those who obey it, it reveals their [or: its] own virtue.

D380 (B245) Stobaeus, *Anthology*

The laws would not prevent each person from living as he pleased, if one man did not do harm to another. For envy is at the origin of strife.

D381 (B257) Stobaeus, *Anthology*

In respect of certain animals (?), this is how it is regarding killing them and not killing them: He who kills those that commit an injustice [i.e. that cause damage] and wish to commit injustice should not be penalized. And for the sake of well-being it is better to do this than not to.[1]

---

[1] What the other animals are, besides those for which their justice or injustice determines whether they may be killed or not, is unclear. Perhaps those animals are meant that may not be killed at all, whether they are just or unjust, or perhaps those animals that may be killed even if they are just (e.g. sacrificial animals). The grammar of this passage is difficult and the text may be uncertain.

D382 (B258) Stob. 4.2.16

κτείνειν χρὴ τὰ πημαίνοντα παρὰ δίκην πάντα περὶ
παντός· καὶ ταῦτα ὁ ποιῶν εὐθυμίης[1] καὶ δίκης καὶ
θάρσεος καὶ κτήσεως[2] ἐν παντὶ κόσμῳ μέζω μοῖραν
μεθέξει.

1 ἐπιθυμίης mss., corr. Wakefield apud Gaisford
2 κτήσεως dub. Diels: κτάσεως mss.: alii aliter

D383 (B259) Stob. 4.2.17

ὅκωσπερ περὶ κιναδέων τε καὶ ἑρπετέων γεγράπται[1]
τῶν πολεμίων, οὕτω καὶ κατὰ ἀνθρώπων δοκεῖ μοι
χρεὼν εἶναι ποιεῖν· κατὰ νόμους τοὺς πατρίους κτείνειν πολέμιον ἐν παντὶ κόσμῳ, ἐν ᾧ μὴ νόμος ἀπείρ-
γει· ἀπείργει δὲ[2] ἱερὰ ἑκάστοισιν ἐπιχώρια καὶ σπον-
δαὶ καὶ ὅρκοι.

1 γεγράπται Natorp: γεγράφαται mss.: ⟨νόμοι⟩ γεγράφαται Diels   2 ἀπείργει δὲ Deichgräber: νόμος δὲ ἀπείργει
mss.: φόνον δὲ ἀπείργει dub. Diels, alii aliter

D384 (B260) Stob. 4.2.18

κιξάλλην καὶ λῃστὴν πάντα κτείνων τις ἀθῷος ἂν εἴη
καὶ αὐτοχειρίῃ καὶ κελεύων καὶ ψήφῳ.

D385 (B181) Stob. 2.31.59

κρείσσων ἐπ᾽ ἀρετὴν φανεῖται προτροπῇ χρώμενος

D382 (B258) Stobaeus, *Anthology*

*One must kill the ones [i.e. the animals] that cause damage unjustly, all of them, above all. And he who does this will have a larger share of contentment (*euthumiê*), justice, courage, and property in every [scil. political] order.*

D383 (B259) Stobaeus, *Anthology*

Just as a law has been made regarding hostile foxes and reptiles, it seems to me to be necessary to act in the same way against human beings too: in conformity with the ancestral laws, to kill an enemy in every [scil. political] order in which a law does not forbid this. It is forbidden by temples that are local for each people, and by treaties and oaths.

D384 (B260) Stobaeus, *Anthology*

Anyone who kills any brigand or pirate should not be penalized, whether he does so by his own hand, by ordering it done, or by his vote.

D385 (B181) Stobaeus, *Anthology*

Better, for guiding toward virtue, will turn out to be the

καὶ λόγου πειθοῖ ἤπερ νόμῳ καὶ ἀνάγκῃ. λάθρῃ μὲν
γὰρ ἁμαρτέειν εἰκὸς τὸν εἰργμένον ἀδικίης ὑπὸ νόμου,
τὸν δὲ ἐς τὸ δέον ἠγμένον πειθοῖ οὐκ εἰκὸς οὔτε λάθρῃ
οὔτε φανερῶς ἔρδειν τι πλημμελές· διόπερ συνέσει τε
καὶ ἐπιστήμῃ ὀρθοπραγέων τις ἀνδρεῖος ἅμα καὶ εὐ-
θύγνωμος γίγνεται.

D386 (B264) Stob. 4.5.46

μηδέν τι μᾶλλον τοὺς[1] ἀνθρώπους αἰδεῖσθαι ἑωυτοῦ
μηδέ τι μᾶλλον ἐξεργάζεσθαι κακόν, εἰ μέλλει μηδεὶς
εἰδήσειν ἢ οἱ πάντες ἄνθρωποι· ἀλλ' ἑωυτὸν μάλιστα
αἰδεῖσθαι, καὶ τοῦτον νόμον τῇ ψυχῇ καθεστάναι,
ὥστε μηδὲν ποιεῖν ἀνεπιτήδειον.

[1] τοὺς <ἄλλους> Diels

D387 (B41) Stob. 3. 1. 95 (= Democrat., *Sent.* 7)

μὴ διὰ φόβον, ἀλλὰ διὰ τὸ δέον ἀπέχεσθαι χρεὼν
ἁμαρτημάτων.

Home and Family (D388–D399)

D388 (< A170) Clem. Alex. *Strom.* 2.138.3

Δημόκριτος δὲ γάμον καὶ παιδοποιίαν παραιτεῖται
διὰ τὰς πολλὰς ἐξ αὐτῶν ἀηδίας τε καὶ ἀφολκὰς ἀπὸ
τῶν ἀναγκαιοτέρων.

man who uses exhortation and the persuasion of speech rather than law and constraint. For it is plausible that someone who is kept away from injustice by law commits it in secret, while it is not plausible that someone who is led to act as he ought to by persuasion does something wrong either in secret or openly. And that is why someone who acts rightly by virtue of his understanding and knowledge is courageous and at the same time straight-judging.

D386 (B264) Stobaeus, *Anthology*

One should not feel more of a sense of shame with regard to people than with regard to oneself and should not act worse either, whether no one is going to know about it or whether all people will. But one should feel a sense of shame most of all with regard to oneself, and establish this law for one's soul, so as to do nothing harmful.

D387 (B41) Stobaeus, *Anthology* (attributed to Demo-crates)

One must refrain from wrong actions not from fear but from duty.

Home and Family (D388–D399)

D388 (< A170) Clement of Alexandria, *Stromata*

Democritus advises against marrying and having children because of the many unpleasantnesses and distractions that ensue with regard to matters that are more urgent.

D389 (B288) Stob. 4.40.21

νόσος οἴκου καὶ βίου γίνεται ὅκως περ καὶ σκήνεος.

D390 (B270) Stob. 4.19.45

οἰκέταισιν ὡς μέρεσι τοῦ σκήνεος χρῶ ἄλλῳ πρὸς ἄλλο.

D391 (B111) Stob. 4.23.39 (= Democrat. *Sent.* 78)

ὑπὸ γυναικὸς ἄρχεσθαι ὕβρις ἀνδρὶ[1] ἐσχάτη.

[1] ἀνδρὶ mss.: ἄν εἴη Corp. Par.: ἀνανδρίη Democrat.: ἄν ἀνδρὶ εἴη Diels

D392 (B275) Stob. 4.24.29

τεκνοτροφίη σφαλερόν· τὴν μὲν γὰρ ἐπιτυχίην ἀγῶνος μεστὴν καὶ φροντίδος κέκτηται, τὴν δὲ ἀποτυχίην ἀνυπέρθετον ἑτέρῃ ὀδύνῃ.

D393 (B276) Stob. 4.24.31

οὐ δοκεῖ μοι χρῆναι παῖδας κτᾶσθαι· ἐνορῶ γὰρ ἐν παίδων κτήσει[1] πολλοὺς μὲν καὶ μεγάλους κινδύνους, πολλὰς δὲ λύπας, ὀλίγα δὲ τὰ εὐθηλέοντα καὶ ταῦτα λεπτά τε καὶ ἀσθενέα.

[1] κτίσει mss., corr. Gesner

D389 (B288) Stobaeus, *Anthology*

There is illness of the house and of life just as of the body.

D390 (B270) Stobaeus, *Anthology*

Use household slaves like parts of your body, one for one thing, another for another.

D391 (B111) Stobaeus, *Anthology* (attributed to Democrates)

To be ruled by a woman: the worst outrage (hubris) *for a man.*

D392 (B275) Stobaeus, *Anthology*

Raising children is a slippery affair: for it involves a success filled with struggle and anxiety, or a failure unsurpassed by any other pain.

D393 (B276) Stobaeus, *Anthology*

It does not seem to me that it is necessary to have children. For I observe in having children many great risks, many sufferings, and few gains—and these slight and weak.

D394 (B277) Stob. 4.24.32

ὅτεῳ χρήμη τεά[1] ἐστι παῖδα ποιήσασθαι, ἐκ τῶν φίλων τεύ μοι[2] δοκεῖ ἄμεινον εἶναι. καὶ τῷ μὲν παῖς
ἔσται τοιοῦτος, οἷος ἂν βούληται· ἔστι γὰρ ἐκλέξα-
σθαι οἷον ἐθέλει· καὶ ὃς ἂν δοκῇ ἐπιτήδειος εἶναι, κἂν[3]
μάλιστα κατὰ φύσιν ἔποιτο. καὶ τοῦτο τοσοῦτον διαφέρει, ὅσον ἐνταῦθα μὲν ἔστι τὸν παῖδα λαβεῖν κατα-
θύμιον ἐκ πολλῶν, οἷον[4] ἂν δέῃ.[5] ἢν δέ τις ποιῆται[6]
ἀπὸ ἑωυτοῦ, πολλοὶ ἔνεισι κίνδυνοι· ἀνάγκη γάρ, ὃς
ἂν γένηται, τούτῳ χρῆσθαι.

> [1] χρήματα mss., corr. Diels   [2] τ᾽ ἐμοὶ mss., corr. Diels
> [3] καὶ mss., corr. Diels   [4] ὧν mss., corr. Diels   [5] δέῃ
> Gaisford: δεῖ SA: δῇ M   [6] ἢν ... ποιῆται MA: εἰ ... ποι-
> εῖται S

D395 (B278) Stob. 4.24.33

ἀνθρώποισι τῶν ἀναγκαίων δοκεῖ εἶναι παῖδας κτή-
σασθαι ἀπὸ φύσιος καὶ καταστάσιός τινος ἀρχαίης.
δῆλον δὲ καὶ τοῖς ἄλλοις ζῴοισι. πάντα γὰρ ἔκγονα
κτᾶται κατὰ φύσιν, ἐπωφελείης[1] γε οὐδεμιᾶς εἵνεκα·
ἀλλ᾽ ὅταν γένηται, ταλαιπωρεῖ καὶ τρέφει ἕκαστον ὡς
δύναται καὶ ὑπερδέδοικε,[2] μέχρι σμικρὰ ᾖ,[3] καὶ ἤν τι
πάθῃ ἀνιᾶται. ἡ μὲν φύσις τοιαύτη πάντων ἐστὶν
ὅσσα[4] ψυχὴν ἔχει· τῷ δὲ δὴ ἀνθρώπῳ νομίζον[5] ἤδη
πεποίηται, ὥστε καὶ ἐπαύρεσίν τινα γίγνεσθαι ἀπὸ
τοῦ ἐκγόνου.

D394 (B277) Stobaeus, *Anthology*

For anyone who has some kind of need to have a child, it seems to me better [scil. to get it] from one of his friends. His child will be of the sort that he wishes; for he can pick out the kind he wants. And the one that seems suitable to him will follow him most of all, in accordance with its nature. And the difference is that in this case it is possible to choose the child out of many, just as he desires, of the sort that he needs. But if one makes one oneself, there are many risks involved: for, whatever is born, one must deal with that.

D395 (B278) Stobaeus, *Anthology*

People think that to have children is one of the things that are necessary because of nature and an ancient condition. And this is clear for the other animals. For all have off-spring in conformity with nature, but not for the sake of any utility: for when each one is born, they work hard and nourish it as far as possible, and they fear greatly for it as long as it is small and suffer if anything happens to it. The nature of all things that have life is of this sort; but for the human being it has become a general belief by now that some kind of benefit comes about from offspring.

---

¹ ἐπὶ ὠφελείης mss., corr. Schaeffer   ² ὑπερδέδυκε mss., corr. Gesner   ³ σμικρὰ ᾖ Schaeffer: σμικρᾶς mss.   ⁴ οὖσα mss., corr. Diels   ⁵ νόμιμον Natorp

D396 (B208) Stob. 3.5.24

πατρὸς σωφροσύνη μέγιστον τέκνοις παράγγελμα.

D397 (B280) Stob. 4.26.26

ἔξεστιν οὐ πολλὰ τῶν σφετέρων ἀναλώσαντας παιδεῦσαί τε τοὺς παῖδας καὶ τεῖχός τε καὶ σωτηρίην περιβαλέσθαι τοῖς τε χρήμασι καὶ τοῖς σώμασιν αὐτῶν.

D398 (B279) Stob. 4.26.25

τοῖς παισὶ μάλιστα χρὴ τῶν ἀνυστῶν δατεῖσθαι τὰ χρήματα, καὶ ἅμα ἐπιμέλεσθαι αὐτῶν, μή τι ἀτηρὸν ποιέωσι[1] διὰ χειρὸς ἔχοντες· ἅμα μὲν γὰρ πολλὸν[2] φειδότεροι γίγνονται ἐς τὰ χρήματα καὶ προθυμότεροι κτᾶσθαι καὶ ἀγωνίζονται ἀλλήλοισιν. ἐν γὰρ τῷ ξυνῷ τὰ τελεύμενα οὐκ ἀνιᾷ ὥσπερ ἰδίῃ οὐδ' εὐθυμεῖ τὰ ἐπικτώμενα, ἀλλὰ πολλῷ ἧσσον.

[1] ποιέωσι Wakefield: τοι (τι ed. Trincav.) ἔωσι S
[2] πολλῶν ms., corr. Wakefield

D399 (B272) Stob. 4.22.108

Δημόκριτος ἔφη ὡς γαμβροῦ ὁ[1] μὲν ἐπιτυχὼν εὗρεν υἱόν, ὁ δὲ ἀποτυχὼν ἀπώλεσε καὶ θυγατέρα.

[1] γαμβροῦ ὁ Max Conf., *Loc.* 18.35: ὁ γαμβροῦ mss.

D396 (B208) Stobaeus, *Anthology*

Their father's temperance is the greatest instruction for children.

D397 (B280) Stobaeus, *Anthology*

It is possible, without spending much of what one has, to educate one's children and to build a bulwark and protection around their possessions and their bodies.

D398 (B279) Stobaeus, *Anthology*

*Among one's children it is necessary, as far as is at all possible, to divide one's wealth, and at the same time to pay attention to them to make sure that they not do anything ruinous when they have taken possession of it. For they become at the same time much thriftier with regard to wealth and more eager to acquire it, and they compete with each other. For expenses shared in common do not cause distress as do those made on one's own, nor do the profits provide such contentment (*euthumei*), but much less.*

D399 (B272) Stobaeus, *Anthology*

Democritus said that whoever has had good luck with his son-in-law has found a son, but whoever has had bad luck with him has lost a daughter too.

Farm Management (D400–D402)

D400 (B27) Colum. *Agric.* 3.12.5

[. . .] Democrito [. . .] caeli plagam septentrionalem, quia existiment ei subiectas feracissimas fieri vineas, quae tamen bonitate vini superentur.

D401 (B27a) Colum. *Agric.* 9.14.6

progenerari posse apes iuvenco perempto Democritus [. . .].

D402 (B28) Colum. *Agric.* 11.3.2

Democritus in eo libro quem Georgicon appellavit parum prudenter censet eos facere, qui hortis exstruant munimenta, quod neque latere fabricata maceries perennare possit pluviis ac tempestatibus plerumque infestata, eque lapide supra rei dignitatem poscat inpensa; si vero amplum modum sepire quis velit, patrimonio esse opus.

Education (D403–D412)

D403 (B33) Stob. 2.31.65 (cf. Clem. Alex. *Strom.* 4.149)

ἡ φύσις καὶ ἡ διδαχὴ παραπλήσιόν ἐστι· καὶ γὰρ ἡ διδαχὴ μεταρυσμοῖ[1] τὸν ἄνθρωπον, μεταρυσμοῦσα[2] δὲ φυσιοποιεῖ.[3]

  [1] μετὰ ῥυσμοῦ ms., corr. Mullach (μεταρυθμίζει Clem.)
  [2] μετὰ ῥυσμοῦ ms., corr. Mullach (μεταρυθμοῦσα Clem.)

Farm Management (D400–D402)

D400 (B27) Columella, *On Agriculture*

[. . .] Democritus and [. . .] [scil. praise] the northern part of the sky because they think that vineyards exposed in this direction are most productive, even if the quality of the wine is inferior.

D401 (B27a) Columella, *On Agriculture*

That bees can be generated from a bull that has been killed, Democritus [. . .] [scil. has reported].

D402 (B28) Columella, *On Agriculture*

Democritus, in the book that he entitled *Georgic* [*On Agriculture*], thinks that those people who build protective walls around their gardens are acting imprudently. For an enclosure constructed out of bricks cannot resist for years when it is often assailed by rain and storms, while one made out of stones requires expenses greater than the thing's value. And if someone wants to enclose a large piece of land, he will have to use up his patrimony.

Education (D403–D412)

D403 (B33) Stobaeus, *Anthology*

Nature and instruction are very similar. For instruction modifies the configuration (*metarhusmoi*) of a man, and, modifying his configuration, produces a nature.

---

³ φυσιοποιεῖ Clem.: φύσιν (ις ss.) ποιεῖ ms.: ⟨καὶ⟩ φύσις π. Usener

D404 (B178) Stob. 2.31.56

πάντων κάκιστον ἡ εὐπετείη παιδεῦσαι τὴν νεότητα,
αὕτη γάρ ἐστι ἢ τίκτει τὰς ἡδονὰς ταύτας,[1] ἐξ ὧν ἡ
κακότης γίνεται.

[1] φαύλας Hense

D405 (B179) Stob. 2.31.57

†ἐξωτικῶς† μὴ[1] πονέειν παῖδες ἀνιέντες (?), οὔτε γράμ-
ματ᾽ ἂν μάθοιεν οὔτε μουσικὴν οὔτε ἀγωνίην, οὐδ᾽,
ὅπερ μάλιστα τὴν ἀρετὴν συνέχει, τὸ αἰδεῖσθαι·
μάλα γὰρ ἐκ τούτων φιλέει γίγνεσθαι ἡ αἰδώς.

[1] ἐξωτικῶς μὴ ms.: ζηλωτικῶς ὁμῆ Meineke-Wachsmuth,
ἔξω τί κως ἢ Diels, alii aliter

D406 (B180) Stob. 2.31.58

ἡ παιδεία εὐτυχοῦσι μέν ἐστι κόσμος, ἀτυχοῦσι δὲ
καταφύγιον.

D407 (B182) Stob. 2.31.66

τὰ μὲν καλὰ χρήματα τοῖς πόνοις ἡ μάθησις ἐξεργά-
ζεται, τὰ δ᾽ αἰσχρὰ ἄνευ πόνων αὐτόματα καρποῦται·[1]
καὶ γὰρ οὖν οὐκ ἐθέλοντα πολλάκις ἐξείργει τοιοῦτον
εἶναι· †οὕτω μεγάλης τε τῆς φυτικῆς ἐστι†.[2]

[1] ⟨ἡ ἀμαθίη⟩ καρποῦται Usener: καρποῦνται Meineke
[2] locus desperatus

D404 (B178) Stobaeus, *Anthology*

The worst thing of all is laxity in educating youth. For this is what gives birth to those pleasures from which wickedness comes about.

D405 (B179) Stobaeus, *Anthology*

If children †in a foreign manner† neglected (?) to exert themselves, they would not learn the alphabet nor music nor competitiveness, nor what most of all contains virtue, the feeling of a sense of shame. For it is above all from acts of this sort that a sense of shame tends to come about.

D406 (B180) Stobaeus, *Anthology*

Education is an adornment for successful people and a refuge for unsuccessful ones.

D407 (B182) Stobaeus, *Anthology*

It is by effort that learning produces fine things, but ignoble ones are reaped by themselves without effort. For they often oblige someone, even if he does not want to, to be like that †. . .†.

D408 (B183) Stob. 2.31.72

ἔστι που νέων ξύνεσις καὶ γερόντων ἀξυνεσίη· χρόνος
γὰρ οὐ διδάσκει φρονεῖν, ἀλλ' ὡραίη τροφὴ καὶ φύσις.

D409 (B185) Stob. 2.31.94

κρέσσονές εἰσιν αἱ τῶν πεπαιδευμένων ἐλπίδες ἢ ὁ
τῶν ἀμαθῶν πλοῦτος.

D410 (B77) Stob. 3.4.82 (= Democrat. *Sent.* 42)

δόξα καὶ πλοῦτος ἄνευ ξυνέσιος οὐκ ἀσφαλέα κτή-
ματα.

D411 (B242) Stob. 3.29.66

πλέονες ἐξ ἀσκήσιος ἀγαθοὶ γίγνονται ἢ ἀπὸ φύσιος.

D412 (B59) Stob. 2.31.71 (= Democrat. *Sent.* 24)

οὔτε τέχνη οὔτε σοφίη ἐφικτόν, ἢν μὴ μάθῃ τις.[1]

---

[1] μάθῃ τις Democrat.: μάθησις ms.

D408 (B183) Stobaeus, *Anthology*

*In a certain way, understanding belongs to young men and lack of understanding to old men. For it is not time that teaches how to think (*phronein*), but early upbringing and one's nature.*

D409 (B185) Stobaeus, *Anthology*

The hopes of educated people are stronger than the wealth of uneducated ones.

D410 (B77) Stobaeus, *Anthology* (attributed to Democrates)

Renown and wealth without understanding are not stable possessions.

D411 (B242) Stobaeus, *Anthology*

More people become good by training than by their nature.

D412 (B59) Stobaeus, *Anthology* (attributed to Democrates)

Neither a craft nor wisdom can be attained unless one learns.

ATOMISTS
(LEUCIPPUS [67 DK],
DEMOCRITUS [68 DK])

For Leucippus, references to DK take the form 67 Ax or Bx; for Democritus, references are generally by only Ax, Bx, or Cx.

R

Titles of Ancient Works Dedicated to
Democritus (R1–R2)
Works Concerning His Doctrines (R1)

R1 (A34a)

a Arist. (Diog. Laert. 5.26 et 27)

26. Προβλήματα ἐκ τῶν Δημοκρίτου β′
27. Πρὸς Δημόκριτον α′

b Theophr. (Diog. Laert. 5.43 et 49)

43. Περὶ τῆς Δημοκρίτου ἀστρολογίας α′
49. Περὶ Δημοκρίτου α′

ATOMISTS
(LEUCIPPUS, DEMOCRITUS)

R

Titles of Ancient Works Dedicated to
Democritus (R1–R2)
Works Concerning His Doctrines (R1)

R1 (A34a)

a Aristotle

26. *Problems derived from the writings of Democritus,* two
books
27. *Against Democritus,* one book

b Theophrastus

43. *On the Astronomy of Democritus,* one book
49. *On Democritus,* one book

c Heracl. Pont. (Diog. Laert. 5.87 et 88)

87. Πρὸς Δημόκριτον[1]

  [1] post Δημόκριτον hab. περὶ τῶν οὐρανῶν mss.

88. Πρὸς τὸν[1] Δημόκριτον ἐξηγήσεις α′

  [1] πρὸς τὸν ed. Frob.: πρῶτον BP: πρώτων (et δημοκρι-τίων) F

d Epicur. (Philod. *Lib. dic.*, Frag. 20.7–9)

ἐν [. . .] τοῖς πρὸς Δημόκριτον . . .

e Colotes

See **R88–R89**

f Metrod. (Diog. Laert. 10.24)

Πρὸς Δημόκριτον

g Cleanth. (Diog. Laert. 7.134 et 174)

134. Περὶ τῶν ἀτόμων
174. Πρὸς Δημόκριτον

c Heraclides of Pontus

87. *Against Democritus*

88. *Explanations, Against Democritus,* one book

d Epicurus[1]

in [. . .] his writings against Democritus

> [1] It is uncertain whether this was an independent book (cf. H. Usener, *Epicurea*, Leipzig 1877, p. 97).

e Colotes

See **R88–R89**

f Metrodorus (of Lampsacus, the Epicurean)

Against Democritus

g Cleanthes

134. *On Atoms*[1]
174. *Against Democritus*

> [1] It is possible that this book was directed against Epicurus rather than against the ancient Atomists. The same applies to the work of Sphaerus listed just below, as well as to the preceding title in the list of Sphaerus' works, *On the Minima.*

h Sphaer. (Diog. Laert. 7.178)

Πρὸς τὰς ἀτόμους καὶ τὰ εἴδωλα

Works Concerning His Language (R2)

R2 (A32)

a Callim. (*Suda* K.227)

Πίναξ τῶν Δημοκρίτου¹ γλωσσῶν καὶ συνταγμάτων

¹ Δημοκρίτου Adler: Δημοκράτους mss.

b Heges. Gramm. (Steph. Byz. s.v. Τρωάς)
Περὶ τῆς Δημοκρίτου λέξεως βιβλίον ἐν

Democritus' Language and Style (R3–R9)
Morphological Notices (R3)

R3

a (B13) Apoll. Dysc. *Pronom.*, p. 65.15

καὶ Φερεκύδης ἐν τῇ θεολογίᾳ καὶ ἔτι Δημόκριτος ἐν τοῖς Περὶ ἀστρονομίας καὶ ἐν τοῖς ὑπολειπομένοις συντάγμασι συνεχέστερον χρῶνται τῇ **ἐμεῦ** καὶ ἔτι τῇ **ἐμέο**.

b (B29a) Apoll. Dysc. *Pronom.*, p. 92.20

αἱ πληθυντικαὶ κοινολεκτοῦνται κατ᾽ εὐθεῖαν πρός τε

h Sphaerus

Against the Atoms and Images

Works Concerning His Language (R2)

R2 (A32)

a Callimachus

Catalog of the Rare Words (glôssai) *and Phrases* (suntagmata) *of Democritus*[1]

> [1] The mss. have 'Democrates.'

b Hegesianax the Grammarian

On Democritus' Style (lexis), one book

Democritus' Language and Style (R3–R9)
Morphological Notices (R3)

R3

a (B13) Apollonius Dyscolus, *On Pronouns*

Both Pherecydes in his *Theology* [cf. **PHER. R8a**] and also Democritus in his books on astronomy and in his remaining treatises often use **'emeu'** and also **'emeo'** ('my,' both the contracted and uncontracted forms).

b (B29a) Apollonius Dyscolus, *On Pronouns*

In the nominative, the plural forms *hêmeis, humeis, spheis*

Ἰώνων καὶ Ἀττικῶν, ἡμεῖς, ὑμεῖς, σφεῖς, ἔστι ⟨δὲ⟩[1]
πιστώσασθαι καὶ τὸ ἀδιαίρετον τῆς εὐθείας παρ' Ἴω-
σιν ἐκ τῶν περὶ Δημόκριτον, Φερεκύδην [. . .].

[1] ⟨δὲ⟩ Wilamowitz

c (B129a) *Epimer. Hom.* 396.11

καὶ παρὰ τὸ κλίνω **κέκλιται** παρὰ τῷ Δημοκρίτῳ χωρὶς τοῦ ν.

d (B19) Eust. *In Il.* 3.1, vol. 1, p. 584.3–4

τὸ γάμμα στοιχεῖον **γέμμα** φασὶν Ἴωνες καὶ μάλιστα
Δημόκριτος, ὃς καὶ τὸ μῦ **μῶ** λέγει.

e (B128) Hdn. *Prosod. cath.*, vol. 1, p. 355.11

τὸ γὰρ **ἰθύτρην** παρὰ Δημοκρίτῳ βεβίασται.

f (B131) Hesych. A.5840

ἀπάτητον· τὸ ἀνωμάλως συγκείμενον. παρὰ Δημοκρίτῳ.

g (B20) Schol. in Dion. Thrax, p. 184.3 et 23

τὰ ὀνόματα τῶν στοιχείων ἄκλιτά εἰσιν [. . .] παρὰ
Δημοκρίτῳ δὲ κλίνονται· λέγει γὰρ **δέλτατος** καὶ **θή-**
τατος.

('we,' 'you,' 'they') are used in common by both Ionians and Attics, but the uncontracted form of the nominative can also be documented among the Ionians from the works of Democritus, Pherecydes [cf. **PHER. R8b**] [. . .].

c (B129a) *Homeric Epimerisms*

And from *klinô* ('I cause to lean') [scil. is derived] ***keklitai*** ('is leaning') in Democritus without the *nu*.

d (B19) Eustathius, *Commentary on Homer's* Iliad

The Ionians call the letter *gamma* **'gemma,'** and especially Democritus, who also calls *mu* **'mô.'**

e (B128) Herodian, *General Prosody*

The form **'ithutrên'** ('straight-bored') in Democritus is an unnatural coinage.

f (B131) Hesychius, *Lexicon*

apatêton ('untrodden'): compounded irregularly; in Democritus.

g (B20) Scholia on Dionysius of Thrace's *Art of Grammar*

The names of the letters are not declined [. . .] but they are declined in Democritus. For he says **'deltatos'** ('of *delta*') and **'thêtatos'** ('of *theta*').

Lexical Notices (R4)

R4

a (cf. B298) Phot. *Lex.* A.1

[*scil. ἅ·*] βραχέως δὲ καὶ δασέως ἐκφερόμενον [. . .] σημαίνει, παρὰ δὲ Δημοκρίτῳ ἴδια [. . .].

b (B29) Apoll. Cit. *In Hipp. Artic.*, p. 28.2–7

[. . .] ὁ Βακχεῖος [. . .] ἐν τοῖς[1] Περὶ τῶν Ἱπποκρατείων λέξεων [. . .] φησὶν πάλιν· "ἀναγέγραπται δὲ καὶ ὡς ὁ Δημόκριτος εἴη καλῶν τῆς ἴτυος τὴν τῷ κοίλῳ περικειμένην ὀφρὺν ἄμβην."

[1] ἐν τοῖς Diels: ουτως L: οὕτως ‹ἐν τοῖς› Schoene

c (B139a) Hesych. A.3564

ἀμειψίχρον·[1] μεταβάλλοντα ‹τὴν χρόαν›.[2]

[1] ἀμειψίχροον Kuster   [2] ‹τὴν χρόαν› Kuster

d (B130) Hesych. A.3988

ἀμφιδήτιοι· ὡς κρίκοι διάκενοι, παρὰ Δημοκρίτῳ.

ATOMISTS (LEUCIPPUS, DEMOCRITUS)

Lexical Notices[1] *(R4)*

[1] For further lexical notices from the grammatical tradition concerning Democritus, see also **D34b**, **D38**, **D83b**, **D146**, **D167**, **D180**, **D182**, **D215**, **D218**, **D232**.

R4

a (cf. B298) Photius, *Lexicon*

[scil. *alpha*] pronounced short and with rough breathing [i.e. '**ha**'] means [. . .], 'one's own things' in Democritus.

b (B29) Apollonius of Citium, *Commentary on Hippocrates'* On Joints

[. . .] Bacchius [scil. of Tanagra] [. . .] in his *Hippocratic Lexicon* [. . .] says again, "It is also registered that Democritus calls the rim lying around the hollow of a shield '**ambê**' ('circuit')."

c (B139a) Hesychius, *Lexicon*

ameipsikhron: 'changing ⟨the color⟩.'

d (B130) Hesychius, *Lexicon*

amphidêtioi: like empty rings, in Democritus.

e (B144a) Phot. *Lex.* A.1406

ἀναβήσομαι· Δημόκριτος ἀντὶ τοῦ ἐπανελεύσομαι
⟨ἐπὶ τὰ⟩¹ ἐξ ἀρχῆς.

¹ ⟨ἐπὶ τὰ⟩ Diels

f (B132) Hesych. A.7691

ἀσκαληνές·¹ ἰσόπλευρον, παρὰ Δημοκρίτῳ.

¹ ἀσκαληρές H, corr. Diels

g (B133) Hesych. B.1215

βροχμώδης· ἡ νοτερὰ καὶ ἁπαλή, Δημόκριτος.

h (B134) Hesych. B.1218

βρόχος· ἀγκύλη,¹ Δημόκριτος.² ἀγχόνη, δεσμός.

¹ ἀγκοίλη mss., corr. Musurus   ² ἀγκοίλη, Δημόκριτος
del. Soping

i (B136) Hesych. Δ.2498

δυοχοῖ· πωματίζει παρὰ Δημοκρίτῳ, ἤγουν πωμάζει,
σκεπάζει.

j (B121) Eust. *In Od.* 2.190, p. 1441.18

Δημόκριτος δὲ ἐπιτηδειέστατόν φησι.

e (B144a) Photius, *Lexicon*

***anabêsomai*:** Democritus instead of 'I shall go back ‹to›
the beginning.'

f (B132) Hesychius, *Lexicon*

askalênes: 'equilateral,' in Democritus.

g (B133) Hesychius, *Lexicon*

brokhmôdês: 'moist and soft,' Democritus.

h (B134) Hesychius, *Lexicon*

brokhos: 'noose,' Democritus. Strangling, bond.

i (B136) Hesychius, *Lexicon*

duokhoi: 'he/it covers with a lid' in Democritus, or 'cover
up,' 'protect.'

j (B121) Eustathius, *Commentary on Homer's* Odyssey

Democritus says **'*epitêdeiestatos*'** ('most suitable').

k (B122) *Etym. Gen.* A.399 s.v. ἀλαπάξαι

[. . .] καὶ Δημόκριτος τοὺς παρὰ τῶν κυνηγετῶν γινο-
μένους βόθρους ‹λα›πάθους[1] καλεῖ διὰ τὸ κεκενῶ-
σθαι.

  [1] ‹λα›πάθους Lasserre-Livadaras

l (B137) Hesych. Σ.2156

συγγονή· σύστασις. Δημόκριτος.

His Style (R5–R9)

R5 (A34) Cic. *De orat.* 1.11.49

si ornate locutus est, sicut et fertur et mihi videtur,
physicus ille Democritus, materies illa fuit physici de qua
dixit, ornatus vero ipse verborum oratoris putandus est.

R6 (A34) Cic. *Orat.* 20.67

itaque video visum esse non nullis Platonis et Democriti
locutionem etsi absit a versu, tamen quod incitatius fera-
tur et clarissimis verborum luminibus utatur, potius poema
putandum quam comicorum poetarum [. . .].

R7 (A34) Cic. *Div.* 2.64.133

valde Heraclitus obscurus, minime Democritus.

k (B122) Etymologicum Genuinum

[. . .] and Democritus calls the pits made by hunters '*<la>pathoi*' because they are hollowed out.

l (B137) Hesychius, *Lexicon*

sungonê: 'composition.' Democritus.

His Style (R5–R9)

R5 (A34) Cicero, *On the Orator*

If the celebrated natural philosopher Democritus has expressed himself in an ornamented style, as is reported and as seems to me to be the case, the material about which he spoke belonged to natural philosophy, but the ornament of the words itself must be thought to belong to the orator.

R6 (A34) Cicero, *The Orator*

I see that some people have thought that the style of Plato and Democritus, even if it is free of poetic meter, nevertheless, since it moves along with great rapidity and makes use of the most brilliant verbal ornaments, is more to be considered a [scil. real] poem than those of the comic poets [. . .].

R7 (A34) Cicero, *On Divination*

Heraclitus is extremely obscure [cf. **HER. R5–R11**], Democritus not at all.

361

R8 (A34) Dion. Hal. *Comp. verb.* 24

[. . .] φιλοσόφων δὲ κατ᾽ ἐμὴν δόξαν Δημόκριτός τε καὶ Πλάτων καὶ Ἀριστοτέλης· τούτων γὰρ¹ ἑτέρους εὑρεῖν ἀμήχανον ἄμεινον κεράσαντας τοὺς λόγους.

¹ γὰρ F: δὲ PMV

R9 (< A77) Plut. *Quaest. conv.* 5.7.6 683A

[. . .] τῇ δὲ λέξει δαιμονίως λέγειν καὶ μεγαλοπρεπῶς.

Anaxagoras' Attitude Toward Democritus (R10)

R10 (< 59 A1) Diog. Laert. 2.14

ἔδοξε δέ πως καὶ Δημοκρίτῳ ἀπεχθῶς ἐσχηκέναι, ἀποτυχὼν τῆς πρὸς αὐτὸν κοινολογίας.

Plato's Attitude Toward Democritus (R11)

R11 (< A1) Diog. Laert. 9.40

Ἀριστόξενος δ᾽ ἐν τοῖς Ἱστορικοῖς ὑπομνήμασί φησι [Frag. 131 Wehrli] Πλάτωνα θελῆσαι συμφλέξαι τὰ Δημοκρίτου συγγράμματα, ὁπόσα ἐδυνήθη συναγαγεῖν, Ἀμύκλαν δὲ καὶ Κλεινίαν τοὺς Πυθαγορικοὺς

R8 (A34) Dionysius of Halicarnassus, *On Word Order*

[. . .] among the philosophers, in my opinion, Democritus, Plato, and Aristotle [scil. are the greatest writers in the intermediate style]. For it is impossible to find anyone else who has mixed the [scil. kinds of] discourse better than these.

R9 (< A77) Plutarch, *Table Talk*

[. . .] but the style he uses when he speaks is divine and sublime.

Anaxagoras' Attitude Toward Democritus (R10)

R10 (< 59 A1) Diogenes Laertius

He [i.e. Anaxagoras] seemed in some way to feel hostile toward Democritus, since he had failed to enter into a discussion with him.[1]

> [1] The relation between this report and Diog. Laert. 9.34–35 (**ANAXAG. R2; ATOM. P25**) is problematic: was it Anaxagoras who rejected Democritus, or was it the other way around?

Plato's Attitude Toward Democritus (R11)

R11 (< A1) Diogenes Laertius

Aristoxenus says in his *Historical Memoirs* that Plato wanted to burn all the writings of Democritus that he was able to collect, but that the Pythagoreans Amyclas and Clinias prevented him on the grounds that this would be

κωλῦσαι αὐτόν, ὡς οὐδὲν ὄφελος· παρὰ πολλοῖς γὰρ
εἶναι ἤδη τὰ βιβλία. καὶ δῆλον δέ· πάντων γὰρ σχεδὸν τῶν ἀρχαίων μεμνημένος ὁ Πλάτων οὐδαμοῦ Δημοκρίτου διαμνημονεύει, ἀλλ' οὐδὲ ἔνθα[1] ἀντειπεῖν τι[2]
αὐτῷ δέοι, δῆλον <ὅτι>[3] εἰδὼς ὡς πρὸς τὸν ἄριστον
αὐτῷ[4] τῶν φιλοσόφων <ὁ ἀγὼν> ἔσοιτο.[5]

[1] ἔνθα <ἂν> Long   [2] ἀντειπεῖν τι Β (ἀντιπεῖν) P[1]: ἀντι-
πίπτειν F P[4] in marg.   [3] <ὅτι> Reiske   [4] αὐτῷ Cobet:
οὕτω mss.   [5] <ὁ ἀγὼν> ἔσοιτο Casaubon: ἐρίσοι Lapini: an
οὕτω . . . εἴσιοι vel αὐτῷ . . . εἰσιτέον?

The Atomists in Aristotle and the
Peripatetic Tradition (R12–R67)

Cf. **R1a, b, c**

Parallels (R12–R21)
With the Natural Philosophers in General (R12)

R12 (cf. ad 28 B8) Arist. *Phys.* 1.5 188a19–26

πάντες δὴ τἀναντία ἀρχὰς ποιοῦσιν [. . .] (καὶ γὰρ
Παρμενίδης θερμὸν καὶ ψυχρὸν ἀρχὰς ποιεῖ [. . .]) καὶ
οἱ μανὸν καὶ πυκνόν, καὶ Δημόκριτος τὸ πλῆρες[1] καὶ
κενόν, ὧν τὸ μὲν ὡς ὂν τὸ δὲ ὡς οὐκ ὂν εἶναί φησιν·
ἔτι θέσει, σχήματι, τάξει· ταῦτα δὲ γένη ἐναντίων·
θέσεως ἄνω κάτω, πρόσθεν ὄπισθεν, σχήματος γεγωνιωμένον[2] ἀγώνιον,[3] εὐθὺ περιφερές.

[1] πλῆρες E[1]I: στερεὸν E[2]FJ   [2] γεγωνιωμένον FI:
γωνία EJ   [3] ἀγώνιον om. mss. plerique

useless, since many people already possessed the books. And this is clearly the case: for although Plato mentions almost all the ancients, he never makes mention of Democritus anywhere, even where it would have been necessary for him to contradict him, clearly because he knew that ⟨the struggle⟩ would oppose him to the greatest of philosophers.

The Atomists in Aristotle and the Peripatetic Tradition (R12–R67)

Cf. **R1a, b, c**

Parallels (R12–R21) With the Natural Philosophers in General (R12)

R12 (cf. ad 28 B8) Aristotle, *Physics*

They all make the contraries principles [. . .] for Parmenides too makes hot and cold principles, [. . . cf. **PARM. R11**], as well as those who [scil. take as principles] the rarefied and dense, and Democritus [scil. who takes] the solid and the void, of which he says that the one is what is, the other what is not; and who furthermore, [scil. has recourse to] position, shape, and order. And these are genera of contraries: for position, up/down, in front/in back; for shape, with an angle/without an angle, straight/round.[1]

---

[1] Or, with a different reading: "for the shape, an angle, straight or round." For according to Democritus, a sphere is an angle of a certain kind (cf. **D60b**).

With the Pythagoreans (R13–R14)

R13 (67 A15, 68 A120) Arist. *Cael.* 3.4 303a3–10

ἀλλὰ μὴν οὐδ᾽ ὡς ἕτεροί τινες λέγουσιν, οἷον Λεύκιππός τε καὶ Δημόκριτος ὁ Ἀβδηρίτης, εὔλογα τὰ συμ-
βαίνοντα· φασὶ γὰρ εἶναι τὰ πρῶτα μεγέθη πλήθει
μὲν ἄπειρα, μεγέθει δὲ ἀδιαίρετα, καὶ οὔτ᾽ ἐξ ἑνὸς
πολλὰ γίγνεσθαι οὔτε ἐκ πολλῶν ἕν, ἀλλὰ τῇ τούτων
συμπλοκῇ καὶ ἐπαλλάξει¹ πάντα γεννᾶσθαι [**D45**].
τρόπον γάρ τινα καὶ οὗτοι πάντα τὰ ὄντα ποιοῦσιν
ἀριθμοὺς καὶ ἐξ ἀριθμῶν· καὶ γὰρ εἰ μὴ σαφῶς δη-
λοῦσιν, ὅμως τοῦτο βούλονται λέγειν.

¹ ἐπαλλάξει JHE⁴: περιπλέξει E: περιπαλάξει Diels (cf.
app. ad **D35b** et **D36**)

R14

a (< 101.1 Leszl) Arist. *An.* 1.3 404a16–20

[. . . = **ATOM. D132, D136**] ἔοικε δὲ καὶ τὸ παρὰ τῶν
Πυθαγορείων λεγόμενον τὴν αὐτὴν ἔχειν διάνοιαν·
ἔφασαν γάρ τινες αὐτῶν ψυχὴν εἶναι τὰ ἐν τῷ ἀέρι
ξύσματα, οἱ δὲ τὸ ταῦτα κινοῦν, περὶ δὲ τούτων εἴρηται ὅτι συνεχῶς φαίνεται κινούμενα, κἂν ᾖ νηνεμία
παντελής.

With the Pythagoreans (R13–R14)

R13 (67 A15, 68 A120) Aristotle, *On the Heavens*

But the consequences resulting from the way in which certain others [scil. than the Pythagoreans] speak, like Leucippus and Democritus of Abdera, are not plausible either. For they say that the first magnitudes are unlimited in number, but indivisible in magnitude, and that neither can a plurality come about out of one nor one out of a plurality, but that it is by the interlacing and **intertwining** (*epallaxis*) of these things that all things are generated. For in a certain way these latter too make all beings numbers and constitute them out of numbers. And even if they do not indicate this clearly, all the same it is this that they mean to say.

R14

a (≠ DK) Aristotle, *On the Soul*

[. . .] It seems that what the Pythagoreans say means the same thing [scil. as what Leucippus and Democritus say about the soul, cf. **ATOM. D132, D136**]. For some of them said that the soul is motes (*xusmata*) in the air, others that it is what moves these. People say about these that they are seen to be in constant motion, even if there is a total lack of a breeze [= **PYTHS. ANON. D49**].

367

b (< 101.4 Leszl) Simpl. *In An.*, p. 26.11–19

πότερον δὲ οὕτως ὁ Δημόκριτος ἀπὸ σωμάτων ἐγέννα
τὴν ζωήν, ἢ ἐνδεικτικῶς τὴν νοερὰν ἐβούλετο διὰ
τῆς σφαίρας οὐσίαν, οὐκ ἔχομεν ἀποφήνασθαι. οὐ
δεῖ γὰρ τῇ Ἀριτοτελικῇ ἐπερείδεσθαι ἱστορίᾳ διὰ τὸ
ὡς ἐπίπαν μόνον ἐκτίθεσθαι τὸ φαινόμενον, ὥσπερ
καὶ τὸ περὶ τῶν Πυθαγορείων ἐπαγόμενον. τὸν μὲν
γὰρ Δημόκριτον ἱστορεῖ ὅμοια τοῖς ἐν ἀέρι λέγειν ξύ-
σμασι τὰ στοιχεῖα, τινὰς δὲ τῶν Πυθαγορείων αὐτὰ
ταῦτα, οὐκ ἂν ταῦτα οἰηθέντων ποτὲ τῶν Πυθαγορείων ἀνδρῶν, ἐνδεικνυμένων δὲ ἴσως τὴν ἤδη
μεριζομένην τῆς ψυχῆς οὐσίαν καὶ εἰς τὸ φανερὸν
προϊοῦσαν.

With Anaxagoras (R15–R16)

R15 (> 59 A45) Arist. *Phys.* 3.4 203a19–24, a33–b2

ὅσοι δ' ἄπειρα ποιοῦσι τὰ στοιχεῖα, καθάπερ Ἀναξαγόρας καὶ Δημόκριτος, ὁ μὲν ἐκ τῶν ὁμοιομερῶν, ὁ δ'
ἐκ τῆς πανσπερμίας τῶν σχημάτων, τῇ ἁφῇ συνεχὲς
τὸ ἄπειρον εἶναί φασιν [**D46**]. καὶ ὁ μὲν ὁτιοῦν τῶν
μορίων εἶναι μίγμα ὁμοίως τῷ παντὶ διὰ τὸ ὁρᾶν
ὁτιοῦν ἐξ ὁτουοῦν γιγνόμενον· [. . .] Δημόκριτος δ' οὐδὲν ἕτερον ἐξ ἑτέρου γίγνεσθαι τῶν πρώτων φησίν·
ἀλλ' ὅμως γε αὐτῷ τὸ κοινὸν σῶμα πάντων ἐστὶν
ἀρχή, μεγέθει κατὰ μόρια καὶ σχήματι διαφέρον.

b (≠ DK) Simplicius, *Commentary on Aristotle's* On the Soul

Whether Democritus was generating life in this way on the basis of bodies, or whether he wished to indicate the intelligible substance by means of the sphere [cf. **ATOM. D132**], we are not able to assert. For one should not rely on Aristotle's report since, as he does in general, he only explains the appearance, as also in what he mentions regarding the Pythagoreans. For he reports that Democritus says that the elements are similar to motes (*xusmata*) in the air, and that some Pythagoreans [scil. say] exactly the same thing, whereas never would the Pythagorean men have thought this, but they were surely showing the substance of the soul already divided and progressing toward its manifestation.

With Anaxagoras (R15–R16)

R15 (> 59 A45) Aristotle, *Physics*

Those [scil. natural philosophers] who posit that the elements are unlimited [scil. in number], like Anaxagoras and Democritus, constituted for the former out of the homoeomers, for the latter out of the 'universal seminal reserve' (*panspermia*) of the shapes, say that the unlimited exists as continuous by virtue of contact. And the former says that any one of the parts is a mixture in the same way as the whole, because it is seen that every thing comes about from every thing. [. . .] But Democritus says that none of the first [scil. elements] comes about out of another of them; but all the same, the common body is for him the principle of all things, differing in its parts by its magnitude and shape.

R16 (< 57 Leszl) Arist. *Metaph.* Γ5 1009a25–30

εἰ οὖν μὴ ἐνδέχεται γενέσθαι τὸ μὴ ὄν, προυπῆρχεν
ὁμοίως τὸ πρᾶγμα ἄμφω ὄν, ὥσπερ καὶ Ἀναξαγόρας
μεμῖχθαι πᾶν ἐν παντί φησι καὶ Δημόκριτος· καὶ γὰρ
οὗτος τὸ κενὸν καὶ τὸ πλῆρες ὁμοίως καθ' ὁτιοῦν
ὑπάρχειν μέρος, καίτοι τὸ μὲν ὄν τούτων εἶναι τὸ δὲ
μὴ ὄν.

With Protagoras (R17)

R17 (< 57.3 Leszl) Alex. *In Metaph.*, pp. 271.38–272.2

ἕπεται δὲ τοῦτο καὶ τοῖς λέγουσιν ἑκάστῳ τὸ φαινόμενον καὶ εἶναι τοιοῦτον, ὧν εἶεν ἂν οἵ τε περὶ Δημόκριτον καὶ Πρωταγόραν.

With Plato and the Platonists (R18–R21)

R18 (67 A7) Arist. *GC* 1.8 325b25–33

τοσοῦτον γὰρ διαφέρει τοῦ μὴ τὸν αὐτὸν τρόπον Λευκίππῳ λέγειν, ὅτι ὁ μὲν στερεὰ ὁ δ' ἐπίπεδα λέγει τὰ
ἀδιαίρετα, καὶ ὁ μὲν ἀπείροις ὡρίσθαι σχήμασι τῶν
ἀδιαιρέτων στερεῶν ἕκαστον ὁ δὲ ὡρισμένοις, ἐπεὶ
ἀδιαίρετά γε ἀμφότεροι λέγουσι καὶ ὡρισμένα σχήμασιν. ἐκ δὴ τούτων αἱ γενέσεις καὶ αἱ διακρίσεις,
Λευκίππῳ μὲν δύο τρόποι ἂν εἶεν, διά τε τοῦ κενοῦ καὶ

R16 (≠ DK) Aristotle, *Metaphysics*

If then it is not possible that what is not came to be, the thing must have existed before, being both [scil. contraries] alike, as Anaxagoras says that everything is mixed in everything [cf. **ANAXAG. D25**] as well as Democritus: for the latter too says that the void and the full are found alike in any part, even if one of these is being and the other nonbeing.

With Protagoras (R17)

R17 (≠ DK) Alexander of Aphrodisias, *Commentary on Aristotle's* Metaphysics

This consequence [i.e. the negation of the principle of contradiction] follows for those who say that what appears to each person is also what kind of thing it is; among these are Democritus and Protagoras.

With Plato and the Platonists (R18–R21)

R18 (67 A7) Aristotle, *On Generation and Corruption*

He [i.e. Plato] only differs from Leucippus' way of speaking insofar as the latter says that the indivisibles are solids, the former that they are surfaces [cf. *Timaeus* 53c–55c], and that for the former each of the indivisible solids is delimited by shapes that are unlimited [scil. in number], while for the latter they are limited, since both speak of entities that are indivisible and limited by shapes. It is on the basis of these that generations and dissociations occur; for Leucippus, there would be two ways, by the void and

διὰ τῆς ἁφῆς (ταύτῃ γὰρ διαιρετὸν ἕκαστον), Πλάτωνι
δὲ κατὰ τὴν ἁφὴν μόνον· κενὸν γὰρ οὐκ εἶναί φησιν.

R19 (47.3 Leszl) Simpl. *In Cael.*, p. 576.10–19

ἀλλὰ τί, φησίν, διοίσει τῆς Δημοκρίτου δόξης ἡ ἐκ
τῶν ἐπιπέδων λέγουσα, εἴπερ καὶ αὐτὴ κατὰ τὰ σχήματα εἰδοποιεῖσθαι τὰ φυσικὰ σώματά φησι; ῥᾴδιον
δὴ καὶ πρὸς τοῦτο λέγειν, ὅτι κατὰ τοῦτο μὲν οὐδὲν
διαφέρει· καὶ γάρ, ὅπερ καὶ πρότερον εἶπον [cf.
p. 564.24–26 = **D57a**], Δημόκριτον ὁ Θεόφραστος
ἱστορεῖ ὡς ἰδιωτικῶς ἀποδιδόντων τῶν κατὰ τὸ θερμὸν καὶ τὸ ψυχρὸν καὶ τὰ τοιαῦτα αἰτιολογούντων
ἐπὶ τὰς ἀτόμους ἀναβῆναι· διαφέρει δὲ ἴσως ταύτης
ἐκείνη ἡ δόξα καὶ τῷ ἁπλούστερόν τι τῶν σωμάτων
προϋποτεθέσθαι τὸ ἐπίπεδον τῶν ἀτόμων σωμάτων οὐσῶν καὶ τῷ συμμετρίας καὶ ἀναλογίας δημιουργικὰς
τοῖς σχήμασιν ἐνιδεῖν καὶ τῷ περὶ τῆς γῆς ἀλλοίως
διαιτᾶσθαι.[1]

[1] διαιτᾶσθαι Heiberg: διατᾶσθαι A¹: διατάττεσθαι A²DEF

R20 Arist. *An.*

a (≠ DK) 1.4 409a10–15

δόξειε δ᾿ ἂν οὐθὲν διαφέρειν μονάδας λέγειν ἢ σω-
μάτια μικρά· καὶ γὰρ ἐκ τῶν Δημοκρίτου σφαιρίων
ἐὰν γένωνται στιγμαί, μόνον δὲ μένῃ τὸ ποσόν, ἔσται
τι ἐν αὐτῷ τὸ μὲν κινοῦν τὸ δὲ κινούμενον, ὥσπερ ἐν

by contact (for it is in this way that each thing can be divided); for Plato, according to contact alone (for he says that there is no void).

R19 (≠ DK) Simplicius, *Commentary on Aristotle's* On the Heavens

But, he [i.e. Alexander of Aphrodisias] says, in what regard will the opinion speaking on the basis of surfaces differ from Democritus', if indeed this latter too states that physical bodies have their specifications (*eidopoieisthai*) on the basis of the shapes? It is quite easy to reply to this that in this regard they do not differ at all; for, as I said earlier [cf. **D57a**], Theophrastus reports [scil. in his *Physics*] that Democritus went back to the atoms, on the idea that those who invoke as causes cold and warmth and these kinds of things are giving idiosyncratic explanations; but surely the other opinion differs from this one by positing the surface as something simpler than bodies, atoms being bodies, by seeing demiurgic symmetries and analogies in the shapes, and by judging differently regarding the earth [cf. Plato, *Timaeus*, 55d–e].

R20 Aristotle, *On the Soul*

a (≠ DK)

It would seem to make no difference whether one speaks of unities (*monades*) [scil. like such Platonists as Xenocrates, who define the soul as a self-moving number] or of small corpuscles. For if one makes the little spheres of Democritus points, and only quantity remains, there will be in it [i.e. the point] one part that imparts motion and

τῷ συνεχεῖ· οὐ γὰρ διὰ τὸ μεγέθει διαφέρειν ἢ μικρότητι συμβαίνει τὸ λεχθέν, ἀλλ' ὅτι ποσόν.

b (> A104a) 1.5 409a31–b4

συμβαίνει δέ [. . .] τῇ μὲν ταὐτὸ λέγειν τοῖς σῶμά τι
λεπτομερὲς αὐτὴν τιθεῖσι, τῇ δ', ὥσπερ Δημόκριτος
κινεῖσθαί φησιν ὑπὸ τῆς ψυχῆς, ἴδιον τὸ ἄτοπον. εἴπερ γάρ ἐστιν ἡ ψυχὴ ἐν παντὶ τῷ αἰσθανομένῳ
σώματι, ἀναγκαῖον ἐν τῷ αὐτῷ δύο εἶναι σώματα, εἰ
σῶμά τι ἡ ψυχή· τοῖς δ' ἀριθμὸν λέγουσιν [. . .].

R21 (< A135) Theophr. *Sens.* 60–61

[60] Δημόκριτος δὲ καὶ Πλάτων ἐπὶ πλεῖστόν εἰσιν
ἡμμένοι, καθ' ἕκαστον γὰρ ἀφορίζουσι, πλὴν ὁ μὲν
οὐκ ἀποστερῶν τῶν αἰσθητῶν τὴν φύσιν, Δημόκριτος
δὲ πάντα πάθη τῆς αἰσθήσεως ποιῶν. [. . .] Δημόκριτος μὲν οὖν οὐχ ὁμοίως λέγει περὶ πάντων, ἀλλὰ τὰ
μὲν τοῖς μεγέθεσι, τὰ δὲ τοῖς σχήμασιν, ἔνια δὲ τάξει
καὶ θέσει διορίζει. Πλάτων δὲ σχεδὸν ἅπαντα πρὸς
τὰ πάθη καὶ τὴν αἴσθησιν ἀποδίδωσιν. ὥστε δόξειεν
ἂν ἑκάτερος ἐναντίως τῇ ὑποθέσει λέγειν. [61] ὁ μὲν
γὰρ πάθη ποιῶν τῆς αἰσθήσεως καθ' αὑτὰ διορίζει
τὴν φύσιν· ὁ δὲ καθ' αὑτὰ ποιῶν ταῖς οὐσίαις πρὸς
τὰ πάθη τῆς αἰσθήσεως ἀποδίδωσι. [. . . = **D69**]

another that is moved, just as in the continuum. For it is not because of a difference in largeness or smallness that what we have described occurs, but because there is quantity.

b (> A104a) What happens [. . .] is that on the one hand they [i.e. the proponents of the Platonic theory] say the same thing as those who posit that it [i.e. the soul] is a kind of subtle body, and that on the other, just as Democritus claims that it [i.e. the body] is moved by the soul, [scil. they say] their own particular absurdity. For if the soul is present throughout the whole perceiving body, there must exist two bodies in the same place if the soul is a body. And as for those who say it is a number [. . .].

R21 (< A135) Theophrastus, *On Sensations*

[60] Democritus and Plato have most deeply studied the question [i.e. of the nature of perceptibles], for they provide a definition in every case, except that the latter does not deprive the perceptible realities of their nature, while Democritus makes all of them affections of sensation. [. . .] Democritus does not speak in the same way about all the phenomena, but defines some by magnitudes, others by shapes, and some by order and position. Plato, by contrast, explains almost all of them in relation to affection and sensation. So that each of them would seem to contradict his hypothesis. [61] For the one who makes them affections of sensation defines them in their nature as realities in themselves; while the one who makes them, by their substance, realities in themselves explains them in relation to affections of sensation. [. . .]

Praise (R22–R23)

R22 (24.3 Leszl) Arist. *GC* 1.2 316a5–14

αἴτιον δὲ τοῦ ἐπ᾽ ἔλαττον δύνασθαι τὰ ὁμολογούμενα
συνορᾶν ἡ ἀπειρία. διὸ ὅσοι ἐνῳκήκασι μᾶλλον ἐν
τοῖς φυσικοῖς, μᾶλλον δύνανται ὑποτίθεσθαι τοιαύτας
ἀρχὰς αἳ ἐπὶ πολὺ δύνανται συνείρειν· οἱ δ᾽ ἐκ τῶν
λόγων πολλῶν ἀθεώρητοι τῶν ὑπαρχόντων ὄντες,
πρὸς ὀλίγα βλέψαντες, ἀποφαίνονται ῥᾷον. ἴδοι δ᾽ ἄν
τις καὶ ἐκ τούτων ὅσον διαφέρουσιν οἱ φυσικῶς καὶ
λογικῶς σκοποῦντες· περὶ γὰρ τοῦ ἄτομα εἶναι μεγέθη οἱ μέν φασιν διότι αὐτὸ τὸ τρίγωνον πολλὰ
ἔσται, Δημόκριτος δ᾽ ἂν φανείη οἰκείοις καὶ φυσικοῖς
λόγοις πεπεῖσθαι.

R23 (A42) Arist. *Metaph.* Z13 1039a7–11

[. . .] εἰ ἡ οὐσία ἕν, οὐκ ἔσται ἐξ οὐσιῶν ἐνυπαρχου-
σῶν καὶ κατὰ τοῦτον τὸν τρόπον, ὃν λέγει Δημόκριτος ὀρθῶς· ἀδύνατον γὰρ εἶναί φησιν ἐκ δύο ἓν ἢ ἐξ
ἑνὸς δύο γενέσθαι· τὰ γὰρ μεγέθη τὰ ἄτομα τὰς οὐσίας ποιεῖ.

Criticisms (R24–R67)
Regarding Definition (R24–R25)

R24 (B165) Arist. *PA* 1.1 640b29–35

εἰ μὲν οὖν τῷ σχήματι καὶ τῷ χρώματι ἕκαστόν ἐστι

Praise (R22–R23)

R22 (≠ DK) Aristotle, *On Generation and Corruption*

The reason for a diminished capability of seeing the agreed facts is lack of experience. And that is why those who live more among physical phenomena are more capable of positing such principles as can be connected together more fully; while those who because of a multitude of arguments become unobservant of what happens look at only a few cases and make pronouncements too easily. One can see from this too how much those who study things physically are different from those who do so dialectically. For on the question of the existence of indivisible magnitudes, the ones say that there will be a multiplicity of triangles in themselves, whereas Democritus would seem to have been persuaded by appropriate arguments, that is, physical ones.

R23 (A42) Aristotle, *Metaphysics*

[. . .] if substance is one, it will not be composed out of inherent substances, and this in accordance with the argument that Democritus states correctly. For he says that it is impossible that one come from two, or two from one; for he makes substances indivisible magnitudes.

Criticisms (R24–R67)
Regarding Definition (R24–R25)

R24 (B165) Aristotle, *Parts of Animals*

If then each animal and each of its parts consisted in shape

τῶν τε ζῴων καὶ τῶν μορίων, ὀρθῶς ἂν Δημόκριτος
λέγοι· φαίνεται γὰρ οὕτως ὑπολαβεῖν. φησὶ γοῦν
παντὶ δῆλον εἶναι οἷόν τι τὴν μορφήν ἐστιν ὁ ἄνθρωπος, ὡς ὄντος αὐτοῦ τῷ τε σχήματι καὶ τῷ χρώματι
γνωρίμου. καίτοι καὶ ὁ τεθνεὼς ἔχει τὴν αὐτὴν τοῦ
σχήματος μορφήν, ἀλλ᾽ ὅμως οὐκ ἔστιν ἄνθρωπος.

R25 (< A135) Theophr. *Sens.* 82

[. . . = **R59**] περὶ δὲ ὀσμῆς προσαφορίζειν παρῆκεν[1]
πλὴν τοσοῦτον, ὅτι τὸ λεπτὸν ἀπορρέον ἀπὸ τῶν
βαρέων[2] ποιεῖ τὴν ὀδμήν. ποῖον δέ τι τὴν φύσιν ὂν ὑπὸ
τίνος πάσχει, οὐκέτι προσέθηκεν, ὅπερ[3] ἴσως ἦν κυ-
ριώτατον. Δημόκριτος μὲν οὖν οὕτως ἔνια παραλείπει.

---

[1] παρῆκεν Schneider: εἴρηκέ γε mss.   [2] θερμῶν Usener:
παχέων Mullach   [3] ὥσπερ mss., corr. Stephanus

Regarding Causes (R26–R31)

R26 (> A65) Arist. *Phys.* 8.1 252a32–b5

ὅλως δὲ τὸ νομίζειν ἀρχὴν εἶναι ταύτην ἱκανήν, εἴ τι
αἰεὶ ἢ ἔστιν οὕτως ἢ γίγνεται, οὐκ ὀρθῶς ἔχει ὑπολαβεῖν, ἐφ᾽ ὃ Δημόκριτος ἀνάγει τὰς περὶ φύσεως αἰτίας, ὡς οὕτω καὶ τὸ πρότερον ἐγίγνετο· τοῦ δὲ ἀεὶ
οὐκ ἀξιοῖ ἀρχὴν ζητεῖν, λέγων ἐπί τινων ὀρθῶς, ὅτι
δ᾽ ἐπὶ πάντων, οὐκ ὀρθῶς. καὶ γὰρ τὸ τρίγωνον ἔχει
δυσὶν ὀρθαῖς ἀεὶ τὰς γωνίας ἴσας, ἀλλ᾽ ὅμως ἐστίν τι
τῆς ἀιδιότητος ταύτης ἕτερον αἴτιον· τῶν μέντοι ἀρχῶν οὐκ ἔστιν ἕτερον αἴτιον ἀιδίων οὐσῶν.

and color, Democritus would be speaking correctly [scil. when he defines man]. For he seems to think in this way; at least he says that it is clear to everyone what sort of thing a man is with regard to his shape [= **D26a**], on the idea that he is knowable by shape and color. And yet a corpse too has the same form of the shape, but all the same is not a man.

R25 (< A135) Theophrastus, *On Sensations*

With regard to smell, he has neglected to provide its definition, except that it is the subtle efflux from heavy things that causes odor [**D67**]. Regarding what kind of thing it is by nature and by what thing it undergoes the effect, he has not added anything further—and yet this was perhaps the most important thing. Thus Democritus omits a number of matters.

Regarding Causes (R26–R31)

R26 (> A65) Aristotle, *Physics*

In general, to think that it is a sufficient principle if something always is or becomes in such and such a way, is not a correct supposition. But it is to this that Democritus reduces the causes concerning nature when he says that this happened in the same way previously too [cf. **R27**]. But he does not think it necessary to seek a principle of the 'always,' so that it is only about certain cases that he speaks correctly, but when he applies it to all he does so incorrectly. For a triangle always has its angles equal to two right angles, but all the same there is a different reason for this 'always'; whereas of principles there is not a different cause, since they always exist.

R27 (< 42.1 Leszl) Arist. *GA* 2.6 742b17–21

οὐ καλῶς δὲ λέγουσιν οὐδὲ τοῦ διὰ τί τὴν ἀνάγκην,
ὅσοι λέγουσιν ὅτι οὕτως ἀεὶ γίνεται, καὶ ταύτην εἶναι
νομίζουσιν ἀρχὴν ἐν αὐτοῖς, ὥσπερ Δημόκριτος ὁ
Ἀβδηρίτης, ὅτι τοῦ μὲν ἀεὶ καὶ ἀπείρου οὐκ ἔστιν
ἀρχή [. . . cf. **D79**].

R28 (< A36) Arist. *PA* 1.1 642a24–28

αἴτιον δὲ τοῦ μὴ ἐλθεῖν τοὺς προγενεστέρους ἐπὶ τὸν
τρόπον τοῦτον, ὅτι τὸ τί ἦν εἶναι καὶ τὸ ὁρίσασθαι
τὴν οὐσίαν οὐκ ἦν, ἀλλ᾽ ἥψατο μὲν Δημόκριτος πρῶτος, ὡς οὐκ ἀναγκαίου δὲ τῇ φυσικῇ θεωρίᾳ, ἀλλ᾽
ἐκφερόμενος ὑπ᾽ αὐτοῦ τοῦ πράγματος [. . .].

R29 (< A106) Arist. *Resp.* 4

a 471b30–472a3

Δημόκριτος δ᾽ ὅτι μὲν ἐκ τῆς ἀναπνοῆς συμβαίνει τι
τοῖς ἀναπνέουσι λέγει, φάσκων κωλύειν ἐκθλίβεσθαι
τὴν ψυχήν· οὐ μέντοι ὡς τούτου γ᾽ ἕνεκα ποιήσασαν
τοῦτο τὴν φύσιν οὐθὲν εἴρηκεν· ὅλως γὰρ ὥσπερ καὶ
οἱ ἄλλοι φυσικοί, καὶ οὗτος οὐθὲν ἅπτεται τῆς τοιαύτης αἰτίας [. . .].

R27 (≠ DK) Aristotle, *Generation of Animals*

They do not speak well nor do they explain the necessity of the cause, those who say that it [i.e. the generation and growth of animals] always occurs this way and who think, like Democritus of Abdera, that this is a principle in them, since there is not a principle [i.e. a beginning, *arkhê*] of the always and unlimited [. . .].

R28 (< A36) Aristotle, *Parts of Animals*

The reason our predecessors did not arrive at this kind [scil. of cause, the formal or final one] is that what the being of a thing is (*to ti ên einai*) and the definition of its essence (*ousia*) were lacking. It was Democritus who was the first to approach the question, not as being necessary for the theory of nature, but because he was brought to it by the things themselves [. . .].

R29 (< A106) Aristotle, *On Respiration*

a

Democritus says that something comes about from respiration for beings that breathe, when he asserts that it prevents the soul from being expelled [cf. **D136**]. But he has not said anything at all about nature doing this for that reason. For in general he does not approach a cause of this sort any more than the other natural philosophers do [. . .].

b 472a16–18

τὴν δ' αἰτίαν διὰ τί ποτε πᾶσι μὲν ἀναγκαῖον ἀποθανεῖν, οὐ μέντοι ὅτε ἔτυχεν ἀλλὰ κατὰ φύσιν μὲν γήρᾳ,
βίᾳ δὲ παρὰ φύσιν, οὐθὲν δεδήλωκεν [. . .].

R30 (> A66) Arist. *GA* 5.8 789b2–8 et 12–15

Δημόκριτος δὲ τὸ οὗ ἕνεκα ἀφεὶς λέγειν, πάντα ἀνάγει εἰς ἀνάγκην οἷς χρῆται ἡ φύσις, οὖσι μὲν τοιού-
τοις, οὐ μὴν ἀλλ' ἕνεκά τινος οὖσι, καὶ τοῦ περὶ
ἕκαστον βελτίονος χάριν. ὥστε γίνεσθαι μὲν οὐθὲν
κωλύει οὕτω καὶ ἐκπίπτειν, ἀλλ' οὐ διὰ ταῦτα, ἀλλὰ
διὰ τὸ τέλος· ταῦτα δ' ὡς κινοῦντα καὶ ὄργανα καὶ ὡς
ὕλη αἴτια [. . .]. ὅμοιον δ' ἔοικε τὸ λέγειν τὰ αἴτια ἐξ
ἀνάγκης κἂν εἴ τις διὰ τὸ μαχαίριον οἴοιτο τὸ ὕδωρ
ἐξεληλυθέναι μόνον τοῖς ὑδρωπιῶσιν, ἀλλ' οὐ διὰ τὸ
ὑγιαίνειν οὗ ἕνεκα τὸ μαχαίριον ἔτεμεν.

R31 (A67) Simpl. *In Phys.*, p. 327.23–26

ἀλλὰ καὶ Δημόκριτος ἐν οἷς φησι "δεῖνον ἀπὸ τοῦ
παντὸς ἀποκριθῆναι[1] παντοίων εἰδέων" [**D82**] ⟨πῶς
δὲ καὶ ὑπὸ τίνος αἰτίας μὴ λέγει⟩ ἔοικεν ἀπὸ ταὐτομάτου καὶ τύχης γεννᾶν αὐτόν.

[1] ἀποκριθῆναι E: ἀποκρίνεσθαι DF

b

But the cause for which it is necessary that all [scil. living beings] die one day, not by chance, but in conformity with nature because of old age, or against nature by violence, he has not indicated clearly [. . .].

R30 (> A66) Aristotle, *Generation of Animals*

Democritus neglects to speak about the final cause and reduces to necessity all the processes that nature makes use of—which are indeed of this sort [i.e. necessary], but yet they are for a final cause and for what is better in every case. So that nothing prevents them [i.e. teeth] from growing and falling out in this way, but not for these reasons [i.e. material ones], but for the sake of the end: these factors are causes as moving, instruments, and as matter [. . .]. But he seems to speak of necessary causes in the same way as if one thought that the lancet alone were the cause of the water being drawn off from patients with dropsy, and not the condition of healthiness, for the sake of which the lancet made its incision.

R31 (A67) Simplicius, *Commentary on Aristotle's* Physics

Democritus too [scil. like Empedocles], when he says, **"A vortex of all kinds of forms became detached from the whole"** [= **D82**] (but without saying either how or by what cause), seems to generate it by a spontaneous process [*automaton*] and by chance [*tukhê*].

*Criticism of the Atomist Hypothesis: A Digression
in Aristotle's* Generation and Corruption *(R32)*

R32 (> A 60) Arist. *GC* 1.8

a 325b33–326a24

περὶ δὴ τῶν ἀδιαιρέτων στερεῶν τὸ μὲν ἐπὶ πλέον
θεωρῆσαι τὸ συμβαῖνον [35] ἀφείσθω τὸ νῦν, ὡς δὲ
μικρὸν παρεκβᾶσιν εἰπεῖν, ἀναγκαῖον ἀπαθές τε ἕκαστον λέγειν τῶν ἀδιαιρέτων (οὐ γὰρ οἷόν [326a1] τε
πάσχειν ἀλλ᾽ ἢ διὰ τοῦ κενοῦ) καὶ μηθενὸς ποιητικὸν
πάθους· οὔτε γὰρ ψυχρὸν οὔτε σκληρὸν[1] οἷόν τ᾽ εἶναι.
καίτοι τοῦτό γε ἄτοπον, τὸ μόνον ἀποδοῦναι τῷ περι-
φερεῖ σχήματι τὸ θερμόν· ἀνάγκη γὰρ καὶ τοὐναντίον
τὸ ψυχρὸν ἄλλῳ τινὶ [5] προσήκειν τῶν σχημάτων.
ἄτοπον δὲ κἂν εἰ ταῦτα μὲν ὑπάρχῃ, λέγω δὲ θερ-
μότης καὶ ψυχρότης, βαρύτης δὲ καὶ κουφότης καὶ
σκληρότης καὶ μαλακότης μὴ ὑπάρξει· καίτοι βαρύτερόν γε κατὰ τὴν ὑπεροχήν φησιν εἶναι Δημόκριτος
ἕκαστον τῶν ἀδιαιρέτων, ὥστε δῆλον ὅτι καὶ θερμότε-
ρον. [10] τοιαῦτα δ᾽ ὄντα μὴ πάσχειν ὑπ᾽ ἀλλήλων
ἀδύνατον, οἷον ὑπὸ τοῦ πολὺ ὑπερβάλλοντος θερμοῦ
τὸ ἠρέμα ψυχρόν.[2] ἀλλὰ μὴν εἰ σκληρόν, καὶ μαλακόν, τὸ δὲ μαλακὸν τῷ πάσχειν τι λέγεται· τὸ γὰρ
ὑπεικτικὸν μαλακόν.

ἀλλὰ μὴν ἄτοπον καὶ εἰ μηθὲν ὑπάρχει ἀλλὰ μόνον
σχῆμα· [15] καὶ εἰ ὑπάρχει, ἓν δὲ μόνον, οἷον τὸ μὲν
σκληρὸν τὸ δὲ θερμόν· οὐδὲ γὰρ ἂν μία τις εἴη φύσις

*Criticism of the Atomist Hypothesis: A Digression
in Aristotle's* Generation and Corruption *(R32)*

R32 (> A 60) Aristotle, *On Generation and Corruption*

a [The problem of affection]

Concerning indivisible solids, let us set aside for the moment a fuller examination of their consequences; but to speak a little as a digression, it is necessary to state that each of the indivisibles is both impassible (for it is not possible [326a1] to be acted upon if not by means of the void) and does not produce any affections: for it cannot be either cold or hard [or perhaps: hot].[1] And yet this is very strange, to assign heat only to the round shape [cf. **D59**]. For it is necessary that the contrary as well, cold,[2] [5] belong to some other shape. And it is also very strange that these, I mean heat *and* cold, belong to them, but heaviness *and* lightness, hardness *and* softness do not belong to them. In fact Democritus says that each of the indivisibles is at least heavier in virtue of its excess, so that it is clear that it is also warmer. [10] But being such, it is impossible that they not be affected by each other, for example that the slightly cold [scil. not be affected] by the excessively hot. But on the other hand, if there is hard, there is also soft, and the soft is called that because of a certain affection—for soft is what yields.

But it is also very strange that nothing belongs to them except for shape; [15] and also that if others do belong to them, that there is only one for each, so that the one is

---

[1] σκληρὸν] calidum coni. Asulanus   [2] ψυχρόν E[1]LMHJV: θερμόν FW

αὐτῶν. ὁμοίως δὲ ἀδύνατον καὶ εἰ πλείω τῷ ἑνί· ἀδιαίρετον γὰρ ὂν ἐν τῷ αὐτῷ ἕξει τὰ πάθη· ὥστε καὶ
ἐὰν πάσχῃ, εἴπερ ψύχεται, ταύτῃ τί³ καὶ ἄλλο ποιήσει
ἢ πείσεται; τὸν αὐτὸν δὲ [20] τρόπον καὶ ἐπὶ τῶν
ἄλλων παθημάτων· τοῦτο γὰρ καὶ τοῖς στερεὰ καὶ
τοῖς ἐπίπεδα λέγουσιν ἀδιαίρετα συμβαίνει τὸν αὐτὸν
τρόπον· οὔτε γὰρ μανότερα οὔτε πυκνότερα οἷόν τε
γίνεσθαι κενοῦ μὴ ὄντος ἐν τοῖς ἀδιαιρέτοις.

³ τί Rashed: τι vel τοι mss. plerique

b 326a24–326b2

ἔτι δ' ἄτοπον καὶ τὸ μικρὰ μὲν ἀδιαίρετα εἶναι, μεγάλα δὲ μή· νῦν μὲν [25] γὰρ εὐλόγως τὰ μεγάλα
θραύεται μᾶλλον τῶν μικρῶν· τὰ μὲν γὰρ διαλύεται
ῥᾳδίως, οἷον τὰ μεγάλα· προσκόπτει γὰρ πολλοῖς· τὸ
δὲ ἀδιαίρετον ὅλως διὰ τί μᾶλλον ὑπάρχει τῶν μεγάλων τοῖς μικροῖς; ἔτι δὲ πότερον μία πάντων φύσις
ἐκείνων τῶν στερεῶν, ἢ διαφέρει θάτερα τῶν ἑτέρων,
[30] ὥσπερ ἂν εἰ τὰ μὲν εἴη πύρινα, τὰ δὲ γήινα τὸν
ὄγκον; εἰ μὲν γὰρ μία φύσις ἁπάντων, τί τὸ χωρίσαν;
ἢ διὰ τί οὐ γίγνεται ἁψάμενα ἕν, ὥσπερ ὕδωρ ὕδατος
ὅταν θίγῃ; οὐδὲν γὰρ διαφέρει τὸ ὕστερον τοῦ προ-
τέρου. εἰ δ' ἕτερα, ποῖα ταῦτα; καὶ δῆλον ὡς ταύτας
θετέον ἀρχὰς καὶ αἰτίας τῶν [35] συμβαινόντων μᾶλλον ἢ τὰ σχήματα. ἔτι δέ, διαφέροντα [326b1] τὴν
φύσιν, κἂν ποιοῖ κἂν πάσχοι θιγγάνοντα ἀλλήλων.

hard and the other hot—for if so, their nature would not be one. But it is likewise impossible that several [scil. affections] belong to only one [scil. indivisible]. For, being indivisible, it will possess the affections in the same place; so that, when it is affected, if it is cooled, what other action or affection will happen at this place? And in the same way [20] for the other affections as well. For the same thing applies to those who say that the indivisibles are solids or surfaces [cf. Plato, *Timaeus* 53c–55d]. For the indivisibles could not become either more rarefied or more dense, since there is no void in them.

b [The problem of indivisibility]

[326a24] It is also very strange that small things are indivisible but large ones are not. For as it is, it is reasonable that large things break apart more than small ones; for they decompose easily, given that they are large, for they collide with many things. But why in general does indivisibility belong to small things more than to large ones? Again, is there just one nature of all those solids, or do they differ from each other, [30] so that the ones would be fiery, the others a mass of earth? For if there is only one nature for all of them, what is it that separates them? Or why, when they come into contact, do they not become one, like water when it touches water? For this latter case does not differ at all from the earlier one. But if they are different, of what sort are they? And it is clear that these are what should be posited as principles and causes for what happens rather than the shapes. Furthermore, if they differ [326b1] in their nature, they would both act and be acted upon [scil. all at once] when they touched each other.

c 326b2–6

ἔτι δὲ τί τὸ κινοῦν; εἰ μὲν γὰρ ἕτερον, παθητικά· εἰ δ᾿
αὐτὸ αὑτὸ ἕκαστον, ἢ διαιρετὸν ἔσται, κατ᾿ ἄλλο μὲν
κινοῦν κατ᾿ ἄλλο δὲ κινούμενον, ἢ κατὰ ταὐτὸ τἀναντία ὑπάρξει, καὶ [5] ἡ ὕλη οὐ μόνον ἀριθμῷ ἔσται μία
ἀλλὰ καὶ δυνάμει.

d 326b5–27

ὅσοι μὲν οὖν διὰ τῆς ⟨διὰ⟩[1] τῶν πόρων κινήσεώς
φασι τὰ πάθη συμβαίνειν, εἰ μὲν καὶ πεπληρωμένων
τῶν πόρων, περίεργον οἱ πόροι· εἰ γὰρ ταύτῃ τι πάσχει τὸ πᾶν, κἂν μὴ πόρους ἔχον ἀλλ᾿ αὐτὸ συνεχὲς
ὂν πάσχοι τὸν αὐτὸν τρόπον. ἔτι δὲ πῶς ἐνδέχεται
περὶ τοῦ διορᾶν συμβαίνειν ὡς λέγουσιν; [10] οὔτε
γὰρ κατὰ τὰς ἀφὰς ἐνδέχεται διιέναι διὰ τῶν δια-
φανῶν, οὔτε διὰ τῶν πόρων, εἰ πλήρης ἕκαστος· τί
γὰρ διοίσει τοῦ μὴ ἔχειν πόρους; πᾶν γὰρ ὁμοίως
ἐστὶν πλῆρες. ἀλλὰ μὴν εἰ κενὰ μὲν ταῦτα, ἀνάγκη
δὲ σώματα ἐν αὑτοῖς ἔχειν, ταὐτὸ συμβήσεται πάλιν.
εἰ δὲ τηλικαῦτα τὸ [15] μέγεθος ὥστε μὴ δέχεσθαι
σῶμα μηδέν, γελοῖον τὸ μικρὸν μὲν οἴεσθαι κενὸν
εἶναι, μέγα δὲ μὴ μηδ᾿ ὁπηλικονοῦν, ἢ τὸ κενὸν ἄλλο
τι οἴεσθαι λέγειν πλὴν χώραν σώματος, ὥστε δῆλον
ὅτι παντὶ σώματι τὸν ὄγκον ἴσον ἔσται κενόν.

ὅλως δὲ τὸ πόρους ποιεῖν περίεργον· εἰ μὲν γὰρ

[1] ⟨διὰ⟩ Mugler

388

c [The problem of motion]

Again, what is it that sets them in motion? For if it is something different from themselves, then they will be capable of being acted upon; but if each one [scil. moves] itself, then either it will be divisible (setting in motion in this part, being set in motion in that one) or else contrary properties will belong to it in the same respect, and [5] its matter will be one not only in number but also in potentiality.

d [The problem of vision and the passages]

So for all those who say that the affections are produced by motion ‹through› passages, if this happens even when the passages are filled, then the passages are superfluous. For if the whole is affected in this way, it would be affected in the same way even if it did not possess passages but were itself continuous. Furthermore, how is it possible for vision to occur in the way they assert? [10] For it is not possible to penetrate through transparent bodies by their points of contact, nor through the passages if each one is full. For in what way will that be different from not having passages? For the whole is full in the same way. But if these [i.e. the passages] are empty, but it is necessary that they contain bodies within themselves, then the same consequence will ensue once again. And if they are of such a [scil. small] size [15] that they cannot receive any body, it is ridiculous to think that a small void exists but a large one, of whatever size, does not, or to suppose that 'void' means anything other than the place of a body, so that it is clear that for every body there will be a void equal in volume.

In general, to posit passages is superfluous. For if

389

μηδὲν ποιεῖ [20] κατὰ τὴν ἁφήν, οὐδὲ διὰ τῶν πόρων
ποιήσει διιόν· εἰ δὲ τῷ ἅπτεσθαι, καὶ μὴ πόρων ὄντων
τὰ μὲν πείσεται τὰ δὲ ποιήσει τῶν πρὸς ἄλληλα τοῦτον τὸν τρόπον πεφυκότων.

ὅτι μὲν οὖν οὕτως λέγειν τοὺς πόρους, ὥς τινες
ὑπολαμβάνουσιν, ἢ ψεῦδος ἢ μάταιον, φανερὸν ἐκ
τούτων ἐστίν· διαιρετῶν [25] δ' ὄντων πάντῃ τῶν σωμάτων πόρους ποιεῖν γελοῖον· ᾗ γὰρ διαιρετά, δύναται χωρίζεσθαι.

Regarding the Unlimited Number of Atoms (R33)

R33 (< 67 A15 et > 68 A60a) Arist. *Cael.* 3.4 303a3–5 et
a17–b8

[303a3] ἀλλὰ μὴν οὐδ' ὡς ἕτεροί τινες λέγουσιν, οἷον
Λεύκιππός τε καὶ Δημόκριτος ὁ Ἀβδηρίτης, εὔλογα
τὰ συμβαίνοντα· [. . . = **D45**]. [303a17] πρῶτον μὲν οὖν
ταὐτὸν καὶ τούτοις ἁμάρτημα τὸ μὴ πεπερασμένας
λαβεῖν τὰς ἀρχάς, ἐξὸν ἅπαντα ταὐτὰ λέγειν. ἔτι δ'
εἰ μὴ ἄπειροι τῶν σχημάτων αἱ διαφοραί, δῆλον ὅτι
οὐκ ἔσται τὰ στοιχεῖα ἄπειρα. πρὸς δὲ τούτοις ἀνάγκη
[20] μάχεσθαι ταῖς μαθηματικαῖς ἐπιστήμαις ἄτομα
σώματα λέγοντας, καὶ πολλὰ τῶν ἐνδόξων καὶ τῶν
φαινομένων κατὰ τὴν αἴσθησιν ἀναιρεῖν, περὶ ὧν
εἴρηται πρότερον ἐν τοῖς περὶ χρόνου καὶ κινήσεως.
ἅμα δὲ καὶ ἐναντία λέγειν αὐτοὺς αὐτοῖς ἀνάγκη· ἀδύ-

something does not act [20] by contact, then neither will it do so by penetrating through passages. But if it does so by making contact, then, even if there are no passages, some things will be acted upon and others will act if their nature is such that they behave in this way with regard to each other.

Therefore it is manifest from these considerations that to speak in this way about passages, as some people suppose them to be, is either false or useless. Since bodies are divisible [25] in every place, it is ridiculous to posit passages; for insofar as they are divisible they can be divided into separate parts.

Regarding the Unlimited Number of Atoms (R33)

R33 (< 67 A15 and > 68 A60a) Aristotle, *On the Heavens*

[303a3] But neither does what is said by certain others [scil. than Anaxagoras], like Leucippus and Democritus of Abdera, lead to reasonable consequences [. . .]. [303a17] First, these too commit the same error of not conceiving the principles as limited, even though it would be possible [scil. even in this case] for them to say exactly the same things. Furthermore, if the differences of the shapes are not unlimited, it is evident that the elements will not be unlimited. In addition, those who admit indivisible bodies must necessarily enter into conflict [20] with the mathematical sciences and abolish many accepted views (*endoxa*) and phenomena relating to sensation, about which we spoke earlier in our studies on time and motion [cf. *Phys.* 6.1–2]. At the same time it is necessary that they contradict themselves. For it is impossible, if the elements

391

νατον γὰρ ἀτόμων ὄντων τῶν στοιχείων μεγέθει [25]
καὶ μικρότητι διαφέρειν ἀέρα καὶ γῆν καὶ ὕδωρ· οὐ
γὰρ οἷόν τ᾽ ἐξ ἀλλήλων γίγνεσθαι· ὑπολείψει γὰρ ἀεὶ
τὰ μέγιστα σώματα ἐκκρινόμενα, φασὶ δ᾽ οὕτω γίγνεσθαι ὕδωρ καὶ ἀέρα καὶ γῆν ἐξ ἀλλήλων. ἔτι οὐδὲ
κατὰ τὴν τούτων ὑπόληψιν δόξειεν ἂν ἄπειρα γίγνεσθαι τὰ στοιχεῖα, εἴπερ [30] τὰ μὲν σώματα διαφέρει
σχήμασι, τὰ δὲ σχήματα πάντα σύγκειται ἐκ πυρα-
μίδων, τὰ μὲν εὐθύγραμμα ἐξ εὐθυγράμμων, ἡ δὲ
σφαῖρα ἐξ ὀκτὼ μορίων. [. . .] ἔτι δ᾽ εἰ ἑκάστῳ μὲν τῶν
στοιχείων ἐστί τις οἰκεία κίνησις, καὶ ἡ τοῦ ἁπλοῦ
σώματος ἁπλῆ, μή εἰσι δ᾽ αἱ ἁπλαῖ κινήσεις [303b5]
ἄπειροι διὰ τὸ μήτε τὰς ἁπλᾶς φορὰς πλείους εἶναι
δυοῖν μήτε τοὺς τόπους ἀπείρους, οὐκ ἂν εἴη οὐδ᾽ οὕτως ἄπειρα τὰ στοιχεῖα.

Regarding Atomic Differences (R34)

R34 (< 8.2 Leszl) Simpl. *In Cat.*, pp. 216.31–217.5

καὶ πρὸς Δημόκριτον δὲ καὶ Ἐπίκουρον [Frag. 288
Usener] δικαιολογεῖται, τί δήποτε τινὰς μὲν διαφορὰς
περὶ τὰς ἀτόμους ἀπολείπουσιν, οἷον σχημάτων, βάρους, ναστότητος, σωματότητος, περάτων, μεγέθους,
κινήσεως, οὔτε δὲ χρόαν οὔτε γλυκύτητα οὔτε ζωὴν
ἔχειν οὐδὲ[1] τῶν ἄλλων τῶν τοιούτων λόγους προϋφε-
στηκέναι ἀποφαίνονται· κοινοῦ γὰρ ὄντος τοῦ περὶ

are indivisible, that air, earth, and water differ by largeness [25] and smallness. For it is not possible that they come to be out of each other; for the largest bodies, in separating, will always be lacking—but it is in this way that they say that water, air, and earth come to be out of each other. Furthermore, in accordance with their very conception the elements would seem to be not unlimited, since [30] the bodies differ by their shapes, and all the shapes are composed out of pyramids, the rectilineals out of rectilinear pyramids and the sphere out of eight parts. [. . .] Furthermore, if to each of the elements corresponds its own characteristic motion, and the motion of a simple body is simple, and simple motions are not [303b5] unlimited [scil. in number] because there are not more than two simple locomotions and places are not unlimited [scil. in number], on the basis of this reasoning the elements would not be unlimited [scil. in number] either.

Regarding Atomic Differences (R34)

R34 (≠ DK) Simplicius, *Commentary on Aristotle's* Categories

This is how one pleads the case against Democritus and Epicurus: why then do they admit certain differences in the atoms, such as those of shapes, weight, compactness, corporeality, limits, magnitude, motion, but assert that they do not possess either color or sweetness or life, and that the reasons for the other [scil. characteristics] of this sort do not preexist either? For given that what they say

---

[1] οὐδὲ p. 39.22 in paraphrasi: οὐ mss.

τῶν ἑκτῶν λόγου ἄτοπον μὴ τὰ αὐτὰ περὶ τῶν αὐτῶν
διατάττεσθαι, καὶ ἔτι ἀτοπώτερον τὰς ἀρχηγικωτάτας
δυνάμεις ὑστερογενεῖς ποιεῖν, ὥσπερ ζωὴν καὶ νοῦν
καὶ φύσιν καὶ λόγον καὶ τὰ τοιαῦτα. παραπλησίως δὲ
ἀδύνατον καὶ ἀπὸ τῆς συνόδου ταῦτα ἀποτελεῖσθαι·
νόμῳ γὰρ ἔστι[2] χροιὴ κατὰ τὸν Δημόκριτον καὶ τὰ
ἄλλα ὁμοίως, τῇ ἀληθείᾳ δὲ ἄτομα καὶ κενόν.

2 ἔσται mss., corr. Usener

Regarding the Void (R35–R36)

R35 (30.4 Leszl) Arist. *Phys.* 4.1 208b25–27

ἔτι οἱ τὸ κενὸν φάσκοντες εἶναι τόπον λέγουσιν· τὸ
γὰρ κενὸν τόπος ἂν εἴη ἐστερημένος σώματος.

R36 (< A60) Arist. *Cael.* 4.2 309b24–28

ἄλογον δὲ καὶ τὸ χώραν τῷ κενῷ ποιεῖν, ὥσπερ οὐκ
αὐτὸ χώραν τινὰ οὖσαν· ἀναγκαῖον δ', εἴπερ κινεῖται
[25] τὸ κενόν, εἶναι αὐτοῦ τινα τόπον, ἐξ οὗ μεταβάλ-
λει καὶ εἰς ὅν. πρὸς δὲ τούτοις τί τῆς κινήσεως αἴτιον;
οὐ γὰρ δὴ τό γε κενόν· οὐ γὰρ αὐτὸ κινεῖται μόνον,
ἀλλὰ καὶ τὸ στερεόν.

regarding external things is shared in common, it is very strange not to assign the same things to the same things, and it is even more strange to posit that the most principal powers, like life, intellect, nature, reason, and things of this sort, are born later. And similarly, it is impossible to produce these [scil. characteristics] out of collection. For by convention there is color according to Democritus and similarly with the other things, but in truth atoms and void [cf. **D14**].

Regarding the Void (R35–R36)

R35 (≠ DK) Aristotle, *Physics*

Those who posit the existence of the void say that it is a place, because the void would be a place deprived of body.

R36 (< A60) Aristotle, *On the Heavens*

It is also absurd to explain place by the void, as though this latter were not itself some kind of place. And it is necessary, given that the void moves, that it have some place from which and into which it makes the change. And besides these considerations, what is the cause of motion? For it is obviously not the void: for it is not the only thing that is moved, but so too is the solid.

Regarding Motion (R37–R43)

R37 (67 A18) Arist. *Metaph.* Λ6 1071b31–34

διὸ ἔνιοι ποιοῦσιν ἀεὶ ἐνέργειαν, οἷον Λεύκιππος καὶ
Πλάτων· ἀεὶ γὰρ εἶναί φασι κίνησιν. ἀλλὰ διὰ τί καὶ
τίνα οὐ λέγουσιν οὐδ' ὡδὶ ‹ἢ ὡδί›, οὐδὲ[1] τὴν αἰτίαν.

[1] οὐδ' ὡδὶ ‹ἢ ὡδί›, οὐδὲ Fazzo: οὐδὲ ὡδὶ οὐδὲ mss.: οὐδ',
εἰ ὡδὶ ‹ἢ ὡδί› Diels

R38 (> 67 A6) Alex. *In Metaph.*, p. 36.21–27

οὗτοι γὰρ λέγουσιν ἀλληλοτυπούσας καὶ κρουομένας
πρὸς ἀλλήλας κινεῖσθαι τὰς ἀτόμους· πόθεν μέντοι ἡ
ἀρχὴ τῆς κινήσεως τοῖς κατὰ φύσιν, οὐ λέγουσιν· ἡ
γὰρ κατὰ τὴν ἀλληλοτυπίαν βίαιός ἐστι κίνησις καὶ
οὐ κατὰ φύσιν, ὑστέρα δὲ ἡ βίαιος τῆς κατὰ φύσιν.
οὐδὲ γὰρ τὸ πόθεν ἡ βαρύτης ἐν ταῖς ἀτόμοις λέ-
γουσι· τὰ γὰρ ἀμερῆ τὰ ἐπινοούμενα ταῖς ἀτόμοις καὶ
μέρη ὄντα αὐτῶν ἀβαρῆ φασιν εἶναι· ἐκ δὲ ἀβαρῶν
συγκειμένων πῶς ἂν βάρος γένηται;[1]

[1] γίνοιτο coni. Bonitz

R39 (> 67 A19) Arist. *Cael.* 1.7 275b29–276a12

εἰ δὲ μὴ συνεχὲς τὸ πᾶν, ἀλλ' ὥσπερ λέγει Δημόκριτος καὶ Λεύκιππος, διωρισμένα τῷ [30] κενῷ, μίαν
ἀναγκαῖον εἶναι πάντων τὴν κίνησιν. διώρισται μὲν
γὰρ τοῖς σχήμασιν· τὴν δὲ φύσιν φασὶν αὐτῶν εἶναι

Regarding Motion (R37–R43)

R37 (67 A18) Aristotle, *Metaphysics*

That is why some people say that there is always activity,
like Leucippus and Plato. For they say that there is always
motion. But for what reason and because of what factors,
they do not say, nor [scil. that the motion is] this way ⟨or
that way⟩, nor the reason [scil. why it is this way or that
way].

R38 (> 67 A6) Alexander of Aphrodisias, *Commentary on
Aristotle's* Metaphysics

They [scil. Leucippus and Democritus] say that the atoms
move by hitting one another and striking against one another, but where the principle of motion comes from for
the things that exist by nature, they do not say. For motion
due to hitting one another is motion by force and not according to nature, and motion by force is posterior to motion according to nature. And they have not said either
where the heaviness in the atoms comes from. For they
say that what thought conceives of as partlessness in the
atoms and is [scil. in fact] parts of them is without weight.
But how could weight come about out of what is composed
of things without weight? [cf. **D50–D51**]

R39 (> 67 A19) Aristotle, *On the Heavens*

If the whole is not continuous but, as Democritus and
Leucippus say, [scil. things are] distinguished by the [30]
void, it is necessary that the motion of all of them be only
one. For, to be sure, they are distinguished by the shapes;
but they say that their nature is only one, as if they were

μίαν, ὥσπερ ἂν εἰ χρυσὸς ἕκαστον εἴη κεχωρισμένος.
τούτων δέ, [276a1] καθάπερ λέγομεν, ἀναγκαῖον εἶναι
τὴν αὐτὴν κίνησιν· ὅπου γὰρ μία βῶλος, καὶ ἡ σύμ-
πασα γῆ φέρεται, καὶ τό τε πᾶν πῦρ καὶ σπινθὴρ εἰς
τὸν αὐτὸν τόπον. ὥστ᾽ οὔτε κοῦφον ἁπλῶς οὐθὲν
ἔσται τῶν σωμάτων, εἰ πάντ᾽ ἔχει βάρος· εἰ δὲ [5]
κουφότητα, βαρὺ οὐδέν. ἔτι εἰ βάρος ἔχει ἢ κουφότητα, ἔσται ἢ ἔσχατόν τι τοῦ παντὸς ἢ μέσον.
τοῦτο δ᾽ ἀδύνατον ἀπείρου γ᾽ ὄντος. ὅλως δ᾽, οὗ μή
ἐστι μέσον μηδ᾽ ἔσχατον, μηδὲ τὸ μὲν ἄνω τὸ δὲ
κάτω, τόπος οὐθεὶς ἔσται τοῖς σώμασι τῆς φορᾶς.
τούτου δὲ μὴ ὄντος κίνησις οὐκ ἔσται· ἀνάγκη γὰρ
[10] κινεῖσθαι ἤτοι κατὰ φύσιν ἢ παρὰ φύσιν, ταῦτα
δ᾽ ὥρισται τοῖς τόποις τοῖς τ᾽ οἰκείοις καὶ τοῖς ἀλλο-
τρίοις.

R40 (36.1 Leszl) Arist. *Phys.* 4.8 214b28–33 et a19–22

συμβαίνει δὲ τοῖς λέγουσιν εἶναι κενὸν ὡς ἀναγκαῖον,
εἴπερ ἔσται κίνησις, τοὐναντίον μᾶλλον, ἄν τις ἐπι-
σκοπῇ, μὴ ἐνδέχεσθαι μηδὲ ἓν κινεῖσθαι, ἐὰν ᾖ κενόν·
ὥσπερ γὰρ οἱ διὰ τὸ ὅμοιον φάμενοι τὴν γῆν ἠρεμεῖν,
οὕτω καὶ ἐν τῷ κενῷ ἀνάγκη ἠρεμεῖν· οὐ γὰρ ἔστιν οὗ
μᾶλλον ἢ ἧττον κινηθήσεται [. . .] [214a19] ἔτι οὐδεὶς
ἂν ἔχοι εἰπεῖν διὰ τί κινηθὲν στήσεταί που· τί γὰρ
μᾶλλον ἐνταῦθα ἢ ἐνταῦθα; ὥστε ἢ ἠρεμήσει ἢ εἰς
ἄπειρον ἀνάγκη φέρεσθαι, ἐὰν μή τι ἐμποδίσῃ κρεῖτ-
τον.

each gold in a separate state. But of these things, [276a1] as we say, it is necessary that the motion be the same. For where a single lump of earth moves to, so too does the whole earth; and both the whole fire and a spark [scil. move] to the same place. So that none of the bodies will be purely and simply light, if all possess heaviness; and if [5] it is lightness [scil. that all possess], then none will be heavy. Furthermore, if they possess heaviness or lightness, there will either be some extreme limit of the whole or some middle. But this is impossible, if it is unlimited. In general, that of which there is neither a middle nor an extreme limit, neither upward nor downward, will not provide bodies with a place for their locomotion. And if this does not exist, there will not be motion. For it is necessary [10] that motion be either in conformity with nature or against nature, and this is defined by places, proper ones and alien ones.

R40 (≠ DK) Aristotle, *Physics*

If one examines the question, it is instead the contrary that comes about for those who say that it is necessary that the void exists if there is to be motion, namely that it is not possible for even a single thing to move if there is void. For just as for those who say that the earth is at rest because of similarity [cf. **ANAXIMAND. D30**], so too it is necessary that there be rest in the void as well. For there is no place where there will be more or less motion. [. . .] [214a19] Furthermore, no one could say why something in motion should stop somewhere: for why here rather than there? So that either it will be at rest or else it is necessary that its movement be infinite, at least if something stronger does not prevent it.

R41 (30.6 Leszl) Simpl. *In Phys.*, p. 533.14–19

διὸ καὶ ὁ Εὔδημος ἐν τρίτῳ τῶν Φυσικῶν παρακολου-
θῶν τοῖς ἐνταῦθα λεγομένοις καὶ ὡς ὁμολογούμενον
ἕκαστον τῶν αἰτίων ἀφαιρῶν τοῦ τόπου "ἀλλ᾽ ἀρά
γε," φησίν, "ὡς τὸ κινῆσαν; ἢ οὐδὲ οὕτως ἐνδέχεται,
ὦ Δημόκριτε· δεῖ γὰρ κινητικὸν εἶναι καὶ ἔχειν τινὰ
δύναμιν" [Frag. 75 Wehrli]. τὸ γὰρ κενὸν τόπον εἶπεν ὁ
Δημόκριτος, ὅπερ τῇ ἑαυτοῦ φύσει κενὸν ὄντως καὶ
ἀδύνατον καὶ ἀδρανὲς ἂν ἦν.

R42 (> 67 A16) Arist. *Cael.* 3.2 300b 8–11 et 14–16

διὸ καὶ Λευκίππῳ καὶ Δημοκρίτῳ, τοῖς λέγουσιν ἀεὶ
κινεῖσθαι τὰ πρῶτα σώματα ἐν τῷ κενῷ καὶ τῷ
ἀπείρῳ, λεκτέον τίνα κίνησιν καὶ τίς ἡ κατὰ φύσιν
[10] αὐτῶν κίνησις. [. . .] [300b14] εἰς ἄπειρον γὰρ εἶ-
σιν, εἰ μή τι ἔσται κατὰ φύσιν κινοῦν πρῶτον, ἀλλ᾽
ἀεὶ τὸ [15] πρότερον βίᾳ κινούμενον κινήσει.

R43 (< 64.1 Leszl) Arist. *Cael.* 3.2 301a6–13

ἀλλὰ μὴν καὶ τοῦτο ἄτοπον καὶ ἀδύνατον, τὸ ἄπειρον
ἄτακτον ἔχειν κίνησιν· ἔστι γὰρ φύσις ἐκείνη τῶν
πραγμάτων οἵαν ἔχει τὰ πλείω καὶ τὸν πλείω χρόνον·
συμβαίνει οὖν αὐτοῖς τοὐναντίον τὴν μὲν ἀταξίαν εἶναι κατὰ φύσιν, τὴν δὲ τάξιν καὶ τὸν κόσμον παρὰ
φύσιν· καίτοι οὐδὲν ὡς ἔτυχε γίγνεται τῶν κατὰ φύ-

R41 (≠ DK) Simplicius, *Commentary on Aristotle's Physics*

And this [scil. because place is not an efficient cause] is why Eudemus says in the third book of his *Physics,* following what is said here [Arist., *Phys.* 4.1 209a18–22] and denying, as being generally agreed upon, each of the causes for place: "But will it be then as the moving cause? Or else this is not possible either, Democritus. For it must impart motion and possess some power." For Democritus said that the void is place, which, being in reality void by its own nature, must be without power and without force.

R42 (> 67 A16) Aristotle, *On the Heavens*

That is why Leucippus and Democritus, who say that the first bodies are in perpetual motion in the void and the unlimited, ought to say what kind of motion this is and what their natural motion is. [. . .] For it will go on to infinity if there is not some first mover in conformity with nature, but instead it is always something that is moved earlier by force that imparts motion.

R43 (≠ DK) Aristotle, *On the Heavens*

But this too is absurd and impossible, that the unlimited have a disordered motion. For the nature of things is such as most things possess and for most of the time. So what comes about for them [scil. those who posit, in the unlimited, bodies unlimited in number] is the contrary, namely that disorder is in conformity with nature and that order and the organized world (*kosmos*) are against nature. And yet none of the things that are in conformity with nature happens by chance. This point at least, Anaxagoras seems

401

σιν. ἔοικε δὲ τοῦτό γε αὐτὸ καλῶς Ἀναξαγόρας λα-
βεῖν· ἐξ ἀκινήτων γὰρ ἄρχεται κοσμοποιεῖν.

Regarding Weight (R44–R46)

R44 (< A60) Arist. *Cael.* 4.2 309a11–18

[. . . = **D40**] λέγουσι μὲν οὖν τοῦτον τὸν τρόπον, ἀνάγκη δὲ προσθεῖναι τοῖς οὕτω διορίζουσι μὴ μόνον τὸ
κενὸν ἔχειν πλεῖον, ἂν ᾖ κουφότερον, ἀλλὰ καὶ τὸ
στερεὸν ἔλαττον· εἰ γὰρ ὑπερέξει τῆς τοιαύτης ἀναλογίας, οὐκ ἔσται κουφότερον. διὰ γὰρ τοῦτο καὶ τὸ
πῦρ εἶναί φασι κουφότατον, ὅτι πλεῖστον ἔχει κενόν.
συμβήσεται οὖν μικροῦ πυρὸς πολὺν χρυσὸν πλεῖον
ἔχοντα τὸ κενὸν εἶναι κουφότερον, εἰ μὴ καὶ στερεὸν
ἕξει πολλαπλάσιον· ὥστε τοῦτο λεκτέον.

R45 (< A60) Arist. *Cael.* 4.2 309a27–32 et 309b17–18

ἀναγκαῖον δὲ καὶ τοῖς περὶ τῆς τοῦ πυρὸς κουφότητος
αἰτιωμένοις τὸ πολὺ κενὸν ἔχειν σχεδὸν ἐν ταῖς αὐταῖς
ἐνέχεσθαι δυσχερείαις. ἔλαττον μὲν γὰρ ἕξει στερεὸν
τῶν ἄλλων σωμάτων, καὶ τὸ κενὸν πλεῖον· ἀλλ' ὅμως
ἔσται [30] τι πυρὸς πλῆθος ἐν ᾧ τὸ στερεὸν καὶ τὸ
πλῆρες ὑπερβάλλει τῶν περιεχομένων στερεῶν ἔν τινι
μικρῷ πλήθει γῆς. [. . .] [309b17] ἄτοπον δὲ καὶ εἰ διὰ
τὸ κενὸν μὲν ἄνω φέρονται, τὸ δὲ κενὸν αὐτὸ μή.

to have grasped quite well: for he begins the production of the world from immobile things [cf. **ANAXAG. D29**].

Regarding Weight (R44–R46)

R44 (< A60) Aristotle, *On the Heavens*

[. . .] This then is how they speak, but it is necessary, for those who define things in this way, to add that something possess not only more void if it is lighter, but also less solid: for if it exceeds this proportion, it will not be lighter. For that is why they say that fire is the lightest thing, because it possesses the most void. But it will follow then that a large amount of gold, since it possesses more void than a small fire, will be lighter than this, unless it also possesses much more solid. So that this is how one should speak.

R45 (< A60) Aristotle, *On the Heavens*

It is necessary that those too who give as the cause for the lightness of fire the abundance of void in it are caught in just about the same difficulties [scil. as Anaxagoras and Empedocles, cf. **ANAXAG. D59; EMP. R15b**]. For it will possess less solid than the other bodies, and more void; but all the same there will be a certain quantity of fire in which the solid and the full exceed the solids contained in some small quantity of earth. [. . .] It is also very strange that they move upward because of the void while the void itself does not.

R46 (< A135) Theophr. *Sens.* 68

[. . . = **D65**] ἄτοπον δ᾽ ἂν φανείη πρῶτον μὲν τὸ μὴ
πάντων ὁμοίως ἀποδοῦναι τὰς αἰτίας, ἀλλὰ βαρὺ¹ μὲν
καὶ κοῦφον καὶ μαλακὸν καὶ σκληρὸν καὶ μεγέθει καὶ
σμικρότητι² καὶ τῷ μανῷ καὶ πυκνῷ, θερμὸν δὲ καὶ
ψυχρὸν καὶ τὰ ἄλλα τοῖς σχήμασιν.³ ἔπειτα βαρέος
μὲν καὶ κούφου καὶ σκληροῦ καὶ μαλακοῦ καθ᾽ αὑτὰ
ποιεῖν φύσεις (μέγεθος μὲν γὰρ καὶ σμικρότης καὶ τὸ
πυκνὸν καὶ τὸ μανὸν οὐ πρὸς ἕτερόν ἐστι), θερμὸν δὲ
καὶ ψυχρὸν καὶ τὰ ἄλλα⁴ πρὸς τὴν αἴσθησιν, καὶ
ταῦτα πολλάκις λέγοντα, διότι τοῦ χυλοῦ⁵ τὸ σχῆμα
σφαιροειδές. [. . . = **R56**]

¹ βαρὺ Philippson: δριμὺ mss.   ² σκληρότητι mss., corr.
Wimmer   ³ post σχήμασιν lac. pos. Schneider e.g. ‹διορί-
ζειν›   ⁴ θερμῶν δὲ καὶ ψυχρῶν καὶ τῶν ἄλλων mss., corr.
Usener   ⁵ χυμοῦ mss., corr. Schneider

Regarding Generation and Other
Kinds of Change (R47)

R47 (> A38) Arist. *GC* 1.9 327a14–26

ὅλως δὲ τὸ τοῦτον γίνεσθαι τὸν τρόπον μόνον σχιζο-
μένων τῶν σωμάτων, ἄτοπον· ἀναιρεῖ γὰρ οὗτος ὁ
λόγος ἀλλοίωσιν, ὁρῶμεν δὲ τὸ αὐτὸ σῶμα συνεχὲς
ὂν ὁτὲ μὲν ὑγρὸν ὁτὲ δὲ πεπηγός, οὐ διαιρέσει καὶ
συνθέσει τοῦτο παθόν, οὐδὲ *τροπῇ καὶ* **διαθιγῇ**, καθάπερ λέγει Δημόκριτος· οὔτε γὰρ μεταταχθὲν οὔτε
μετατεθὲν τὴν φύσιν πεπηγὸς ἐξ ὑγροῦ γέγονεν, οὐδὲ

R46 (< A135) Theophrastus, *On Sensations*

It would seem absurd, first of all, not to explain the causes of all [scil. perceptible phenomena] in the same way, but [scil. to explain] heavy, light, soft, and hard by means of largeness, smallness, looseness, and density, but hot, cold, and the others by means of the shapes. And then to posit heavy, light, hard, and soft natures as existing by themselves (for largeness, smallness, density, and looseness are not relative to something else), but [scil. to refer] hot, cold, and the other ones to sensation—and this although he says a number of times that the shape of flavor is spherical.[...]

Regarding Generation and Other
Kinds of Change (R47)

R47 (> A38) Aristotle, *On Generation and Corruption*

In general, it is absurd that this [i.e. acting and being acted upon] happen only in this way, namely when bodies are split apart. For this thesis abolishes alteration, but we see that the same body, even though remaining continuous, is at one time liquid, at another solid, and that it undergoes this affection not because of separation and reunification, nor because of **"turning"** and **"contact,"** as Democritus says [cf. **D72**]. For it is not because there has been a change of disposition or of placement in its nature that it

νῦν ὑπάρχει σκληρὰ καὶ πεπηγότα ἀδιαίρετα τοὺς
ὄγκους· ἀλλ᾽ ὁμοίως ἅπαν ὑγρόν, ὁτὲ δὲ σκληρὸν καὶ
πεπηγός ἐστιν. ἔτι δ᾽ οὐδ᾽ αὔξησιν οἷόν τ᾽ εἶναι καὶ
φθίσιν· οὐ γὰρ ὁτιοῦν ἔσται γεγονὸς μεῖζον, εἴπερ
ἐστὶ πρόσθεσις, καὶ μὴ πᾶν μεταβεβληκός, ἢ μιχθέν-
τος τινὸς ἢ καθ᾽ αὐτὸ μεταβάλλοντος.

Regarding the Plurality of Worlds (R48)

R48

a (≠ DK) Arist. *Phys.* 4.10 218b3–5

ἔτι δ᾽ εἰ πλείους ἦσαν οἱ οὐρανοί, ὁμοίως ἂν ἦν ὁ
χρόνος ἡ ὁτουοῦν αὐτῶν κίνησις, ὥστε πολλοὶ χρόνοι
ἅμα.

b (78.7 Leszl) Simpl. *In Phys.*, p. 701.30–32

"εἰ γὰρ πλείους ἦσαν" φησὶν "οὐρανοί," τουτέστι κόσμοι, ὥσπερ ὑποτίθενται οἱ περὶ Δημόκριτον [. . .].

Regarding the Sea (R49)

R49 (< A100) Arist. *Meteor.* 2.3 356b9–15

τὸ δὲ νομίζειν ἐλάττω τε γίγνεσθαι τὸ πλῆθος, ὥσπερ
φησὶ Δημόκριτος, καὶ τέλος ὑπολείψειν, τῶν Αἰσώπου
μύθων οὐθὲν διαφέρειν ἔοικεν ὁ πεπεισμένος οὕτως·
καὶ γὰρ ἐκεῖνος ἐμυθολόγησεν ὡς δὶς μὲν ἡ Χάρυβδις

has changed from being liquid to becoming solidified, nor do there now [i.e. in this state] exist within it hard and solidified bodies indivisible in their masses; but just as it is entirely liquid, it is sometimes hard and solidified. Moreover, it is not possible that there be growth and diminution. For it is not every part that will have become larger, if there is addition, and the whole will not have been transformed, if something has been mixed or it has itself been transformed.

Regarding the Plurality of Worlds (R48)

R48

a (≠ DK) Aristotle, *Physics*

Again, if there were a plurality of heavens, in the same way the movement of each of them would be a time, so that many times would coexist.

b (≠ DK) Simplicius, *Commentary on Aristotle's* Physics

"If there were," he says, "a plurality of heavens," i.e. worlds, as Democritus and his followers suppose [. . .].

Regarding the Sea (R49)

R49 (< A100) Aristotle, *Meteorology*

To think that it [i.e. the sea] decreases in volume, as Democritus says, and at the end will cease to exist [**D122**] —anyone who believes this seems not to be at all different from the fables of Aesop. For he told the myth that

407

ἀναρροφήσασα τὸ μὲν πρῶτον τὰ ὄρη ἐποίησε φα-
νερά, τὸ δὲ δεύτερον τὰς νήσους, τὸ δὲ τελευταῖον
ῥοφήσασα ξηρὰν ποιήσει πάμπαν.

Regarding the Magnet (R50)

R50 (< A165) Alex. (?) *Quaest.* 2.23, p. 73.7–11

ἀλλὰ τὸ μὲν τὴν λίθον καὶ τὸν σίδηρον ἐξ ὁμοίων
συγκεῖσθαι δέξαιτ᾽ ἄν τις, πῶς δὲ καὶ[1] τὸ ἤλεκτρον
καὶ τὸ ἄχυρον;[2] ὅταν δὲ καὶ ἐπ᾽ ἐκείνων λέγῃ τις[3]
ταύτην τὴν αἰτίαν, ἔστι[4] πολλὰ ἑλκόμενα ὑπὸ τοῦ
ἠλέκτρου, οἷς πᾶσιν εἰ ἐξ ὁμοίων σύγκειται, κἀκεῖνα
ἐξ ὁμοίων ἀλλήλοις συγκείμενα ἕλκοι <ἂν>[5] ἄλληλα.

[1] καὶ Bruns: εἰς mss.   [2] sign. interrog. post αἰτίαν pos.
mss., post ἄχυρον Bruns   [3] ὅταν. . . λέγῃ τις Diels: ὅτι. . .
λέγεται mss.   [4] ἔστι Diels: ἔτι mss.   [5] <ἂν> Bruns

Regarding the Soul (R51)

R51 (< 103.3 Leszl) Arist. *An.* 1.3 406b22–25

[. . . = **D131**] ἡμεῖς δ᾽ ἐρωτήσομεν εἰ καὶ ἠρέμησιν
ποιεῖ τοῦτ᾽ αὐτό· πῶς δὲ ποιήσει, χαλεπὸν ἢ ἀδύνατον
εἰπεῖν. ὅλως δὲ οὐχ οὕτω φαίνεται κινεῖν ἡ ψυχὴ τὸ
ζῷον, ἀλλὰ διὰ προαιρέσεώς τινος καὶ νοήσεως.

Charybdis, having swallowed them twice, the first time
made the mountains appear, the second time the islands,
but that swallowing a final time, she will make it completely dry.[1]

[1] The fable in question is not extant.

Regarding the Magnet (R50)

R50 (< A165) Alexander of Aphrodisias (?), *Problems and
Solutions (Questions) on Nature*

But that the magnet and iron are composed of similar [scil.
atoms]—one could accept this, but how could it be the
same for amber and chaff? And if someone says that this
is the cause for the latter two as well, there are many things
that are attracted by amber; and if it is composed of [scil.
atoms] similar to all of these, these latter too, being composed out of [scil. atoms] similar to each other, would have
to attract each other.

Regarding the Soul (R51)

R51 (≠ DK) Aristotle, *On the Soul*

[. . .] As for us, we shall ask whether this same thing [i.e.
the atoms, which are always in motion] also produces rest;
but how it will produce this, it is difficult or impossible to
say. In general, the soul does not seem to impart motion
to the animal in this way, but thanks to a certain choice
and thought.

Regarding Sensation and Its Objects (R52–R66)
In General (R52–R56)

R52 (57 Leszl) Arist. *Metaph.* Γ5 1009b9–12

ποῖα οὖν τούτων ἀληθῆ ἢ ψευδῆ, ἄδηλον· οὐθὲν γὰρ
μᾶλλον τάδε ἢ τάδε ἀληθῆ, ἀλλ᾽ ὁμοίως. διὸ Δημόκριτός γέ φησιν ἤτοι οὐθὲν εἶναι ἀληθὲς ἢ ἡμῖν γ᾽
ἄδηλον.

R53 (cf. A112) Arist. *Metaph.* Γ5 1009b12–17

ὅλως δὲ διὰ τὸ ὑπολαμβάνειν φρόνησιν μὲν τὴν
αἴσθησιν, ταύτην δ᾽ εἶναι ἀλλοίωσιν, τὸ φαινόμενον
κατὰ τὴν αἴσθησιν ἐξ ἀνάγκης ἀληθές εἶναί φασιν·
ἐκ τούτων γὰρ καὶ Ἐμπεδοκλῆς καὶ Δημόκριτος καὶ
τῶν ἄλλων ὡς ἔπος εἰπεῖν ἕκαστος τοιαύταις δόξαις
γεγένηνται ἔνοχοι.

R54 (A119) Arist. *Sens.* 4 442a29–b3

Δημόκριτος δὲ καὶ οἱ πλεῖστοι τῶν φυσιολόγων, ὅσοι
λέγουσι περὶ αἰσθήσεως, ἀτοπώτατόν τι ποιοῦσιν·
πάντα γὰρ τὰ αἰσθητὰ ἁπτὰ ποιοῦσιν. καίτοι εἰ τοῦτο
οὕτως ἔχει, δῆλον ὡς καὶ τῶν ἄλλων αἰσθήσεων
ἑκάστη ἁφή τίς ἐστιν·

R55 (< A135) Theophr. *Sens.* 49

[49] Δημόκριτος δὲ περὶ μὲν αἰσθήσεως οὐ διορίζει,

410

ATOMISTS (LEUCIPPUS, DEMOCRITUS)

Regarding Sensation and Its Objects (R52–R66)
In General (R52–R56)

R52 (≠ DK) Aristotle, *Metaphysics*

So which kinds of these [i.e. sensations] are true or false is unclear. For these are not more true than those, but similarly so. And that is why, as for Democritus, he says that nothing is true or else that it is not clear, at least for us.

R53 (cf. A112) Aristotle, *Metaphysics*

And in general it is because they suppose that thought is sensation and that this latter is an alteration, that they say that what appears with regard to sensation is necessarily true. For it is for these reasons that Empedocles, Democritus, and practically every one of the others have fallen under the grip of such opinions.

R54 (A119) Aristotle, *On Sensation*

Democritus and most of the natural philosophers who speak about sensation do something that is extremely strange: for they make all perceptibles objects of touch. But if this is how it is, it is clear that each of the other sensations will also be a certain kind of touching too.

R55 (< A135) Theophrastus, *On Sensations*

[49] On the subject of sensation, Democritus does not

411

πότερα τοῖς ἐναντίοις ἢ τοῖς ὁμοίοις ἐστίν. εἰ μὲν γὰρ
<τῷ>¹ ἀλλοιοῦσθαι ποιεῖ τὸ αἰσθάνεσθαι, δόξειεν ἂν
τοῖς διαφόροις· οὐ γὰρ ἀλλοιοῦται τὸ ὅμοιον ὑπὸ τοῦ
ὁμοίου· πάλιν δ' <εἰ>² τὸ μὲν αἰσθάνεσθαι καὶ ἁπλῶς
ἀλλοιοῦσθαι <τῷ>³ πάσχειν, ἀδύνατον δέ, φησί, τὰ⁴
μὴ ταὐτὰ πάσχειν, ἀλλὰ κἂν ἕτερα ὄντα ποιῇ οὐχ
<ἧ>⁵ ἕτερα ἀλλ' ἧ ταὐτόν τι ὑπάρχει,⁵ τοῖς ὁμοίοις. διὸ
περὶ μὲν τούτων ἀμφοτέρως ἔστιν ὑπολαβεῖν. περὶ
ἑκάστης δ' ἤδη αὐτῶν ἐν μέρει πειρᾶται λέγειν [... =
D147].

¹ <τῷ> Camotius   ² <εἰ> Wimmer   ³ <τῷ> Philippson
⁴ τῷ vel τὸ mss., corr. Zeller   ⁵ ἀλλὰ καὶ ἕτερα ὄντα ποιεῖν
οὐχ ἕτερα ἀλλ' ἧ ταὐτόν τι πάσχει mss., corr. Diels conl. Arist.
GC 1.7. 323b13

R56

a (< A135) Theophr. *Sens.* 69–72

[... = **R46**] [69] ὅλως δὲ μέγιστον ἐναντίωμα καὶ κοινὸν ἐπὶ πάντων, ἅμα μὲν πάθη ποιεῖν τῆς αἰσθήσεως,
ἅμα δὲ τοῖς σχήμασι διορίζειν, καὶ τὸ αὐτὸ φαίνεσθαι τοῖς μὲν πικρόν, τοῖς δὲ γλυκύ, τοῖς δ' ἄλλως.¹
οὔτε γὰρ οἷόν <τε>² τὸ σχῆμα πάθος εἶναι οὔτε ταὐτὸν
τοῖς μὲν σφαιροειδές, τοῖς δ' ἄλλως. ἀνάγκη δ'³ ἴσως,
εἴπερ⁴ τοῖς μὲν γλυκύ, τοῖς δὲ πικρόν, οὐδὲ κατὰ τὰς
ἡμετέρας ἕξεις μεταβάλλειν τὰς μορφάς. ἁπλῶς δὲ τὸ
μὲν σχῆμα καθ' αὑτό ἐστι, τὸ δὲ γλυκὺ καὶ ὅλως τὸ

define whether it is produced by what is contrary or by what is similar. For if he explains sensation by an alteration, it would seem that this occurs by what is different; for what is similar is not altered by what is similar. But on the other hand, if sensation and, in general, being altered is the result of an affection, and if it is impossible, as he says, that things that are not identical be affected, but, even if they are other, they act not insofar as they are other but insofar as they have something in common, [scil. it would seem that this occurs] by what is similar. For this reason it is possible to admit both hypotheses on this subject. He then tries to discuss each of them in turn [. . .].

R56

a (< A135) Theophrastus, *On Sensations*

[. . .] [69] In general, the greatest contradiction, and one that is common to all [scil. the perceptibles], is simultaneously to make them affections of sensation but to define them by the shapes, and [scil. to maintain] that the same thing appears bitter to some, sweet to others, and different to others. For it is not possible either that the shape be an affection, or that the same thing be spherical to some and different to others (but this is surely necessary if it is to be sweet to some and bitter to others), and not that the shapes change according to our conditions either. In short, the shape exists by itself, but sweetness and in general the

---

¹ ἄλλοις mss., corr. Diels   ² οἷον οὔτε γὰρ mss., corr. et suppl. Diels   ³ εἴπερ post δ᾿ hab. mss., secl. Stephanus
⁴ εἴπερ ὡς εἶπεν Wimmer (qui post πικρὸν lac. sign.)

αἰσθητὸν πρὸς ἄλλο καὶ ἐν ἄλλοις, ὥς φησιν. ἄτοπον
δὲ καὶ τὸ πᾶσιν ἀξιοῦν ταὐτὸ φαίνεσθαι τῶν αὐτῶν
αἰσθανομένοις καὶ τούτων τὴν ἀλήθειαν ἐλέγχειν, καὶ
ταῦτα εἰρηκότα πρότερον τὸ τοῖς⁵ ἀνομοίως διακειμέ-
νοις ὅμοια⁶ φαίνεσθαι⁷ καὶ πάλιν τὸ μηθὲν μᾶλλον
ἕτερον ἑτέρου τυγχάνειν τῆς ἀληθείας.

⁵ τούτοις mss., corr. Wimmer   ⁶ ἀνόμοια Koraïs
⁷ φαίνεται mss., corr. Stephanus

[70] εἰκὸς γὰρ τὸ βέλτιον τοῦ χείρονος καὶ τὸ ὑγιαῖ-
νον τοῦ κάμνοντος· κατὰ φύσιν γὰρ μᾶλλον. ἔτι δὲ
εἴπερ μὴ ἔστι φύσις τῶν αἰσθητῶν διὰ τὸ μὴ ταὐτὰ
πᾶσι φαίνεσθαι, δῆλον ὡς οὐδὲ τῶν ζῴων οὐδὲ τῶν
ἄλλων σωμάτων· οὐδὲ γὰρ περὶ τούτων ὁμοδοξοῦσι.
καίτοι εἰ μὴ καὶ διὰ τῶν αὐτῶν γίνεται πᾶσι τὸ γλυκὺ
καὶ τὸ πικρόν, ἀλλ᾽ ἥ γε φύσις τοῦ πικροῦ καὶ τοῦ
γλυκέος ἡ αὐτὴ φαίνεται πᾶσιν. ὅπερ καὶ αὐτὸς ἂν
δόξειεν ἐπιμαρτυρεῖν. πῶς γὰρ ἂν τὸ ἡμῖν πικρὸν ἄλλοις ἦν γλυκὺ καὶ στρυφνόν, εἰ μή τις ἦν ὡρισμένη
φύσις αὐτῶν;
[71] ἔτι δὲ ποιεῖ σαφέστερον, ἐν οἷς φησι γίνεσθαι
μὲν ἕκαστον καὶ εἶναι κατ᾽ ἀλήθειαν, ἰδίως δ᾽ ἐπὶ μι-
κροῦ¹ "μοῖραν ἔχειν² συνέσεως." ὥστε διά τε³ τούτων
ἐναντίον ἂν φανείη τὸ μὴ ποιεῖν φύσιν τινὰ τῶν αἰσθητῶν καὶ πρὸς τούτοις, ὅπερ ἐλέχθη καὶ πρότερον,

¹ πικροῦ Schneider   ² ἔχει vel ἔχῃ mss., corr. Stephanus
³ τι mss., corr. Schneider

414

perceptible exists in relation to something else and in other things, as he says. It is also as absurd to suppose that the same [scil. impression] appears to all those who perceive the same [scil. things] and to refute the truth of these latter—and this, after having said earlier that there appear similar (?) [scil. impressions] to people with dissimilar dispositions—as it is to maintain, inversely, that the one does not touch upon the truth any more than the other does.

[70] For it is likely that the better is superior to the worse and the healthy person to the sick one; for that is more in conformity with nature. Furthermore, if indeed it is true that there is not a nature of perceptibles, given that they do not appear the same to all, it is clear that there is not one either for animals and other bodies; for people are not of the same opinion about these either. And yet even if the sweet and the bitter do not come about for all from the same causes, nonetheless at least the nature itself of the bitter and the sweet appears to be the same for all. He himself would seem to bear witness to this. For how could what is bitter for us be sweet and sour for others, if there were not some determinate nature for them?

[71] He makes this even clearer where he says that each thing becomes and exists according to truth, but, with regard to what is small, in a particular way, that it **"possesses a share of understanding."**[1] So that it would seem contradictory not to admit a nature of perceptibles, both for these last reasons and, besides these, as was also

---

[1] The correction, adopted by all the editors, of 'small' (*mikron*) to 'bitter' (*pikron*), is not an improvement. This seems to be a general epistemological proposition (cf. **D22**).

ὅταν σχῆμα μὲν ἀποδιδῷ τῆς οὐσίας[1] ὥσπερ καὶ τῶν
ἄλλων, μὴ εἶναι δὲ λέγῃ φύσιν· ἢ γὰρ οὐδενὸς ὅλως
ἢ καὶ τούτων ἔσται τῆς αὐτῆς γε ὑπαρχούσης αἰτίας.
ἔτι δὲ τὸ θερμόν τε καὶ ψυχρόν, ἅπερ ἀρχὰς τιθέασιν,
εἰκὸς ἔχειν τινὰ φύσιν, εἰ δὲ ταῦτα καὶ τὰ ἄλλα. νῦν
δὲ σκληροῦ μὲν καὶ μαλακοῦ καὶ βαρέος καὶ κούφου
ποιεῖ τιν'[2] οὐσίαν, ἅπερ[3] οὐχ ἧττον ἔδοξε λέγεσθαι
πρὸς ἡμᾶς, θερμοῦ δὲ καὶ ψυχροῦ καὶ τῶν ἄλλων
οὐδενός· καίτοι τό γε βαρὺ καὶ κοῦφον ὅταν διορίζῃ
τοῖς μεγέθεσιν, ἀνάγκη τὰ ἁπλᾶ πάντα τὴν αὐτὴν
ἔχειν ὁρμὴν τῆς φορᾶς, ὥστε μιᾶς τινος ἂν ὕλης εἴη
καὶ τῆς αὐτῆς φύσεως.
[72] ἀλλὰ περὶ μὲν τούτων ἔοικε συνηκολουθηκέναι
τοῖς ποιοῦσιν ὅλως τὸ φρονεῖν κατὰ τὴν ἀλλοίωσιν,
ἥπερ ἐστὶν ἀρχαιοτάτη δόξα. πάντες γὰρ οἱ παλαιοὶ
καὶ[4] ποιηταὶ καὶ σοφοὶ κατὰ τὴν διάθεσιν ἀποδιδόασι
τὸ φρονεῖν [. . . = **D159a**].

[1] θερμασίας coni. Usener   [2] τὴν mss., corr. Diels
[3] ἅπερ Schneider: ὅπερ mss.
[4] οἱ post καὶ hab. mss., del. Diels

b (< A163) Theophr. *CP* 6.17.11

ἐπεὶ τά γε σχήματα Δημοκρίτου [. . .] τεταγμένας
ἔχοντα τὰς μορφὰς τεταγμένα καὶ τὰ πάθη καὶ τ⟨ὰς
αἰσθήσεις ἐ⟩χρῆν[1] ποιεῖν.

[1] lac. in mss. UM suppl. Diels: τοι γε οὐκ ἐχρῆν P

said earlier, when on the one hand he explains the form of their substance, just as for the others [scil. perceptibles], but on the other hand despite this he denies the existence of a nature. For either no thing at all will have one, or else these will have one too, given that the cause is the same kind. Furthermore, it is plausible that the hot and the cold, which they posit as principles, possess a nature; and if these do, then so too do the others. Now, he establishes that the hard and the soft, the heavy and the light—things that did not seem to be less defined with relation to us— have a certain substance, but not the hot and the cold, nor any of the other [scil. perceptibles]. And yet when he determines the heavy and the light by magnitudes, it follows necessarily that all the simple [scil. bodies] have the same impulse of movement, so that there would be a single kind of matter, endowed with the same nature.

[72] But in these matters he seems to have followed those people who in general explain thinking as a function of alteration, which is an extremely ancient opinion; for all the ancients, both the poets and the sages, give an account of thinking according to the disposition [scil. of the body].

b (< A163) Theophrastus, *Causes of Plants*

For the shapes of Democritus [. . .], since they possess ordered forms, ought also to produce ordered affections and ‹sensations (?)›.

Vision and Colors (R57–R59)

R57 (< A135) Theophr. *Sens.* 51–55

[. . . = **D147**] [51] πρῶτον μὲν οὖν ἄτοπος ἡ ἀποτύπω-
σις ἡ ἐν τῷ ἀέρι. δεῖ γὰρ ἔχειν πυκνότητα καὶ μὴ
θρύπτεσθαι τὸ πυκνούμενον,[1] ὥσπερ καὶ αὐτὸς λέγει
παραβάλλων τοιαύτην εἶναι τὴν ἐντύπωσιν, οἷον εἰ
ἐκμάξειας εἰς κηρόν.[2] ἔπειτα μᾶλλον ἐν ὕδατι τυποῦσθαι δυνατόν, ὅσῳ πυκνότερον· ἧττον δὲ ὁρᾶται,[3]
καίτοι προσῆκε μᾶλλον. ὅλως δὲ ἀπορροὴν ποιοῦντα
τῆς μορφῆς, ὥσπερ ἐν τοῖς περὶ τῶν εἰδῶν,[4] τί δεῖ τὴν
ἀποτύπωσιν ποιεῖν; αὐτῷ γὰρ ἐμφαίνεται τὰ εἴδωλα.[5]

[1] τυπούμενον Zeller   [2] εἰς κηρόν Burchard: εἰς σκληρόν mss.   [3] ὁρᾶσθαι mss., corr. Wimmer   [4] εἰδώλων
Schneider   [5] τί δὴ τὴν ἀποτύπωσιν ποιεῖ, αὐτῷ γὰρ ἐμ-
φαίνει τῷ τὰ εἴδωλα P, rescr. F: corr. Schneider

[52] εἰ δὲ δὴ τοῦτο συμβαίνει καὶ ὁ ἀὴρ ἀπομάττεται
καθάπερ κηρὸς ὠθούμενος καὶ πυκνούμενος, πῶς καὶ
ποία τις ἡ ἔμφασις γίνεται; δῆλον γὰρ ὡς ἐπὶ προσ-
ώπου ⟨ὁ⟩[1] τύπος ἔσται τῷ ὁρωμένῳ καθάπερ ἐν τοῖς
ἄλλοις. τοιούτου δ᾽ ὄντος ἀδύνατον ἐξ ἐναντίας ἔμφασιν γίνεσθαι μὴ στραφέντος τοῦ τύπου. τοῦτο δ᾽ ὑπὸ
τίνος ἔσται καὶ πῶς, δεικτέον· οὐχ οἷόν τε γὰρ ἄλλως
γίνεσθαι τὸ ὁρᾶν. ἔπειτα ὅταν ὁρᾶται πλείονα κατὰ
τὸν αὐτὸν τόπον, πῶς ἐν τῷ αὐτῷ ἀέρι πλείους ἔσον-
ται τύποι; καὶ πάλιν πῶς ἀλλήλους ὁρᾶν ἐνδέχεται;
τοὺς γὰρ τύπους ἀνάγκη συμβάλλειν ἑαυτοῖς, ἑκάτε-

Vision and Colors (R57–R59)

R57 (< A135) Theophrastus, *On the Sensations*

[. . .] [51] First of all, then, the impression produced in the air is absurd. For the body that is condensed must possess a certain density and not be broken into pieces, as he himself proves when he says, as a comparison, that the impression is exactly as if one were to mold a form in wax. And then it is more probable that the impression would be made in water, to the degree that it is denser; but vision occurs less in that case, whereas it ought to occur more. And in general, given that he posits an efflux of the shape, as he does in his discussions about forms, what need does he have to posit the production of the impression? For the images are reflected in it [scil. probably: the eye].

[52] But if indeed this does happen, and the air is modeled like wax that is pressed and condensed, in what way and of what sort is the reflection produced? For it is clear that the impression will be turned to face the object seen, as in the other cases. And since it will be like this, it is impossible that a reflection be produced inversely without the impression being turned around. By what agency this will come about and in what way remains to be demonstrated; for it is not possible that vision come about in any other way. And then, when a plurality of things is seen in the same place, how will there be room for a plurality of impressions in the same air? And again, how is it possible to see each other? For necessarily the impressions will encounter themselves, given that each of them is a mask

---

¹ <ὁ> Schneider

ρον ἀντιπρόσωπον² ὄντα ἀφ' ὧν ἐστιν. ὥστε τοῦτο
ζήτησιν ἔχει.

² ἂν πρόσωπον mss., corr. Stephanus

[53] καὶ πρὸς τούτῳ διὰ τί ποτε ἕκαστος αὐτὸς αὑτὸν
οὐχ ὁρᾷ; καθάπερ γὰρ τοῖς τῶν πέλας ὄμμασιν, οἱ
τύποι καὶ τοῖς ἑαυτῶν¹ ἐμφαίνοιντ' ἄν, ἄλλως τε εἰ καὶ
εὐθὺς ἀντιπρόσωποι κεῖνται καὶ ταὐτὸ συμβαίνει
πάθος ὥσπερ ἐπὶ τῆς ἠχοῦς. ἀνακλᾶσθαι γάρ φησι
καὶ πρὸς αὐτὸν τὸν φθεγξάμενον τὴν φωνήν. ὅλως δὲ
ἄτοπος ἡ τοῦ ἀέρος τύπωσις. ἀνάγκη γὰρ ἐξ ὧν λέγει
πάντα ἐναποτυποῦσθαι τὰ σώματα καὶ πολλὰ ἐναλ-
λάττειν, ὃ καὶ πρὸς τὴν ὄψιν ἐμπόδιον ἂν εἴη καὶ
ἄλλως οὐκ εὔλογον. ἔτι δὲ εἴπερ ἡ τύπωσις διαμένει,
καὶ μὴ φανερῶν ὄντων² μηδὲ πλησίον ὄντων τῶν
σωμάτων ἐχρῆν ὁρᾶν εἰ καὶ μὴ νύκτωρ, ἀλλὰ μεθ'
ἡμέραν. καίτοι τούς γε τύπους οὐχ ἧττον εἰκὸς διαμέ-
νειν νυκτός, ὅσῳ ἐμψυχρότερος³ ὁ ἀήρ.

¹ καὶ τοῖς ἑαυτῶν Diels: καίτοιγε αὐτῶν mss.   ² ὄντων
del. Schneider   ³ ἐμψυχότερος mss., corr. Wimmer

[54] ἀλλ' ἴσως τὴν ἔμφασιν ὁ ἥλιος ποιεῖ καὶ¹ τὸ φῶς
ὥσπερ ἐπιφέρων ἐπὶ τὴν ὄψιν, καθάπερ ἔοικε βούλεσθαι λέγειν· ἐπεὶ τό γε τὸν ἥλιον ἀπωθοῦντα² ἀφ'
ἑαυτοῦ καὶ ἀποπλαττόμενον πυκνοῦν³ τὸν ἀέρα, καθάπερ φησίν, ἄτοπον· διακρίνειν γὰρ πέφυκε μᾶλλον.

ἄτοπον δὲ καὶ τὸ μὴ μόνον τοῖς ὄμμασιν, ἀλλὰ καὶ
τῷ ἄλλῳ σώματι μεταδιδόναι τῆς αἰσθήσεως· φησὶ

corresponding to the features of its source. So that this remains unresolved.

[53] And besides, for what reason does it happen that each person does not see himself? For the impressions would be reflected in their own eyes too just as in the eyes of those who are nearby, especially if they are located immediately facing and the same phenomenon happens as in the case of an echo. For he says that a sound is reverberated back toward the same person who emitted it. In general, the impression in the air is absurd. For from what he says it follows necessarily that all bodies are impressed upon it and that many cross one another—something that would be a hindrance for sight and moreover would not be plausible. Moreover, if it is true that the impression persists even in the case of things that are not seen, it would be necessary that vision take place even when the bodies are not near, if not at night, then at least during the day. And yet it is not less likely that the impressions persist at night, to the degree that the air is cooler then.
[54] But perhaps it is the sun that produces the reflection as well as the light, transporting the former in some way toward sight, as he seems to mean—at least his claim that the sun condenses the air by repelling it and modeling it is absurd. For it is more in its nature to disaggregate.

It is also as absurd to make not only the eyes but also the rest of the body participate in sensation. For he says

---

¹ καὶ del. Vossianus   ² τὸν ἥλιον ἀπωθοῦντα Schneider:
τὸν ὅτι ἀπαθοῦντα mss.   ³ πυκνὸν mss., corr. Schneider

γὰρ διὰ τοῦτο κενότητα καὶ ὑγρότητα ἔχειν δεῖν τὸν ὀφθαλμόν, ἵν᾽ ἐπὶ πλέον δέχηται καὶ τῷ ἄλλῳ σώματι παραδιδῷ.

ἄλογον δὲ καὶ τὸ μάλιστα μὲν ὁρᾶν φάναι τὰ ὁμόφυλα, τὴν δὲ ἔμφασιν ποιεῖν τοῖς ἀλλόχρωσιν ὡς οὐκ ἐμφαινομένων τῶν ὁμοίως.[4] τὰ δὲ μεγέθη καὶ τὰ διαστήματα πῶς ἐμφαίνεται,[5] καίπερ ἐπιχειρήσας λέγειν οὐκ ἀποδίδωσιν.

[55] περὶ μὲν οὖν ὄψεως ἰδίως ἔνια βουλόμενος λέγειν πλείω παραδίδωσι ζήτησιν. [. . . = **D157**]

<hr/>

[4] ὁμοίων Vossianus   [5] φαίνεται mss., corr. Philippson

<hr/>

R58 (> A122) Arist. *An.* 2.7 419a15–21

οὐ γὰρ καλῶς τοῦτο λέγει Δημόκριτος, οἰόμενος, εἰ γένοιτο κενὸν τὸ μεταξύ, ὁρᾶσθαι ἂν ἀκριβῶς καὶ εἰ μύρμηξ ἐν τῷ οὐρανῷ εἴη· τοῦτο γὰρ ἀδύνατόν ἐστιν. πάσχοντος γάρ τι τοῦ αἰσθητικοῦ γίνεται τὸ ὁρᾶν· ὑπ᾽ αὐτοῦ μὲν οὖν τοῦ ὁρωμένου χρώματος ἀδύνατον· λείπεται δὴ ὑπὸ τοῦ μεταξύ, ὥστ᾽ ἀναγκαῖόν τι εἶναι μεταξύ· κενοῦ δὲ γενομένου οὐχ ὅτι ἀκριβῶς, ἀλλ᾽ ὅλως οὐθὲν ὀφθήσεται.

R59 (< A135) Theophr. *Sens.* 79–82

[. . . = **D66**] [79] πρῶτον μὲν οὖν τὸ πλείους ἀποδοῦναι τὰς ἀρχὰς ἔχει τινὰ ἀπορίαν· οἱ γὰρ ἄλλοι τὸ λευκὸν καὶ τὸ μέλαν ὡς τούτων ἁπλῶν ὄντων μόνων. ἔπειτα

that this is why the eye must contain void and moisture, so that it can receive more and transmit to the rest of the body.

It is also unreasonable to assert that one sees better the members of the same species, and to produce the reflection by impressions of different colors, on the pretext that things that appear in a similar way would not be reflected. As for the way in which magnitudes and distances appear, he has tried to explain this but has not succeeded. [55] And so, in trying to make some original assertions about sight, he leaves even more questions unresolved. [. . .]

R58 (> A122) Aristotle, *On the Soul*

Democritus does not speak correctly when he thinks that if the intermediate [scil. space] were void, one would see exactly even if an ant were in the sky [**D149**]. For this is impossible. For vision is produced when the organ of sensation is acted upon in some way. Now, it is impossible that this happen because of the color that is seen itself, so it remains that this be due to the intermediary, so that it is necessary that there be some intermediary. But if this is void, then so far from seeing exactly, one will see nothing at all.

R59 (< A135) Theophrastus, *On Sensations*

[. . .] [79] First of all, admitting a plurality of principles [scil. for explaining colors] presents some difficulty; for other people [scil. explain only] white and black, on the idea that only these [scil. colors] are the simple ones. And

τὸ μὴ πᾶσι τοῖς λευκοῖς μίαν ποιῆσαι τὴν μορφήν,
ἀλλ' ἑτέραν τοῖς σκληροῖς καὶ τοῖς ψαθυροῖς. οὐ[1] γὰρ
εἰκὸς ἄλλην αἰτίαν εἶναι τοῖς διαφόροις κατὰ τὴν
ἁφήν, οὐδ' ἂν ἔτι τὸ σχῆμα αἴτιον εἴη[2] τῆς φορᾶς,[3]
ἀλλὰ μᾶλλον ἡ θέσις· ἐνδέχεται γὰρ καὶ τὰ περιφερῆ
καὶ ἁπλῶς πάντα ἐπισκιάζειν ἑαυτοῖς. σημεῖον δέ· καὶ
γὰρ αὐτὸς ταύτην φέρει τὴν πίστιν, ὅσα τῶν λείων
μέλανα φαίνεται· διὰ γὰρ τὴν σύμφυσιν καὶ τὴν
τάξιν ὡς τὴν αὐτὴν ἔχοντα τῷ μέλανι φαίνεσθαι
τοιαῦτα. καὶ πάλιν ὅσα λευκὰ τῶν τραχέων· ἐκ μεγάλων[4] γὰρ εἶναι ταῦτα καὶ τὰς συνδέσεις οὐ περιφερεῖς,[5] ἀλλὰ προκρόσσας[6] καὶ τῶν σχημάτων τὰς μορφὰς μιγνυμένας,[7] ὥσπερ ἡ ἀνάβασις καὶ τὰ πρὸ τῶν
τειχῶν ἔχει †σώματα†.[8] τοιοῦτον γὰρ ὂν ἄσκιον εἶναι
καὶ οὐ κωλύεσθαι τοῦ λαμπροῦ.[9]

[1] εἰ Diels   [2] εἴη Diels: εἶναι mss.   [3] διαφορᾶς
Mullach   [4] μεγάλων F: μεγάλου P   [5] οὐ περιφερεῖς
F: ὑπερφερεῖς P   [6] προκρόσσας Stephanus: προκόσσας
mss.   [7] ἀγνυμένας Diels   [8] χώματα Mullach   [9] τὸ
λαμπρόν Schneider

[80] πρὸς δὲ τούτοις πῶς λέγει καὶ ἐξ ὧν[1] τὸ λευκὸν
ἐνίων γίνεσθαι μέλαν, εἰ τεθείησαν οὕτως, ὥστ' ἐπισκιάζειν; ὅλως δὲ τοῦ διαφανοῦς καὶ τοῦ λαμπροῦ
μᾶλλον ἔοικε τὴν φύσιν ἢ τοῦ λευκοῦ λέγειν. τὸ γὰρ
εὐδίοπτον εἶναι καὶ μὴ ἐπαλλάττειν[2] τοὺς πόρους τοῦ

[1] ἐξ ὧν mss.: ζώων Usener   [2] ἀπαλλάττειν mss., corr.
Schneider

then, not admitting only one shape for all white things, but one for hard ones and a different one for friable ones; for it is not likely that there would be a different cause for things that differ with regard to touch, and it would no longer be the form that would provide the cause for the difference [scil. between the two whites of different origin], but instead the position—for nothing prevents spherical bodies, and in general all bodies, from casting a shadow upon themselves. And here is evidence: for he himself corroborates this view regarding smooth bodies that appear black; for it is because of their structure and order, to the degree that it is similar to black, that they take on this appearance. And inversely regarding rough bodies that appear white: for these are composed of large elements and their joints are not spherical but protruding, and the forms of their shapes are mixed, like an ascent (?) and †objects† in front of walls.[1] For an arrangement like this does not produce a shadow and is not incompatible with shining brightly.

[1] Text difficult to understand. Are the differences in height on the surface of the atoms being compared with machines permitting the ramparts of a city to be scaled?

[80] And besides, how can he say, and on what basis, that the white color of certain things becomes black if they are placed in such a way as to produce a shadow? In general, he seems to speak about the nature of the diaphanous and the brightly shining more than about that of the white; for

διαφανοῦς· πόσα δὲ λευκὰ τοῦ διαφανοῦς;[3] ἔτι δὲ τὸ
μὲν εὐθεῖς εἶναι τῶν λευκῶν τοὺς πόρους, τῶν δὲ
μελάνων ἐπαλλάττειν, ὡς εἰσιούσης τῆς φύσεως[4] ὑπολαβεῖν ἔστιν· ὁρᾶν δέ φησι[5] διὰ τὴν ἀπορροὴν καὶ
τὴν ἔμφασιν τὴν εἰς τὴν ὄψιν· εἰ δὲ τοῦτό ἐστι, τί
διοίσει τοὺς πόρους κεῖσθαι κατ' ἀλλήλους ἢ ἐπαλλάττειν; οὐδὲ τὴν ἀπορροὴν ἀπὸ τοῦ κενοῦ πως γίνεσθαι[6] ῥᾴδιον ὑπολαβεῖν· ὥστε λεκτέον τούτου τὴν
αἰτίαν. ἔοικε γὰρ ἀπὸ τοῦ φωτὸς ἢ ἀπὸ ἄλλου τινὸς
ποιεῖν τὸ λευκόν. διὸ καὶ τὴν παχύτητα τοῦ ἀέρος
αἰτιᾶται[7] πρὸς τὸ φαίνεσθαι μέλαν.

[3] πόσα δὲ λευκὰ τοῦ διαφανοῦς temptavimus (vel ἔτι δὲ
πόσα δὲ λευκὰ τοῦ διαφανοῦς?): ἐπὶ πόσα δὲ λευκὰ τοῦ διαφανοῦς mss., secl. Wimmer: τοῦ διαφανοῦς ἔστι. πρῶτα δὲ τὰ
λευκὰ τοῦ διαφανοῦ coni. Diels   [4] φάσεως coni.
Philippson, ὄψεως Usener   [5] φασὶ mss.: corr. Schneider
[6] πῶς γίνεται coni. Diels   [7] αἰτιᾶσθαι mss.: corr. Schneider

[81] ἔτι δὲ πῶς[1] τὸ μέλαν ἀποδίδωσιν, οὐ ῥᾴδιον κατα-
μαθεῖν· ἡ σκιὰ γὰρ μέλαν τι καὶ ἐπιπρόσθησίς ἐστι
τοῦ λευκοῦ· διὸ πρῶτον τὸ λευκὸν τὴν φύσιν. ἅμα δὲ
οὐ μόνον τὸ ἐπισκιάζειν, ἀλλὰ καὶ τὴν παχύτητα τοῦ
ἀέρος καὶ τῆς εἰσιούσης ἀπορροῆς αἰτιᾶται καὶ τὴν
ταραχὴν τοῦ ὀφθαλμοῦ. πότερον δὲ ταῦτα συμβαίνει
διὰ τὸ μὴ εὐδίοπτον ἢ μέλαν,[2] ἢ καὶ ἄλλως[3] γίνοιτ' ἂν
καὶ ποίῳ, οὐ διασαφεῖ.

[1] ὡς mss., corr. Usener   [2] ἢ μέλαν post ποίῳ mox,
transp. huc nos: secl. Diels: τὸ μέλαν coni. Wimmer: ἢ μέλανι
Stephanus   [3] ἄλλῳ Diels

it belongs to the diaphanous to be transparent and in its case there is no crossing of the passages; and how many white things belong to the diaphanous?[1] Moreover, to say that the passages of white things are straight while those of black things cross, is to admit that their nature penetrates [scil. into the organ of sight]. But he says that one sees thanks to the efflux and the reflection in the eye. But if this is the case, what difference does it make whether the passages are arranged in such a way that they face one another rather than crossing? Nor is it easy to suppose that the efflux is produced in some way from the void, so that the cause of this remains to be stated. For he seems to make white originate from light or from something else; and it is for this reason that he makes the thickness of the air as well the cause for the black appearance.

[1] Text uncertain.

[81] Moreover, it is not easy to comprehend the way in which he explains black. For a shadow is something black and is something superimposed upon white; and that is why white is first by nature. But at the same time he makes not only the production of a shadow the cause but also the thickness of the air and of the efflux that penetrates [scil. into the organ of sight] as well as the disturbance of the eye. But he does not clarify whether this happens because it is not transparent or is black, and whether it might happen in some other way, and if so in which.

[82] ἄτοπον δὲ καὶ τὸ τοῦ χλωροῦ[1] μὴ ἀποδοῦναι μορφήν, ἀλλὰ μόνον ἐκ τοῦ στερεοῦ καὶ τοῦ κενοῦ ποιεῖν.
κοινὰ γὰρ ταῦτά γε[2] πάντων καὶ ἐξ ὁποίων οὖν ἔσται
σχημάτων. χρῆν δ' ὥσπερ κἂν[3] τοῖς ἄλλοις ἴδιόν τι
ποιῆσαι, καὶ εἰ μὲν ἐναντίον[4] τῷ ἐρυθρῷ, καθάπερ τὸ
μέλαν τῷ λευκῷ, τὴν ἐναντίαν ἔχει[5] μορφήν· εἰ δὲ μὴ[6]
ἐναντίον, αὐτὸ τοῦτ' ἄν τις θαυμάσειεν, ὅτι τὰς ἀρχὰς
οὐκ ἐναντίας[7] ποιεῖ· δοκεῖ γὰρ ἐν πᾶσιν[8] οὕτω. μάλιστα δ' ἐχρῆν τοῦτο διακριβοῦν, ποῖα τῶν χρωμάτων
ἁπλᾶ καὶ διὰ τί τὰ μὲν σύνθετα, τὰ δὲ ἀσύνθετα·
πλείστη γὰρ ἀπορία[9] περὶ τῶν ἀρχῶν. ἀλλὰ τοῦτο μὲν
ἴσως χαλεπόν· ἐπεὶ καὶ τῶν χυμῶν εἴ τις δύναιτο τοὺς
ἁπλοῦς ἀποδοῦναι, μᾶλλον ἂν ὅδε λέγοι. [. . . = **D67,
R25**]

---

[1] τὸ τὸ χλωρὸν mss., corr. Schneider   [2] ταῦτα τε mss.,
corr. Camotius et Vossianus   [3] κἂν Diels: καὶ mss.   [4] ἐναν-
τίῳ mss., corr. Schneider   [5] ἔχειν Diels   [6] εἰ δὲ μὴ
Diels: εἰ δ' ἢ μὴ mss.: εἰ δ' εἴη μὴ Schneider   [7] ἐναντία
mss., corr. Schneider   [8] ἐν πᾶσιν P: ἐκ πᾶσιν F: ἅπασιν
coni. Diels   [9] ἀπειρία mss., corr. Camotius

Hearing (R60–R61)

R60 (< A135) Theophr. *Sens.* 57

[. . . = **D157**] τὸ μὲν οὖν ἀσαφῶς[1] ἀφορίζειν ὁμοίως
ἔχει τοῖς ἄλλοις. ἄτοπον δὲ καὶ ἴδιον[2] <τὸ>[3] κατὰ πᾶν
τὸ σῶμα τὸν ψόφον εἰσιέναι, καὶ ὅταν εἰσέλθῃ διὰ
τῆς ἀκοῆς, διαχεῖσθαι κατὰ πᾶν, ὥσπερ οὐ ταῖς ἀκο-
αῖς, ἀλλ' ὅλῳ τῷ σώματι τὴν αἴσθησιν οὖσαν. οὐ[4]

[82] It is also absurd that he does not assign a shape to greenish-yellow, but defines it only by the solid and the void. For these are elements shared in common by all things and can be composed out of any shapes whatsoever; so it would be necessary to indicate some individual [scil. feature], as in the other cases. And if it is opposed to red, as black is to white, it possesses the opposite shape; but if it is not opposed, one might well be surprised at the very fact that he does not posit the principles as opposites. For this seems to be the case in all things. But above all it would be necessary to determine with precision which colors are the simple ones and for what reason some are composite and others are not; for the greatest uncertainty reigns on the subject of the principles. But this is surely difficult: for with regard to tastes as well, if someone were able to explain which ones are simple, then it would rather be he [i.e. Democritus] who would speak of this.

Hearing (R60–R61)

R60 (< A135) Theophrastus, *On Sensations*

With regard to the lack of precision in his account, he is similar to the others. But one absurdity that is peculiar to him is to suppose that sound penetrates into the whole body, and that when it enters through the ear it is diffused everywhere, as though this sensation were produced not by the ears but by the whole body. For even if it shares the

¹ ἀσαφῶς Diels: σαφῶς mss.   ² καὶ ἴδιον Zeller: καὶ δι᾽ ὧν mss.   ³ ⟨τὸ⟩ Diels   ⁴ οὐ Schneider: εἰ mss.

γὰρ κἂν συμπάσχῃ⁵ τι τῇ ἀκοῇ, διὰ τοῦτο καὶ αἰσθά-
νεσθαι.⁶ πάσαις γὰρ τοῦτό γε ὁμοίως ποιεῖ, καὶ οὐ
μόνον ταῖς αἰσθήσεσιν, ἀλλὰ καὶ τῇ ψυχῇ. [. . . =
D158]

5 καὶ συμπάσχει mss., corr. Diels
6 αἰσθάνεται Schneider

R61 (< A128) Aët. 4.19.3 (Ps.-Plut.) [περὶ φωνῆς]

[. . . = **D156**] ἔχοι δ᾽ ἄν τις πρὸς τούτους εἰπεῖν· πῶς
ὀλίγα θραύσματα πνεύματος μυρίανδρον ἐκπληροῖ
θέατρον;

Flavors and Taste (R62–R66)

R62 (< A135) Theophr. *Sens.* 72

[. . . = **R56b**] τῶν δὲ χυλῶν ἑκάστῳ τὸ σχῆμα ἀποδί-
δωσι¹ πρὸς τὴν δύναμιν ἀφομοιῶν τὴν² ἐν τοῖς πάθε-
σιν· ὅπερ οὐ μόνον ἐξ ἐκείνων, ἀλλὰ καὶ ἐκ τῶν αἰ-
σθητηρίων ἔδει συμβαίνειν ἄλλως τε καὶ εἰ πάθη
τούτων ἐστίν. οὐ γὰρ πᾶν τὸ σφαιροειδὲς οὐδὲ τὰ
ἄλλα σχήματα τὴν αὐτὴν ἔχει δύναμιν, ὥστε κατὰ τὸ
ὑποκείμενον³ ἔδει διορίζειν, πότερον ἐξ ὁμοίων ἢ ἐξ
ἀμφοῖν⁴ ἐστι καὶ πῶς ἡ τῶν αἰσθήσεων ἀλλοίωσις
γίνεται, καὶ πρὸς τούτοις ὁμοίως ἐπὶ πάντων ἀποδοῦ-

1 ἀποδιδόασι mss., corr. Schneider
2 τοῖς mss.: corr. Schneider

affection of hearing for it, it is not because of this that it feels the sensation. For it does this in the same way with all the senses, and not only with them, but also with the soul.

R61 (< A128) Aëtius

[. . .] But one could object to them [i.e. to philosophers like Democritus]: how could a small number of fragments of air completely fill a theater with thousands of places?

Flavors and Taste (R62–R66)

R62 (< A135) Theophrastus, *On Sensations*

[. . .] As for tastes, he [scil. Democritus] attributes to each one the shape that corresponds to its power, making it similar to [scil. the characteristics of] the affections [**D159;** cf. **D65**]—an explanation that should have been derived not only from these [scil. characteristics] but also from the organs of sensation, especially if they [i.e. these characteristics] are affections of these latter. For it is false to suppose that everything spherical possesses the same power, and so too for the other shapes, so that it would have been necessary to determine the substrate [scil. that undergoes the affection] and to establish whether it is composed out of similar [scil. forms] or out of both [scil. kinds], and in what way the alteration of the senses is produced, and besides this to give an explanation in the same way for all

---

3 ὥστε καὶ τὸ κάτω mss., corr. Diels
4 ἀνομοίων Diels

ναι τῶν διὰ τῆς ἁφῆς καὶ μὴ μόνον τὰ περὶ γεῦσιν. ἀλλὰ καὶ ταῦτα μὲν ἤτοι διαφοράν τινα ἔχει πρὸς τοὺς χυλούς, ἣν ἔδει διελεῖν, ἢ καὶ παρεῖται δυνατὸν ὂν ὁμοίως εἰπεῖν. [. . . = **D66**]

R63 (< A130) Theophr. *CP* 6.2.1

[. . . = **D161**] πλὴν ἴσως ἐκεῖνα ἄν τις ἐπιζητήσειε παρὰ¹ τούτων, ὥστε καὶ τὸ ὑποκείμενον ἀποδιδόναι ποῖόν τι· δεῖ γὰρ εἰδέναι μὴ μόνον τὸ ποιοῦν, ἀλλὰ καὶ τὸ πάσχον, ἄλλως τ᾽ εἰ καὶ μὴ πᾶσιν ὁ αὐτὸς ὁμοίως φαίνεται, καθάπερ φησίν.

¹ περὶ Diels

R64 (A131) Theophr. *CP* 6.2.3–4

ἄτοπον δὲ κἀκεῖνο τοῖς τὰ σχήματα λέγουσιν ἢ τῶν ὁμοίων διαφορὰ κατὰ μικρότητα καὶ μέγεθος εἰς τὸ μὴ τὴν αὐτὴν ἔχειν δύναμιν. οὐ γὰρ ἐπὶ¹ τῆς μορφῆς ἀλλὰ τῶν ὄγκων αἱ δυνάμεις, οὓς² εἰς μὲν τὸ διαβιάσασθαι καὶ ἁπλῶς τὸ μᾶλλον καὶ τὸ ἧττον τάχ᾽ ἄν τις ἀποδοίη,³ εἰς δὲ τὸ μὴ ταὐτὸ⁴ δύνασθαι μηδὲ ποιεῖν οὐκ εὔλογον, ἐπεὶ ἐν τοῖς σχήμασιν αἱ δυνάμεις· εἰ γὰρ ὁμοιόσχηματα,⁵ ταὐτὸν ἂν εἴη τὸ ὑπάρχον ὥσπερ καὶ ἐν τοῖς ἄλλοις.

¹ ἔτι Einarson-Link   ² οὓς Schneider: ἃς mss.   ³ ἀποδοίη Wimmer: ἀποδέδωκεν mss.   ⁴ ταὐτὸ Wimmer: αὐτὸ mss.   ⁵ εἰ . . . ὁμοιόσχηματα Uʳᵉᶜ M: εἰ . . . ὁμοιοσχήμονα P: ᾗ . . . ὅμοιος σχήματι Einarson-Link

the phenomena that come about by touch and not only for that belong to taste. But either these [scil. tactile] phenomena present in comparison with taste some difference, which he should have analyzed, or else he is neglecting to provide an explanation in common, even though this would be possible. [. . .]

R63 (< A130) Theophrastus, *Causes of Plants*

[. . .] but surely one could inquire further [scil. of Democritus and Plato] with regard to these subjects [scil. how the shapes explain tastes], how to explain what kind of thing the substrate is. For it is necessary to know not only what causes an affection, but also what undergoes the affection, especially if the same [scil. taste] does not appear in the same way to all people, as he says.

R64 (A131) Theophrastus, *Causes of Plants*

Absurd, too, in those who speak of shapes, is [recurring to] the difference, among those that are similar, with regard to their smallness and largeness, in order [scil. to explain] that they do not possess the same property (*dunamis*). For the properties depend not upon the form but upon the volumes, and one might perhaps use these to explain the forcible penetration [scil. of the soil in germination] and in general the more and the less, but it is not plausible [scil. to use them] with regard to differences in property and in action, since the properties depend upon the shapes. For if these have similar shapes, then their effect would have to be the same, as in the other cases.

R65 (A132) Theophr. *CP* 6.7.2

Δημοκρίτῳ μέν γε πῶς ποτε ἐξ ἀλλήλων ἡ γένεσις,
ἀπορήσειεν ἄν τις. ἀνάγκη γὰρ ἢ τὰ σχήματα μεταρ-
ρυθμίζεσθαι καὶ ἐκ σκαληνῶν καὶ ὀξυγωνίων περιφερῆ γίνεσθαι, ⟨ἢ⟩[1] πάντων ἐνυπαρχόντων οἷον τῶν
τε τοῦ στρυφνοῦ καὶ ὀξέος καὶ γλυκέος τὰ μὲν ἐκκρίνεσθαι τὰ τῶν πρότερον ἀεί, τὰ δ' οἰκεῖα καθ' ἕκαστον, θάτερα δὲ ὑπομένειν,[2] ἢ τρίτον τὰ μὲν ἐξιέναι
τὰ δ' ἐπεισιέναι. ἐπεὶ δ' ἀδύνατον μετασχηματίζεσθαι
(τὸ γὰρ ἄτομον[3] ἀπαθές), λοιπὸν τὰ μὲν εἰσιέναι τὰ
δ' ἐξιέναι ⟨ἢ τὰ μὲν ὑπομένειν τὰ δ' ἐξιέναι⟩·[4] ἄμφω
δὲ ταῦτα ἄλογα· προσαποδοῦναι γὰρ δεῖ καὶ τί τὸ
ἐργαζόμενον ταῦτα καὶ ποιοῦν.

---

[1] ⟨ἢ⟩ Wimmer   [2] θάτερα δὲ ὑπομένειν ⟨τὰ οἰκεῖα καθ'
ἕκαστον⟩ Wimmer   [3] ἄτοπον mss., corr. Scaliger   [4] ⟨ἢ τὰ
μὲν ὑπομένειν τὰ δ' ἐξιέναι⟩ Wimmer: ⟨τὰ μὲν ἐξιέναι, τὰ δ'
οἰκεῖα καθ' ἕκαστον ὑπομένειν⟩ Einarson-Link: ⟨ἢ τὰ μὲν ἐκκρίνεσθαι τὰ δ' οἰκεῖα καθ' ἕκαστον ὑπομένειν⟩ Leszl

R66 (A133) Theophr. *Odor.* 64

τί δή ποτε Δημόκριτος τοὺς μὲν χυμοὺς πρὸς τὴν
γεῦσιν ἀποδίδωσι, τὰς δ' ὀσμὰς καὶ τὰς χρόας οὐχ
ὁμοίως πρὸς τὰς ὑποκειμένας αἰσθήσεις; ἔδει γὰρ ἐκ
τῶν σχημάτων.

R65 (A132) Theophrastus, *Causes of Plants*

One might well see a difficulty [scil. in understanding] in what way for Democritus [scil. tastes] are generated out of one another. For it is necessary either that the shapes alter the configuration of their form and change from irregular and acute-angled to spherical, or else that, all of them being contained within, like those of sour, acid, and sweet, the ones separate out (those that each time are located in front, and those that are characteristic for each [scil. flavor]) while the others remain [scil. inside], or thirdly that the ones go out while the others penetrate within. But since it is impossible that they change their form (for the atom is impassible), it remains that the ones penetrate and the others go out <or that the ones remain and the others go out>. But both of these possibilities are senseless. For it is necessary to explain additionally what brings this about and is its efficient cause.

R66 (A133) Theophrastus, *On Odors*

Why then does Democritus explain flavors with regard to the sense of taste, but not odors and colors in relation to the corresponding senses in the same way? For he should have done this, on the basis of the shapes.

Regarding Animal Physiology (R67)

R67 Arist. *GA* 5.8

a (< A147) 788b9–11, 14–15

εἴρηκε μὲν οὖν περὶ αὐτῶν καὶ Δημόκριτος, οὐ καλῶς
δ᾽ εἴρηκε. οὐ γὰρ ἐπὶ πάντων σκεψάμενος καθόλου
λέγει τὴν αἰτίαν [. . . = **D185**]. καίτοι θηλάζει γε καὶ
ὗς, οὐκ ἐκβάλλει δὲ τοὺς ὀδόντας [. . .].

b (< 98.3 Leszl) 788b24–28

εἰ οὖν συνέβαινεν, ὡς ἐκεῖνος λέγει, πρὸς ἥβην, ἐν-
έλειπεν ἂν ἡ φύσις τῶν ἐνδεχομένων αὐτῇ τι ποιεῖν,
καὶ τὸ τῆς φύσεως ἔργον ἐγίνετ᾽ ἂν παρὰ φύσιν. τὸ
γὰρ βίᾳ παρὰ φύσιν, βίᾳ δέ φησι συμβαίνειν τὴν
γένεσιν τῶν ὀδόντων.

Fourth-Century Democriteans (R68–R78)
Successions and Lines of Descent

See **DOX. T20[15], T21[64.4]**

Metrodorus of Chios [70 DK] (R68–R72)
General Principles (R68–R70)

R68

a (B1) Cic. *Acad.* 2.23.73

is qui hunc maxime est admiratus, Chius Metrodorus

Regarding Animal Physiology (R67)

R67 Aristotle, *Generation of Animals*

a (< A147)

Democritus too has spoken about these [i.e. milk teeth and their shedding], but he has not spoken correctly. For he does not indicate the cause in general on the basis of having examined all the cases [. . .]. And yet the sow too gives milk but does not cause the teeth to be shed [. . .].

b (≠ DK)

If then it [scil. the appearance of the organs necessary for dealing with food] occurred, as he says, around the time of puberty, nature would be failing with regard to what it is possible for it to do, and the action of nature would occur against nature. For what happens by constraint is against nature, and he says that the formation of the [scil. milk] teeth comes about by constraint.

Fourth-Century Democriteans (R68–R78)
Successions and Lines of Descent

See **DOX. T20[15], T21[64.4]**

Metrodorus of Chios [70 DK] (R68–R72)
General Principles (R68–R70)

R68

a (B1) Cicero, *Prior Academics*

Metrodorus of Chios, the man who most admired him [i.e.

initio libri qui est de natura "nego," inquit, "scire nos
sciamusne aliquid an nihil sciamus, ne id ipsum quidem
nescire aut scire nos, nec omnino sitne aliquid an nihil sit."

b (B1, B2) Aristocl. *Phil.* in Eus. *PE* 14.19.8–9

[. . .] καὶ πάντα χρῆναι πιστεύειν ταῖς τοῦ σώματος
αἰσθήσεσιν ὁρισαμένους, ὧν εἶναι Μητρόδωρον τὸν
Χῖον καὶ Πρωταγόραν τὸν Ἀβδηρίτην. [9] τὸν μὲν οὖν
Μητρόδωρον Δημοκρίτου ἔφασαν ἀκηκοέναι, ἀρχὰς
δὲ ἀποφήνασθαι τὸ πλῆρες καὶ τὸ κενόν· ὧν τὸ μὲν
ὄν, τὸ δὲ μὴ ὂν εἶναι. γράφων γέ τοι περὶ φύσεως
εἰσβολῇ ἐχρήσατο τοιαύτῃ· "οὐδεὶς ἡμῶν οὐδὲν οἶδεν, οὐδ᾽ αὐτὸ τοῦτο, πότερον οἴδαμεν ἢ οὐκ οἴδαμεν." ἥτις εἰσβολὴ κακὰς ἔδωκεν ἀφορμὰς τῷ μετὰ
ταῦτα γενομένῳ Πύρρωνι. προβὰς δέ φησιν ὅτι
"πάντα ἐστίν, ὃ ἄν τις νοήσῃ."

R69 (A3) Theophr. *Op. phys.* in Simpl. *In Phys.*,
p. 28.27–30 (< Frag. 229 FHS&G)

καὶ Μητρόδωρος δὲ ὁ Χῖος ἀρχὰς σχεδόν τι τὰς
αὐτὰς τοῖς περὶ Δημόκριτον ποιεῖ, τὸ πλῆρες καὶ τὸ
κενὸν τὰς πρώτας αἰτίας ὑποθέμενος, ὧν τὸ μὲν ὄν,
τὸ δὲ μὴ ὂν εἶναι· περὶ δὲ τῶν ἄλλων ἰδίαν τινὰ ποι-
εῖται τὴν μέθοδον.

Democritus], says in the beginning of his book *On Nature:*
"I say that we do not know whether we know anything or
know nothing, nor do we even know whether we do not
know or know this, nor in general whether anything exists
or nothing exists."

b (B1, B2) Aristocles, *On* Philosophy, in Eusebius, *Evangelical Preparation*

[. . .] those who explained that it is necessary to trust
in all matters the sensations of the body, among whom
were Metrodorus of Chios and Protagoras of Abdera [cf.
PROT. R4]. They said that Metrodorus studied with Democritus; and that he asserted that the full and the empty
are principles, of which the one is being, the other nonbeing. And writing on nature he begins in the following
way: **"None of us knows anything, and not even this,
whether we know it or do not know it."** This beginning
gave bad impulses to Pyrrho, who was born after this. And
later he says, **"All the things that one thinks of exist,
whatever they are."**

R69 (A3) Theophrastus, *Physical Opinions* in Simplicius,
Commentary on Aristotle's Physics

And Metrodorus of Chios posits almost exactly the same
principles as Democritus, making the full and the empty
the first causes, of which the one is being, the other nonbeing. About all other matters he follows his own method.

R70 Aët.

a (A6) 1.5.4 (Stob.) [εἰ ἓν τὸ πᾶν]

Μητρόδωρος, ὁ καθηγητὴς Ἐπικούρου, φησὶν ἄτοπον εἶναι ἐν μεγάλῳ πεδίῳ ἕνα στάχυν γενηθῆναι καὶ ἕνα κόσμον ἐν τῷ ἀπείρῳ. ὅτι δὲ ἄπειροι[1] κατὰ τὸ πλῆθος, δῆλον ἐκ τοῦ ἄπειρα τὰ αἴτια εἶναι. εἰ γὰρ ὁ κόσμος πεπερασμένος, τὰ δ' αἴτια πάντα ἄπειρα ἐξ ὧν ὅδε ὁ κόσμος γέγονεν, ἀνάγκη ἀπείρους εἶναι. ὅπου γὰρ τὰ αἴτια ‹ἄπειρα›,[2] ἐκεῖ καὶ τἀποτελέσματα. αἴτια δὲ ἤτοι αἱ ἄτομοι ἢ τὰ στοιχεῖα.

[1] ἄπειρος mss., corr. Meineke   [2] ‹ἄπειρα› Reiske

b (A7) 2.1.3 (Ps.-Plut.; cf. Stob.) [περὶ κόσμου]

Δημόκριτος, Ἐπίκουρος καὶ ὁ τούτου καθηγητὴς Μητρόδωρος ἀπείρους κόσμους ἐν τῷ ἀπείρῳ κατὰ πᾶσαν περίστασιν.[1]

[1] περίστασιν Plut.: περιαγωγήν Stob.

Explanations of Some Natural Phenomena (R71–R72)

R71 (A9) Aët. 2.17.1 (Stob., Plut.) [πόθεν φωτίζονται οἱ ἀστέρες]

Μητρόδωρος ἅπαντας τοὺς ἀπλανεῖς ἀστέρας ὑπὸ τοῦ ἡλίου προσλάμπεσθαι.

R70 Aëtius

a (A6)

Metrodorus, the teacher of Epicurus, says that it is absurd that [scil. only] one ear of wheat be born in a large plain, and [scil. only] one world in the unlimited. That they [i.e. the worlds] are unlimited in number, is clear from the fact that the causes are unlimited. For if the world were limited, but all the causes out of which this world came about were unlimited, then of necessity they [i.e. the worlds] would be unlimited. For where the causes are unlimited, there the effects are too. The causes are either the atoms or the elements.

b (A7)

Democritus, Epicurus, and his teacher Metrodorus: worlds unlimited [scil. in number] in the unlimited, throughout the entire surrounding area (*peristasis*).

Explanations of Some Natural Phenomena (R71–R72)

R71 (A9) Aëtius

Metrodorus: all the fixed stars are illuminated by the sun.

R72 (A17) Aët. 3.5.12 (Ps.-Plut.) [περὶ ἴριδος]

Μητρόδωρος ὅταν διὰ νεφῶν ἥλιος διαλάμψῃ, τὸ μὲν
νέφος κυανίζειν, τὴν δ᾽ αὐγὴν ἐρυθραίνεσθαι.

Nausiphanes [75 DK] (R73–R75)

R73 (A5) Cic. *Nat. deor.* 1.26.73

ita metuit ne quid umquam didicisse videatur. in Nau-
siphane Democriteo tenetur; quem cum a se non neget
auditum, vexat tamen omnibus contumeliis. atqui si haec
Democritea non audisset, quid audierat? quid est in physicis Epicuri non a Democrito?

R74 (B4) Sen. *Epist.* 88.43

Nausiphanes ait ex his, quae videntur esse, nihil magis
esse quam non esse.

R75 (B3) Clem. Alex. *Strom.* 2.130.5

[. . .] Ναυσιφάνης τὴν ἀκαταπληξίαν·[1] ταύτην γὰρ
ἔφη ὑπὸ Δημοκρίτου ἀθαμβίην λέγεσθαι.

---

[1] ἀκαταπληξίαν Klotz: κατάπληξιν ms.

R72 (A17) Aëtius

Metrodorus: when the sun shines through the clouds, the cloud becomes dark blue while the ray of light becomes red.

See also ad **DIOG. D15**

Nausiphanes [75 DK] (R73–R75)

R73 (A5) Cicero, *On the Nature of the Gods*

He [i.e. Epicurus] was afraid of seeming ever to have learned anything [scil. from someone]. But he is caught out in the case of Nausiphanes the Democritean, whom he attacks with all kinds of abuse even though he does not deny that he studied with him. And yet if he did not learn these doctrines of Democritus from him, what did he learn? What is there in Epicurus' natural philosophy that does not come from Democritus?

R74 (B4) Seneca, *Letters to Lucilius*

Nausiphanes says that, among the things that seem to exist, nothing exists more than it does not exist.

R75 (B3) Clement of Alexandria, *Stromata*

[. . .] Nausiphanes [scil. calls] imperturbability [scil. the goal]; for he says that this is what Democritus called 'unastoundedness' (*athambiê*).

Diotimus of Tyre [76 DK] (R76–R78)

R76 (76.3) Sext. Emp. *Adv. Math.* 7.140

[. . . = **R108**] Διότιμος δὲ τρία κατ᾽ αὐτὸν ἔλεγεν εἶναι
κριτήρια, τῆς μὲν τῶν ἀδήλων καταλήψεως τὰ φαινόμενα—ὄψις γὰρ τῶν ἀδήλων τὰ φαινόμενα, ὥς φησιν
Ἀναξαγόρας, ὃν ἐπὶ τούτῳ Δημόκριτος ἐπαινεῖ—, ζη-
τήσεως δὲ τὴν ἔννοιαν—περὶ παντὸς γάρ, ὦ παῖ, μία
ἀρχὴ τὸ εἰδέναι περὶ ὅτου ἔστιν ἡ ζήτησις—, αἱρέ-
σεως δὲ καὶ φυγῆς τὰ πάθη· τὸ μὲν γὰρ ᾧ προσοι-
κειούμεθα, τοῦτο αἱρετόν ἐστιν, τὸ δὲ ᾧ προσαλλοτρι-
ούμεθα, τοῦτο φευκτόν ἐστιν.

R77 (76.1) Aët. 2.17.3 (Stob.) [πόθεν φωτίζονται οἱ
ἀστέρες]

Διότιμος Τύριος, ὁ Δημοκρίτειος,[1] τὴν αὐτὴν τούτοις
εἰσηνέγκατο γνώμην.

  [1] Δημοκρίτειος Diels: διοκρίτιος mss.: διακριτικὸς Heeren

R78 (76.2) Clem. Alex. *Strom.* 2.130.6

ἔτι πρὸς τούτοις Διότιμος τὴν παντέλειαν τῶν ἀγαθῶν, ἣν εὐεστὼ προσαγορεύεσθαι, τέλος ἀπέφηνεν.

Diotimus of Tyre [76 DK] (R76–R78)

R76 (76.3) Sextus Empiricus, *Against the Logicians*

Diotimus[1] said that according to him [i.e. Democritus] there are three criteria: for grasping invisible things, the appearances ([. . . = **ANAXAG. D6**] as is said by Anaxagoras, whom Democritus praises for this); for inquiry the concept (*ennoia*) ("On every subject, my child, there is only one starting point: to know what it is that we are seeking" [Plato, *Phaedrus* 237B]); for preferring and avoiding, the passions: for what we have become familiar with is what is to be preferred, while what we remain alien from is to be avoided.

[1] It is generally thought that this Diotimus is the Democritean, but it might instead be a Stoic of the same name.

R77 (76.1) Aëtius

Diotimus of Tyre, the Democritean, introduced the same opinion regarding these [i.e. the fixed stars] as these men [i.e. Metrodorus, cf. **R71,** and Strato].

R78 (76.2) Clement of Alexandria, *Stromata*

Besides these [i.e. Democritus, Hecataeus, Apollodorus, Nausiphanes], Diotimus too indicated as the goal **complete perfection with regard to good things,** which was called 'well-being' (*euestô*) [scil. by Democritus, cf. e.g. **ATOM. D229**].

Democritus and the Epicureans (R79–R99)

Cf. **R1d, e**

The Line of Descent (R79)

R79

a (A51) Cic. *Nat. deor.* 1.26.73

quid est in physicis Epicuri non a Democrito? nam etsi quaedam commutavit, ut quod paulo ante de inclinatione atomorum dixi, tamen pleraque dicit eadem, atomos, inane,[1] imagines, infinitatem locorum innumerabilitatemque mundorum, eorum ortus, interitus, omnia fere, quibus naturae ratio continetur.

[1] inane *ed. Ald.*: inanes *mss. plerique*

b (< A70) Lact. *Div. inst.* 1.2

[. . .] cuius sententiae auctor est Democritus, confirmator Epicurus.

Attitude of Epicurus and the Epicureans Toward
Leucippus and Democritus (R80–R93)
Epicurus Denies the Existence of Leucippus
or His Quality as a Philosopher (R80)

R80 (67 A2) Diog. Laert. 10.13

ἀλλ᾽ οὐδὲ Λεύκιππόν τινα γεγενῆσθαί φησι φιλόσο-

Democritus and the Epicureans (R79–R99)

Cf. **R1d, e**

The Line of Descent (R79)

R79

a (A51) Cicero, *On the Nature of the Gods*

What is there in Epicurus' natural philosophy that does not come from Democritus? For even if he has changed some things, for example regarding the swerve of the atoms about which I spoke a little earlier, nonetheless most of what he says is the same—the atoms, the void, the images, the infinity of space and the infinite number of worlds, the destruction of the place they occupy: almost everything the explanation of nature comprises.

b (< A70) Lactantius, *Divine Institutions*

Of this opinion [. . . scil. that all things have been made and are governed by chance] Democritus is the originator, Epicurus the corroborator.

Attitude of Epicurus and the Epicureans Toward
Leucippus and Democritus (R80–R93)
Epicurus Denies the Existence of Leucippus
or His Quality as a Philosopher (R80)

R80 (67 A2) Diogenes Laertius

He himself [i.e. Epicurus] as well as Hermarchus deny

φον [Frag. 232 Usener], οὔτε αὐτὸς οὔτε Ἕρμαρχος
[Frag. 13 Longo], ὃν ἔνιοί φασι καὶ Ἀπολλόδωρος ὁ
Ἐπικούρειος διδάσκαλον Δημοκρίτου γεγενῆσθαι.

Epicurus' Relation to Democritus in
General (R81–R85)

R81 (A52) Diog. Laert. 10.2

φησὶ δ᾿ Ἕρμιππος [Frag. 60 Wehrli] γραμματοδιδά-
σκαλον αὐτὸν γεγενῆσθαι, ἔπειτα μέντοι περιτυχόντα
τοῖς Δημοκρίτου βιβλίοις ἐπὶ φιλοσοφίαν ᾆξαι [. . .].

R82 (A53) Plut. Adv. Col. 3 1108E

καίτοι πολὺν χρόνον αὐτὸς ἑαυτὸν ἀνηγόρευε Δημοκρίτειον ὁ Ἐπίκουρος [cf. Frag. 234 Usener], ὡς ἄλλοι
τε λέγουσι καὶ Λεοντεύς, εἷς τῶν ἐπ᾿ ἄκρον Ἐπικούρου
μαθητῶν, πρὸς Λυκόφρονα γράφων τιμᾶσθαί τέ φησι
τὸν Δημόκριτον ὑπ᾿ Ἐπικούρου διὰ τὸ πρότερον
ἅψασθαι τῆς ὀρθῆς γνώσεως, καὶ τὸ σύνολον τὴν
πραγματείαν Δημοκρίτειον προσαγορεύεσθαι διὰ τὸ
περιπεσεῖν αὐτὸν πρότερον ταῖς ἀρχαῖς περὶ φύσεως.
ὁ δὲ Μητρόδωρος ἄντικρυς ⟨ἐν τῷ⟩[1] Περὶ φιλοσοφίας
εἴρηκεν [Frag. 33 Körte] ὡς, εἰ μὴ προκαθηγήσατο Δημόκριτος, οὐκ ἂν προῆλθεν Ἐπίκουρος ἐπὶ τὴν σο-
φίαν.

[1] ⟨ἐν τῷ⟩ Menagius

that any philosopher Leucippus ever existed, though some people, including Apollodorus the Epicurean, say that he was the teacher of Democritus.

Epicurus' Relation to Democritus in General (R81–R85)

R81 (A52) Diogenes Laertius

Hermippus says that he [i.e. Epicurus] had become an elementary schoolteacher, but then when he ran across the books of Democritus he rushed eagerly toward philosophy [. . .].

R82 (A53) Plutarch, *Against Colotes*

And yet for a long time Epicurus himself called himself a 'Democritean,' as is said by others and in particular by Leonteus, one of Epicurus' chief disciples, in his letter to Lycophron; and he says that Epicurus honored Democritus for having touched upon the correct knowledge before [scil. he had], and that as a whole he called his philosophical approach (*pragmateia*) 'Democritean' because he [i.e. Democritus] had stumbled upon the principles of nature before [scil. he had]. And Metrodorus said directly ‹in his› *On Philosophy* that if Democritus had not been his guide, Epicurus would not have made progress toward wisdom.

R83 (A69) Epicur. *Nat.* 25 (p. 41 Laursen)

[οἱ] δ᾽ αἰτιολο|γήσαντες ἐξ ἀρχῆς ἱκανῶς | καὶ ο[ὐ]
μόν[ο]ν τῶν πρὸ [α]ὐτῶ[ν] | πολὺ διενέγκαντες ἀλλὰ
καὶ τῶν | ὕστερον πολλαπλ[α]σίως ἔλαθον | ἑαυτοῖς,
καίπερ ἐν πολλο[ῖς] με|γάλα κουφίσαντες, ε[ἰ]ς τὸ¹
τ[ὴ]ν ἀ|νάγκην καὶ ταὐτόματ[ο]ν² πάν|τα α[ἰτιᾶσ]θαι.

¹ ε[ἰ]ς τὸ Sedley: ENTO apogr. Oxon.: ἔν· τὸ Gigante
² ταὐτόματον Lucignano, Gomperz: ΤΑΤΤΟΜΕΝ[3/4]
apogr. Neap.: ΤΑΤΤΟΜΕΓ[.]Ν apogr. Oxon.: ταὐτὸ μέν[ο]ν vel
μέν[ει]ν Laursen

R84 (> 0.9.4 Leszl) Philod. *Lib. dic.* Frag. 20.2–9

διὰ [. . .] τὴ[ν] μεριζο|μένην συνγ[ν]ώ[μ]ην ἐν οἷς | δι-
έπεσον, ὡς ἔν τε τοῖς | πρὸς Δημόκριτον ἵστα|ται διὰ
τέλους Ἐπίκουρος [. . .]

R85 (A53) Diog. Laert. 10.8

[. . .] Δημόκριτον Ληρόκριτον [. . .].

R83 (A69) Epicurus, *On Nature*

The first people to have advanced satisfactory causal explanation, and who greatly surpassed not only their predecessors but also, and even more, their successors, forgot themselves, even though on many points they brought great relief, in attributing the cause of everything to necessity and what is spontaneous.

R84 (≠ DK) Philodemus, *On Frank Criticism*

[. . .] because of the pardon granted in the cases in which they [i.e. probably: the adversaries] were mistaken, as Epicurus maintains from one end to the other not only of his books against Democritus [scil. but also . . .]

R85 (A53) Diogenes Laertius

[scil. Epicurus called] Democritus [i.e. 'the judge of the people'] 'Lerocritus' [i.e. 'the judge of balderdash'].

Specific Criticisms of Leucippus' and Democritus'
Doctrines by Epicurus and the
Epicureans (R86–R93)
Epicurus (R86–R87)

R86 (67 A24) Epicur. *ad Pyth.* 89–90 (= Diog. Laert. 10.89–90)

[. . .] καὶ ὁ τοιοῦτος δύναται κόσμος γίνεσθαι καὶ ἐν κόσμῳ καὶ[1] μετακοσμίῳ, ὃ λέγομεν μεταξὺ κόσμων διάστημα, ἐν πολυκένῳ τόπῳ καὶ οὐκ ἐν μεγάλῳ[2] εἰλικρινεῖ καὶ κενῷ, καθάπερ τινές[3] φασιν [. . .]. οὐ γὰρ ἀθροισμὸν δεῖ μόνον γενέσθαι οὐδὲ δῖνον ἐν ᾧ ἐνδέχεται κόσμον γίνεσθαι κενῷ κατὰ τὸ δοξαζόμενον ἐξ ἀνάγκης, αὔξεσθαί τε, ἕως ἂν ἑτέρῳ προσκρούσῃ, καθάπερ τῶν φυσικῶν καλουμένων φησί τις· τοῦτο γὰρ μαχόμενόν ἐστι τοῖς φαινομένοις.

[1] κἂν Usener   [2] μεγάλῳ <καὶ> Brieger
[3] τινὰ mss., corr. Casaubon

R87 (< A160) Cic. *Tusc.* 1.34.82

etsi Democritum insimulat Epicurus [Frag. 17 Usener], Democritii negant.

Colotes (R88–R89)

R88 (cf. 8.1.Leszl) Plut. *Adv. Col.* 8 1111A–B, E–F

[. . .] ἐγκλητέος οὖν ὁ Δημόκριτος οὐχὶ τὰ συμβαί-

Specific Criticisms of Leucippus' and Democritus'
Doctrines by Epicurus and the
Epicureans (R86–R93)
Epicurus (R86–R87)

R86 (67 A24) Epicurus, *Letter to Pythocles*

[. . .] such a world can come about both in a world and in
what we call a *metakosmion,* the space between worlds, in
a place with much void, and not in a large space that
is pure and void, as some people say exist [cf. **D80a,
D80b[31]**] [. . .]. For it is not enough that an aggregate or
a vortex be formed in the void, in which it is agreed that a
world can be formed, by necessity, and then grow until it
strikes against another one, as one of those who are called
natural philosophers says [cf. **D81**]. For this is in contradiction with what is seen to be the case.

R87 (< A160) Cicero, *Tusculan Disputations*

Even if Epicurus accuses Democritus [scil. of saying that
there is sensation after death, cf. **D140–D142**], the Democriteans deny it.

Colotes (R88–R89)

R88 (≠ DK) Plutarch, *Against Colotes*

[. . .] So one must accuse Democritus not of having recog-

453

νοντα ταῖς ἀρχαῖς ὁμολογῶν ἀλλὰ λαμβάνων ἀρχὰς
αἷς ταῦτα συμβέβηκεν. ἔδει γὰρ ἀμετάβλητα μὴ θέσθαι τὰ πρῶτα, θέμενον δὲ δὴ[1] συνορᾶν ὅτι ποιότητος
οἴχεται πάσης γένεσις. [. . .] ἡ δ' ἄτομος αὐτή τε καθ'
ἑαυτὴν ἔρημός ἐστι καὶ γυμνὴ πάσης γονίμου δυνά-
μεως, καὶ πρὸς ἄλλην προσπεσοῦσα βρασμὸν ὑπὸ
σκληρότητος καὶ ἀντιτυπίας ἄλλο δ' οὐδὲν ἔσχεν
οὐδ' ἐποίησε πάθος, ἀλλὰ παίονται καὶ παίουσι τὸν
ἅπαντα χρόνον, οὐχ ὅπως ζῷον ἢ ψυχὴν ἢ φύσιν
ἀλλ' οὐδὲ πλῆθος ἐξ ἑαυτῶν κοινὸν οὐδὲ σωρὸν ἕνα
παλλομένων ἀεὶ καὶ διισταμένων δυνάμεναι παρα-
σχεῖν.

[1] δὴ Wyttenbach: μὴ mss.

R89 (B156) Plut. *Adv. Col.* 4 1108F–1109A

ἐγκαλεῖ δ' αὐτῷ πρῶτον, ὅτι τῶν πραγμάτων ἕκαστον
εἰπὼν[1] οὐ μᾶλλον τοῖον ἢ τοῖον εἶναι συγκέχυκε τὸν
βίον. ἀλλὰ τοσοῦτόν γε Δημόκριτος ἀποδεῖ τοῦ νομίζειν μὴ μᾶλλον εἶναι τοῖον ἢ τοῖον τῶν πραγμάτων
ἕκαστον, ὥστε Πρωταγόρᾳ τῷ σοφιστῇ τοῦτ' εἰπόντι
μεμαχῆσθαι καὶ γεγραφέναι πολλὰ καὶ πιθανὰ πρὸς
αὐτόν. οἷς οὐδ' ὄναρ ἐντυχὼν ὁ Κωλώτης ἐσφάλη
περὶ λέξιν τοῦ ἀνδρός, ἐν ᾗ διορίζεται μὴ μᾶλλον τὸ
'δὲν' ἢ τὸ 'μηδὲν' εἶναι, 'δέν' μὲν ὀνομάζων τὸ σῶμα
'μηδέν' δὲ τὸ κενόν, ὡς καὶ τούτου φύσιν τινὰ καὶ
ὑπόστασιν ἰδίαν ἔχοντος.

[1] ἐπιὼν mss., corr. Xylander

nized the consequences that follow from his principles
but of having posited principles from which these consequences follow. He should not have assumed that the first
[scil. elements] are immutable, but, having posited them,
he should have noticed that the generation of any kind of
quality had thereby been abolished. [. . .] The atom is by
itself deprived and bare of all generative power, and when
it collides with another one it receives an agitation because
of its hardness and resistance, but it does not receive or
produce any other affection; but they are struck and strike
the whole time, and, being constantly agitated and dispersed, they are not capable of producing not only an
animal, a life, or a nature, but not even a quantity of themselves shared in common nor a single heap.

R89 (B156) Plutarch, *Against Colotes*

He [i.e. Colotes] accuses him [i.e. Democritus] first of all
of throwing life into total confusion by saying that every
thing is not more like this than like that [cf. **D31**]. But
Democritus, so far from thinking that every thing is not
more like this than like that, fought against Protagoras the
sophist, who said this himself [cf. e.g. **PROT. R14**], and
he wrote many convincing objections against him. But
Colotes, who has not even read these texts in his dreams,
is mistaken about this man's formulation, in which he defines that the **'something'** (*den*) does not exist more than
the **'nothing'** (*mêden*), calling the body **'something'** and
the void **'nothing,'** on the idea that this too possesses a
certain nature and its own existence [cf. **D33**].

Lucretius (R90–R91)

R90 (cf. A61) 2.225–229 et 235–239

225   quod si forte aliquis credit graviora potesse
      corpora, quo citius rectum per inane feruntur,
      incidere ex supero levioribus atque ita plagas
      gignere quae possint genitalis reddere motus,
      avius a vera longe ratione recedit.
      [. . .]
235   at contra nulli de nulla parte neque ullo
      tempore inane potest vacuum subsistere rei,
      quin, sua quod natura petit, concedere pergat;
      omnia quapropter debent per inane quietum
      aeque ponderibus non aequis concita ferri.

R91 (A108) 3.370–73

      illud in his rebus nequaquam sumere possis,
      Democriti quod sancta viri sententia ponit,
      corporis atque animi primordia singula privis
      apposita alternis variare, ac nectere membra.

      372 privis *Bentley*: primis mss.

Lucretius (R90–R91)

R90 (cf. A61) *On the Nature of Things*

> But if by chance someone thinks that heavier bodies, 225
> Because they move more quickly straight through the
>   void,
> Can fall from above against lighter ones and thereby
>   produce blows
> That can produce generative motions,
> Then he moves far away from correct reason.
> [. . .]
> But by contrast [scil. with motion through a fluid 235
>   medium], nowhere and never
> Can the empty void hold up anything at all,
> But instead—what its own nature seeks—it
>   continually yields place;
> And that is why all things move through the tranquil
>   void,
> Borne along equally even if their weights are
>   unequal.

R91 (A108) *On the Nature of Things*

> By no means could you accept in these matters
> What the sacred opinion of that great man Democri-
>   tus claims:
> That the elements of body and soul, arranged next to
>   each other,
> Alternate and thereby weave together the limbs.

Diogenes of Oenoanda (R92–R93)

R92 (A50) Diog. Oen. Frag. 54.II–III Smith

[Col. II] ἂν γὰ[ρ] τῷ Δημο|κρίτου τις χ[ρ]ήσηται | [5] λόγῳ, μηδεμίαν μὲν | ἐλευθέραν [φ]άσκων | ταῖς ἀτόμ[οι]ς κείνη|σιν εἶναι διὰ τὴν πρὸς | ἀλλήλας σύ[ν]κρουσιν | [10] αὐτῶν, ἔνθεν δὲ φαί|νεσθαι κατ[η]γανκασ|μένως πά[ν]τα κεινεῖσ|θαι, φή[σομ]εν πρὸς | αὐτὸν ὧ[ς "οὐκ οἶδας, ὅσ|τις ποτὲ εἶ, καὶ ἐλευθέ|[Col. III]ραν τινὰ ἐν ταῖς ἀτό|μοις κείνησιν εἶναι, ἣ[ν] | Δημόκριτος μὲν οὐ|[5]χ εὗρεν, Ἐπίκουρος δὲ | εἰς φῶς ἤγαγεν, παρεν|κλιτικὴν ὑπάρχουσαν, | ὡς ἐκ τῶν φαινομέ|νων δείκνυσιν;"

Col. II suppl. Cousin (3, 6,7,11, 13), Usener (4, 9, 12), Smith (14); Col. III Usener (3)

R93 (8.4 Leszl) Diog. Oen. Frag. 7.II–III Smith

ἐσφάλη δ᾽ ἀναξίως ἑαυτοῦ | καὶ Δημόκριτος, τὰς | [5] ἀτόμους μόνας κατ᾽ ἀ|λήθειαν εἰπὼν ὑπάρχειν | ἐν τοῖς οὖσι, τὰ δὲ λοιπὰ | νομιστεὶ ἅπαντα. κατὰ | γὰρ τὸν σὸν λόγον, ὦ Δη|[10]μόκριτε, οὐχ ὅπως τὸ ἀληθὲς εὑρεῖν, ἀλλ᾽ οὐδὲ | ζῆν δυνησόμεθα, μή|τε τὸ πῦρ φυλαττόμε|νοι [μήτε τ]ὴν σφαγὴν | [Col. III] μήτ᾽ [ἄλλην τινὰ δύνα]|μι[ν . . .

Col. III.1–2 suppl. Smith   14 suppl. Cousin

Diogenes of Oenoanda (R92–R93)

R92 (A50) Diogenes of Oenoanda, Epicurean inscription

[Col. II] For if someone uses Democritus' argument and says that the atoms do not have any free motion because of their collision with each other, for which reason it seems that all things move under constraint, we shall say to him, "Do you not know, whoever you are, that there is a free motion [Col. III] in the atoms, which Democritus did not discover, but which Epicurus brought to light, and which consists in a swerve, as he demonstrates on the basis of what is seen to be the case?"

R93 (≠ DK) Diogenes of Oenoanda, Epicurean inscription

Democritus too erred, in a way unworthy of himself, when he said that only the atoms exist in truth in the things that are, while all other things are by convention. For according to what you say, Democritus, we are not capable not only of discovering the truth but even of living, not being able to protect ourselves against either fire or a wound [Col. III] or any other power . . .

Differences between Epicurus and
Democritus (R94–R99)
Regarding the Atom (R94–R96)

R94 (> A47) Aët. 1.3.18 (Ps.-Plut.) [περὶ ἀρχῶν τί εἰ-
σιν]

Ἐπίκουρος [. . .] κατὰ Δημόκριτον φιλοσοφήσας ἔφη
τὰς ἀρχὰς τῶν ὄντων σώματα λόγῳ θεωρητά [. . .].
συμβεβηκέναι δὲ τοῖς σώμασι τρία ταῦτα, σχῆμα
μέγεθος βάρος. Δημόκριτος μὲν γὰρ ἔλεγε δύο, μέγεθός τε καὶ σχῆμα, ὁ δ᾽ Ἐπίκουρος τούτοις καὶ τρίτον,
τὸ βάρος, ἐπέθηκεν· "ἀνάγκη γάρ," φησί, "κινεῖσθαι
τὰ σώματα τῇ τοῦ βάρους πληγῇ· ἐπεὶ οὐ κινηθήσεται." εἶναι δὲ τὰ σχήματα τῶν ἀτόμων ἀπερίληπτα,[1]
οὐκ ἄπειρα· μὴ γὰρ εἶναι μήτ᾽ ἀγκιστροειδεῖς μήτε
τριαινοειδεῖς μήτε κρικοειδεῖς· ταῦτα γὰρ τὰ σχήματα
εὔθραυστά ἐστιν, αἱ δ᾽ ἄτομοι ἀπαθεῖς ἄθραυστοι.

[1] ἀπερίληπτα Duebner: περιληπτὰ ΜΠ: -τικὰ m

R95 (< 67 A13) Simpl. *In Phys.*, p. 925.13–22

[. . .] Λεύκιππος μὲν καὶ Δημόκριτος οὐ μόνον τὴν
ἀπάθειαν αἰτίαν τοῖς πρώτοις σώμασι τοῦ μὴ διαιρεῖ-
σθαι νομίζουσιν, ἀλλὰ καὶ τὸ σμικρὸν καὶ ἀμερές,
Ἐπίκουρος δὲ ὕστερον ἀμερῆ μὲν οὐχ ἡγεῖται, ἄτομα
δὲ αὐτὰ διὰ τὴν ἀπάθειαν εἶναί φησι [Frag. 268
Usener]. καὶ πολλαχοῦ μὲν τὴν Λευκίππου καὶ Δη-

Differences between Epicurus and Democritus (R94–R99)
Regarding the Atom (R94–R96)

R94 (> A47) Aëtius

Epicurus [. . .] who philosophized in conformity with Democritus, said that the principles of the things that are are bodies visible by thought [. . .]. Three properties accompany bodies: shape, size, and weight. For Democritus said [scil. that there were] two, size and shape, but Epicurus added to these a third one, weight. For it is necessary, he says, that bodies move by the striking due to weight; for [scil. otherwise] they will not move. And the shapes of the atoms are in number indefinite, and not unlimited. For there are not any that have the shape of a hook, a trident, or a ring [cf. **D58**]; for these shapes break easily, whereas the atoms are impassible and unbreakable.

R95 (< 67 A13) Simplicius, *Commentary on Aristotle's* Physics

[. . .] Leucippus and Democritus think that impassibility is not the only reason for the indivisibility of the first bodies, but also their smallness and lack of parts; but later, Epicurus does not think that they lack parts but says that they are indivisible (*atoma*) because of their impassibility. Aristotle has refuted the opinion of Leucippus and De-

μοκρίτου δόξαν ὁ Ἀριστοτέλης διήλεγξεν, καὶ δι᾽
ἐκείνους ἴσως τοὺς ἐλέγχους πρὸς τὸ ἀμερὲς ἐνιστα-
μένους ὁ Ἐπίκουρος ὕστερον μὲν γενόμενος, συμ-
παθῶν δὲ τῇ Λευκίππου καὶ Δημοκρίτου δόξῃ περὶ
τῶν πρώτων σωμάτων, ἀπαθῆ μὲν ἐφύλαξεν αὐτά, τὸ
δὲ ἀμερὲς αὐτῶν παρείλετο, ὡς διὰ τοῦτο ὑπὸ τοῦ
Ἀριστοτέλους ἐλεγχομένων.

R96 (< A43) Dion. Alex. *Nat.* in Eus. *PE* 14.23.3

τοσοῦτον δὲ διεφώνησαν ὅσον ὁ μὲν ἐλαχίστας πάσας καὶ διὰ τοῦτο ἀνεπαισθήτους, ὁ δὲ καὶ μεγίστας
εἶναί τινας ἀτόμους ὁ Δημόκριτος ὑπέλαβεν.

*Regarding the Objectivity of the
Perceptibles (R97–R98)*

R97 (53.1 Leszl) Sext. Emp. *Adv. Math.* 8.184–185

[. . .] ὁ μὲν Δημόκριτος μηδὲν ὑποκεῖσθαί φησι τῶν
αἰσθητῶν, ἀλλὰ κενοπαθείας τινὰς αἰσθήσεων εἶναι
τὰς ἀντιλήψεις αὐτῶν, καὶ οὔτε γλυκύ τι περὶ τοῖς
ἐκτὸς ὑπάρχειν, οὐ[1] πικρὸν ἢ θερμὸν ἢ ψυχρὸν ἢ λευκὸν ἢ μέλαν, οὐκ ἄλλο τι τῶν πᾶσι φαινομένων· παθῶν γὰρ ἡμετέρων ἦν[2] ὀνόματα ταῦτα. [185] ὁ δὲ
Ἐπίκουρος πάντα ἔλεγε τὰ αἰσθητὰ τοιαῦτα ὑποκεῖ-
σθαι ὁποῖα φαίνεται καὶ κατ᾽ αἴσθησιν προσπίπτει
[. . .].

mocritus in a number of passages, and it is perhaps because of these objections directed against the lack of parts that Epicurus, who was born later but sympathized with the opinion of Leucippus and Democritus concerning the first bodies, kept them as impassible, but abandoned their lack of parts, on the idea that it was because of this that they had been refuted by Aristotle.

R96 (< A43) Dionysius of Alexandria, *On Nature,* in Eusebius, *Evangelical Preparation*

They [i.e. Epicurus and Democritus] differed to the extent that the one assumed that they [i.e. the natures] are all extremely small and that this is why they are imperceptible, the other, Democritus, that there are also some indivisible [scil. natures] that are extremely large [cf. **D62**].

Regarding the Objectivity of the
Perceptibles (R97–R98)

R97 (≠ DK) Sextus Empiricus, *Against the Logicians*

[. . .] Democritus says that nothing underlies the sensibles, but that their apprehensions are a sort of affection empty of sensations, and that nothing sweet exists among external things, nor bitter, nor hot or cold, nor white or black, nor anything of what appears to all people: for these are names of our affections. But Epicurus said that all the sensibles exist just as they appear and fall under sensation [. . .].

---

[1] οὔτε dub. Kayser   [2] εἶναι dub. Bekker

R98 (> A110) Sext. Emp. *Adv. Math.* 7.369

[. . .] τῶν φυσικῶν οἱ μὲν πάντα ἀνῃρήκασι τὰ φαινόμενα, ὡς οἱ περὶ Δημόκριτον, οἱ δὲ πάντα ἔθεσαν,
ὡς οἱ περὶ τὸν Ἐπίκουρον καὶ Πρωταγόραν.

Regarding Pleasure (R99)

R99 (< A1) Diog. Laert. 9.45

τέλος δ᾽ εἶναι τὴν εὐθυμίαν, οὐ τὴν αὐτὴν οὖσαν τῇ
ἡδονῇ, ὡς ἔνιοι παρακούσαντες ἐξεδέξαντο [. . . cf.
D229].

Democritus, Predecessor of Arcesilaus'
Academy (R100–R101)

R100 (< 59 A95) Cic. *Acad.* 1.12.44

[. . .] earum rerum obscuritate, quae ad confessionem ig-
norationis adduxerant Socratem et iam [. . .] Democritum
[. . .] omnes paene veteres, qui nihil cognosci nihil percipi
nihil sciri posse dixerunt, angustos sensus imbecillos animos brevia curricula vitae et ut Democritus in profundo
veritatem esse demersam [. . .].

R101 (< B165) Cic. *Acad.* 2.23.73

[. . . = **P44a**] atque is non hoc dicit quod nos qui veri esse
aliquid non negamus, percipi posse negamus: ille esse

R98 (> A110) Sextus Empiricus, *Against the Logicians*

[. . .] among the natural philosophers, some have completely abolished all appearances, like Democritus, while others have posited all of them, like Epicurus and Protagoras.

Regarding Pleasure (R99)

R99 (< A1) Diogenes Laertius

The goal is contentment (*euthumia*), which is not the same thing as pleasure, as some people have taken it, on the basis of a misinterpretation [. . .].

Democritus, Predecessor of Arcesilaus'
Academy (R100–R101)

R100 (< 59 A95) Cicero, *Posterior Academics*

[. . .] the obscurity of these matters [. . .] which led Socrates to confess his ignorance and already [. . .] Democritus [. . .] and almost all the ancients, who said that nothing can be either recognized, or perceived, or known: that the senses are constricted, the spirit weak, the course of life brief and, as Democritus said, the truth is sunk in an abyss [. . .] [cf. **D21, D24; ANAXAG. R26**].

R101 (< B165) Cicero, *Prior Academics*

[. . .] But he has not said what we say, we who do not deny that something might be true, but that it could be perceived: he denies completely that there is something true,

465

verum plane negat sensusque idem non obscuros dicit, sed
tenebricosos: sic enim appelat eos.

Democritus and the Pyrrhonian
Skeptics (R102–R108)
Pyrrho's Admiration for Democritus (R102)

R102 (0.8.36 Leszl) Diog. Laert. 9.67

ἀλλὰ καὶ Φίλων ὁ Ἀθηναῖος, γνώριμος αὐτοῦ γεγονώς, ἔλεγεν ὡς ἐμέμνητο μάλιστα μὲν Δημοκρίτου
[. . .].

Does Democritus Belong to the Line of
Descent of Skepticism? (R103–R104)

R103 (< B117) Diog. Laert. 9.72

[. . .] καὶ Δημόκριτος κατ' αὐτοὺς σκεπτικοὶ τυγχάνουσιν [. . .], Δημόκριτος δὲ τὰς ποιότητας ἐκβάλλων, ἵνα
φησὶ "νόμῳ θερμόν [. . .]"· καὶ πάλιν, "[. . .] ἐν βυθῷ
γὰρ ἡ ἀλήθεια" [cf. **D24**].

R104 (A134) Sext. Emp. *Pyrrh. Hyp.* 2.63

ἀμέλει γοῦν ἐκ τοῦ τὸ μέλι τοῖσδε μὲν πικρὸν τοῖσδε
δὲ γλυκὺ φαίνεσθαι ὁ μὲν Δημόκριτος ἔφη μήτε
γλυκὺ αὐτὸ εἶναι μήτε πικρόν [. . .].

and he does not say that the senses are obscure, but that they are 'filled with shadows'[1] [cf. **D20**].

[1] It is in order to accentuate the contrast between the Academic position and that of Democritus that Cicero renders in this way (*tenebricosus*) the term *skotiê*, which in fact means 'obscure' and which is translated so in **D20**.

Democritus and the Pyrrhonian Skeptics (R102–R108)
Pyrrho's Admiration for Democritus (R102)

R102 (≠ DK) Diogenes Laertius

What is more, Philo of Athens, who was his [i.e. Pyrrho's] close friend, said that he mentioned Democritus more than anyone else [. . .].

Does Democritus Belong to the Line of Descent of Skepticism? (R103–R104)

R103 (< B117) Diogenes Laertius

According to them [i.e. the Skeptics] [. . .] and Democritus are Skeptics [. . .]: Democritus when he expels qualities, when he writes, **"by convention hot** [. . .]," and again, **"[. . .] For truth is in an abyss"** [cf. **D24**].

R104 (A134) Sextus Empiricus, *Outlines of Pyrrhonism*

From the fact that honey appears to be bitter to some people and sweet to others, Democritus said that it is neither sweet nor bitter [. . .].

An Unsatisfactory Definition by
Democritus (R105)

R105 (B165) Sext. Emp. *Adv. Math.* 7.265

Δημόκριτος [. . .] ἐπεχείρησε μὲν τὴν ἐπίνοιαν ἐκθέσθαι, πλεῖον δὲ ἰδιωτικῆς ἀποφάσεως οὐδὲν ἴσχυσεν,
εἰπών· "ἄνθρωπός ἐστιν ὃ πάντες ἴδμεν" [cf. **D26b**].

Is Democritus Dogmatic? (R106–R107)

R106 (58.1 Leszl) Sext. Emp. *Pyrrh. Hyp.* 1.213–14 [τίνι
διαφέρει ἡ σκεπτικὴ ἀγωγὴ τῆς Δημοκριτείου φιλοσοφίας;]

ἀλλὰ καὶ ἡ Δημοκρίτειος φιλοσοφία λέγεται κοι-
νωνίαν ἔχειν πρὸς τὴν σκέψιν, ἐπεὶ δοκεῖ τῇ αὐτῇ ὕλῃ
ἡμῖν κεχρῆσθαι· ἀπὸ γὰρ τοῦ τοῖς μὲν γλυκὺ φαίνεσθαι τὸ μέλι τοῖς δὲ πικρὸν τὸν Δημόκριτον ἐπιλογί-
ζεσθαί φασι τὸ μήτε γλυκὺ αὐτὸ εἶναι μήτε πικρόν,
καὶ διὰ τοῦτο ἐπιφθέγγεσθαι τὴν 'οὐ μᾶλλον' φωνὴν
σκεπτικὴν οὖσαν. διαφόρως μέντοι χρῶνται τῇ 'οὐ
μᾶλλον' φωνῇ οἵ τε σκεπτικοὶ καὶ οἱ ἀπὸ τοῦ Δημο-
κρίτου· ἐκεῖνοι μὲν γὰρ ἐπὶ τοῦ μηδέτερον εἶναι τάττουσι τὴν φωνήν, ἡμεῖς δὲ ἐπὶ τοῦ ἀγνοεῖν, πότερον
ἀμφότερα ἢ οὐθέτερόν τι ἔστι τῶν φαινομένων. [214]
ὥστε καὶ κατὰ τοῦτο μὲν διαφέρομεν, προδηλοτάτη δὲ
γίνεται ἡ διάκρισις ὅταν ὁ Δημόκριτος λέγῃ "ἐτεῇ δὲ
ἄτομα καὶ κενόν." "ἐτεῇ" μὲν γὰρ λέγει ἀντὶ τοῦ
"ἀληθείᾳ."

An Unsatisfactory Definition by
Democritus (R105)

R105 (B165) Sextus Empiricus, *Against the Logicians*

Democritus [. . .] tried to explain the concept [scil. of man]
but he did not succeed in providing anything more than
an amateur statement when he said, **"A man is what we
all know"** [= **D26b**].

Is Democritus Dogmatic? (R106–R107)

R106 (≠ DK) Sextus Empiricus, *Outlines of Pyrrhonism*
[In what regard does the Skeptical school differ from
Democritean philosophy?]

Democritean philosophy too is said to have something in
common with Skepticism, since it seems to have recourse
to the same material as we do. For starting out from the
fact that honey seems sweet to some people and bitter to
others, these people say that Democritus inferred from
this that it is neither sweet nor bitter, and that this is why
he pronounced the phrase, "not more than" [cf. **D33**],
which is Skeptical. And yet the Skeptics and those who de-
scend from Democritus use the phrase "not more than" in
different ways. For the latter assign the phrase to its not
being either the one or the other, while we do so to not
knowing whether some phenomenon is both the one and
the other or is neither the one nor the other. So that in this
regard we differ; and the distinction becomes completely
evident when Democritus says, **"in reality atoms and
void"** [cf. **D24**]. For he says **"in reality"** (*eteê*) instead of
"in truth" (*alêtheia*).

R107 (A114) Sext. Emp. *Adv. Math.* 7.389–90

πᾶσαν μὲν οὖν φαντασίαν οὐκ ⟨ἂν⟩[1] εἴποι τις ἀληθῆ
διὰ τὴν περιτροπήν, καθὼς ὅ τε Δημόκριτος καὶ ὁ
Πλάτων ἀντιλέγοντες τῷ Πρωταγόρᾳ ἐδίδασκον· [390]
εἰ γὰρ πᾶσα φαντασία ἐστὶν ἀληθής, καὶ τὸ μὴ πᾶσαν φαντασίαν εἶναι ἀληθῆ, κατὰ φαντασίαν ὑφ-
ιστάμενον, ἔσται ἀληθές, καὶ οὕτω τὸ πᾶσαν φαντασίαν εἶναι ἀληθῆ γενήσεται ψεῦδος.

[1] ⟨ἂν⟩ Bekker

The Context of the Citations of Democritus'
Epistemological Fragments in Sextus Empiricus
(R108)

R108 (ad B9, 6, 7, 8, 11) Sext. Emp. *Adv. Math.* 7.135–39

[135] Δημόκριτος δὲ ὁτὲ[1] μὲν ἀναιρεῖ τὰ φαινόμενα
ταῖς αἰσθήσεσι καὶ τούτων λέγει μηδὲν φαίνεσθαι
κατ' ἀλήθειαν, ἀλλὰ μόνον κατὰ δόξαν, ἀληθὲς δὲ ἐν
τοῖς οὖσιν ὑπάρχειν τὸ ἀτόμους εἶναι καὶ κενόν·
"νόμῳ," γάρ φησι, "γλυκὺ καὶ νόμῳ πικρόν, νόμῳ
θερμόν, νόμῳ ψυχρόν, νόμῳ χροιή· ἐτεῇ δὲ ἄτομα
καὶ κενόν" [**D14**]. ὅπερ ⟨ἔστι⟩·[2] νομίζεται μὲν εἶναι
καὶ δοξάζεται τὰ αἰσθητά, οὐκ ἔστι δὲ κατ' ἀλήθειαν
ταῦτα, ἀλλὰ τὰ ἄτομα μόνον καὶ τὸ κενόν. [136] ἐν δὲ
τοῖς Κρατυντηρίοις, καίπερ ὑπεσχημένος ταῖς αἰσθήσεσι τὸ κράτος τῆς πίστεως ἀναθεῖναι, οὐδὲν ἧττον
εὑρίσκεται τούτων καταδικάζων. φησὶ γὰρ "ἡμεῖς δὲ

R107 (A114) Sextus Empiricus, *Against the Logicians*

One should not say that every representation (*phantasia*) is true, and this is because of self-refutation (*peritropê*), as Democritus and Plato have taught [cf. **PROT. R9–R10**], contradicting Protagoras in this way. For if every representation is true, it will also be true [scil. to say] that every representation is not true, since it results from a representation, and in this way [scil. to say] that every representation is true will be false [= **PROT. R22**].

The Context of the Citations of Democritus'
Epistemological Fragments in Sextus Empiricus
(R108)

R108 (ad B9, 6, 7, 8, 11) Sextus Empiricus, *Against the Logicians*

[135] As for Democritus, he sometimes abolishes what appears to the senses, and says that none of these things appears according to truth but only according to opinion, and that what is true among the things that are is the fact that atoms exist and the void—for he says, **"By convention sweet and by convention bitter, by convention hot, by convention cold, by convention color, but in reality atoms and void"** [**D14**], which means: one accepts and one has the opinion that the objects of the senses exist, but these do not exist in truth, but only the atoms and the void. [136] And in the ***Confirmations,*** although he has promised to attribute to the sensations the force of belief (*pistis*), nonetheless we discover that he is con-

---

vid. app. ad **D15–D21**   ¹ ὅτι mss., corr. Usener
² ⟨ἔστι⟩ Bekker

τῷ μὲν ἐόντι οὐδὲν ἀτρεκὲς συνίεμεν, μεταπίπτον δὲ
κατά τε σώματος διαθήκην καὶ τῶν ἐπεισιόντων καὶ
τῶν ἀντιστηριζόντων" [D15]. καὶ πάλιν φησίν· "ἐτεῇ
μέν νυν ὅτι οἷον ἕκαστον ἔστιν ⟨ἢ⟩ οὐκ ἔστιν οὐ
συνίεμεν, πολλαχῇ δεδήλωται" [D16]. [137] ἐν δὲ τῷ
Περὶ ἰδεῶν· "γιγνώσκειν τε χρή," φησίν, "ἄνθρωπον
τῷδε τῷ κανόνι, ὅτι ἐτεῆς ἀπήλλακται" [D17], καὶ
πάλιν· "δηλοῖ μὲν δὴ καὶ οὗτος ὁ λόγος, ὅτι ἐτεῇ
οὐδὲν ἴσμεν περὶ οὐδενός, ἀλλ' ἐπιρυσμίη ἑκάστοισιν ἡ δόξις" [D18], καὶ ἔτι· "καίτοι δῆλον ἔσται, ὅτι
ἐτεῇ οἷον ἕκαστον γιγνώσκειν ἐν ἀπόρῳ ἐστί"
[D19]. καὶ δὴ ἐν μὲν τούτοις πᾶσαν σχεδὸν κινεῖ[3]
κατάληψιν, ⟨εἰ⟩[4] καὶ μόνον ἐξαιρέτως καθάπτεται τῶν
αἰσθήσεων· [138] ἐν δὲ τοῖς Κανόσι δύο φησὶν εἶναι
γνώσεις, τὴν μὲν διὰ τῶν αἰσθήσεων τὴν δὲ διὰ τῆς
διανοίας, ὧν τὴν μὲν διὰ τῆς διανοίας γνησίην[5] καλεῖ,[6] προσμαρτυρῶν αὐτῇ τὸ πιστὸν εἰς ἀληθείας κρίσιν, τὴν δὲ διὰ τῶν αἰσθήσεων σκοτίην ὀνομάζει,
ἀφαιρούμενος αὐτῆς τὸ πρὸς διάγνωσιν τοῦ ἀληθοῦς
ἀπλανές. [139] λέγει δὲ κατὰ λέξιν· "γνώμης δὲ δύο
εἰσὶν ἰδέαι, ἡ μὲν γνησίη, ἡ δὲ σκοτίη· καὶ σκοτίης
μὲν τάδε σύμπαντα, ὄψις ἀκοὴ ὀδμὴ γεῦσις ψαῦσις·
ἡ δὲ γνησίη, ἀποκεκριμένη δὲ ταύτης" [D20]. εἶτα
προκρίνων σκοτίης τὴν γνησίην ἐπιφέρει λέγων·
"ὅταν ἡ σκοτίη μηκέτι δύνηται μήτε ὁρῆν ἐπ' ἔλατ-

---

3 κρίνει Usener   4 ⟨εἰ⟩ Bekker   5 γνῶσιν mss.,
corr. Fabricius   6 καλεῖ Bekker: κατάγει mss.

demning them. For he says, **"We grasp in actuality not anything that is certain, but something that changes according to the disposition both of the body and of what penetrates and repels"** [**D15**]. And again he says, **"That thus in reality we do not grasp what each thing is or is not, has been made clear in a number of ways"** [**D16**]. [137] And in ***On the Forms*** he says, **"It is necessary to recognize that man by virtue of this criterion is separated from reality"** [**D17**]; and again, **"Certainly this argument too makes it clear that in reality we know nothing about anything, but for each person opinion is a rhythmic afflux"** [**D18**]; and again, **"And yet it will be clear that in reality to recognize of what sort each thing is, belongs to what is impracticable"** [**D19**]. In these passages he virtually uproots all apprehension, even if it is only the sensations that he attacks in particular. [138] But in his ***Criteria,*** he says that there are two kinds of knowledge, one that passes through the senses and another that passes through thought; and of these he calls the one that passes through thought **"genuine,"** testifying to its credibility with regard to the decision of truth, while the other one, the one that passes through the senses, he terms **"obscure,"** refusing to accord it infallibility with regard to the recognition of what is true. [139] For he says verbatim, **"There are two forms of knowledge, the one genuine, the other obscure. And to the obscure one belong all of these: sight, hearing, smell, taste, touch. The other is genuine, and is separated from this one"** [**D20**]. And then, giving his preference to the genuine one over the obscure one, he continues, saying, **"When the one that is obscure is no longer able either to see what**

473

τον μήτε ἀκούειν μήτε ὀδμᾶσθαι μήτε γεύεσθαι
μήτε ἐν τῇ ψαύσει αἰσθάνεσθαι, ἀλλ' ἐπὶ λεπτότερον ‹. . . ›" [**D21**]. οὐκοῦν καὶ κατὰ τοῦτον ὁ λόγος
ἐστὶ κριτήριον, ὃν γνησίην γνώμην καλεῖ [. . . = **R76**].

Arguments of a Stoic Origin Against
Democritus (R109–R110)

Cf. **R1f, g**

R109 Cic. *Acad.*

a (‹ 46.1 Leszl) 2.18.56

primum quidem me ad Democritum vocas, cui non
adsentior potiusque refello[1] propter[2] id quod dilucide
docetur a politioribus physicis, singularum rerum singulas
proprietates esse. [. . .].

[1] potiusque A^2, refello V^2: potius quale fallor *vel. sim. cett.*
[2] propter $V^{2:}$ potest *cett.*

b (› 46.2 Leszl) 2.40.125

sin agis verecundius et me accusas non quod tuis rationibus
non adsentiar sed quod nullis, vincam animum cuique
adsentiar deligam—quem potissimum, quem? Democritum; semper enim, ut scitis, studiosus nobilitatis fui. ur-
gebor iam omnium vestrum convicio: "tune aut inane

is smaller or to hear or to smell or to taste or to perceive by touching, but toward something that is finer ⟨. . .⟩ (?)" [**D21**]. And so, according to him too, the criterion is reason (*logos*), which he calls **"genuine"** thought [. . .].

Arguments of a Stoic Origin Against
Democritus (R109–R110)

Cf. **R1f, g**

R109 Cicero, *Prior Academics*

a (≠ DK) [Lucullus, attacking the Academics, addresses Cicero, who shares some of their views]

First of all, you call me before Democritus, with whom I do not agree, indeed I refute him on the basis of what is lucidly taught by more refined natural philosophers [i.e. the Stoics], that there are singular properties of singular things.

b (≠ DK) [Cicero replies to Lucullus]

But if you do behave more modestly and accuse me not of not agreeing with your own arguments but of not agreeing with anyone's, I will force myself to choose, to whom I can give my assent—whom especially? whom? Democritus: for, as you know I have always been a fan of nobility. I shall now be assailed by reprimands by all of you: "Can

quicquam putes esse, cum ita conpleta et conferta sint
omnia, ut et[1] quod[2] movebitur ‹corpus›[3] corporum[4] cedat
et qua quidque cesserit aliud ilico subsequatur, aut atomos
ullas, e quibus quidquid efficiatur illarum sit dissimil-
limum, aut sine aliqua mente rem ullam effici posse
praeclaram; et, cum in uno mundo ornatus hic tam sit
mirabilis, innumerabilis supra infra dextra sinistra ante
post alios dissimiles alios eiusdem modi mundos esse; et
ut nos nunc simus ad Baulos Puteolosque videamus sic
innumerabiles paribus in locis esse isdem nominibus
honoribus rebus gestis ingeniis formis aetatibus isdem de
rebus disputantes; et, si nunc aut si etiam dormientes
aliquid animo videre videamur, imagines extrinsecus in
animos nostros per corpus inrumpere? tu vero ista ne
asciveris neve fueris commenticiis rebus adsensus; nihil
sentire est melius quam tam prava sentire."

[1] ut et *dett Rom.*: et *AB*: ut *F²N*   [2] quidquid *Reid*
[3] ‹corpus› *Lambinus*: post ‹corpus› *lac. pos. Plasberg* ‹ei
aliquid e numero vicinorum›   [4] corporeum *Reid*

R110 (≠ DK) Plut. *Comm. not.* 39 1079E–F, 1080A

[. . . **D213**] ἐνταῦθα δὴ τὸν Δημόκριτον ἀποφαίνων
ἀγνοοῦντα τὰς μὲν ἐπιφανείας φησὶ [Chrys. *SVF* 2.489]
μήτ᾽ ἴσας εἶναι μήτ᾽ ἀνίσους, ἄνισα δὲ τὰ σώματα τῷ
μήτ᾽ ἴσας εἶναι μήτ᾽ ἀνίσους τὰς ἐπιφανείας. [. . .] "ἃς
γὰρ ὑφορᾶται περὶ τὸν κῶνον ἀναχαράξεις ἡ τῶν
σωμάτων ἀνισότης δήπουθεν οὐχ ἡ τῶν ἐπιφανειῶν
ἀπεργάζεται."

you really suppose that the void is something, when the totality of things is so filled and stuffed that, whatever bodies moves a body, it yields and another body immediately moves into the place it left? Or that there are atoms to which, whatever is made from them, it is completely dissimilar? Or that anything magnificent can be produced without any mind? And that when in a single world there is this order that is so marvelous, there are innumerable worlds above, below, to the right, to the left, in front, behind, some dissimilar to it and others of the same kind? And that just as we are now at Bauli and are looking at Puteoli, in the same way there are innumerable [scil. other people] in the same places [scil. as ours], with the same names, honors, achievements, minds, appearances, and ages, discussing the same subjects? And that, if now or also while we are sleeping we seem to see something with our mind, it is because there are images that burst into our mind from outside through our body? As for you, you must not ascribe to such ideas, or assent to fictitious things: to have no opinion is better than to have such mistaken opinions!"

R110 (≠ DK) Plutarch, *On Common Conceptions*

[. . .] It is at this point that Chrysippus, asserting that Democritus is ignorant, says that the surfaces are neither equal nor unequal, but that the bodies are unequal by reason of the fact that the surfaces are neither equal nor unequal. [. . .] "for the incisions in the cone that he views with suspicion are produced by the inequality of bodies, doubtless, and not by that of surfaces" [cf. **D213**].

Democritus Among the Christians (R111–R114)

R111 (> A26) Tert. *Apol.* 46.11

Democritus excaecando semetipsum, quod mulieres sine concupiscentia aspicere non posset et doleret, si non esset potitus, incontinentiam emendatione profitetur. at Christianus salvis oculis feminas non videt; animo adversus libidinem caecus est.

R112 (9.4 Leszl) Dion. Alex. *Nat.* in Eus. *PE* 14.24.1 et 14.25.1–2

πῶς αὐτῶν ἀνασχώμεθα τυχηρὰ λεγόντων εἶναι συμπτώματα τὰ σοφὰ καὶ διὰ τοῦτο καλὰ δημιουργήματα; [. . .] ἢ τὸν μέγαν τοῦτον οἶκον τὸν ἐξ οὐρανοῦ καὶ γῆς συνεστῶτα καὶ διὰ τὸ μέγεθος καὶ πλῆθος τῆς ἐπιφαινομένης αὐτῷ σοφίας καλούμενον κόσμον ὑπὸ τῶν σὺν οὐδενὶ κόσμῳ φερομένων ἀτόμων κεκοσμῆσθαι καὶ γεγονέναι κόσμον ἀκοσμίαν; πῶς δὲ κινήσεις καὶ ὁδοὺς εὐτάκτους ἐξ ἀτάκτου προάγεσθαι φορᾶς; πῶς δὲ τὴν παναρμόνιον τῶν οὐρανίων χορείαν ἐξ ἀμούσων καὶ ἀναρμόστων συνᾴδειν ὀργάνων;

R113 (9.5 Leszl) Lact. *Ira Dei* 32–33

tanta ergo qui videat et talia, potest existimare nullo effecta esse consilio, nulla providentia, nulla ratione divina, sed ex micis subtilibus et exiguis concreta esse

Democritus Among the Christians (R111–R114)

R111 (> A26) Tertullian, *Apology*

Democritus blinded himself [cf. **P33–P35**] because he was not capable of looking at women without lust and suffered distress if he could not possess them, and by this remedy he confesses his intemperance. By contrast, a Christian can preserve his eyes and still does not see women: he is blind in his soul toward lust.

R112 (≠ DK) Dionysius of Alexandria, *On Nature,* in Eusebius, *Evangelical Preparation,*

How can we endure that they [i.e. Democritus and the Epicureans] say that the works produced by wisdom, which for this very reason are beautiful, are accidents due to chance? [. . .] Or that this great habitation, composed out of the heaven and the earth, and called 'world order' (*kosmos*) on account of the magnitude and abundance of the wisdom manifested in it, has received its order on the basis of atoms moving without any order, and that the absence of order has become order? How is it possible for well-ordered movements and trajectories to be produced out of a disordered motion? How can the harmonious chorus of the heavenly bodies sing together using unmusical and dissonant instruments?

R113 (≠ DK) Lactantius, *On the Wrath of God*

So whoever sees such great things and ones of such a nature [scil. as the world is composed of]—can he believe that they have been produced without plan, without providence, without divine reason, but that such great wonders

tanta miracula? nonne prodigio simile est aut natum esse
hominem qui haec diceret aut extitisse qui crederent, ut
Democritum qui auditor eius fuit, vel Epicurum in quem
vanitas omnis de Leucippi fonte profluxit?

R114 (112.5 Leszl) Aug. *Ad Dioscor. Epist.* 118.27–28

quanto enim melius ne audissem quidem nomen Democriti quam cum dolore cogitarem nescio quem suis
temporibus magnum putatum, qui deos esse arbitraretur
imagines, quae de solidis corporibus fluerent solidaeque
ipsae non essent, easque hac atque hac motu proprio cir-
cumeundo atque illabendo in animos hominum facere ut
vis divina cogitetur, cum profecto illud corpus unde imago
flueret quanto solidius est, tanto praestantius quoque esse
iudicetur!

Two Examples of Apocryphal
Writings (R115–R116)
A Fictitious Autobiographical Statement about
His Travels and Education (R115)

Cf. **P16–P22**

R115 (B299) Clem. Alex. *Strom.* 1.69.4–6 (et al.)

Δημόκριτος γὰρ τοὺς Βαβυλωνίους λόγους ἠθικοὺς[1]
πεποίηται· λέγεται γὰρ τὴν Ἀκικάρου στήλην ἑρμη-

---

[1] ἠθικοὺς ms.: Ἑλληνικοὺς Diels, alii alia

480

are the result of the aggregation of tenuous, tiny particles? Is it not almost a monstrosity, that a man capable of saying these things was born or that people capable of believing them existed, like Democritus, who was his [i.e. Leucippus'] student, or Epicurus, into whom this whole vacuity flowed down from the fountain of Leucippus?

R114 (≠ DK) Augustine, *Letter to Dioscorus*

How much better it would have been if I had never even heard the name of Democritus than that I would have to think with pain that in his times someone was considered to be a great man who believed that gods were images that flowed from solid bodies without being solid themselves [cf. **D154**], and that such images, wandering here and there by their own motion and slipping into men's souls, made them think of divine power, for surely that body from which the image flows, the more solid it is, is considered to be more excellent too.

Two Examples of Apocryphal Writings (R115–R116)
A Fictitious Autobiographical Statement about His Travels and Education (R115)

Cf. **P16–P22**

R115 (B299) Clement of Alexandria, *Stromata*

For Democritus has made the discourses of the Babylonians ethical (?). For he is said to have inserted a transla-

νευθεῖσαν τοῖς ἰδίοις συντάξαι συγγράμμασι κἄστιν
ἐπισημήνασθαι ⟨τὰ⟩² παρ' αὐτοῦ, "τάδε λέγει Δημόκριτος" γράφοντος.³ [5] ναὶ μὴν καὶ περὶ αὐτοῦ⁴
σεμνυνόμενός φησί που ἐπὶ τῇ πολυμαθίᾳ· "ἐγὼ δὲ
τῶν κατ' ἐμαυτὸν ἀνθρώπων γῆν πλείστην ἐπεπλανη-
σάμην, ἱστορέων τὰ μήκιστα, καὶ ἀέρας τε καὶ γέας
πλείστας εἶδον, καὶ λογίων ἀνθρώπων πλείστων ἐπήκουσα,⁵ καὶ γραμμέων συνθέσι⁶ μετὰ ἀποδείξεως οὐ-
δείς κώ με παρήλλαξεν, οὐδ' οἱ Αἰγυπτίων καλεόμενοι
Ἀρπεδονάπται,⁷ σὺν τοῖς δ'⁸ ἐπὶ πᾶσιν ἐπ' ἔτε᾽ †ὀγδώ-
κοντα†⁹ ἐπὶ ξείνης ἐγενήθην." [6] ἐπῆλθε γὰρ Βαβυ-
λῶνά τε καὶ Περσίδα καὶ Αἴγυπτον τοῖς τε Μάγοις
καὶ τοῖς ἱερεῦσι μαθητεύων.

2 ⟨τὰ⟩ Jackson   3 κἄστιν . . . γράφοντος ms.: κᾷτα
. . . γράφων Bernays   4 ἢ hab. ms. post αὐτοῦ, del. Stählin:
δὴ Schwartz   5 ἐπήκουσα Eus. PE 10.4.23: ἐσ- ms.

6 συνθέσι Dindorf: συνθέσιος ms.: καὶ ⟨περὶ⟩ γρ. συνθέσιος Schwartz   7 ἀρπεδοναύται Eus.   8 σὺν τοῖς δ'
ms.: οἷς Eus.: post τοῖς lac. stat. Wilamowitz   9 ὀγδώκοντα
mss.: πέντε coni. Stählin e Diod. Sic. 1.98.3

A Letter to Hippocrates (R116)

R116 (< C6) Ps.-Hipp. Epist. 23 (9.392–93 Littré)

Δημόκριτος Ἱπποκράτει περὶ φύσιος ἀνθρώπου.

χρὴ πάντας ἀνθρώπους ἰητρικὴν τέχνην ἐπίστασθαι, ὦ Ἱππόκρατες, καλὸν γὰρ ἅμα καὶ

tion of the stela of Akikaros[1] into his own writings; and one can distinguish what derives from him by his writing, "Democritus says the following." Indeed, he also says somewhere, putting on airs about his polymathy, "I myself, of all the men of my times, have traveled through the most of the world, investigating the farthest, and I have seen the most airs and lands and have listened to the most men of learning, and in the composition of demonstrative writings no one has ever surpassed me, not even the so-called Harpedonapts [i.e. the 'Cord-Stretchers' or geometers] of the Egyptians. With these I spent as many as †eighty† years abroad on all subjects."[2] For he went to Babylon, Persia, and Egypt, studying with the Magi and the priests.

[1] A legendary Babylonian sage to whom many proverbs were attributed in a number of ancient cultures.   [2] The sentence is obscure and probably corrupt. In any case it is easy to correct '80' to '5' in Greek.

A Letter to Hippocrates (R116)

R116 (< C6) Ps.-Democritus, *Letter to Hippocrates*

Democritus to Hippocrates on the nature of man.

All men ought to know the art of medicine, Hippocrates, for it is a fine thing and at the same time

ξυμφέρον ἐς τὸν βίον, τουτέων δὲ μάλιστα τοὺς
παιδείας καὶ λόγων ἴδριας γεγενημένους. ἱστο-
ρίην σοφίης γὰρ δοκέω ἰητρικῆς ἀδελφὴν καὶ
ξύνοικον· σοφίη μὲν γὰρ ψυχὴν ἀναρύεται πα-
θέων, ἰητρικὴ δὲ νούσους σωμάτων ἀφαιρέεται
[. . .].

Democritus and Bolus of Mendes (R117–R120)

R117 (< B300.3) Colum. *Agric.* 7.5.17

sed Aegyptiae gentis auctor memorabilis Bolus Mendesius,
cuius commenta quae appellantur graece Χειρόκμητα
sub nomine Democriti falso produntur [. . .].

R118

a (B300.1) *Suda* B.482

Βῶλος, Μενδήσιος, Πυθαγόρειος. Περὶ τῶν ἐκ τῆς
ἀναγνώσεως τῶν ἱστοριῶν εἰς ἐπίστασιν ἡμᾶς ἀγόν-
των, Περὶ θαυμασίων, Φυσικὰ δυναμερά· ἔχει δὲ περὶ
συμπαθειῶν καὶ ἀντιπαθειῶν λίθων κατὰ στοιχεῖον·
Περὶ σημείων τῶν ἐξ ἡλίου καὶ σελήνης καὶ ἄρκτου
καὶ λύχνου καὶ ἴριδος.

useful for life, and belongs most of all to those men who have become expert in education and discourses. For I think that the search for wisdom is the sister and housemate of medicine. For wisdom rescues the soul from passions, while medicine removes illnesses from bodies [. . .].

Democritus and Bolus of Mendes[1] *(R117–R120)*

[1] A Neopythagorean philosopher, probably active in Egypt in the third century BC, to whom numerous esoterical and paradoxographical treatises were attributed. He was said to have been a Democritean, and some of his writings were attributed to Democritus himself.

R117 (< B300.3) Columella, *On Agriculture*

But the celebrated Egyptian author Bolus of Mendes, whose treatises, entitled *Artifices (Kheirokmêta)* in Greek, circulate under the pseudonym of Democritus [. . .].

R118

a (B300.1) *Suda*

Bolus of Mendes, Pythagorean. *On Passages from Reading Histories That Attract Our Attention; On Marvels; Potent Natural Remedies* (it contains [scil. material] on sympathies and antipathies of stones, arranged alphabetically); *On the Signs from the Sun, the Moon, the Great Bear, the Lantern* (?), *and the Rainbow.*

485

b (B300.1) *Suda* B.481

Βῶλος, Δημοκρίτειος,[1] φιλόσοφος. Ἱστορίαν καὶ Τέχνην ἰατρικήν. ἔχει δὲ ἰάσεις φυσικὰς ἀπό τινων βοηθημάτων τῆς φύσεως.

[1] Δημόκριτος mss., corr. Holstenius

c (78. vol. II, p. 251.21–23) Apoll. *Mir.* 31

ἄψυνθος [. . .] ἔστι καὶ εἶδος φυτοῦ, περὶ οὗ Βῶλος ὁ Δημοκρίτειος [. . .].

R119

a (B300.4) Schol. in Nic. *Ther.* 764a

Βῶλος[1] δὲ ὁ Δημοκρίτειος ἐν τῷ Περὶ συμπαθειῶν καὶ ἀντιπαθειῶν [. . .].

[1] Ῥῶλος codd., corr. Holstenius

b (B300.10) Tat. *Orat. ad Graecos* 16.17

[. . .] περὶ γὰρ τῶν κατὰ τὸν Δημόκριτον ξυμπαθειῶν τε καὶ ἀντιπαθειῶν τί καὶ λέγειν ἔχομεν ἢ τοῦθ᾽ ὅτι κατὰ τὸν κοινὸν λόγον ἀβδηρολόγος ἐστὶν ὁ ἀπὸ τῶν Ἀβδήρων ἄνθρωπος;

b (B300.1) *Suda*

Bolus, Democritean, philosopher. *History* and *The Art of Medicine* (it contains natural remedies deriving from certain resources provided by nature).

c (78. vol. II, p. 251.21–23) Apollonius, *Wonders*

Apsynthus: [. . .] there is also a species of plant about which Bolus the Democritean [scil. speaks] [. . .].

R119

a (B300.4) Scholia on Nicander's *Theriaca*

Bolus the Democritean in his work *On Sympathies and Antipathies* [. . .].[1]

> [1] There are many other testimonia to the extraordinary popularity of the work on sympathies and antipathies that was attributed to Democritus.

b (B300.10) Tatian, *Oration to the Greeks*

[. . .] For with regard to the sympathies and antipathies according to Democritus, what can we say except that that man from Abdera is, to use the common expression, a prattler of stupidities (*abdêrologos*)?[1]

> [1] A play on words on the name of Abdera, Democritus' native city.

R120 (B300.7)

a Plin. *Nat. hist.* 28.112

[. . .] chamaeleonem, peculiari volumine dignum existimatum Democrito [. . .].

b Aul. Gell. *Noct.* 10.12.6–8

his portentis atque praestigiis a Plinio Secundo scriptis non dignum[1] esse cognomen Democriti puto [. . .]. multa autem videntur ab hominibus istis male sollertibus huiuscemodi commenta in Democritii nomen data nobilitatis auctoritatisque eius perfugio utentibus.

[1] indignum B

Democritus the Doctor (R121–R124)

R121 (188.5 Leszl) Ruf. Ephes. in Oribas. *Coll. med.* 44.14.1

[. . .] περὶ τούτου Δημόκριτός φησιν ὅτι μολύβδου μετὰ φοινικηίου[1] περιαφθέντος ἢ τὸ παράπαν ἀφλέγματος γίνεται ἢ πολλῷ δὴ ῥηίζει.

[1] φοινικίου R, corr. Raeder

R122 (B300.7) Aul. Gell. *Noct.* 4.13.3

viperarum morsibus tibicinium scite modulateque adhibitum mederi refert etiam Democriti liber, qui inscri-

R120 (B300.7)

a Pliny, *Natural History*[1]

[. . .] the chameleon, which was deemed by Democritus to merit his dedicating a whole volume to it [. . .].

[1] This is only one of numerous references by Pliny to 'Democritus' = (Ps.-) Democritus, cf. B300.8 DK.

b Aulus Gellius, *Attic Nights*

I think that the name of Democritus is unworthy of these marvels and delusions of which Pliny the Elder speaks in his writings [. . .]. But many forgeries seem to have been published in this way under the name of Democritus by men lacking in intelligence who wanted to take advantage of the safety provided by his celebrity and authority.

Democritus the Doctor (R121–R124)

R121 (≠ DK) Rufus of Ephesus in Oribasius, *Medical Collections*

[. . .] about this [i.e. a kind of swelling sometimes accompanied by fever], Democritus says that if lead is applied around the area together with the fruit of a date palm, he [i.e. the patient] is completely freed of fever or certainly is very much relieved.

R122 (B300.7) Aulus Gellius, *Attic Nights*

A book of Democritus too, entitled ⟨. . .⟩, reports that snakebites can be cured if pipes are played expertly and

bitur ⟨. . .⟩¹ in quo docet plurimis hominum morbidis
medicinae fuisse incentiones tibiarum.

¹ ⟨Περὶ λοιμῶν⟩ Hertz: ⟨Περὶ συμπαθειῶν⟩ Diels

R123 (cf. B300.10) Cael. Aurel. *Celer. pass.*

a 3.15.120

[. . .] Democritus [. . .] non solum hanc memoravit
esse passionem, sed etiam eius causam tradidit, cum de
opisthotonicis scriberet.

b 3.14.112

vicina etiam quaestio est supradictae, quisnam in hydro-
phobicis locus corporis patiatur. e⟨t⟩ quidem¹ Democritus,
cum de emprosthotonicis diceret, nervos inquit, coniciens
hoc ex corporis conductione atque veretri² tentigine.

¹ equidem *ed. Guinterii, corr. Bendz*   ² veretri coni. *ed.
Rovilliana*: veteri *ed. Guinterii*

c 3.16.132–33

antiquorum autem medicorum nullus istius passionis
tradidit curationem. [. . .] Democritus vero iubet origani
decoctionem dari atque ipsum poculum, quod¹ bibunt, in
sphaerae rotunditatem formari. [133] est autem hoc genus

¹ quo *ed. Rovilliana*

rhythmically; in this book he explains that for many sick men the melodies of pipes were medicinal.[1]

[1] **R122** and **R123** are both assigned by DK to Bolus.

R123 (cf. B300.10) Caelius Aurelianus, *Acute Maladies*

a

[. . .] Democritus [. . .] not only mentioned this disease [i.e. hydrophobia], but he also indicated its cause when he wrote about those who suffer from a general contraction of the extensor muscles (*opisthotonos*).

b

A question closely connected with the one mentioned above [scil. whether hydrophobia is a disease of the soul or of the body] is which part of the body is affected in hydrophobic patients. And Democritus, when he wrote about those who suffer from a general contraction of the flexor muscles (*emprosthotonos*), said it was the nerves, inferring this from the contraction of the body and from the tension of the penis.

c

Of the ancient medical writers, no one has indicated a treatment for this disease [i.e. hydrophobia]. [. . .] But Democritus says that a decoction of oregano should be administered and that the cup itself from which they drink should have the shape of a sphere. But this kind of decoc-

decoctionis acerrimum atque stomachum vexans et in-
cendens. in quo etiam idem sibi repugnare perspicitur: ait
enim hydrophobiam esse incendium nervorum.

R124 (B300.20) P. Lugd. Bat. J 384 (*PGM* 12.351–64)

Δημοκρίτου Σφαῖρα. προγνωστικὸν ζωῆς καὶ θανάτου.
γνῶθι πρὸς τίνα¹ σελήνην ἀνέπεσε νοσῶν καὶ τὸ
ὄνομα τὸ ἐκ γενετῆς² συνψήφισον τῇ σελήνῃ καὶ
βλέπε, πόσαι³ τρ‹ι›ακάδες γίνονται, καὶ τὰ περιλει-
πόμενα τοῦ ἀριθμοῦ κατανόησον εἰς τὴν 'σφαῖραν'·
καὶ ἂν ᾖ ἄνω ἡ ψῆφος, ζήσει, ἐὰν δὲ κάτω, τελευτή-
σει.

α	ι	ιθ
β	ια	κ
γ	ιγ	κγ
δ	ιδ	κε
ζ	ιϛ	κϛ
θ	ιζ	κζ
ε	ιε	κβ
ϛ	ιη	κη
η	κα	κθ
ιβ	κδ	λ

¹ τὴν pap., corr. Diels   ² γεννετῆς pap., corr. Leemans
³ ποσταια pap., corr. Dieterich

tion is very sharp, and it irritates and inflames the stomach. So one sees that he contradicts himself on this point: for he says that hydrophobia is an inflammation of the nerves.

R124 (B300.20) Leiden Magical Papyrus

Democritus' *Sphere.* Prognostic for life and death. Find out at what moon [i.e. on which day of the month] he took to bed sick, add [scil. the number represented by the letters of] his birth name[1] to the moon, see how many periods of thirty are produced [i.e. how many times 30 can be divided into the result], and check the remainder of the number in the 'sphere': if the number calculated falls in its higher part he will live, but if in the lower one he will die.

1	10	19
2	11	20
3	13	23
4	14	25
7	16	26
9	17	27
5	15	22
6	18	28
8	21	29
12	24	30

[1] In ancient Greece, numbers were represented by letters, and hence the numerical values of the letters in a name could be added up to produce a sum.

Democritus the Alchemist (R125–R127)

Alleged Egyptian Sources (R125)

R125

a (< B300.16) Sync. *Chron.*, pp. 297–98

ἐν Αἰγύπτῳ μυηθεὶς ὑπὸ Ὀστάνου τοῦ Μήδου [. . .] ἐν τῷ ἱερῷ τῆς Μέμφεως σὺν ἄλλοις ἱερεῦσι καὶ φιλο-σόφοις, ἐν οἷς ἦν καὶ Μαρία τις Ἑβραία σοφὴ καὶ Παμμένης, συνέγραψε περὶ χρυσοῦ καὶ ἀργύρου καὶ λίθων καὶ πορφύρας λοξῶς, ὁμοίως δὲ καὶ Μαρία. ἀλλ᾽ οὗτοι μὲν Δημόκριτος καὶ Μαρία ἐπηνέθησαν παρὰ Ὀστάνου[1] ὡς πολλοῖς καὶ σοφοῖς αἰνίγμασι κρύψαντες τὴν τέχνην, Παμμένους δὲ κατέγνωσαν ἀφθόνως γράψαντος.

[1] παρὰ στάνου mss., corr. Goar

b (B300.17) Ps.-Synes. *ad Diosc. Comm. in Democritum* (p. 57.6–8, 8–15 *Coll. Alchim.*)

Δημόκριτος ἐλθὼν ἀπὸ Ἀβδήρων φυσικὸς ὢν καὶ πάντα τὰ φυσικὰ ἐρευνήσας καὶ συγγραψάμενος τὰ ὄντα κατὰ φύσιν. [. . .] ἐγένετο δὲ ἀνὴρ λογιώτατος, ὃς ἐλθὼν ἐν Αἰγύπτῳ ἐμυσταγωγήθη παρὰ τοῦ με-γάλου Ὀστάνου ἐν τῷ ἱερῷ τῆς Μέμφεως σὺν καὶ πᾶσι τοῖς ἱερεῦσιν Αἰγύπτου. ἐκ τούτου λαβὼν ἀφορ-μὰς συνεγράψατο βίβλους τέσσαρας βαφικάς, περὶ χρυσοῦ καὶ ἀργύρου καὶ λίθων καὶ πορφύρας. λέγω

ATOMISTS (LEUCIPPUS, DEMOCRITUS)

Democritus the Alchemist (R125–R127)[1]

[1] We provide only a few brief excerpts in order to give some sense of the nature of these texts. Cf. Martelli, *Scritti alchemici* (see the introduction to this chapter).

Alleged Egyptian Sources (R125)

R125

a (< B300.16) Syncellus, *Chronicle*

He [i.e. Democritus], having been initiated into the mysteries in Egypt by Ostanes[1] the Mede [. . .] in the temple of Memphis, together with other priests and philosophers, among whom was also a wise Jewish woman named Maria, and Pammenes, wrote about gold, silver, precious stones, and purple dye, in a riddling style, just as Maria did too. But whereas Democritus and Maria were praised by Ostanes for having concealed their craft by means of many wise enigmas, they condemned Pammenes for having written about it unreservedly.

[1] A legendary Persian mage and alchemist.

b (B300.17) Ps.-Synesius, *To Dioscorus, Commentary on Democrates*

Democritus, who came from Abdera, was a natural philosopher and investigated all natural phenomena and wrotes treatises about the things that exist according to nature [. . .]. He became a most learned man: he came to Egypt and was initiated into the mysteries by the great Ostanes in the temple of Memphis, together with all the priests of Egypt. Taking his inspiration from him, he composed four books on dyes, on gold, silver, precious stones,

495

δή, τὰς ἀφορμὰς λαβὼν συνεγράψατο παρὰ[1] τοῦ με-
γάλου Ὀστάνου. ἐκεῖνος γὰρ ἦν πρῶτος ὁ γράψας ὅτι
"ἡ φύσις τῇ φύσει τέρπεται καὶ ἡ φύσις τὴν φύσιν
κρατεῖ καὶ ἡ φύσις τὴν φύσιν νικᾷ [. . .]."

[1] συνεγράψατο γὰρ Fabricius

c (B300.18) Ps.-Democr. *Lib. 5 ad Leucippum* (pp. 53.18–
54.11 *Coll. Alchim.*)

ἰδοὺ μὲν ὃ ἦν, ὦ Λεύκιππε, περὶ τουτέων τῶν τεχνῶν
τῶν Αἰγυπτίων <ἐν ταῖς τῶν>[1] προφητέων Περσικαῖς[2]
βίβλοις, ἔγραψα τῇ κοινῇ διαλέκτῳ, πρὸς ἣν δὴ μάλιστα ἁρμόζονται· ἡ δὲ βίβλος οὐκ ἔστι κοινή. αἰνί-
γματα γὰρ ἔχει μυστικὰ παλαιά τε καὶ ὠγύγια[3] ἅπερ
οἱ πρόγονοι καὶ θεῖοι[4] Αἰγύπτου βασιλεῖς τοῖς Φοίνιξι
ἀνέθεντο.[5] ἐγὼ δὲ ὁ φίλος σου ὠγυγίοις[6] αἰνίγμασιν
χρήσομαι ἃ δὴ γεγράφαταί[7] μοι τοῖς Αἰγυπτίων παι-
σίν. ἀλλὰ σοί, ἰατρέ, καὶ δι᾽ ἑρμηνέως[8] πάντα οὐ παύ-
σομαι ἀναφανδὸν ἐνεξηγούμενος. περιέχει δὲ ἡ συγ-
γραφὴ λεύκωσίν τε καὶ ξάνθωσιν ἢ χαλκολίθου τε
μαλάξιας καὶ ἑψήσιας καὶ ἕως βαφικῆς, ὕστερον δὲ
ὅσα πάλιν παράδοξα γίγνεται ἐξ αὐτοῦ τοῦ χαλκοῦ
καὶ κινναβάρεως, ἔχε ποιῆσαι χρυσὸν <ἐκ τῆς>[9] καδ-
μίας τε καὶ ἄλλων εἰδῶν, καὶ καύσεων πάλιν <καὶ>[10]
ἐπιπλοκῶν ὅσα παράδοξα γίγνεται.

[1] <ἐν ταῖς τῶν> Ruelle   [2] προφήταις Περσικοῖς ms.,
corr. Diels   [3] ὅσα ὑγιᾶ ms., corr. dub. Diels   [4] θεία ms.,
corr. Diels   [5] τῆς πηλιξοι αὐταιθήντο ms., corr. Ruelle

and purple dye. And I say indeed that he wrote them under the inspiration of the great Ostanes. For he [i.e. Ostanes] was the first one to write that "nature takes pleasure in nature and nature is stronger than nature and nature conquers nature" [cf. **R127b**].

c (B300.18) Ps.-Democritus, *Book 5, Addressed to Leucippus*

Look, Leucippus, at what there was about all those crafts of the Egyptians ⟨contained in the⟩ Persian books of the prophets: I have written them in the common dialect, which is the most appropriate one for them. But the book is not common. For it contains ancient and primeval mystical enigmas, which the ancestral and divine kings of Egypt bestowed upon the Phoenicians. I myself, your friend, shall make use of the primeval enigmas that the sons of the Egyptians wrote down for me. But for you, doctor, I shall not cease to explain them all clearly by interpreting them. The treatise includes dyeing white and dyeing yellow, and ways to soften copper and to boil it and even to dye it, and then all of the astonishing things that are produced in turn out of the bronze itself and cinnabar: be able to make gold ⟨out of⟩ cadmia[1] and other varieties, and again all the astonishing things that are produced out of burnings ⟨and⟩ alloyings.

[1] An oxide of zinc.

---

6 ὡς ὑγείης ms., corr. dub. Diels   7 οὐδεὶς γεγράφατέ ms., corr. Diels   8 διηγερμένος ms., corr. Diels   9 ⟨ἐκ τῆς⟩ Ruelle   10 ⟨καὶ⟩ Ruelle

Renown for His Magical Practices (R126)

R126

a (B300.6) Petron. *Sat.* 88.2

priscis enim temporibus, cum adhuc nuda virtus placeret, vigebant artes ingenuae summumque certamen inter homines erat, ne quid profuturum saeculis diu lateret. itaque hercule herbarum omnium sucos Democritus expressit, et ne lapidum virgultorumque vis lateret, aetatem inter experimenta consumpsit.

b (B300.14) Sen. *Epist.* 90.32–33

"Democritus" inquit [scil. Posidonius, cf. Frag. 284 Edelstein-Kidd] "invenisse dicitur fornicem, ut lapidum curvatura paulatim inclinatorum medio saxo alligaretur." hoc dicam falsum esse: necesse est enim ante Democritum et pontes et portas fuisse, quarum fere summa curvantur. excidit porro vobis eundem Democritum invenisse quemadmodum ebur molliretur, quemadmodum decoctus calculus in zmaragdum converteretur, qua hodieque coctura inventi lapides ⟨in⟩[1] hoc utiles colorantur.

---

[1] ⟨in⟩ Schweighäuser

Renown for His Magical Practices (R126)

R126

a (B300.6) Petronius, *Satyricon*

In ancient times, when naked virtue was still pleasing, the liberal arts flourished and the greatest contention among men was to prevent anything that might benefit the ages from remaining hidden for long. And so, by god, Democritus extracted the juice of all the herbs and spent his whole life performing experiments in order to prevent the power of stones and bushes from remaining hidden.

b (B300.14) Seneca, *Letters to Lucilius*

"Democritus," he [i.e. Posidonius] says, "is reported to have invented the arch, whereby the curvature of stones leaning little by little would be held fast by a keystone." This I would declare to be false: for of necessity there existed before Democritus both bridges and gates, the top parts of which are generally curved. Furthermore, you seem to have forgotten that this same Democritus discovered how ivory could be softened, how a pebble could be transformed into an emerald by being boiled—the very same procedure by which even today stones are colored that have been found to be useful for this purpose.

A Few Sample Recipes (R127)

R127

a (< B300.19) Δημοκρίτου Παίγνια (P. Lond. 121 =
PGM 7.167–75)

[1] τὰ χαλκᾶ χρυσᾶ ποιῆσαι φαίνεσθαι· θεῖον ἄπυρον
μετὰ τῆς[1] κρητηρίας μείξας ἔκμασσε.

[2] ὠὸν ὅμιον μήλῳ[2] γενέσθαι· ζέσας τὸ ὠὸν χρεῖε
κρόκῳ μείξας μετ᾽ οἴνου.

[3] μάγειρον μὴ δύνασθαι τὴν πυρὰν ἀνάψαι· βοτά-
νην ἀεί[ζω]ον[3] θὲς αὐτοῦ εἰς τὴν ἑστίαν.

[4] φαγόντα σκόρδον μὴ ὄζειν· [ῥ]ίζας <σ>εύτλου[4]
ὀπτήσας φάγε.

[5] γραῦν μήτε πολλὰ λαλεῖν μήτε πολλὰ πίνειν· πί-
τυν κόψας βάλε αὐτῆς εἰς τὸ κράμμα.[5]

---

[1] γῆς Wessely   [2] μηλον pap., corr. Wessely   [3] suppl.
Wessely   [4]]ιζασευγλου pap., suppl. et corr. Wessely et
Dieterich   [5] κρᾶμα Dieterich

b (p. 192.97–107 Martelli) Δημοκρίτου περὶ πορφύρας
καὶ χρυσοῦ ποιήσεως· φυσικὰ καὶ μυστικὰ 9–10

[9] τὴν κιννάβαριν λευκὴν ποίει δι᾽ ἐλαίου ἢ ὄξους ἢ
μέλιτος ἢ ἅλμης ἢ στυπτηρίας· εἶτα ξανθὴν διὰ μί-
σνος ἢ σώρεως ἢ χαλκάνθου ἢ θείου ἀπύρου ἢ ὡς
ἐπινοεῖς. καὶ ἐπίβαλλε ἀργύρῳ· καὶ χρυσὸς ἔσται,
ἐὰν χρυσὸν καταβάπτῃς·[1] ἐὰν χαλκόν, ἤλεκτρον. ἡ
φύσις τῇ φύσει τέρπεται.

ATOMISTS (LEUCIPPUS, DEMOCRITUS)

A Few Sample Recipes (R127)

R127

a (< B300.19) *Democritus' Games*

[1] To make bronze seem to be gold: mix unburned sulfur with chalk (?), then wipe it off [scil. after having smeared it on].

[2] An egg to become similar to an apple: boil the egg, then smear it with egg yolk mixed with wine.

[3] To make a cook unable to light his fire: put some house-leek into his hearth.

[4] To eat garlic without stinking: cook beetroots and eat them.

[5] So that an old woman neither talks a lot nor drinks a lot: chop up some pine and throw it into her mixed wine.[1]

---

[1] The papyrus goes on to provide seven other (partially illegible) recipes.

b (≠ DK) Democritus, *On the Fabrication of Purple and Gold: Natural and Mystical Matters*

[9] Make cinnabar white with oil, vinegar, honey, brine, or alum; then make it yellow with copper ore, melanterite, chalcanthite, unburned sulfur, or as you please. And throw it on silver: and gold will be formed if you dip gold into it;[1] or electrum, if you dip copper. Nature takes pleasure in nature.

---

[1] The expression is strange and the text may be corrupt: cf. Martelli, *Scritti alchemici*, pp. 312–13, n. 55.

---

[1] καταβάπτῃ mss., corr. Martelli

[10] τὴν δὲ Κυπρίαν καδμίαν, τὴν ἐξωσμένην λέγω, λεύκαινε ὡς ἔθος. εἶτα ποίει ξανθὴν· ξανθώσεις δὲ χολῇ μοσχείᾳ ἢ τερεβινθίνῃ ἢ κικίνῳ ἢ ῥαφανίνῳ ἢ ᾠῶν λεκίθοις, ξανθῶσαι αὐτὴν δυναμένοις, καὶ ἐπίβαλλε ἀργύρῳ· χρυσὸς γὰρ ἔσται διὰ τὸν χρυσὸν καὶ διὰ τὸ χρυσοζώμιον. ἡ γὰρ φύσις τὴν φύσιν νικᾷ.

Two Aphorisms Attributed to Democritus in Syriac (R128)

R128

a (B303) *Studia Sinaitica* 1, pp. 34–35

b (B304) *Studia Sinaitica* 1, p. 38

<hr>

[1] Translated from the French translation by Henri Hugonnard-Roche.

[10] Whiten Cyprian cadmia, I mean that which has been expelled [scil. from the mineral], as is customary. Then make it yellow: turning it yellow with calf's bile, terebinth resin, castor oil, beet juice, or egg yolk, substances that possess the property of turning it yellow, and throw it on silver. For gold will be formed thanks to the gold and the gold liquor. Nature conquers nature.

Two Aphorisms Attributed to Democritus in Syriac (R128)

R128 From a Syriac collection of Greek sayings

a (B303)

Democritus said, "Wise people, when they go to a foreign country that is not their own, should gather information silently and tranquilly, watching and listening to the reputation belonging to the condition of the sages who live there: how they are, and whether they themselves can measure up to these sages, by secretly weighing their words in comparison with their own. And when they have weighed them and seen which group is better than the other one, only then should they reveal the wealth of their wisdom, in order to be praised for the treasure that they possess, enriching the others by its means. And when their own is too small for them to be able to spend anything from it, then they take from the others and leave."

b (B304)

Democritus said, "I myself know that I do not know anything."[1]

Leucippus and Democritus in The Assembly of
Philosophers *(R129)*

R129 (≠ DK) *Turba Phil.* Sermo VI, p. 63.1–13 Plessner

ait Lucas: "vos non nisi de his quatuor naturis loquimini,
et unumquemque vestrum iam aliquid video dixisse. ego
autem vobis notifico quod Deus creavit omnia ex his
naturis, et quae ex his creata sunt, ad eas revertuntur; in
quibus creaturae et generantur et moriuntur, et omnia
prout Deus praedestinavit."

inquit Democritos qui Lucae est discipulus: "bene
dixisti, magister."

ait Arisleus: "quoniam, Democrites, a Luca habuisti,
non deberes praesumere magistri tui sociis te miscere."

respondit Lucas: "non solum a me scientiam habuit
Democrites, immo ab Indorum et Babilonicorum philo-
sophis. Et puto ipsum suos contemporaneos in scientia
posse superare."

respondit Turba: "veniens ad aetatem non parum pla-
cebit; non tamen adhuc fari debet."

Leucippus and Democritus in The Assembly of
Philosophers *(R129)*

R129 (≠ DK) *The Assembly of Philosophers*

Lucas [i.e. Leucippus] said: "You all speak about nothing
except about these four natures, and I see that each one
of you has already said something. But I inform you that
God created all things from these natures and that what is
created from them returns to them; it is in these things
that creatures are both generated and destroyed, and all
as God has predestined them."

Democritus, who is Lucas' student, said: "You have
spoken well, Master."

Arisleus [i.e. Archelaus] said: "Since, Democritus, you
have this from Lucas, you should not make so bold as to
join in with the comrades of your teacher."

Lucas answered: "Not only from me has Democritus
obtained knowledge, but also from the philosophers of the
Indians and Babylonians. And I believe that he is capable
of surpassing his contemporaries in knowledge."

The Assembly answered: "When he arrives at maturity
he will be pleasing in no small measure; but for the time
being he should not speak."